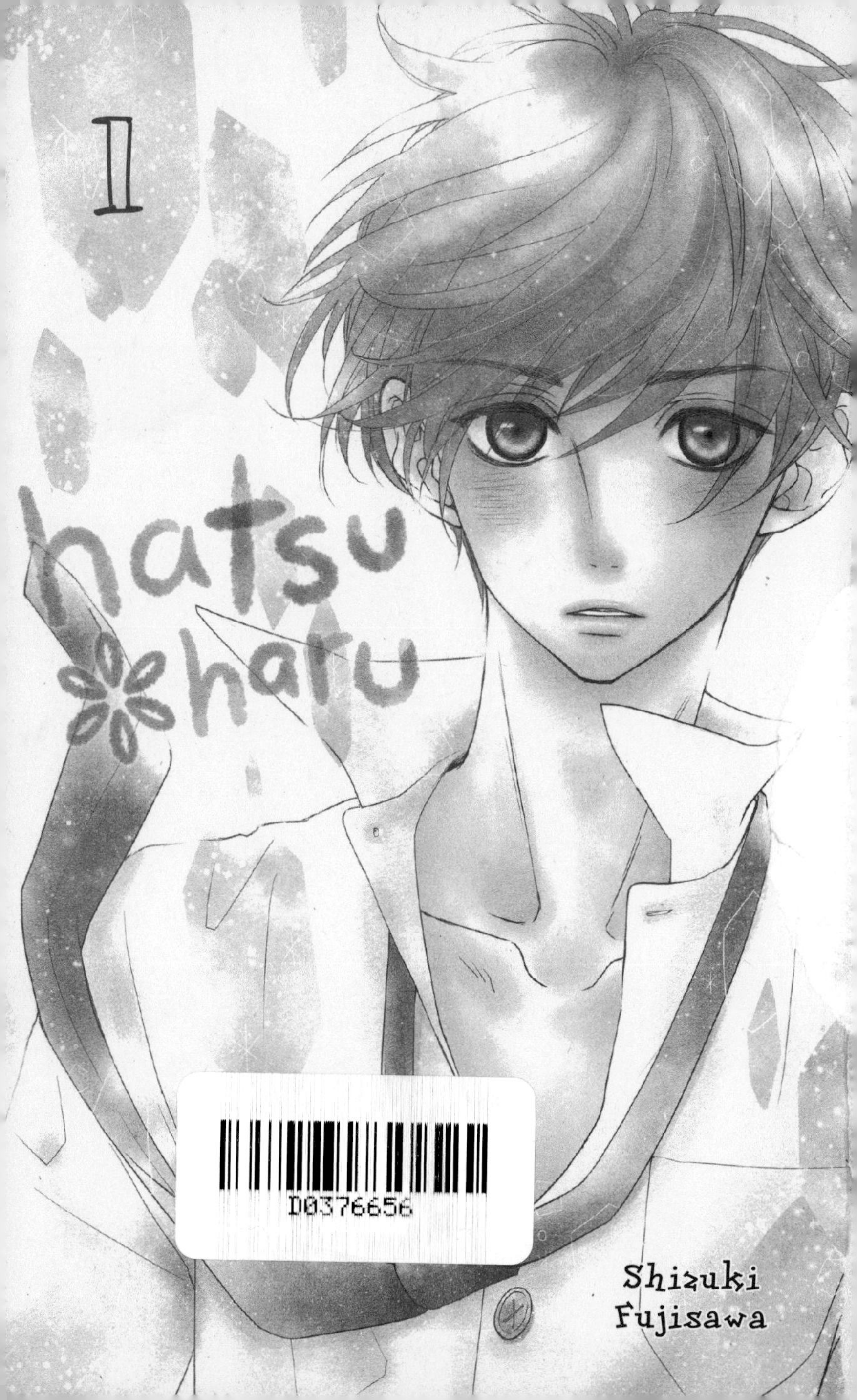
1
hatsu haru
Shizuki Fujisawa

CONTENTS

hatsu*haru
1

CHAPTER 1 3

CHAPTER 2 53

CHAPTER 3 98

CHAPTER 4 145

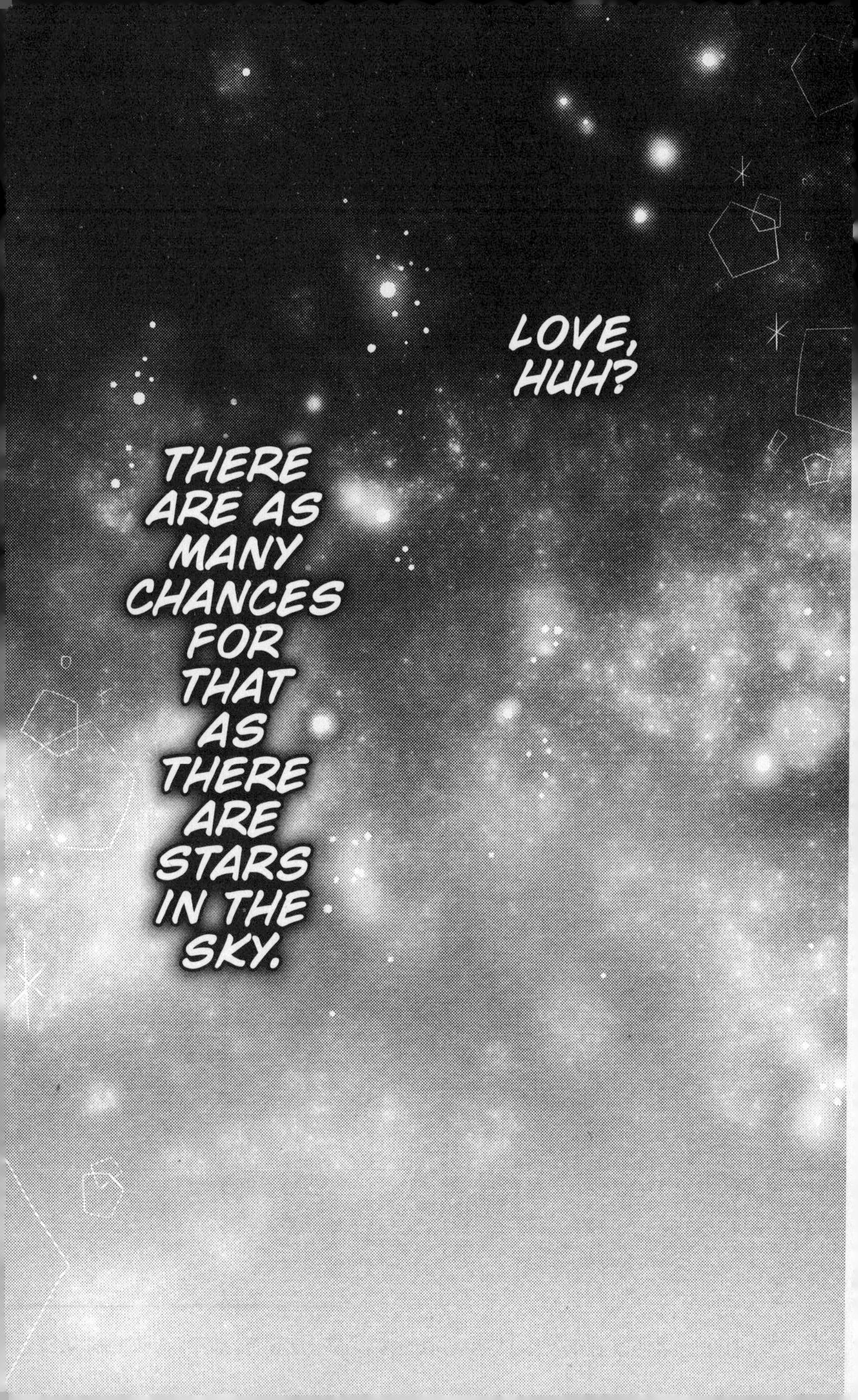
LOVE, HUH?
THERE ARE AS MANY CHANCES FOR THAT AS THERE ARE STARS IN THE SKY.

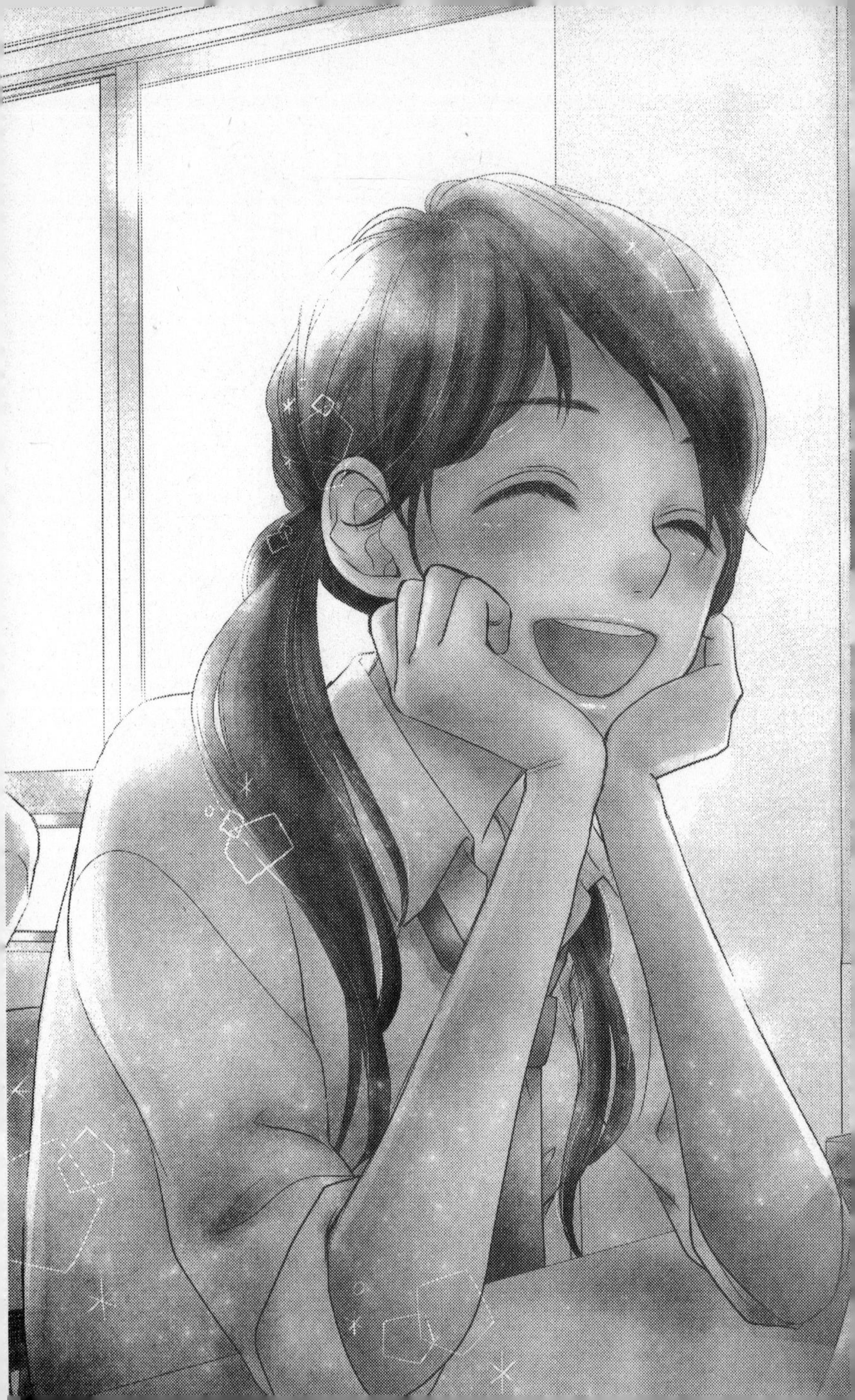

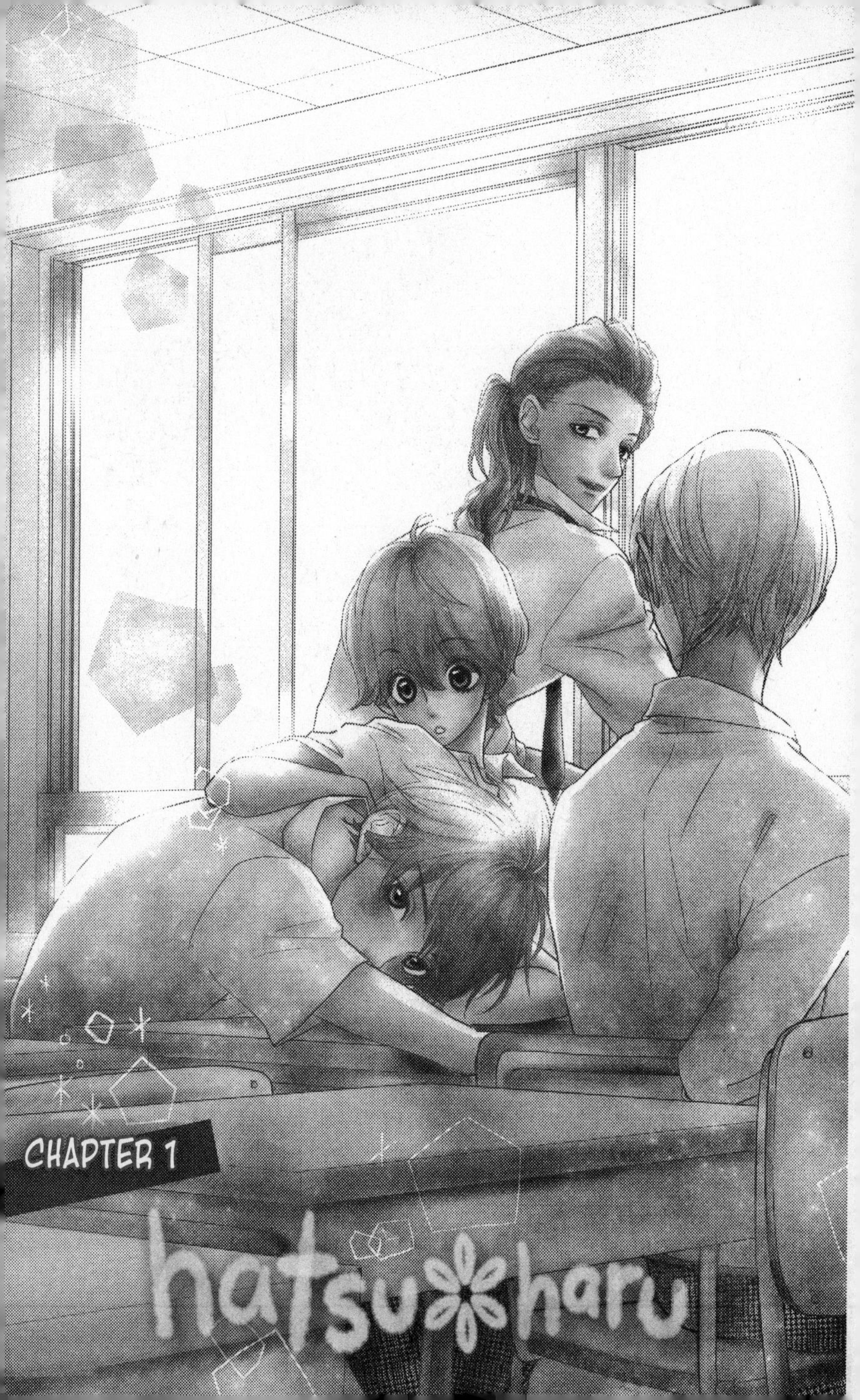

CHAPTER 1
hatsu haru

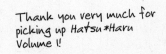

Thank you very much for picking up Hatsu*Haru Volume 1!

The main character is a boy, and the heroine has violent tendencies, but I hope you still enjoy it.

Please read on.

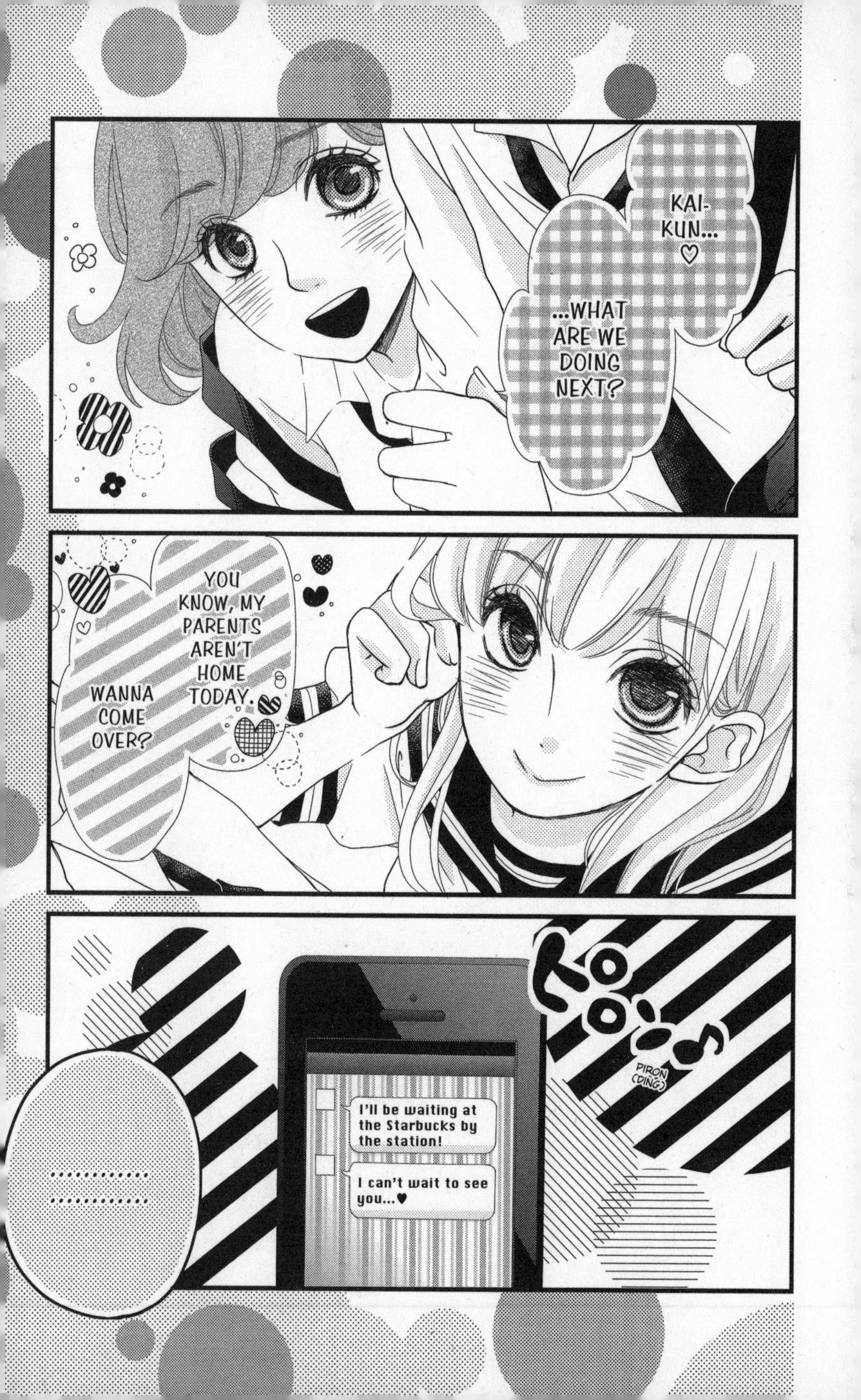
KAI-KUN... ♡
...WHAT ARE WE DOING NEXT?
YOU KNOW, MY PARENTS AREN'T HOME TODAY.
WANNA COME OVER?
PIRON (DING)
I'll be waiting at the Starbucks by the station!
I can't wait to see you...♥
…………
…………

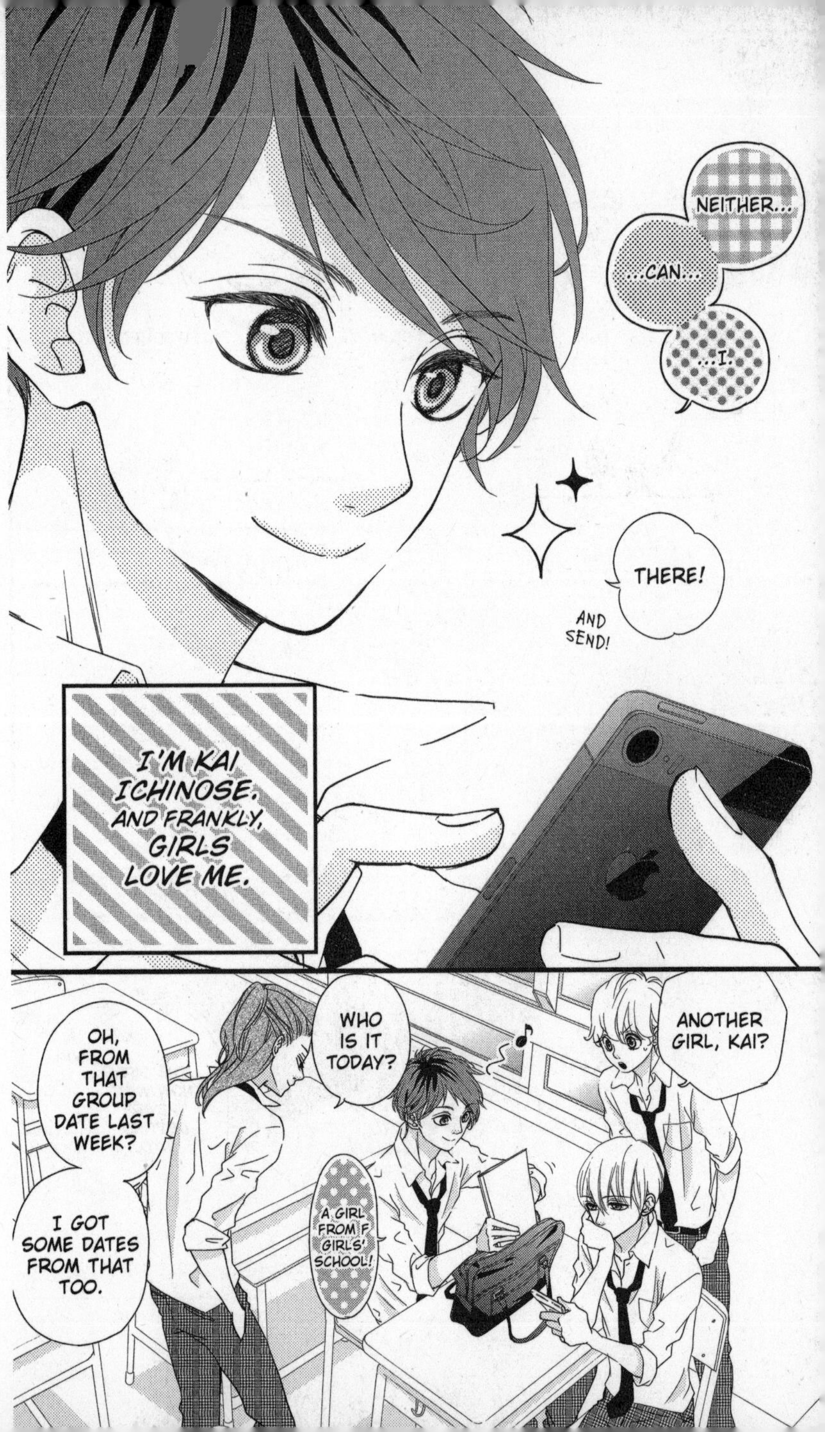
NEITHER...
...CAN...
...I.
THERE!
AND SEND!
I'M KAI ICHINOSE. AND FRANKLY, GIRLS LOVE ME.
ANOTHER GIRL, KAI?
WHO IS IT TODAY?
OH, FROM THAT GROUP DATE LAST WEEK?
A GIRL FROM F GIRLS' SCHOOL!
I GOT SOME DATES FROM THAT TOO.

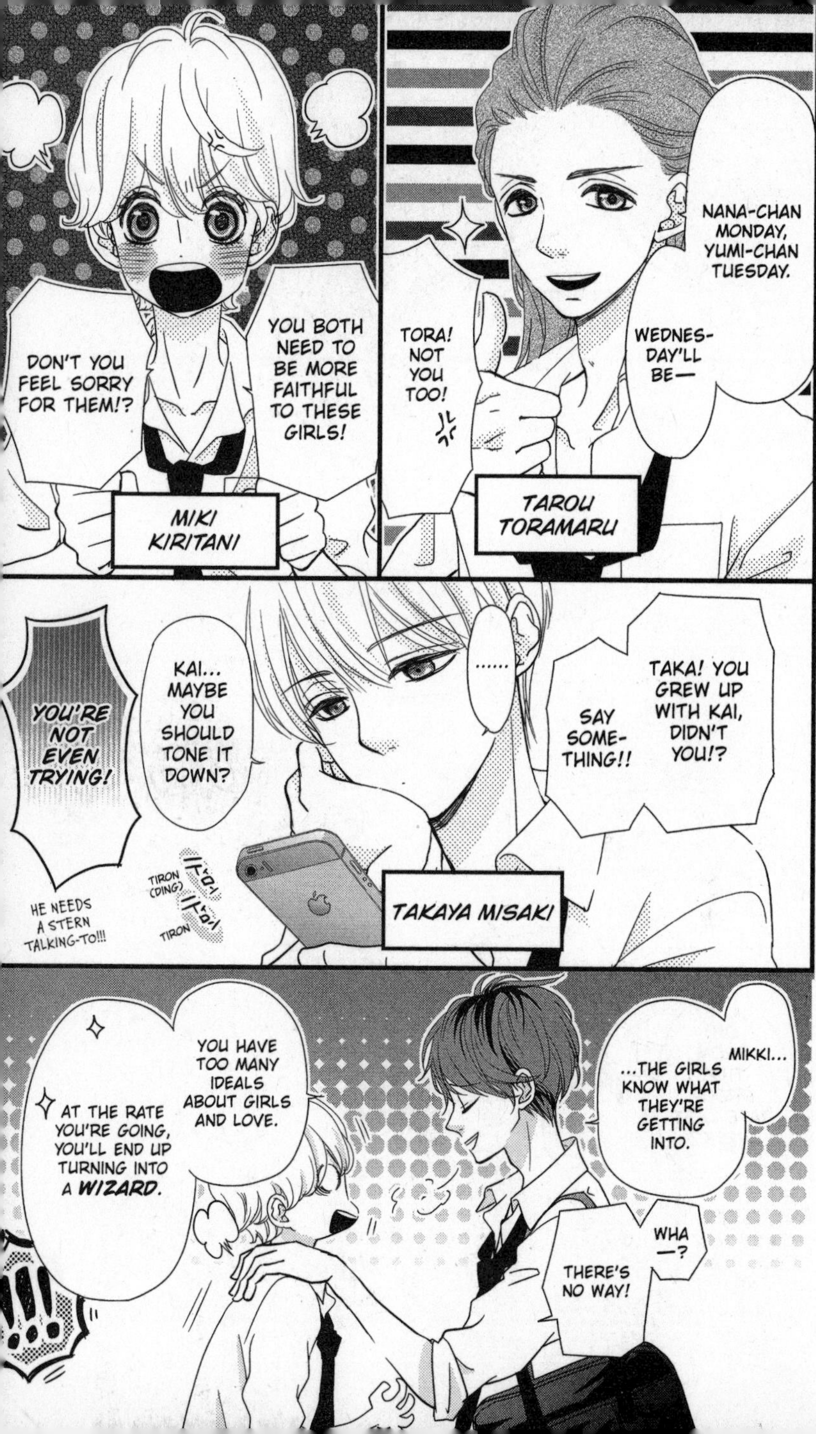
NANA-CHAN MONDAY, YUMI-CHAN TUESDAY.
WEDNES-DAY'LL BE—
TORA! NOT YOU TOO!
TAROU TORAMARU
YOU BOTH NEED TO BE MORE FAITHFUL TO THESE GIRLS!
DON'T YOU FEEL SORRY FOR THEM!?
MIKI KIRITANI
TAKA! YOU GREW UP WITH KAI, DIDN'T YOU!?
SAY SOME-THING!!
......
TAKAYA MISAKI
KAI... MAYBE YOU SHOULD TONE IT DOWN?
TIRON (DING)
TIRON
YOU'RE NOT EVEN TRYING!
HE NEEDS A STERN TALKING-TO!!!
MIKKI...
...THE GIRLS KNOW WHAT THEY'RE GETTING INTO.
YOU HAVE TOO MANY IDEALS ABOUT GIRLS AND LOVE.
AT THE RATE YOU'RE GOING, YOU'LL END UP TURNING INTO A **WIZARD**.
WHA—?
THERE'S NO WAY!

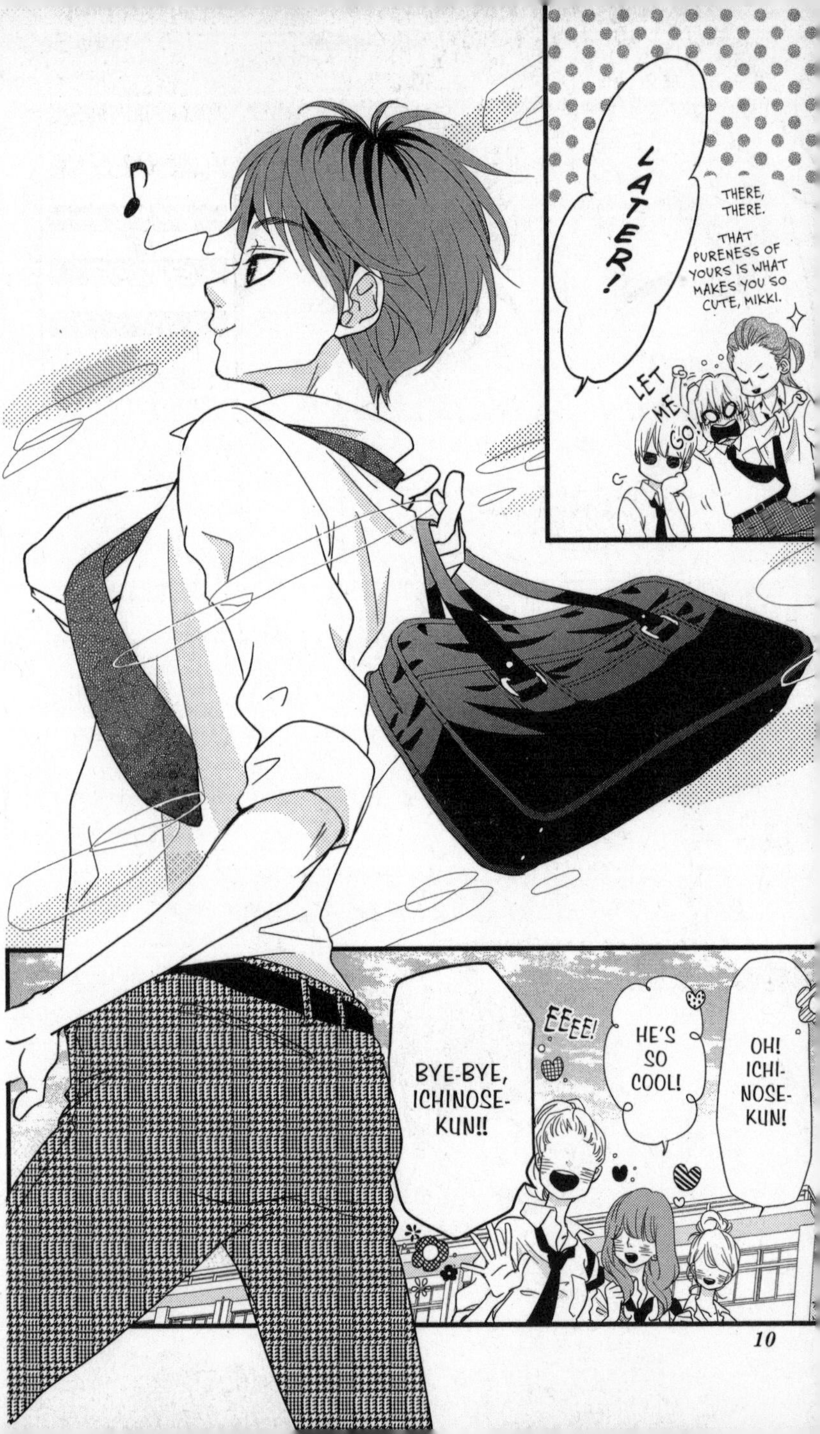
THERE, THERE.
THAT PURENESS OF YOURS IS WHAT MAKES YOU SO CUTE, MIKKI.
LET ME GO!
LATER!
OH! ICHINOSE-KUN!
HE'S SO COOL!
EEEE!
BYE-BYE, ICHINOSE-KUN!!

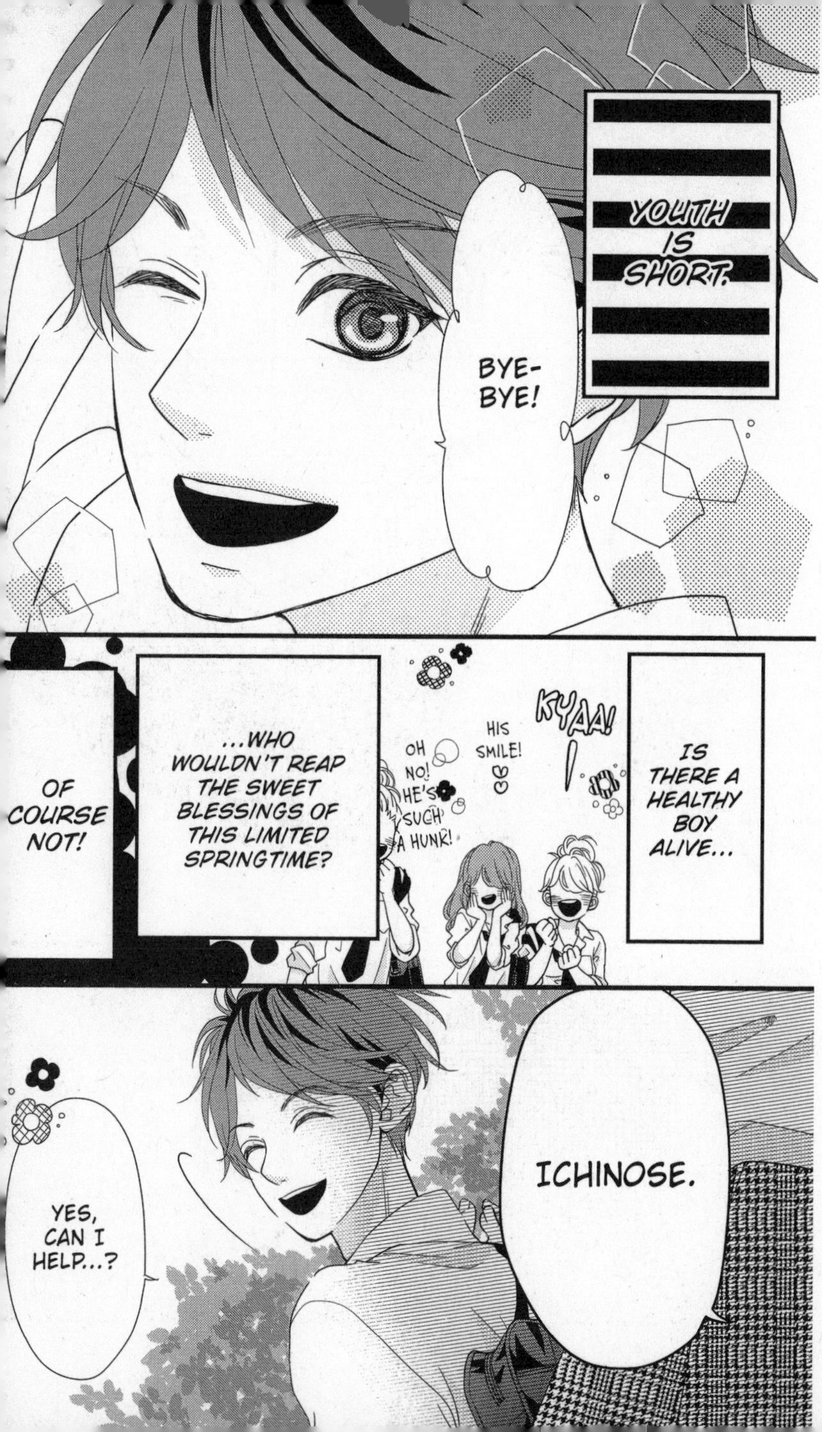
YOUTH IS SHORT.
BYE-BYE!
IS THERE A HEALTHY BOY ALIVE...
KYAA!
HIS SMILE!
OH NO! HE'S SUCH A HUNK!
...WHO WOULDN'T REAP THE SWEET BLESSINGS OF THIS LIMITED SPRINGTIME?
OF COURSE NOT!
ICHINOSE.
YES, CAN I HELP...?

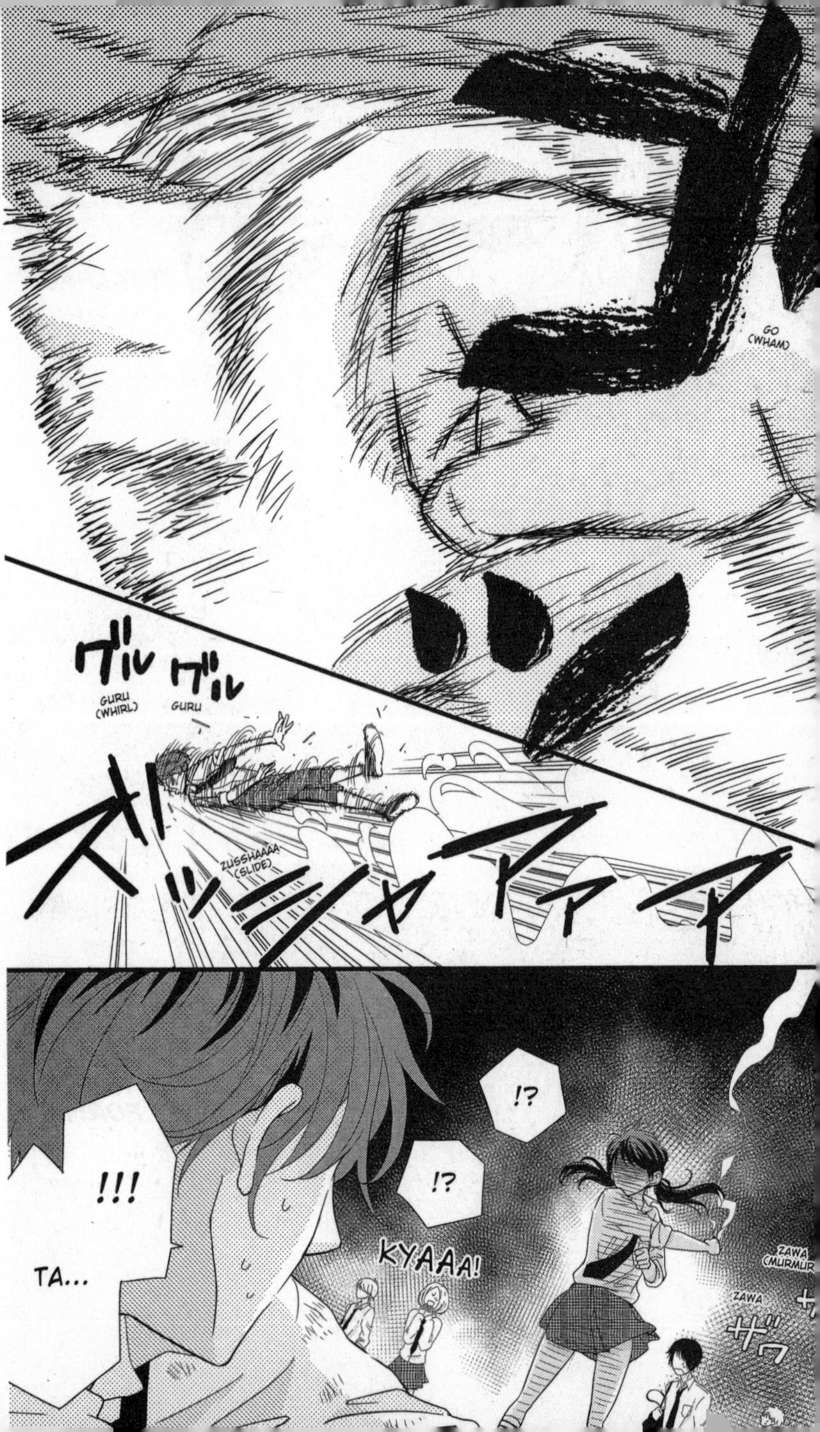
GO
(WHAM)
グル グル
GURU
(WHIRL)
GURU
ZUSSHAAAA
(SLIDE)
ZAWA
(MURMUR)
ZAWA
ザワ
!?
!?
KYAAA!
!!!
TA...

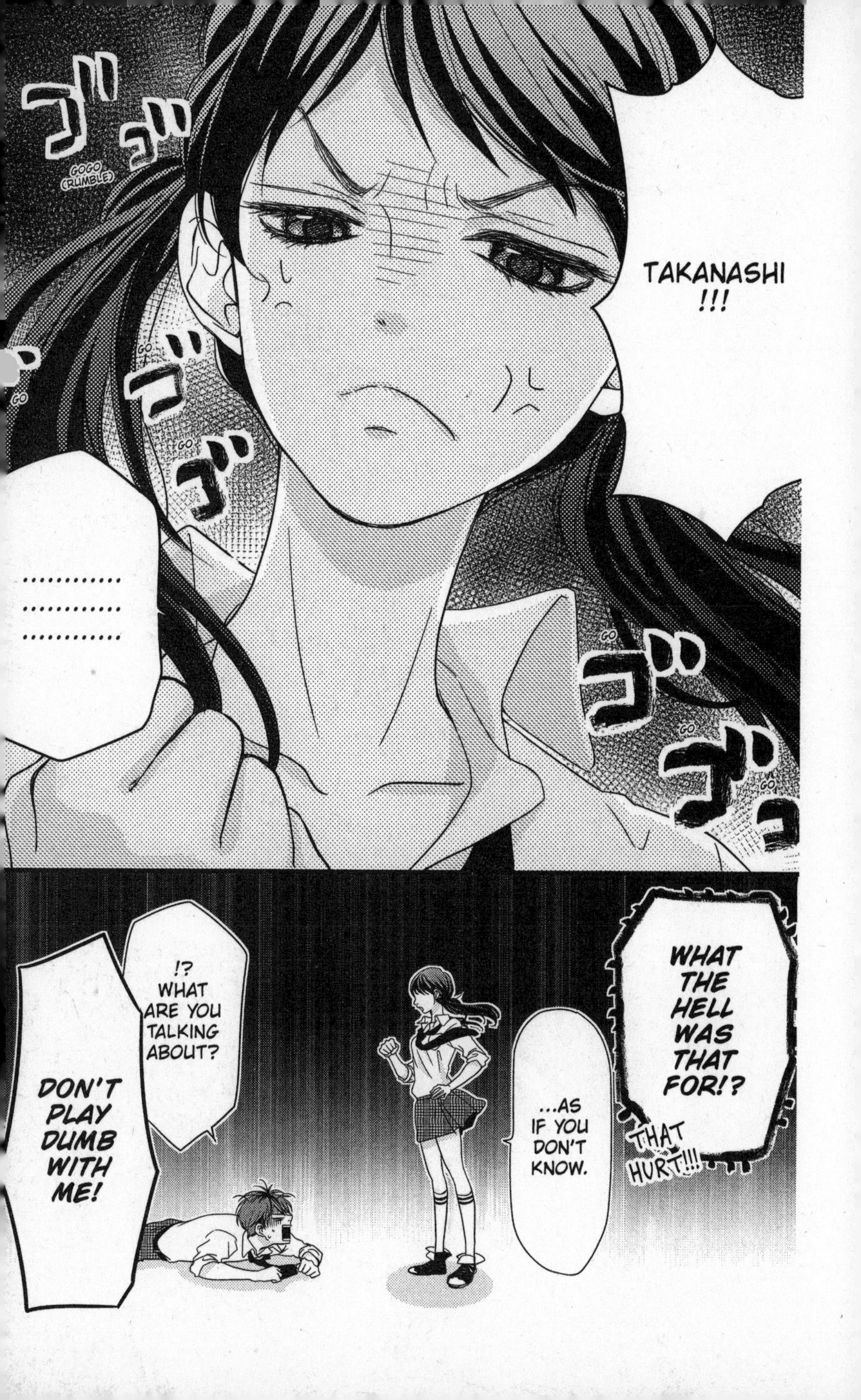

TAKANASHI !!!
GOGO (RUMBLE)
GO
GO
GO
GO
GO
GO
....
WHAT THE HELL WAS THAT FOR!?
THAT HURT!!!
...AS IF YOU DON'T KNOW.
!? WHAT ARE YOU TALKING ABOUT?
DON'T PLAY DUMB WITH ME!

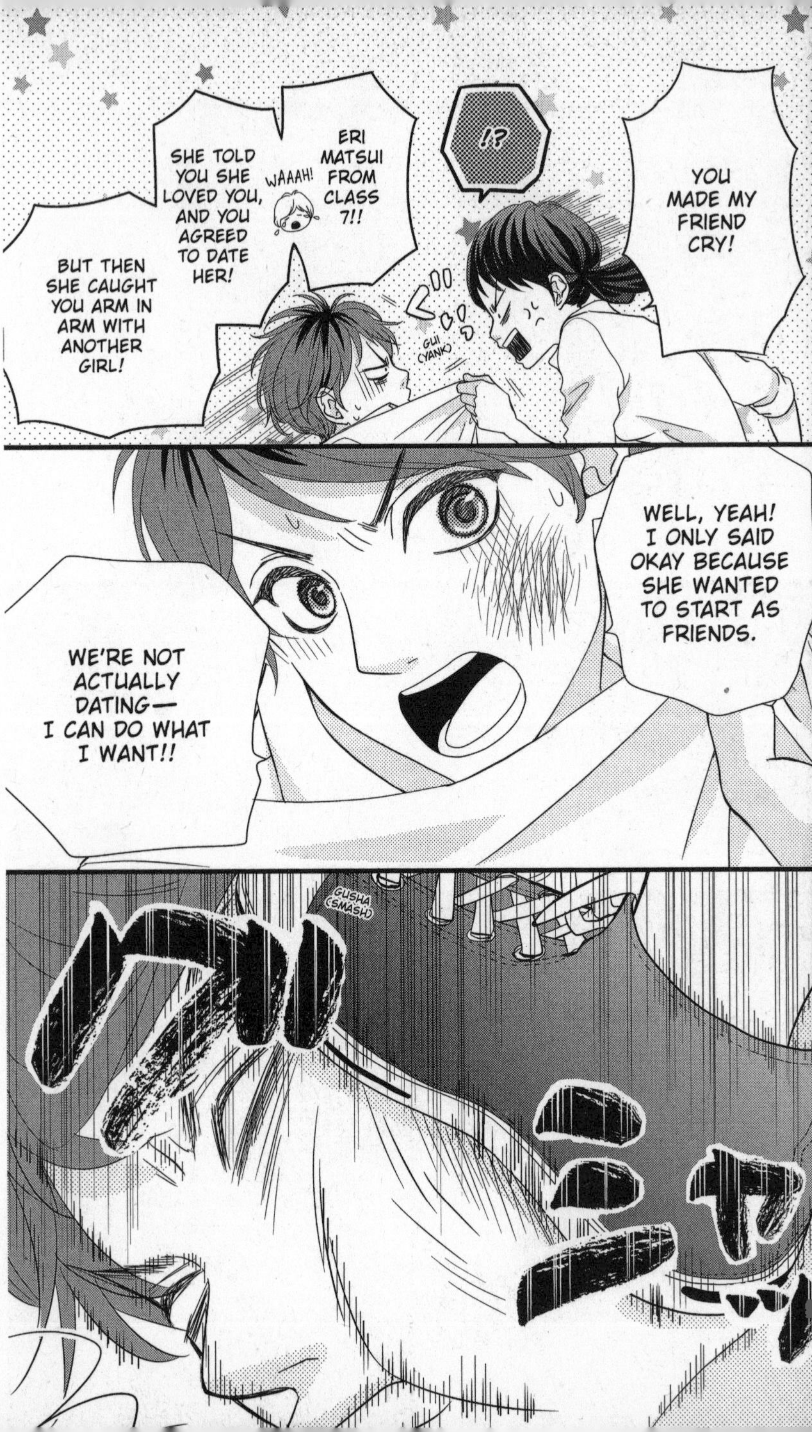
YOU MADE MY FRIEND CRY!
!?
ERI MATSUI FROM CLASS 7!!
WAAAH!
SHE TOLD YOU SHE LOVED YOU, AND YOU AGREED TO DATE HER!
BUT THEN SHE CAUGHT YOU ARM IN ARM WITH ANOTHER GIRL!
GUI (YANK)
WELL, YEAH! I ONLY SAID OKAY BECAUSE SHE WANTED TO START AS FRIENDS.
WE'RE NOT ACTUALLY DATING— I CAN DO WHAT I WANT!!
GUSHA (SMASH)

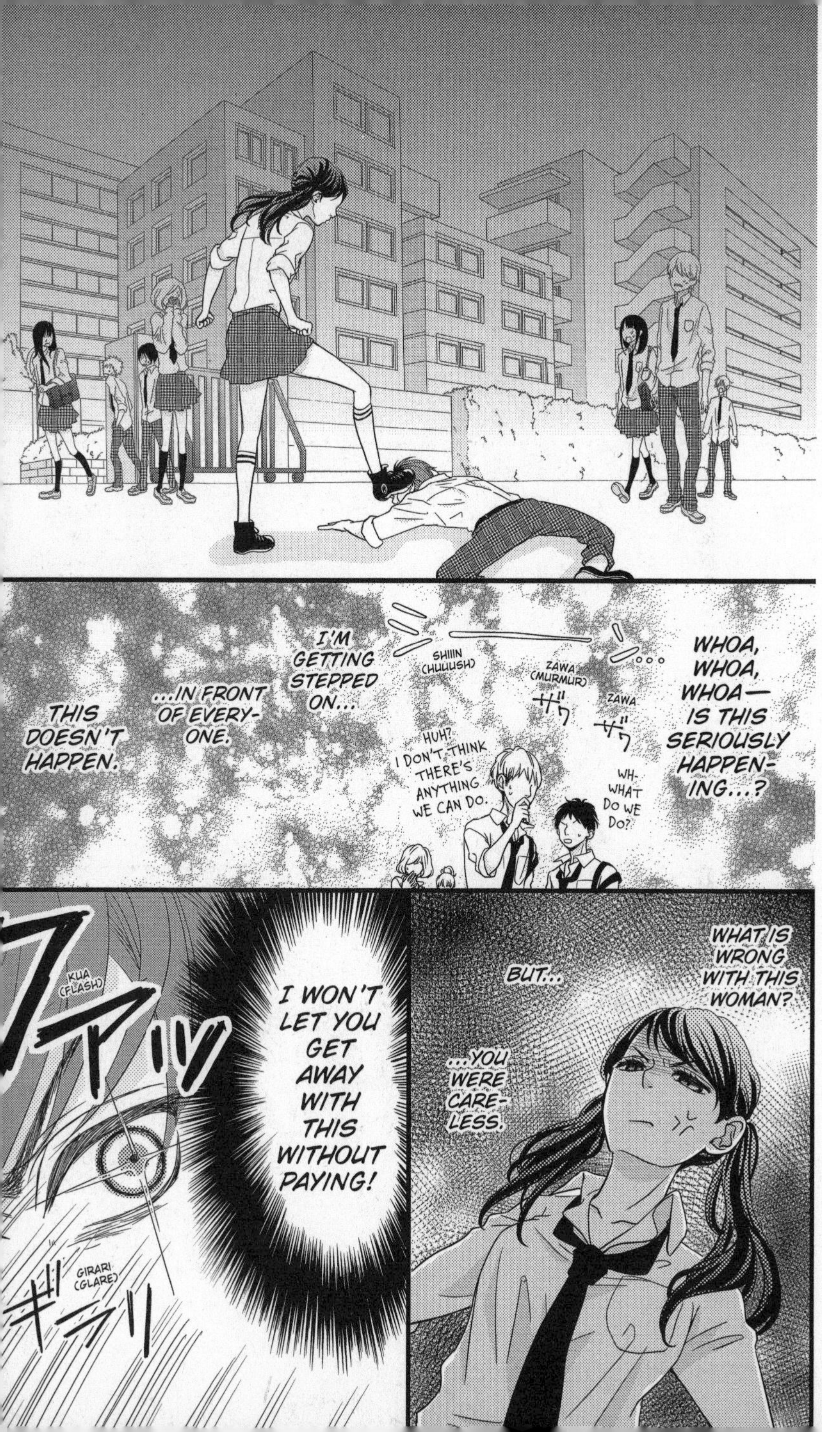
WHOA, WHOA, WHOA— IS THIS SERIOUSLY HAPPEN-ING...?
WH-WHAT DO WE DO?
ZAWA
ZAWA (MURMUR)
HUH? I DON'T THINK THERE'S ANYTHING WE CAN DO.
SHIIIN (HUUUSH)
I'M GETTING STEPPED ON...
...IN FRONT OF EVERY-ONE.
THIS DOESN'T HAPPEN.
WHAT IS WRONG WITH THIS WOMAN?
BUT...
...YOU WERE CARE-LESS.
I WON'T LET YOU GET AWAY WITH THIS WITHOUT PAYING!
KUA (FLASH)
GIRARI (GLARE)

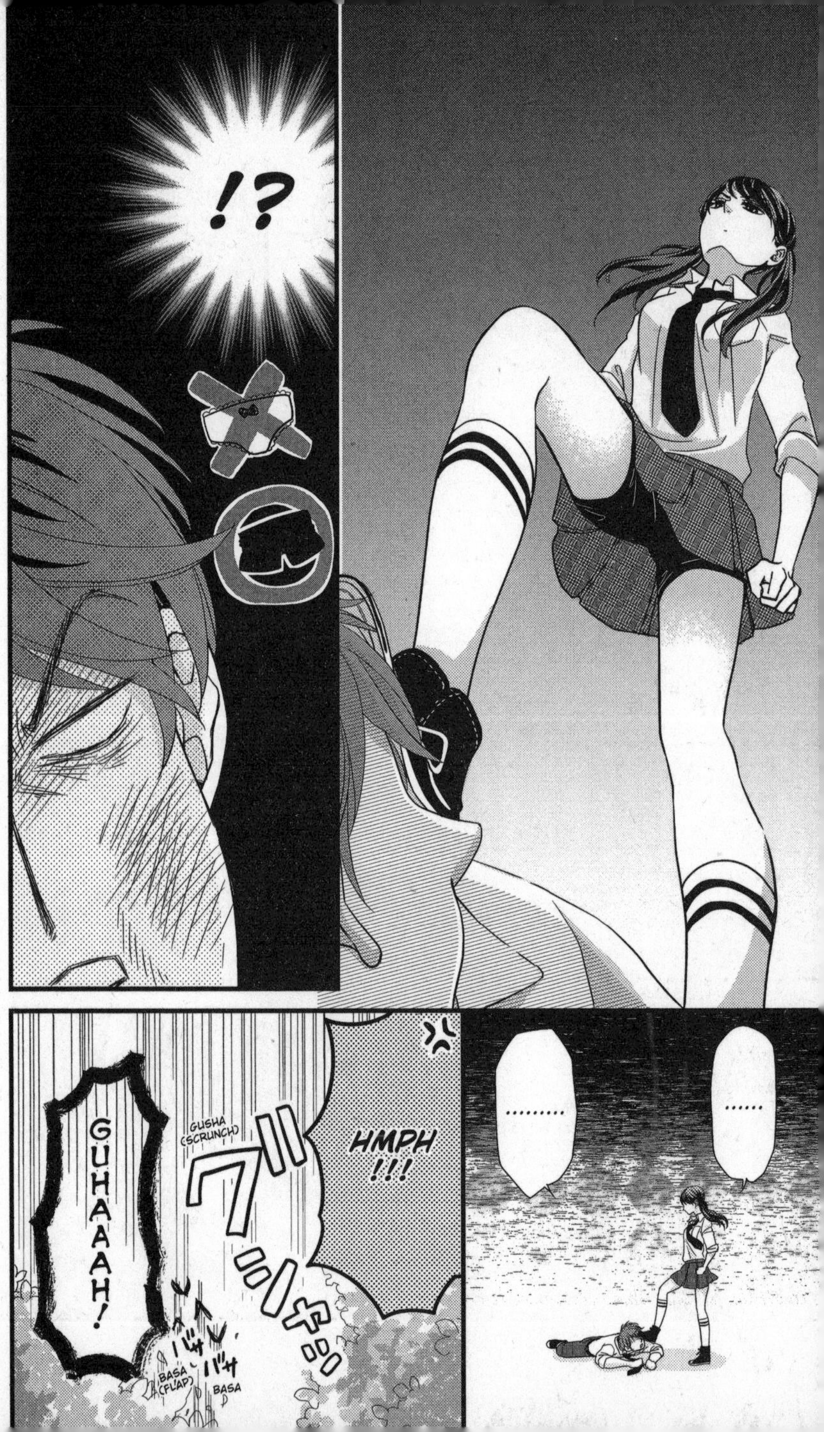
!?
......
....
GUSHA (SCRUNCH)
HMPH!!!
GUHAAAH!
BASA (FLAP)
BASA

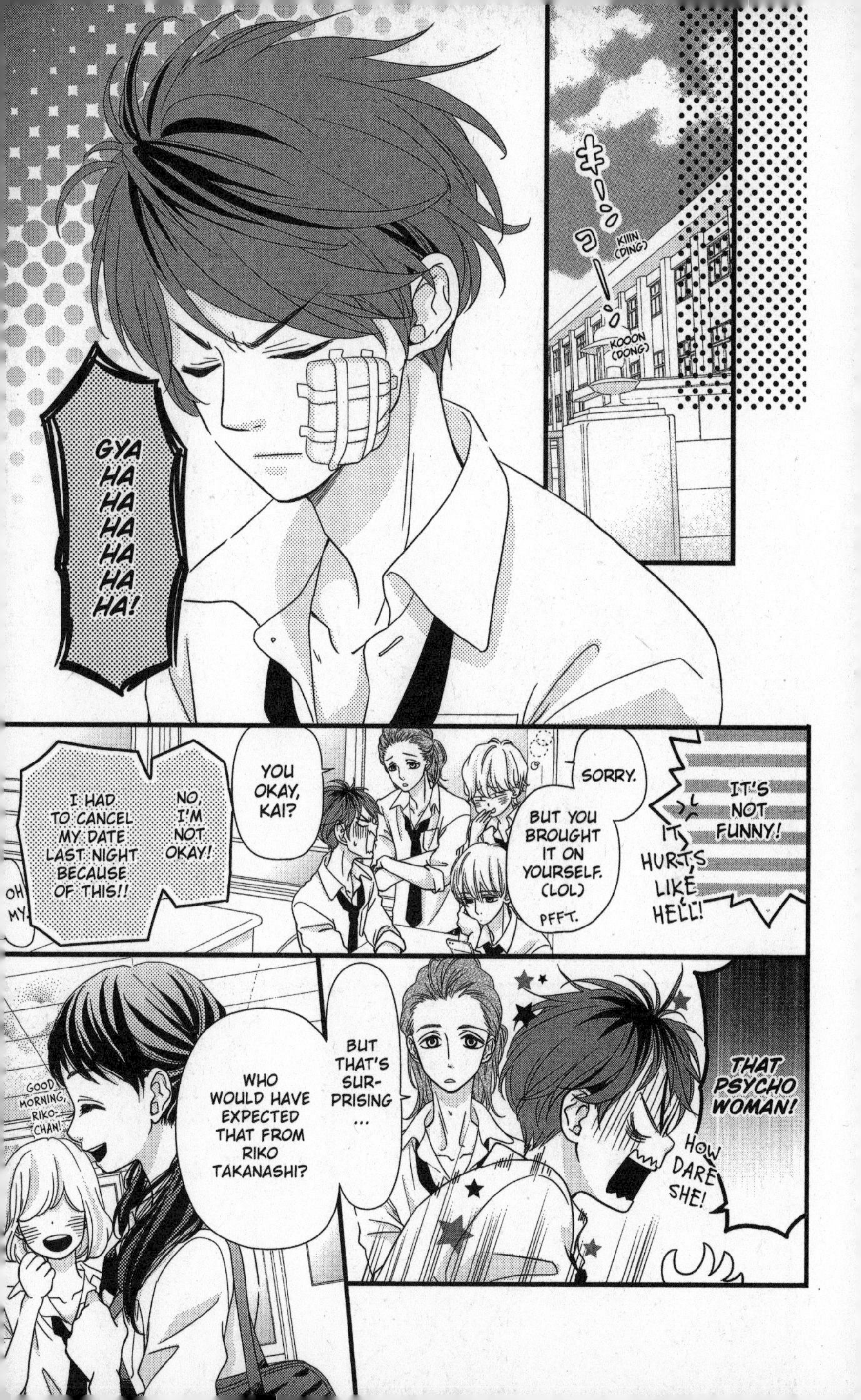
KIIN (DING)
KOOON (DONG)
GYA HA HA HA HA HA HA!
IT'S NOT FUNNY!
IT HURTS LIKE HELL!
SORRY.
BUT YOU BROUGHT IT ON YOURSELF. (LOL)
PFFT.
YOU OKAY, KAI?
NO, I'M NOT OKAY!
I HAD TO CANCEL MY DATE LAST NIGHT BECAUSE OF THIS!!
OH MY.
THAT PSYCHO WOMAN!
HOW DARE SHE!
BUT THAT'S SUR-PRISING...
WHO WOULD HAVE EXPECTED THAT FROM RIKO TAKANASHI?
GOOD MORNING, RIKO-CHAN!

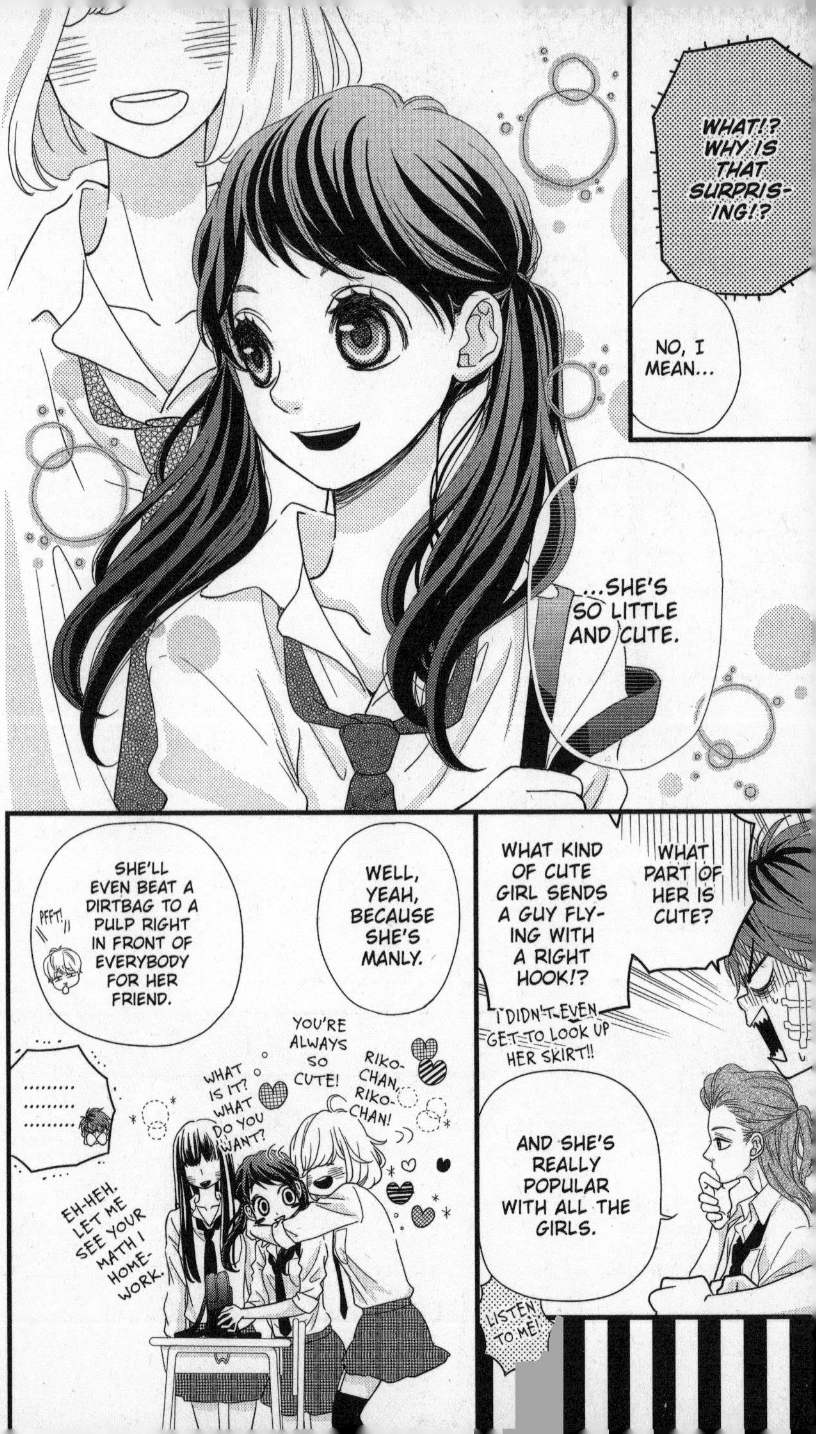
WHAT!? WHY IS THAT SURPRISING!?
NO, I MEAN...
...SHE'S SO LITTLE AND CUTE.
WHAT PART OF HER IS CUTE?
WHAT KIND OF CUTE GIRL SENDS A GUY FLYING WITH A RIGHT HOOK!?
I DIDN'T EVEN GET TO LOOK UP HER SKIRT!!
AND SHE'S REALLY POPULAR WITH ALL THE GIRLS.
LISTEN TO ME!
WELL, YEAH, BECAUSE SHE'S MANLY.
SHE'LL EVEN BEAT A DIRTBAG TO A PULP RIGHT IN FRONT OF EVERYBODY FOR HER FRIEND.
PFFT!
...
....
....
....
YOU'RE ALWAYS SO CUTE!
RIKO-CHAN, RIKO-CHAN!
WHAT IS IT? WHAT DO YOU WANT?
EH-HEH. LET ME SEE YOUR MATH HOMEWORK.

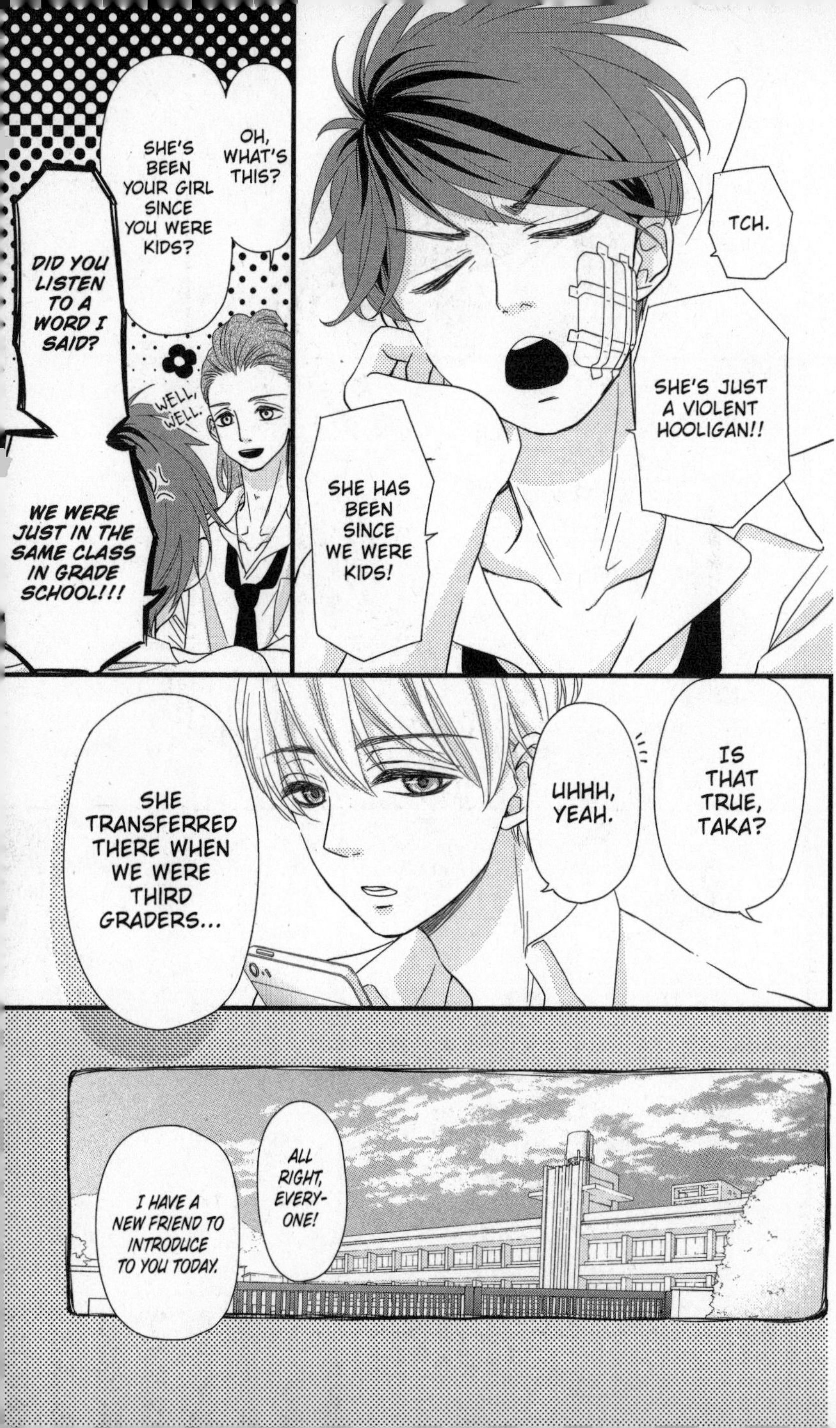
TCH.
SHE'S JUST A VIOLENT HOOLIGAN!!
SHE HAS BEEN SINCE WE WERE KIDS!
OH, WHAT'S THIS?
SHE'S BEEN YOUR GIRL SINCE YOU WERE KIDS?
WELL, WELL.
DID YOU LISTEN TO A WORD I SAID?
WE WERE JUST IN THE SAME CLASS IN GRADE SCHOOL!!!
IS THAT TRUE, TAKA?
UHHH, YEAH.
SHE TRANSFERRED THERE WHEN WE WERE THIRD GRADERS...
ALL RIGHT, EVERY-ONE!
I HAVE A NEW FRIEND TO INTRODUCE TO YOU TODAY.

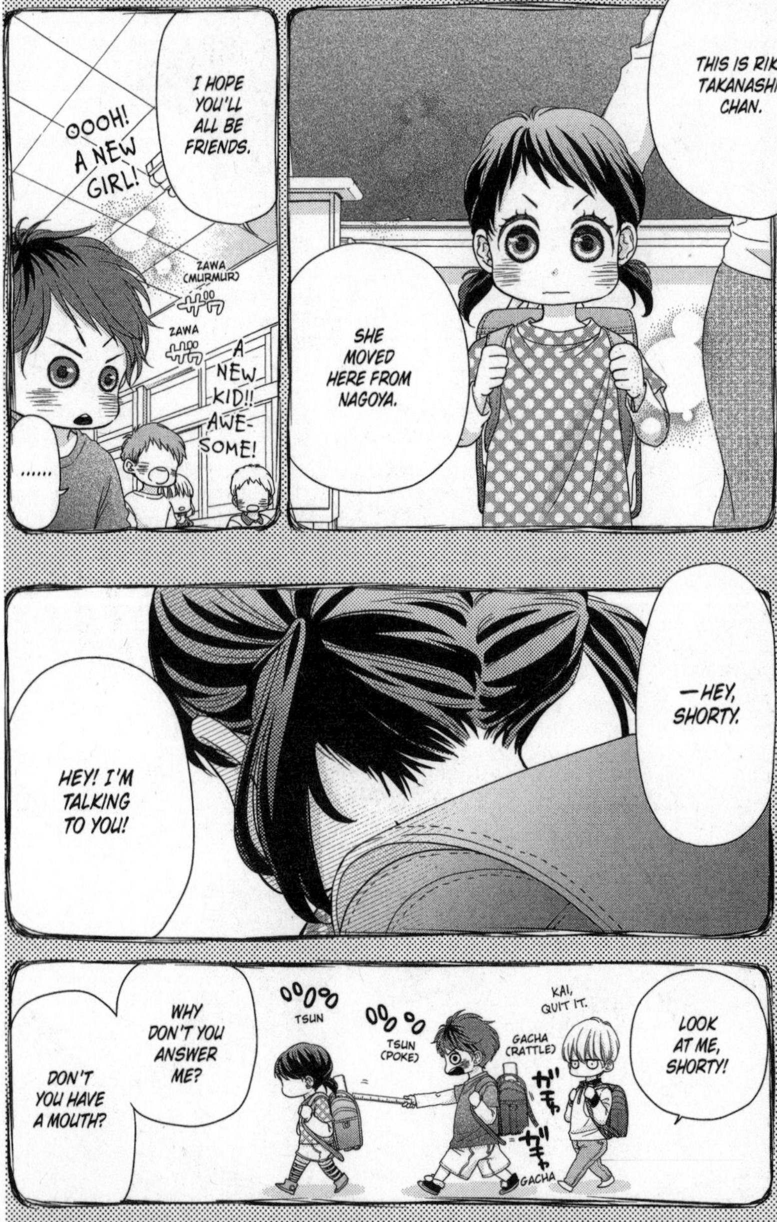
THIS IS RIKO TAKANASHI-CHAN.
SHE MOVED HERE FROM NAGOYA.
I HOPE YOU'LL ALL BE FRIENDS.
OOOH! A NEW GIRL!
ZAWA (MURMUR)
ZAWA
A NEW KID!! AWESOME!
......
—HEY, SHORTY.
HEY! I'M TALKING TO YOU!
LOOK AT ME, SHORTY!
KAI, QUIT IT.
GACHA (RATTLE)
GACHA
TSUN (POKE)
TSUN
WHY DON'T YOU ANSWER ME?
DON'T YOU HAVE A MOUTH?

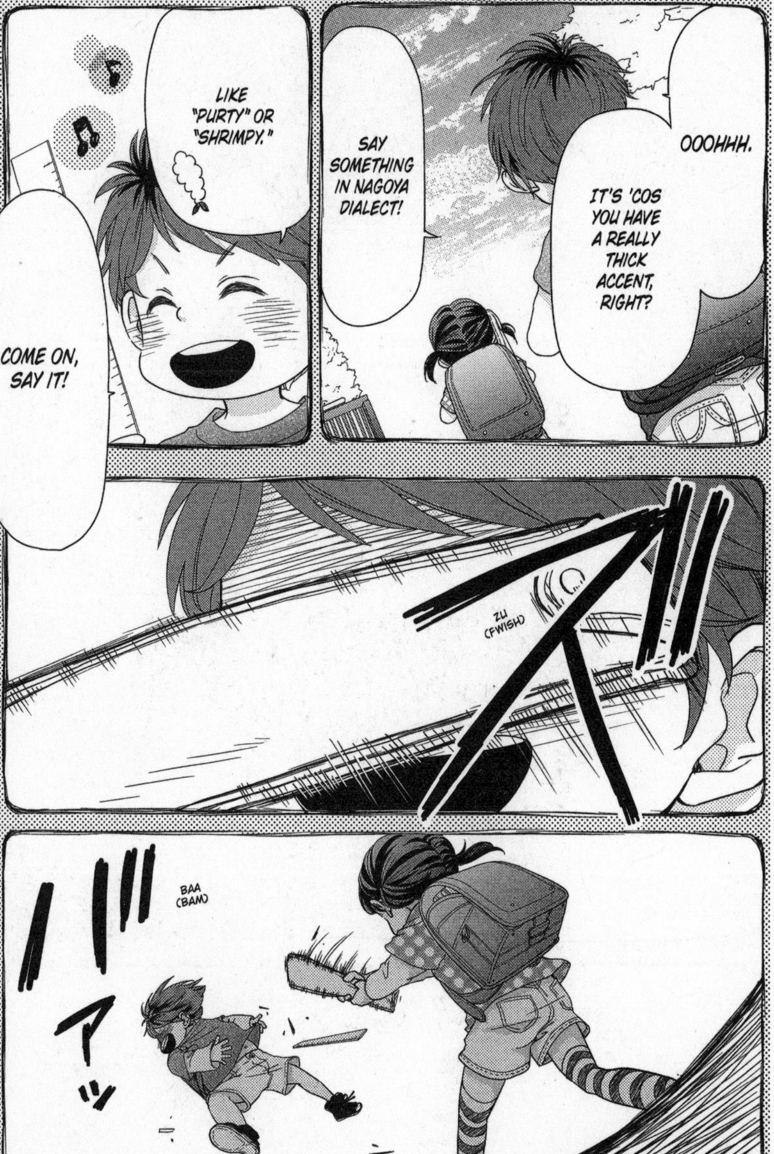
OOOHHH.
IT'S 'COS YOU HAVE A REALLY THICK ACCENT, RIGHT?
SAY SOMETHING IN NAGOYA DIALECT!
LIKE "PURTY" OR "SHRIMPY."
COME ON, SAY IT!
ZU (FWISH)
BAA (BAM)

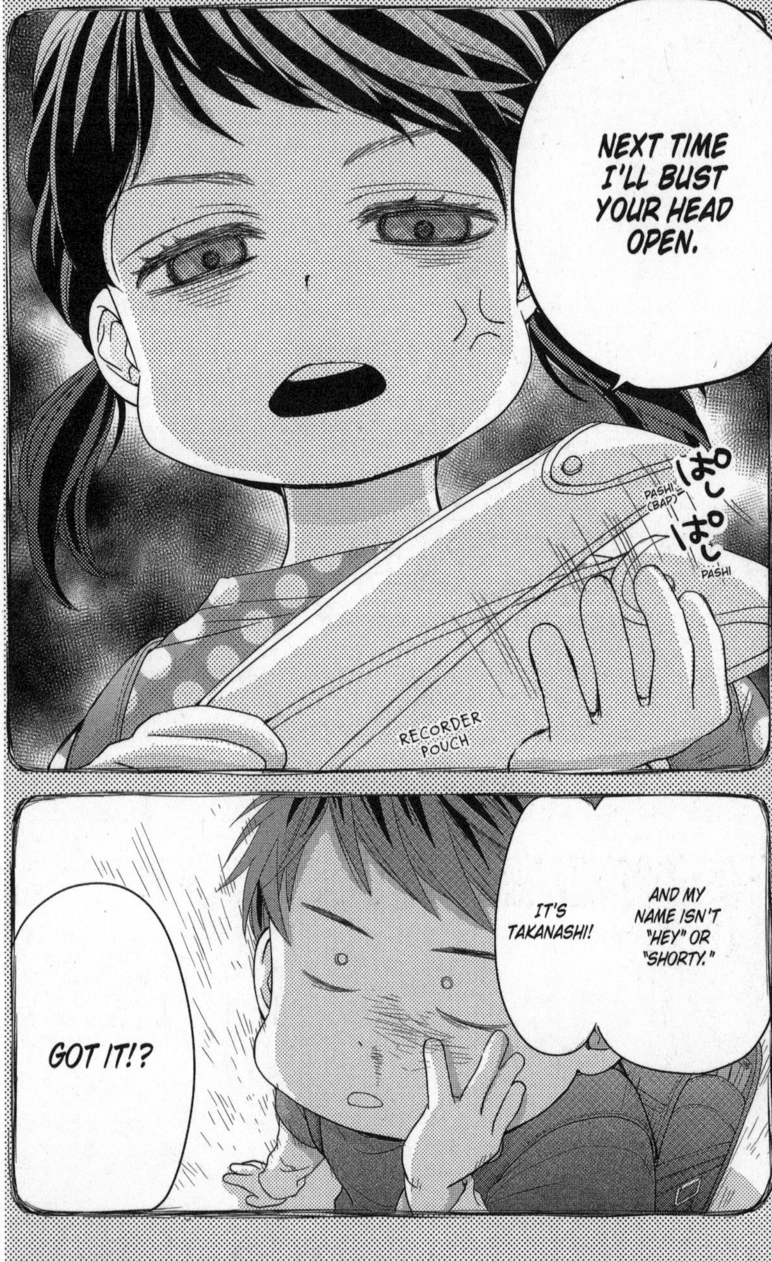
NEXT TIME I'LL BUST YOUR HEAD OPEN.
ぱし PASHI (BAP)
ぱし PASHI
RECORDER POUCH
AND MY NAME ISN'T "HEY" OR "SHORTY."
IT'S TAKANASHI!
GOT IT!?

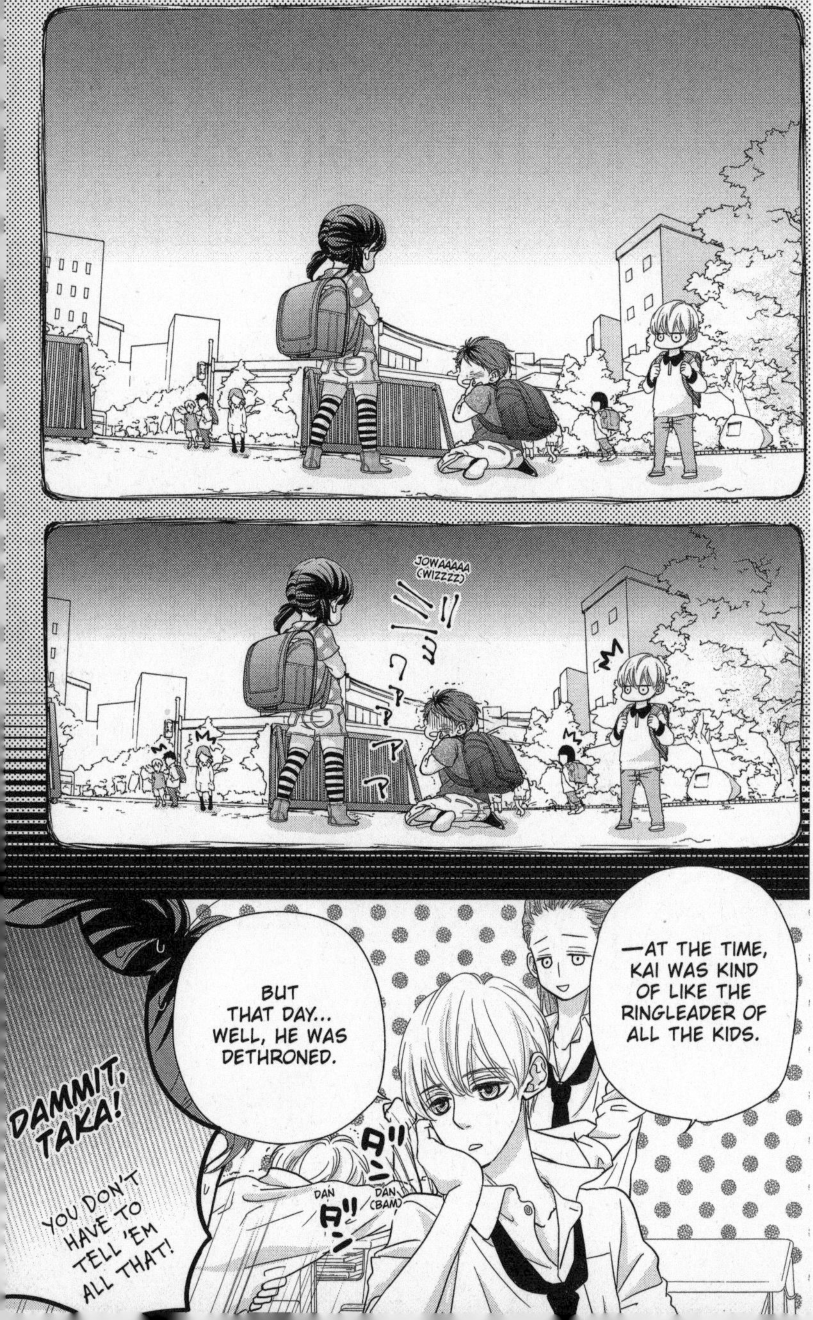
JOWAAAAA (WIZZZZ)
—AT THE TIME, KAI WAS KIND OF LIKE THE RINGLEADER OF ALL THE KIDS.
BUT THAT DAY... WELL, HE WAS DETHRONED.
DAN DAN (BAM)
DAMMIT, TAKA!
YOU DON'T HAVE TO TELL 'EM ALL THAT!

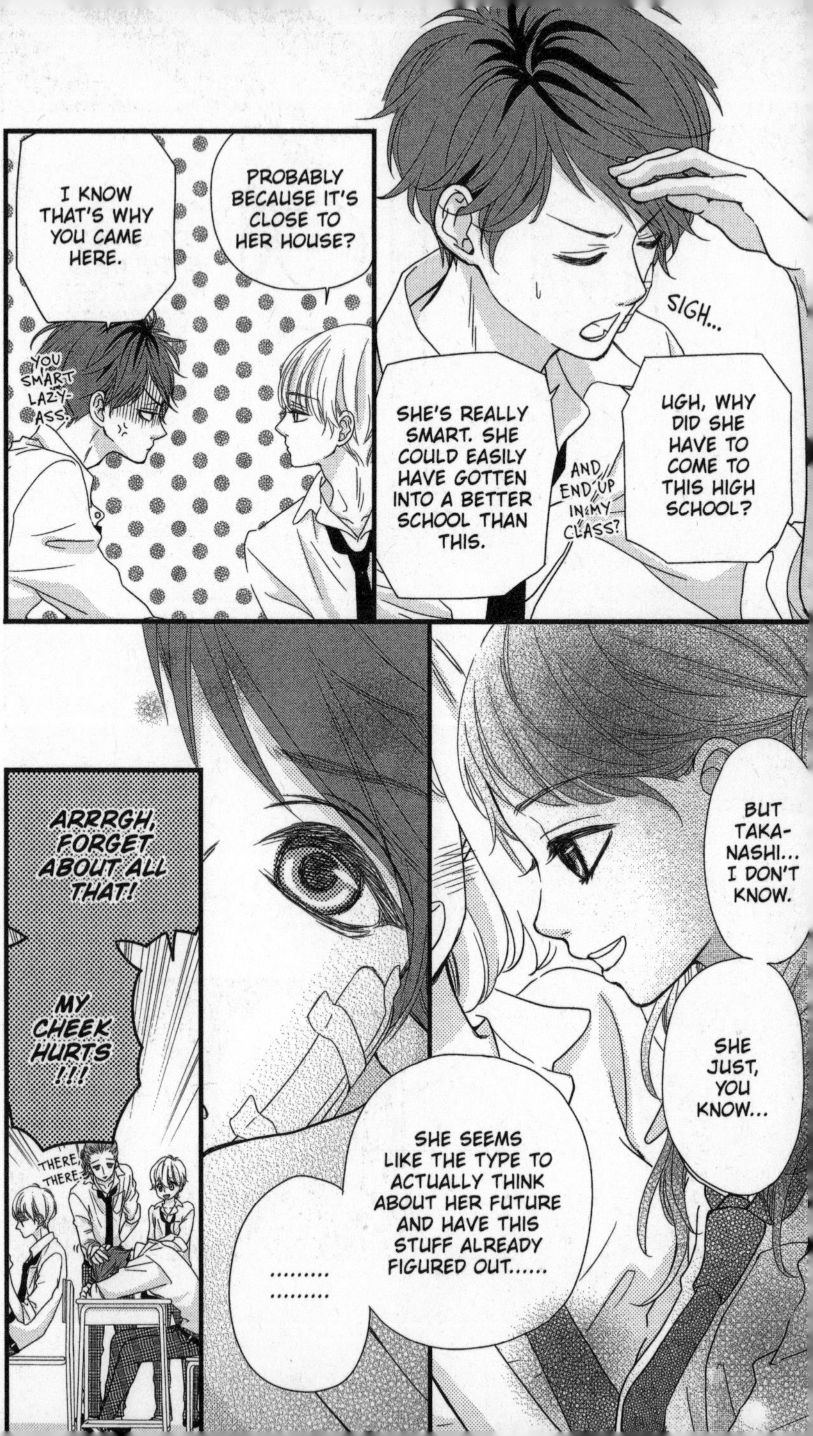
SIGH...
UGH, WHY DID SHE HAVE TO COME TO THIS HIGH SCHOOL?
AND END UP IN MY CLASS?
SHE'S REALLY SMART. SHE COULD EASILY HAVE GOTTEN INTO A BETTER SCHOOL THAN THIS.
PROBABLY BECAUSE IT'S CLOSE TO HER HOUSE?
I KNOW THAT'S WHY YOU CAME HERE.
YOU SMART LAZY-ASS.
BUT TAKA-NASHI... I DON'T KNOW.
SHE JUST, YOU KNOW...
SHE SEEMS LIKE THE TYPE TO ACTUALLY THINK ABOUT HER FUTURE AND HAVE THIS STUFF ALREADY FIGURED OUT......
....
ARRRGH, FORGET ABOUT ALL THAT!
MY CHEEK HURTS!!!
THERE, THERE

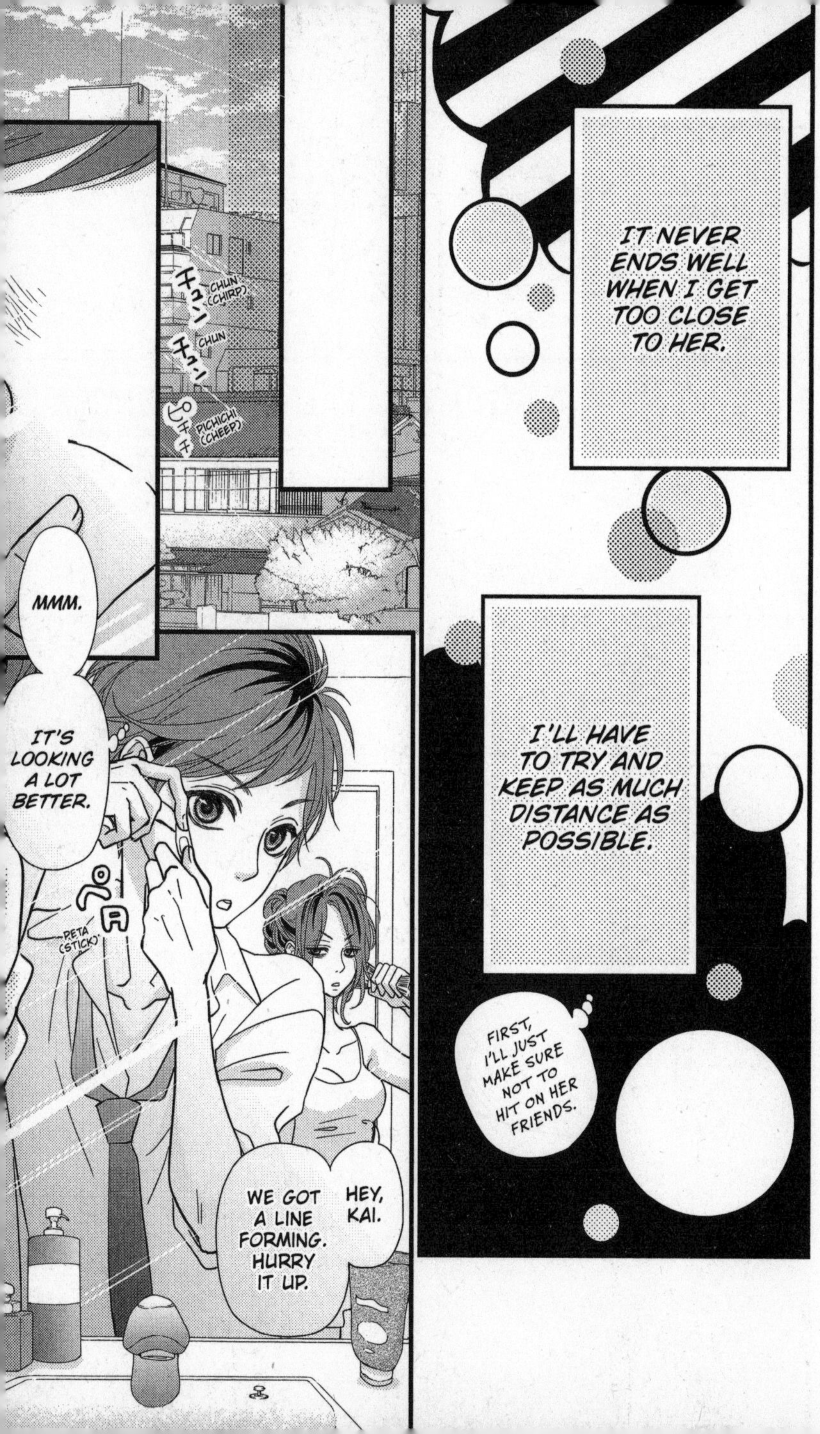
IT NEVER ENDS WELL WHEN I GET TOO CLOSE TO HER.
I'LL HAVE TO TRY AND KEEP AS MUCH DISTANCE AS POSSIBLE.
FIRST, I'LL JUST MAKE SURE NOT TO HIT ON HER FRIENDS.
チュン CHUN (CHIRP)
チュン CHUN
ピチチ PICHICHI (CHEEP)
MMM.
IT'S LOOKING A LOT BETTER.
ペタ PETA (STICK)
HEY, KAI.
WE GOT A LINE FORMING. HURRY IT UP.

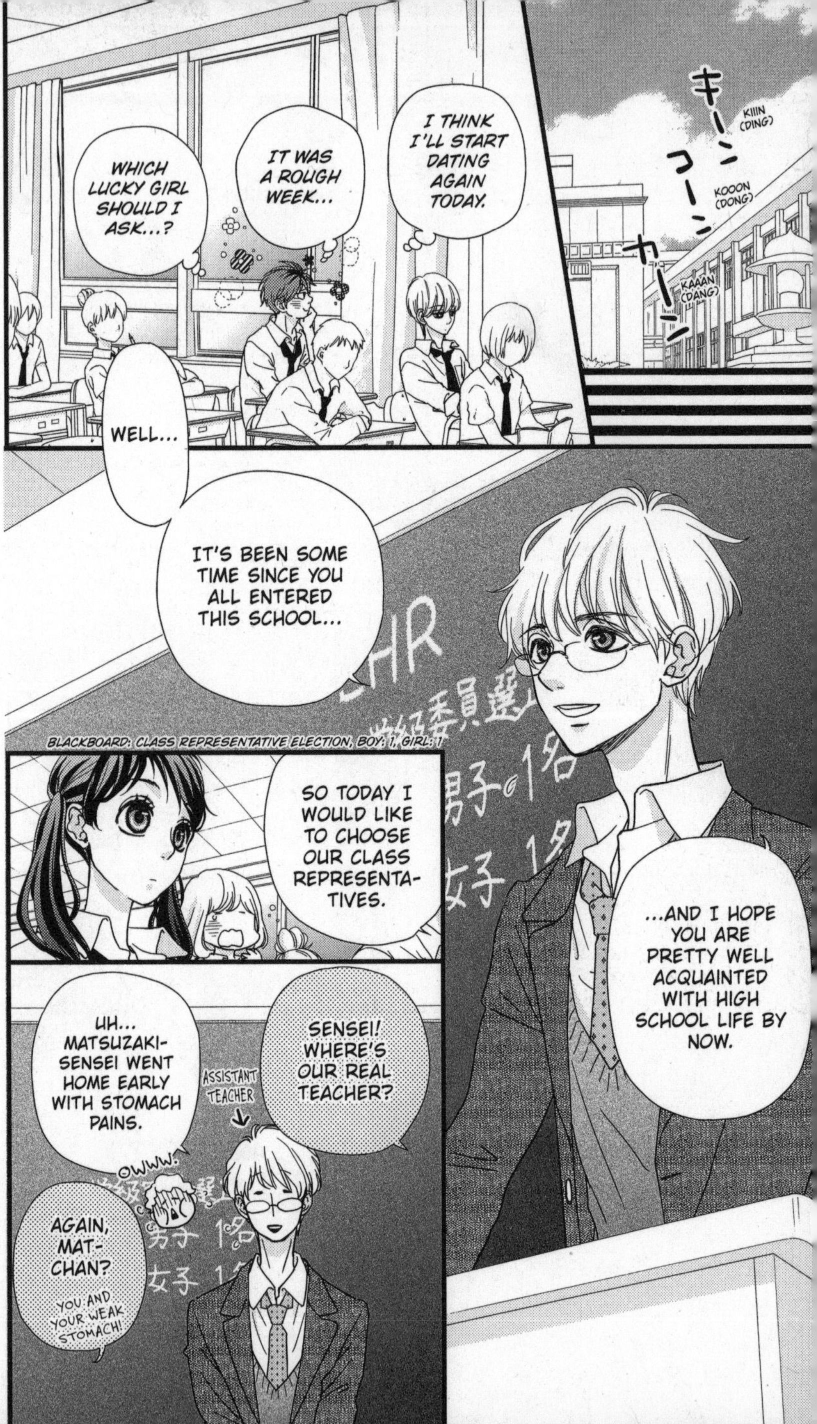
KIIN (DING)
KOOON (DONG)
KAAAN (DANG)
I THINK I'LL START DATING AGAIN TODAY.
IT WAS A ROUGH WEEK...
WHICH LUCKY GIRL SHOULD I ASK...?
WELL...
IT'S BEEN SOME TIME SINCE YOU ALL ENTERED THIS SCHOOL...
...AND I HOPE YOU ARE PRETTY WELL ACQUAINTED WITH HIGH SCHOOL LIFE BY NOW.
BLACKBOARD: CLASS REPRESENTATIVE ELECTION, BOY: 1, GIRL: 1
SO TODAY I WOULD LIKE TO CHOOSE OUR CLASS REPRESENTATIVES.
SENSEI! WHERE'S OUR REAL TEACHER?
UH... MATSUZAKI-SENSEI WENT HOME EARLY WITH STOMACH PAINS.
ASSISTANT TEACHER
OWWW.
AGAIN, MAT-CHAN?
YOU AND YOUR WEAK STOMACH!

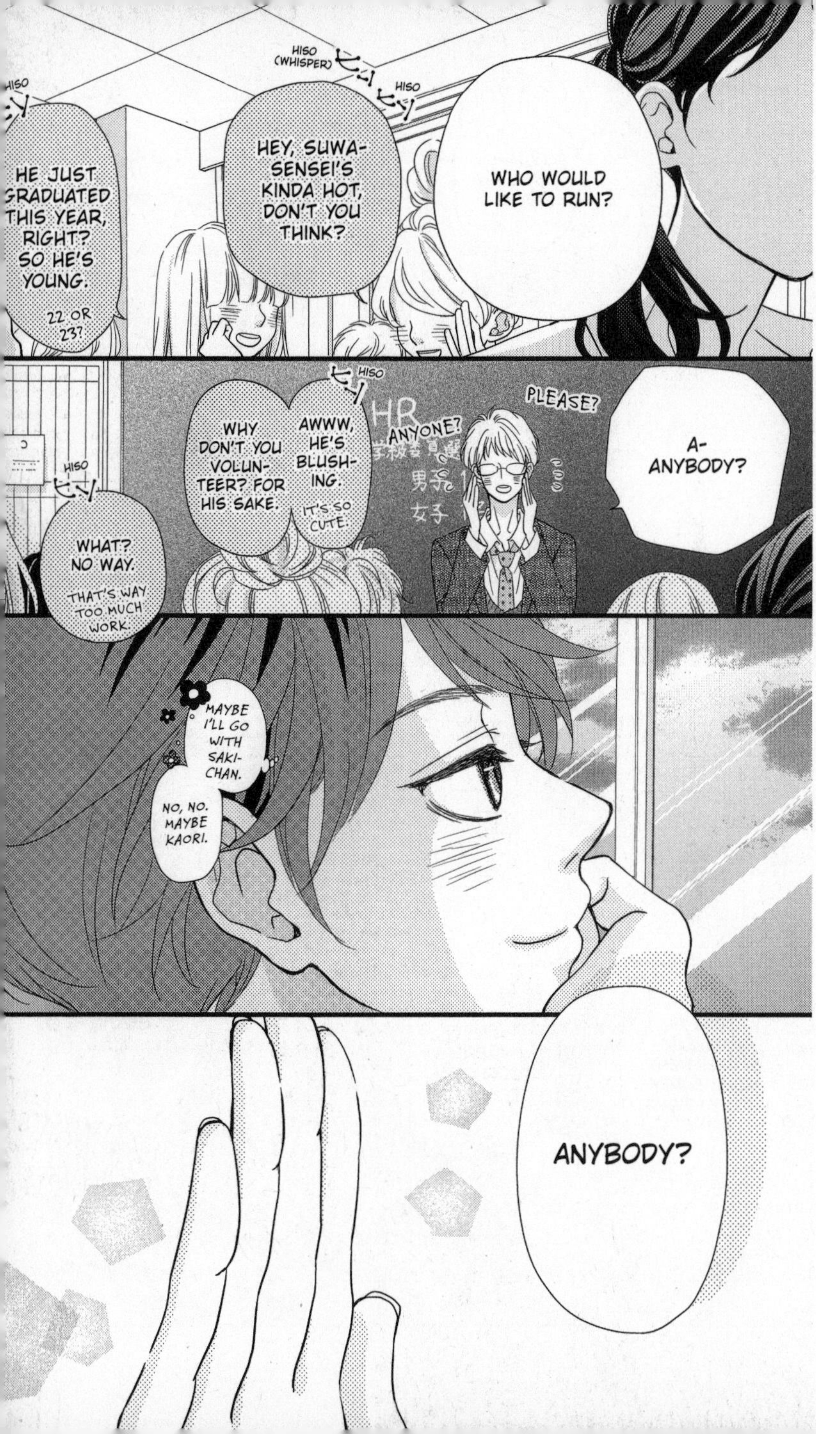
WHO WOULD LIKE TO RUN?
HISO (WHISPER)
HISO
HEY, SUWA-SENSEI'S KINDA HOT, DON'T YOU THINK?
HISO
HE JUST GRADUATED THIS YEAR, RIGHT? SO HE'S YOUNG.
22 OR 23?
A-ANYBODY?
PLEASE?
ANYONE?
HR
HISO
AWWW, HE'S BLUSHING.
IT'S SO CUTE.
WHY DON'T YOU VOLUNTEER? FOR HIS SAKE.
HISO
WHAT? NO WAY.
THAT'S WAY TOO MUCH WORK.
MAYBE I'LL GO WITH SAKI-CHAN.
NO, NO. MAYBE KAORI.
ANYBODY?

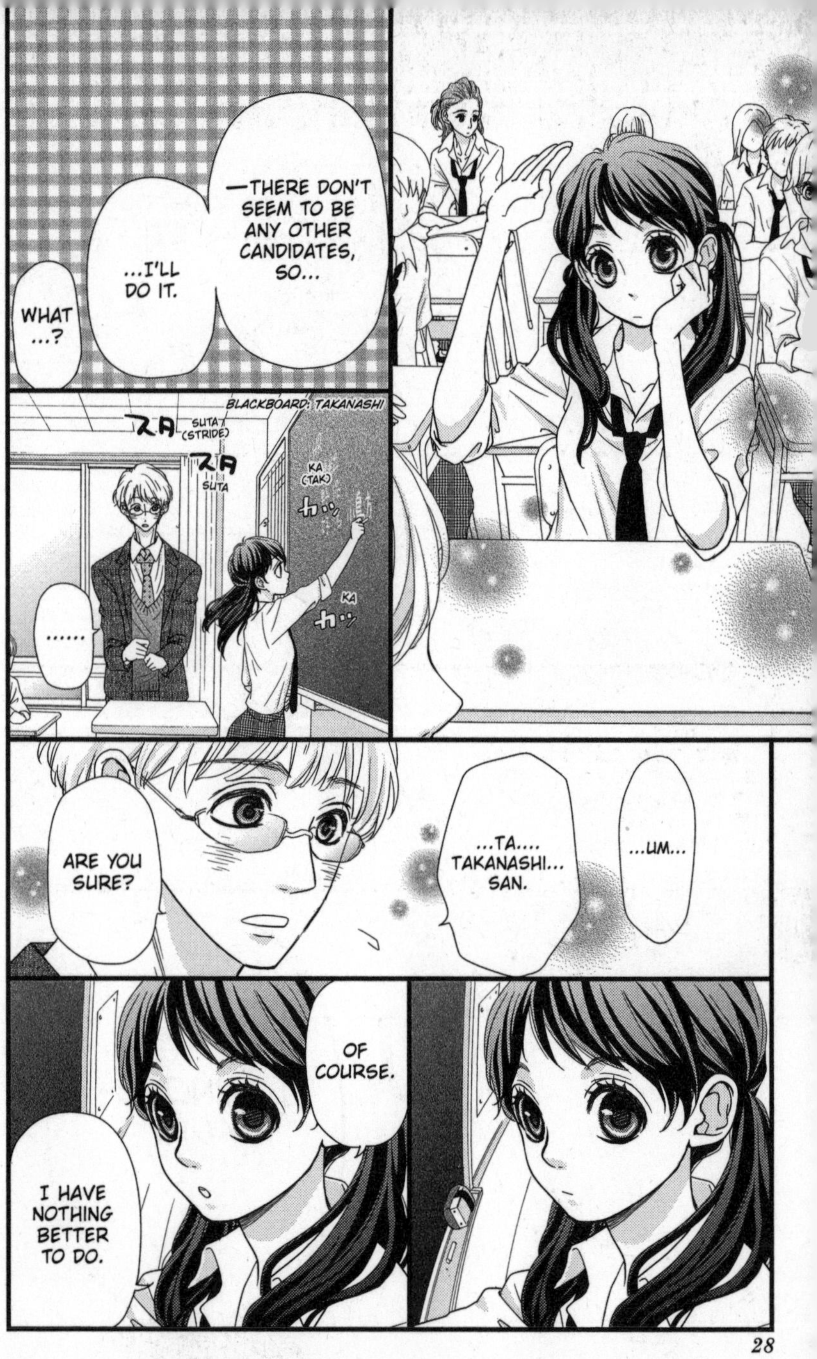
—THERE DON'T SEEM TO BE ANY OTHER CANDIDATES, SO...
...I'LL DO IT.
WHAT ...?
BLACKBOARD: TAKANASHI
SUTA (STRIDE)
SUTA
KA (TAK)
KA
......
...UM...
...TA.... TAKANASHI... SAN.
ARE YOU SURE?
OF COURSE.
I HAVE NOTHING BETTER TO DO.

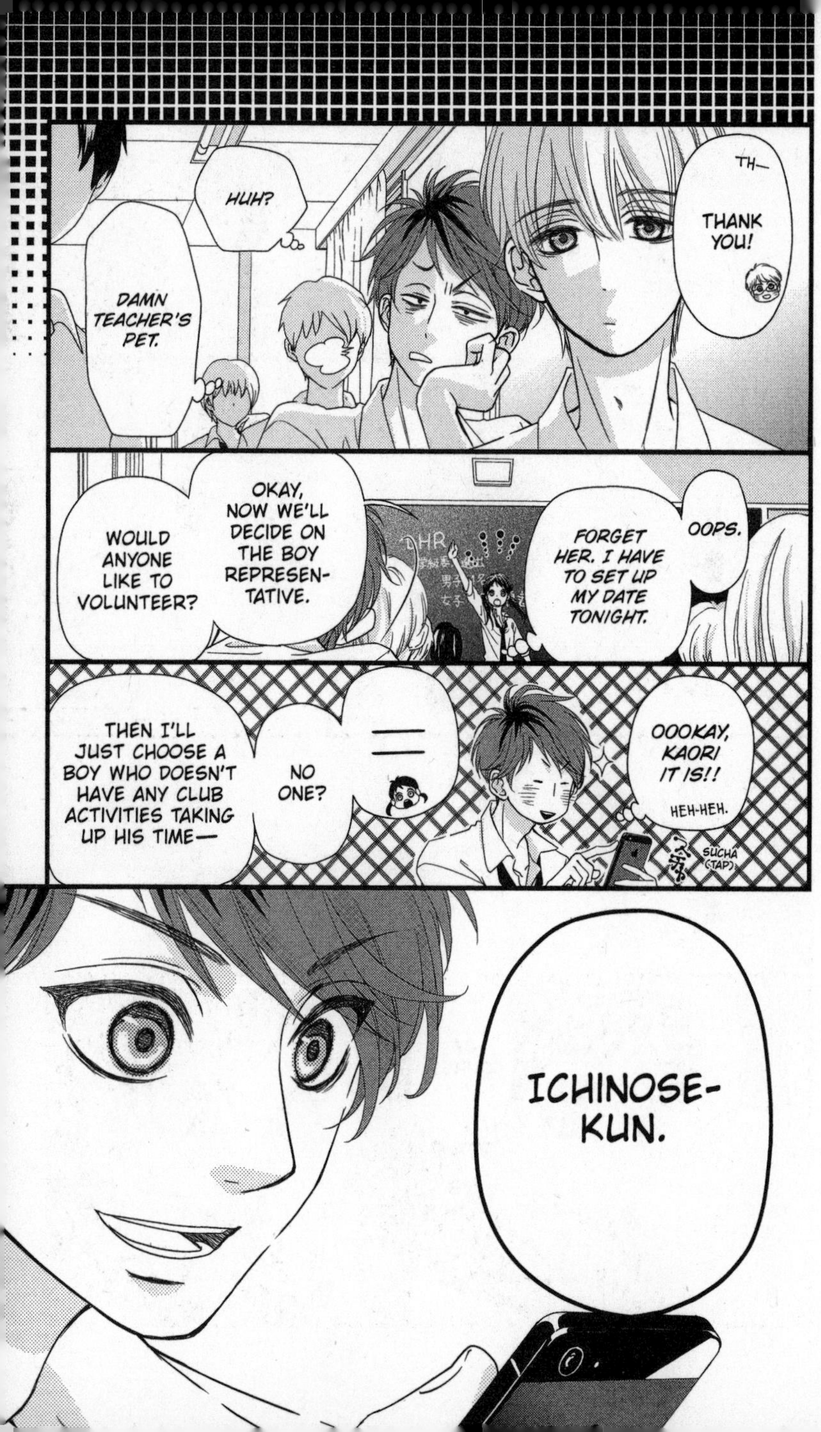
TH—
THANK YOU!
HUH?
DAMN TEACHER'S PET.
OOPS.
FORGET HER. I HAVE TO SET UP MY DATE TONIGHT.
OKAY, NOW WE'LL DECIDE ON THE BOY REPRESENTATIVE.
WOULD ANYONE LIKE TO VOLUNTEER?
OOOKAY, KAORI IT IS!!
HEH-HEH.
SUCHA (TAP)
NO ONE?
THEN I'LL JUST CHOOSE A BOY WHO DOESN'T HAVE ANY CLUB ACTIVITIES TAKING UP HIS TIME—
ICHINOSE-KUN.

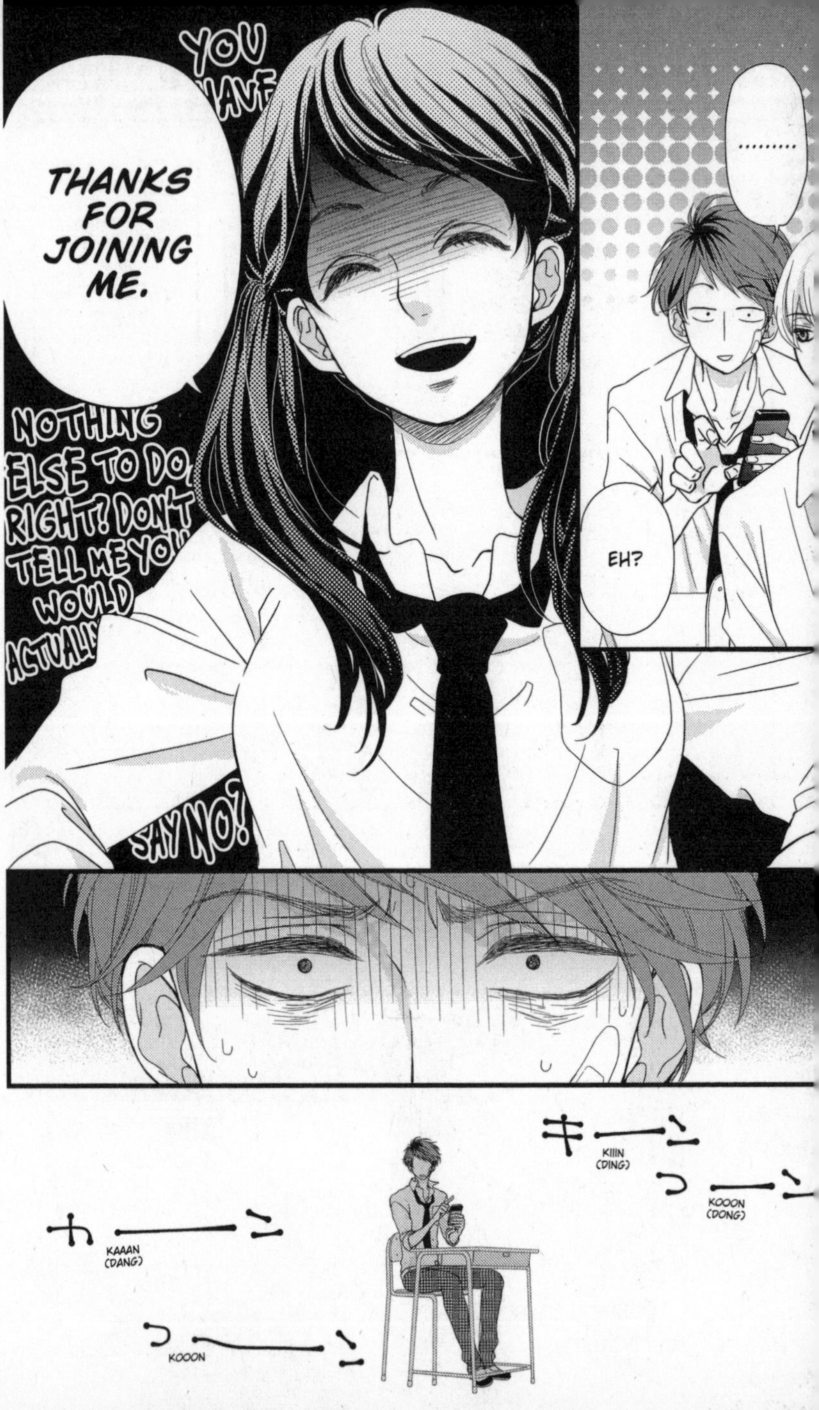
....
EH?
THANKS FOR JOINING ME.
YOU HAVE
NOTHING ELSE TO DO, RIGHT? DON'T TELL ME YOU WOULD ACTUAL
SAY NO?
キーン
KIIIN (DING)
コーン
KOOON (DONG)
カーン
KAAAN (DANG)
コーン
KOOON

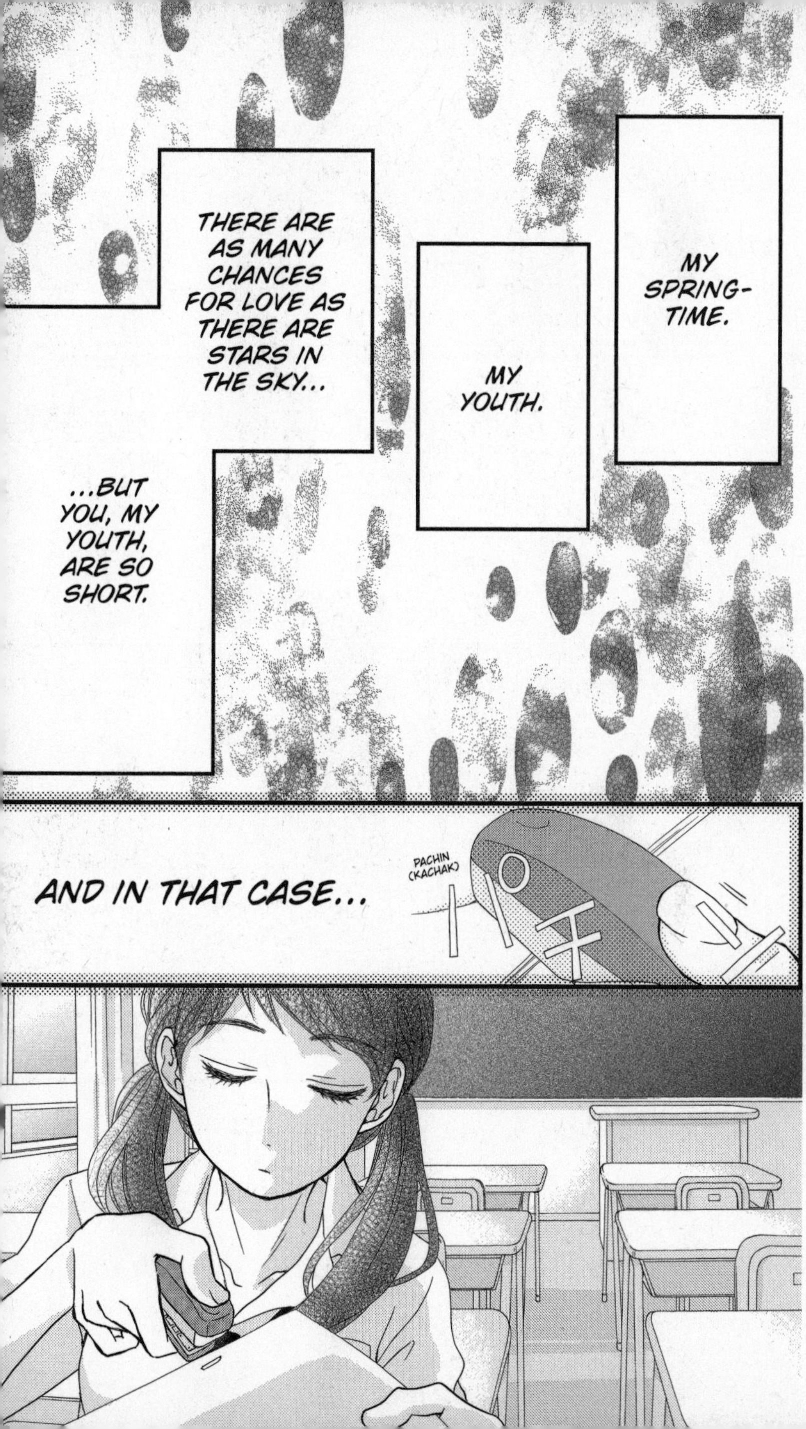
MY SPRING-TIME.
MY YOUTH.
THERE ARE AS MANY CHANCES FOR LOVE AS THERE ARE STARS IN THE SKY...
...BUT YOU, MY YOUTH, ARE SO SHORT.
PACHIN (KACHAK)
AND IN THAT CASE...

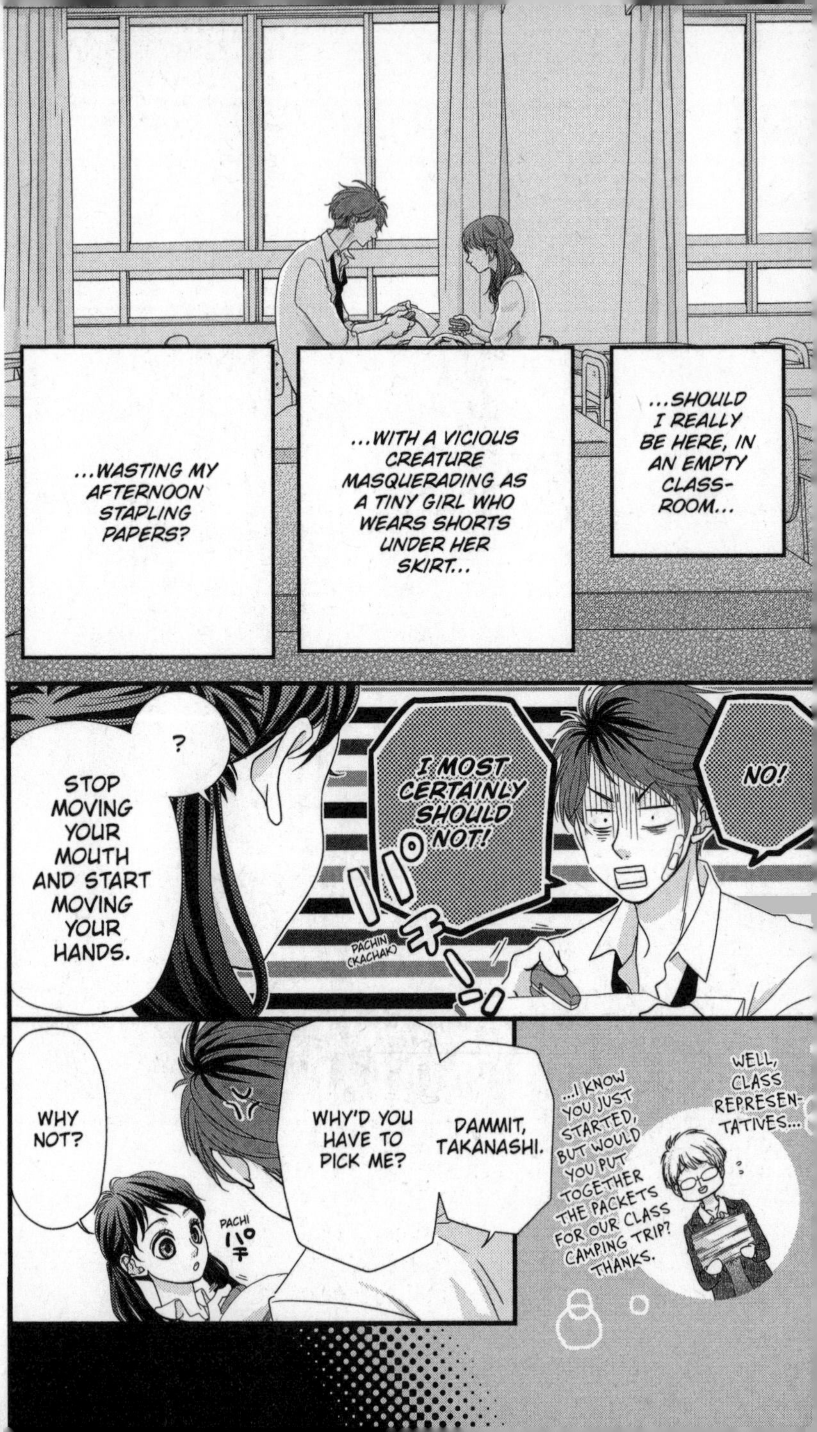
...SHOULD I REALLY BE HERE, IN AN EMPTY CLASS-ROOM...
...WITH A VICIOUS CREATURE MASQUERADING AS A TINY GIRL WHO WEARS SHORTS UNDER HER SKIRT...
...WASTING MY AFTERNOON STAPLING PAPERS?
NO!
I MOST CERTAINLY SHOULD NOT!
PACHIN (KACHAK)
?
STOP MOVING YOUR MOUTH AND START MOVING YOUR HANDS.
WELL, CLASS REPRESEN-TATIVES...
...I KNOW YOU JUST STARTED, BUT WOULD YOU PUT TOGETHER THE PACKETS FOR OUR CLASS CAMPING TRIP? THANKS.
DAMMIT, TAKANASHI.
WHY'D YOU HAVE TO PICK ME?
PACHI
WHY NOT?

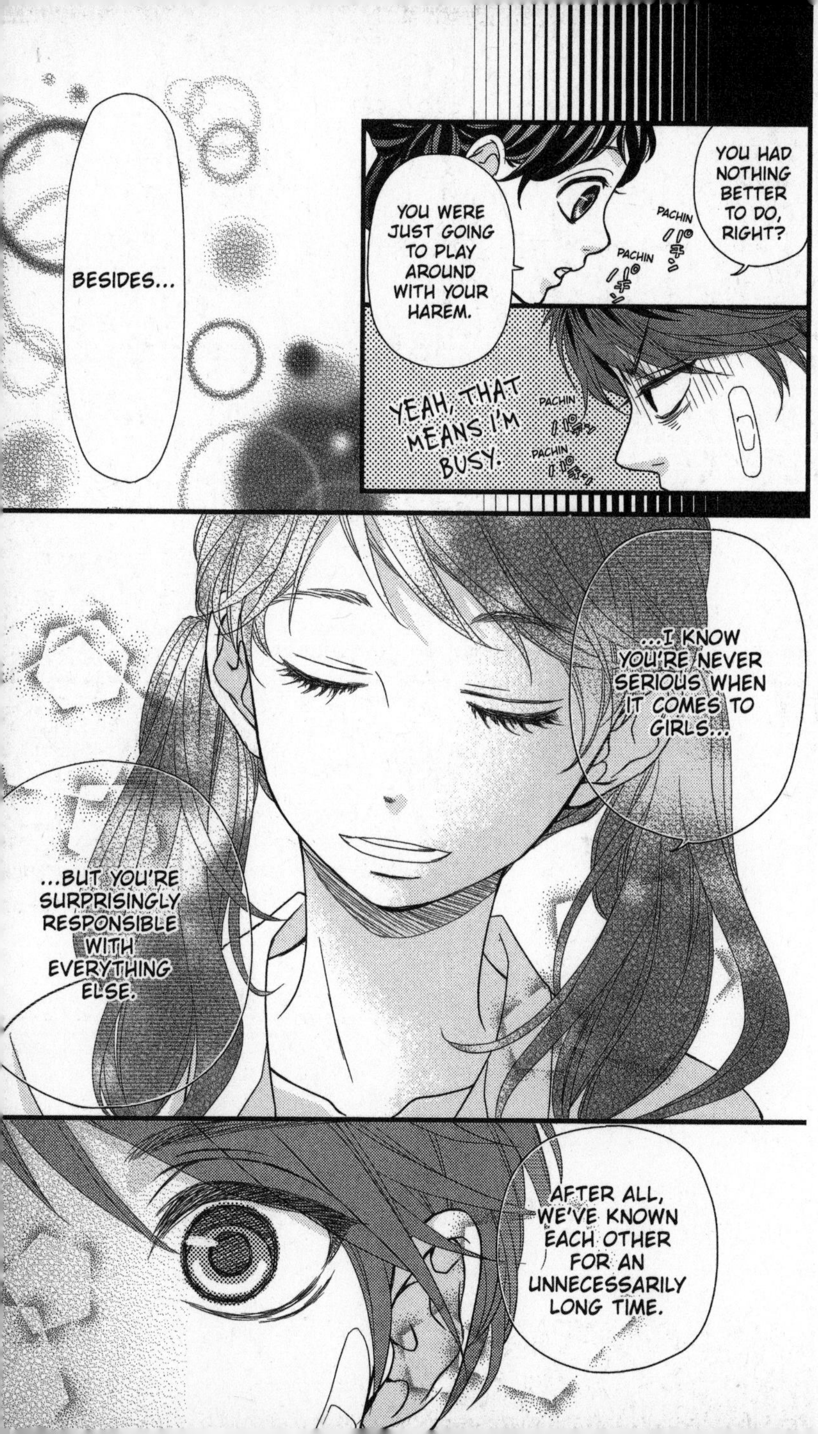
YOU HAD NOTHING BETTER TO DO, RIGHT?
PACHIN
PACHIN
YOU WERE JUST GOING TO PLAY AROUND WITH YOUR HAREM.
PACHIN
PACHIN
YEAH, THAT MEANS I'M BUSY.
BESIDES...
...I KNOW YOU'RE NEVER SERIOUS WHEN IT COMES TO GIRLS...
...BUT YOU'RE SURPRISINGLY RESPONSIBLE WITH EVERYTHING ELSE.
AFTER ALL, WE'VE KNOWN EACH OTHER FOR AN UNNECESSARILY LONG TIME.

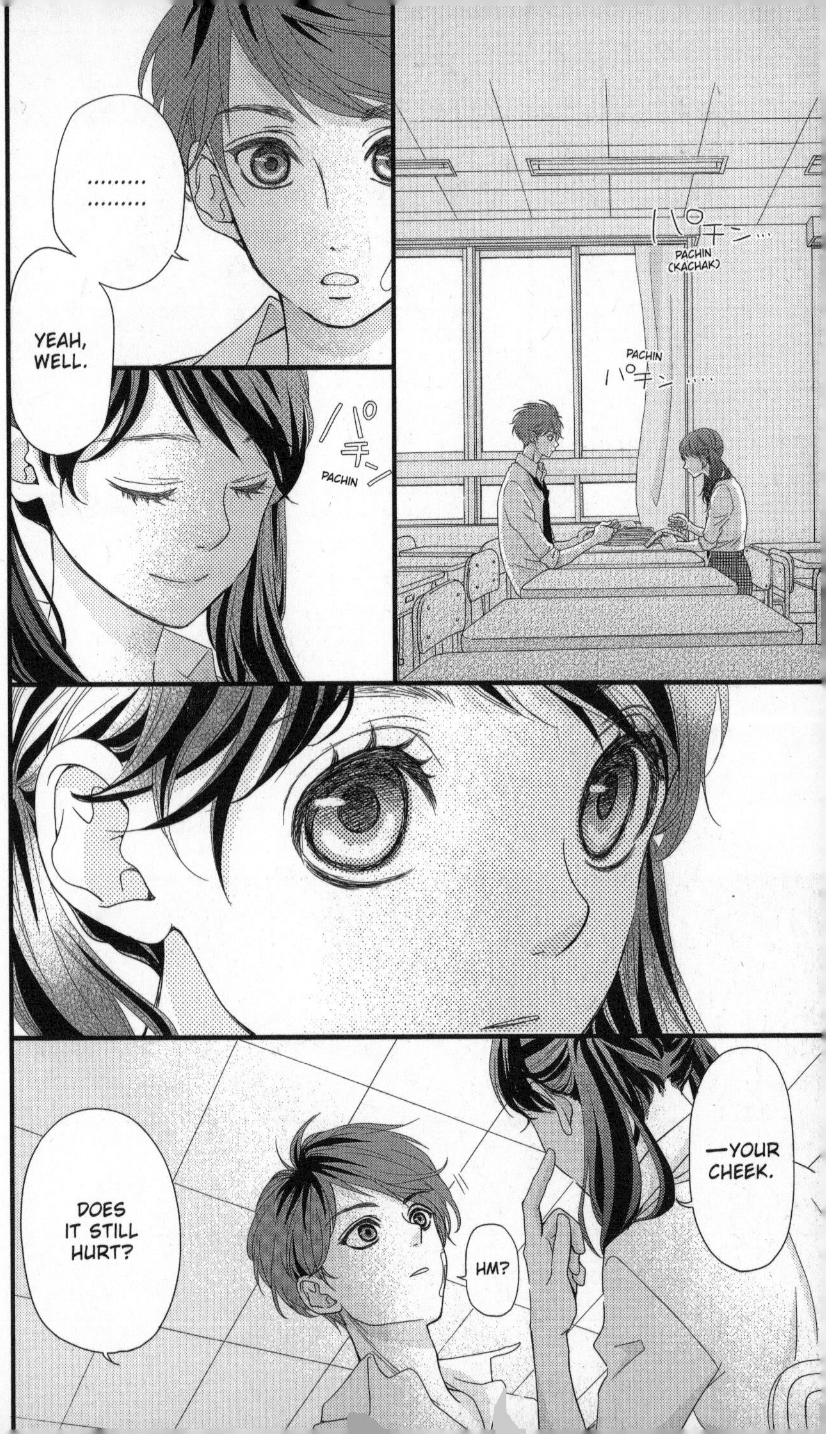
パチン…
PACHIN (KACHAK)
PACHIN
パチン……
....
....
YEAH, WELL.
パチン
PACHIN
—YOUR CHEEK.
HM?
DOES IT STILL HURT?

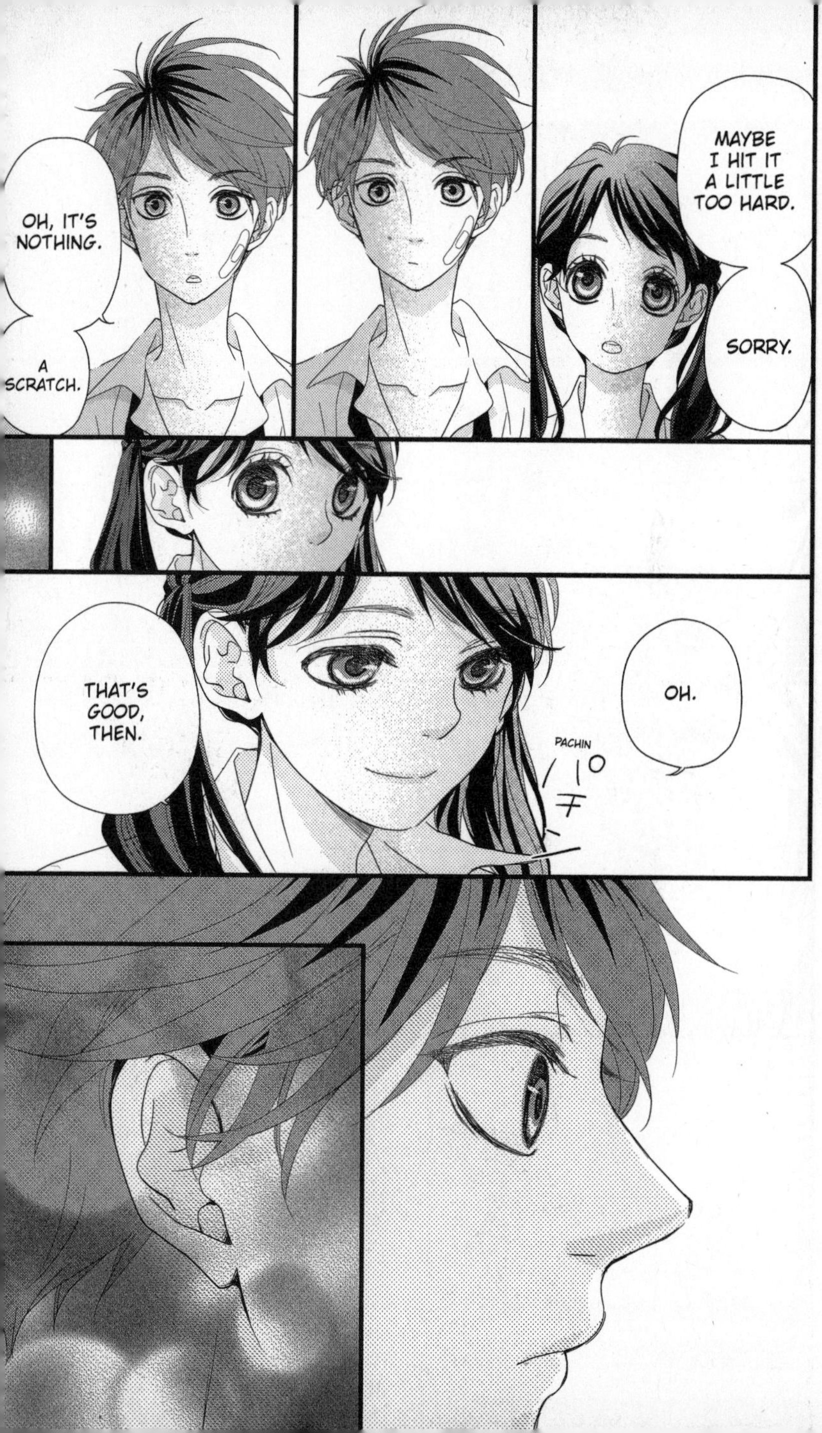
MAYBE I HIT IT A LITTLE TOO HARD.
SORRY.
OH, IT'S NOTHING.
A SCRATCH.
OH.
PACHIN
THAT'S GOOD, THEN.

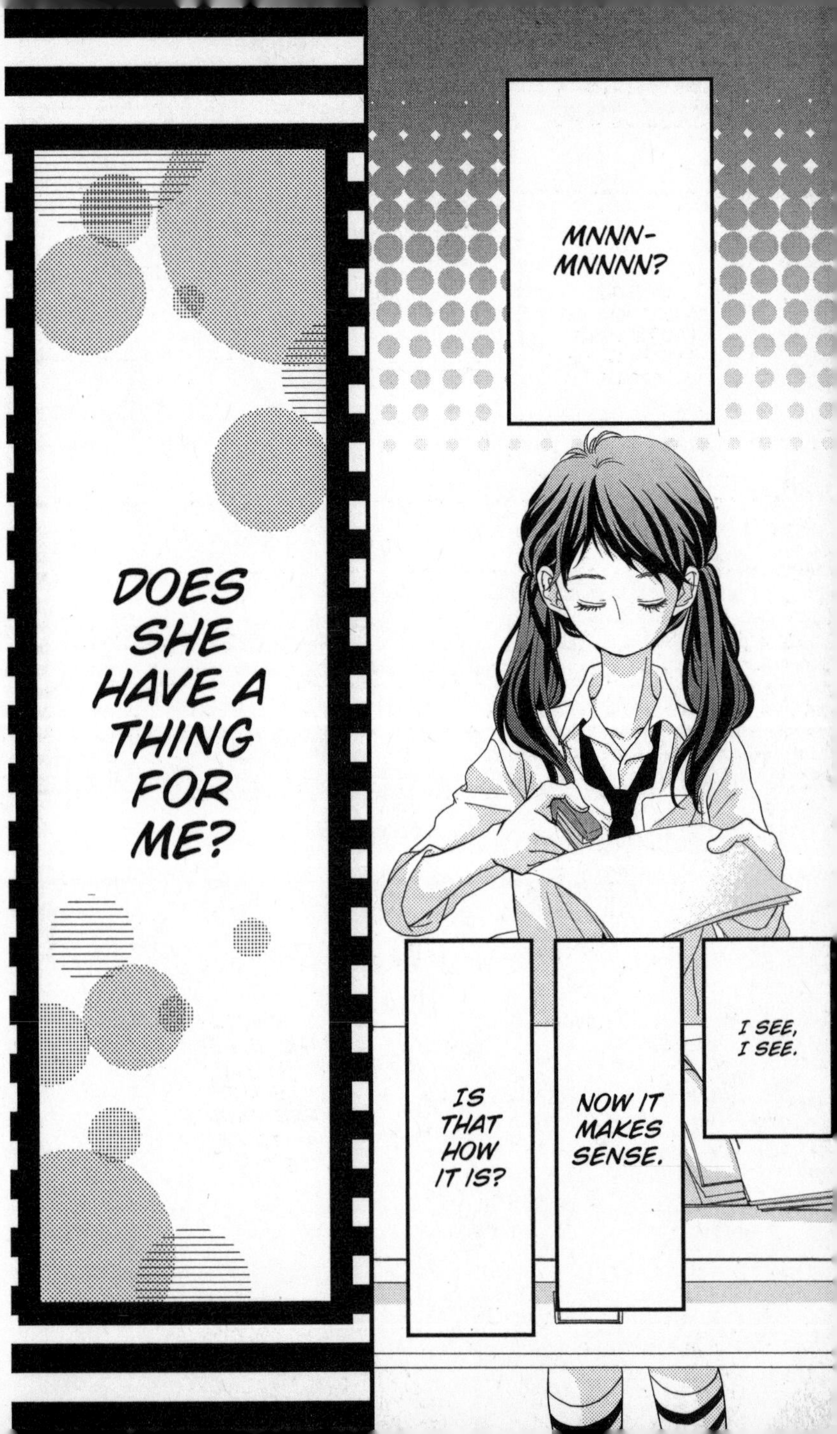
MNNN-MNNNN?
I SEE, I SEE.
NOW IT MAKES SENSE.
IS THAT HOW IT IS?
DOES SHE HAVE A THING FOR ME?

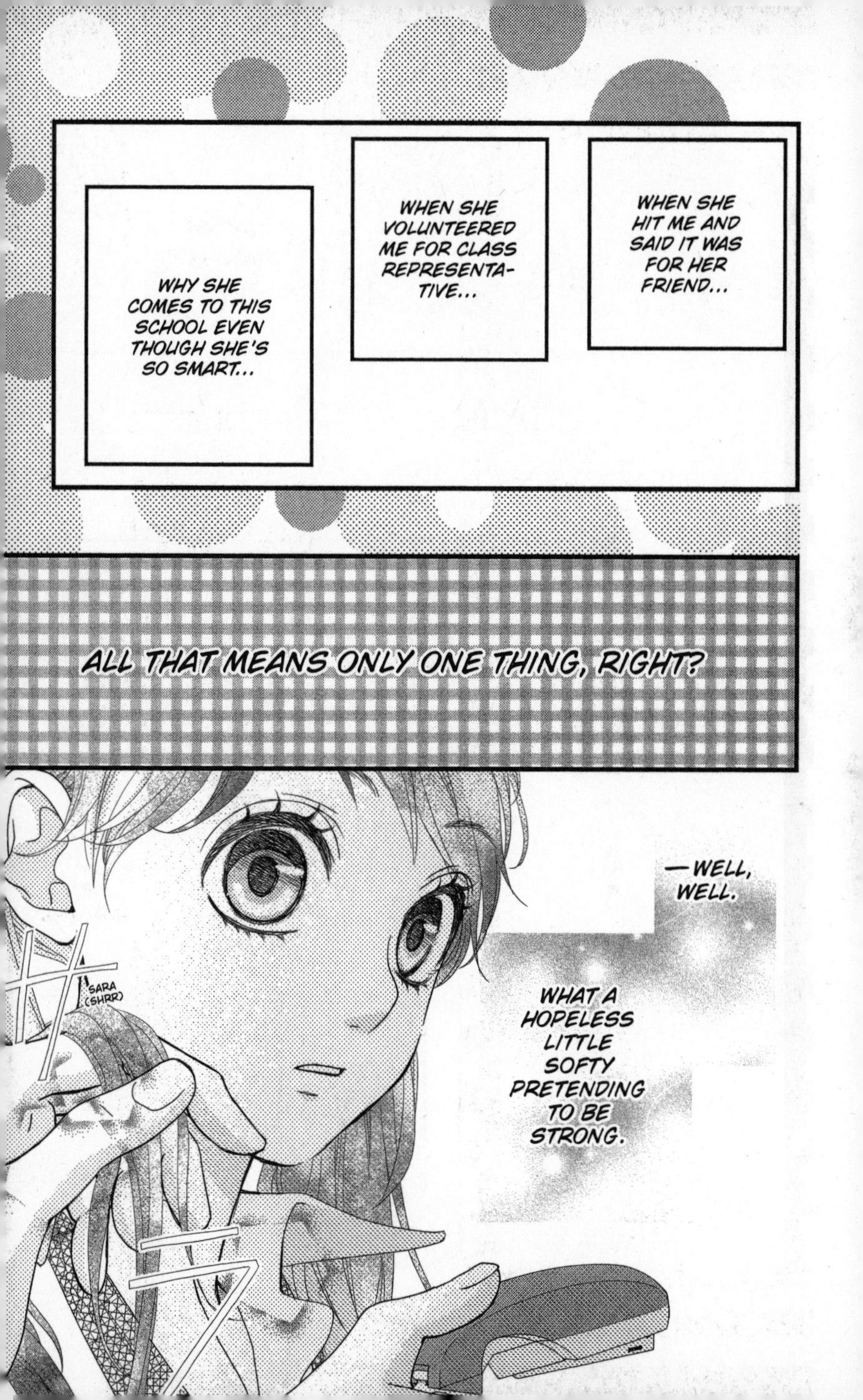
WHEN SHE HIT ME AND SAID IT WAS FOR HER FRIEND...
WHEN SHE VOLUNTEERED ME FOR CLASS REPRESENTATIVE...
WHY SHE COMES TO THIS SCHOOL EVEN THOUGH SHE'S SO SMART...
ALL THAT MEANS ONLY ONE THING, RIGHT?
—WELL, WELL.
WHAT A HOPELESS LITTLE SOFTY PRETENDING TO BE STRONG.
SARA (SHRR)

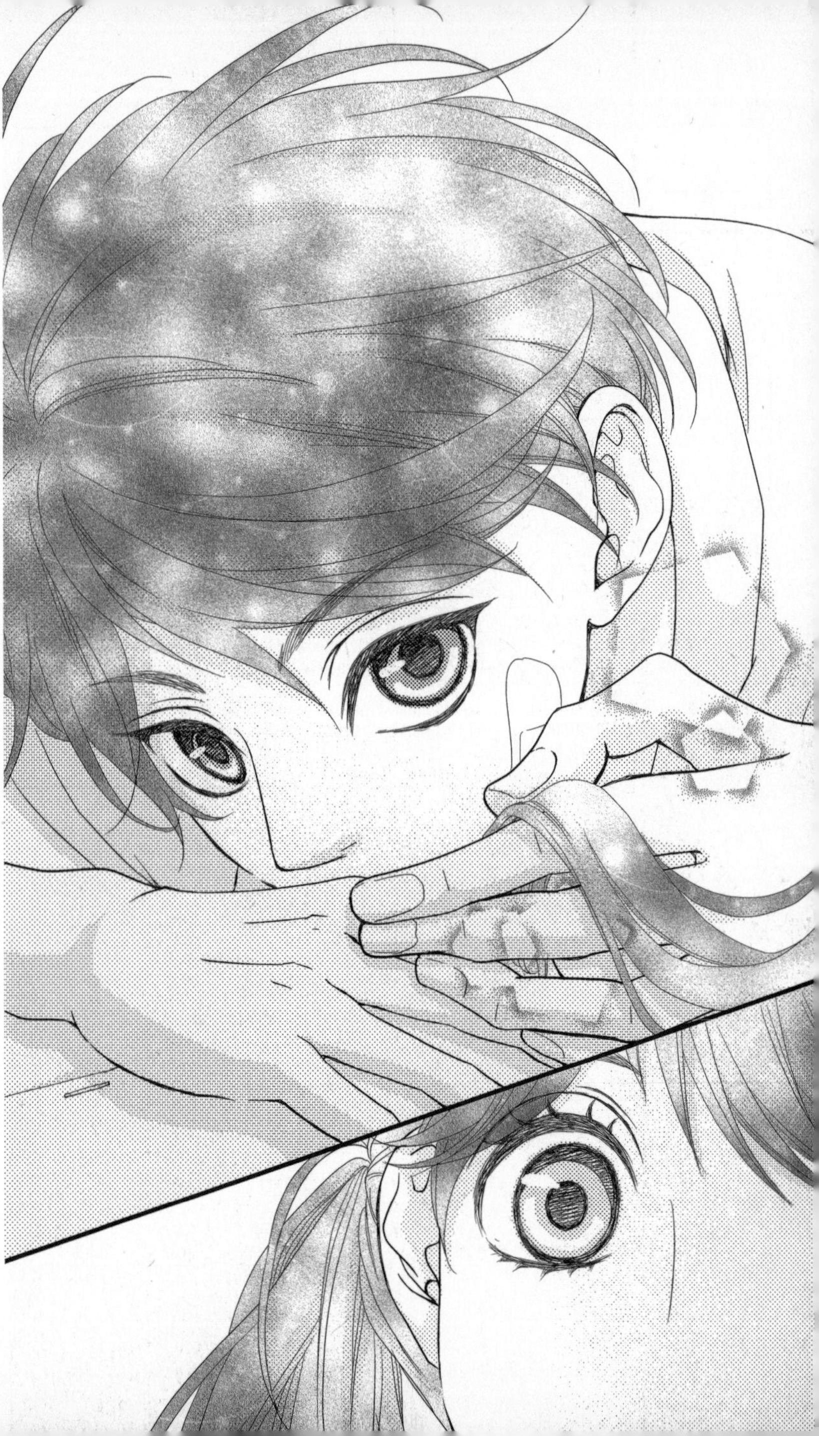

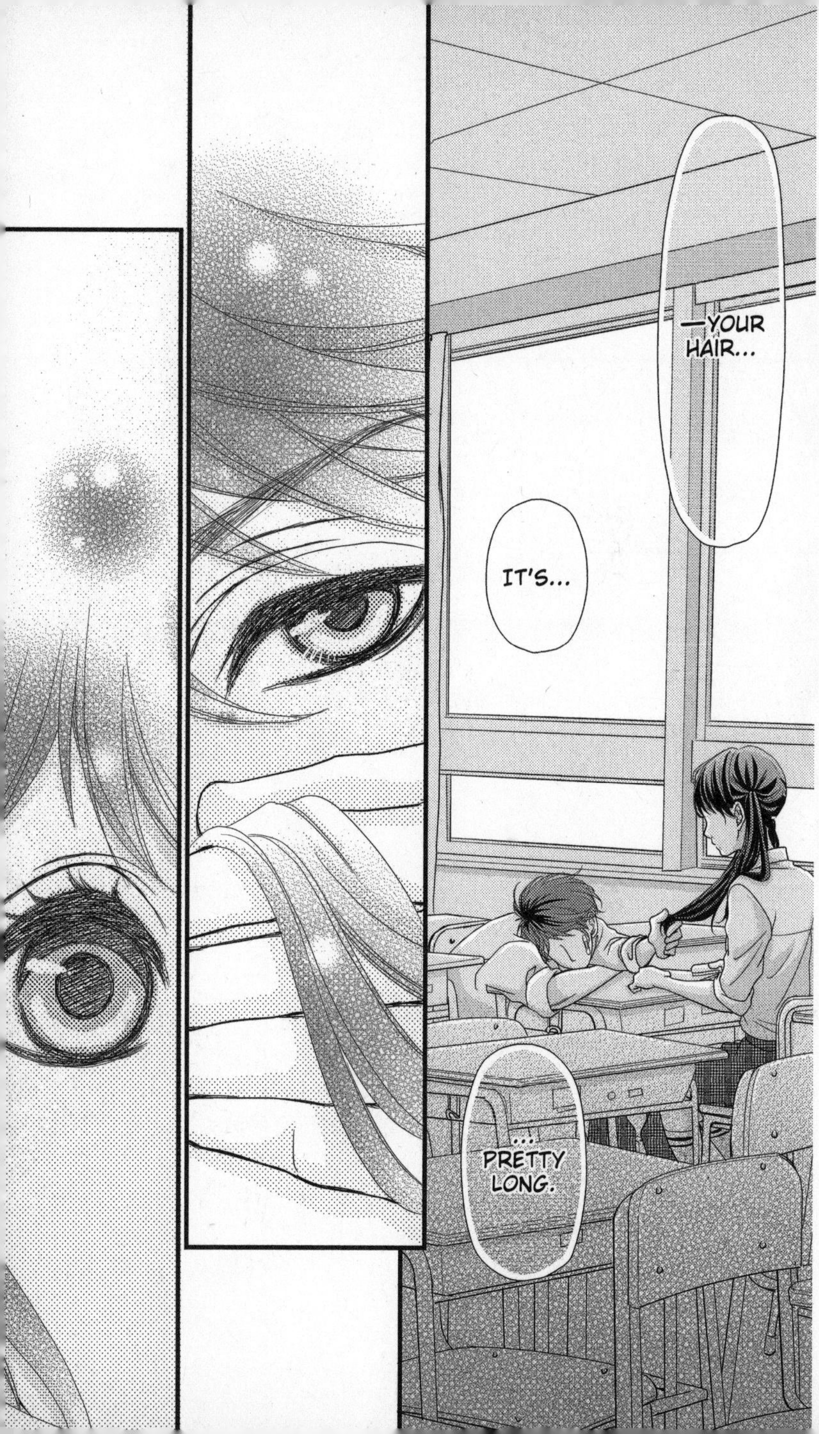
—YOUR HAIR...
IT'S...
... PRETTY LONG.

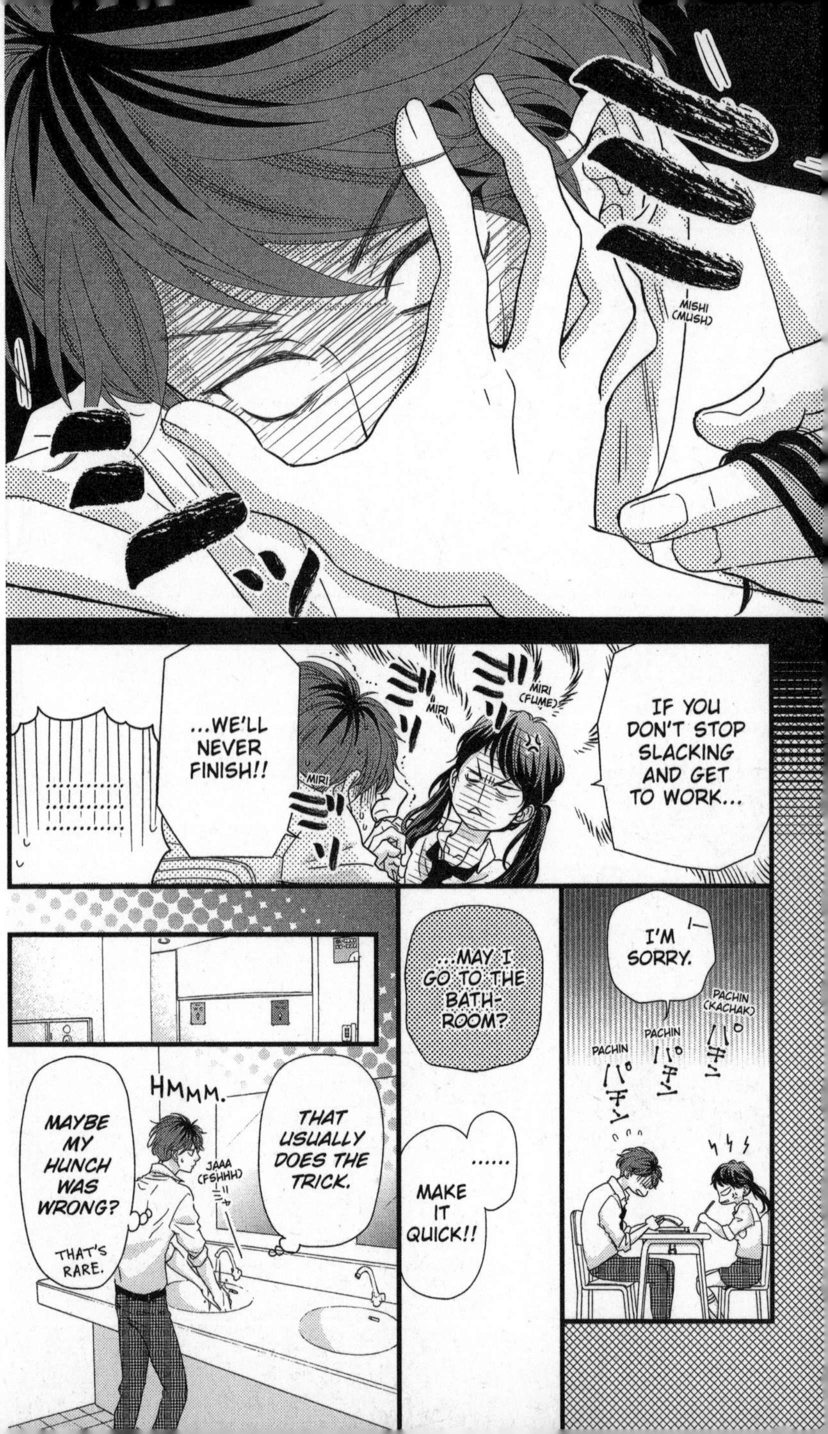
MISHI (MUSH)
IF YOU DON'T STOP SLACKING AND GET TO WORK...
MIRI (FUME)
MIRI
MIRI
...WE'LL NEVER FINISH!!
I'M SORRY.
PACHIN (KACHAK)
PACHIN
PACHIN
...MAY I GO TO THE BATH-ROOM?
......
MAKE IT QUICK!!
HMMM.
THAT USUALLY DOES THE TRICK.
JAAA (FSHHH)
MAYBE MY HUNCH WAS WRONG?
THAT'S RARE.

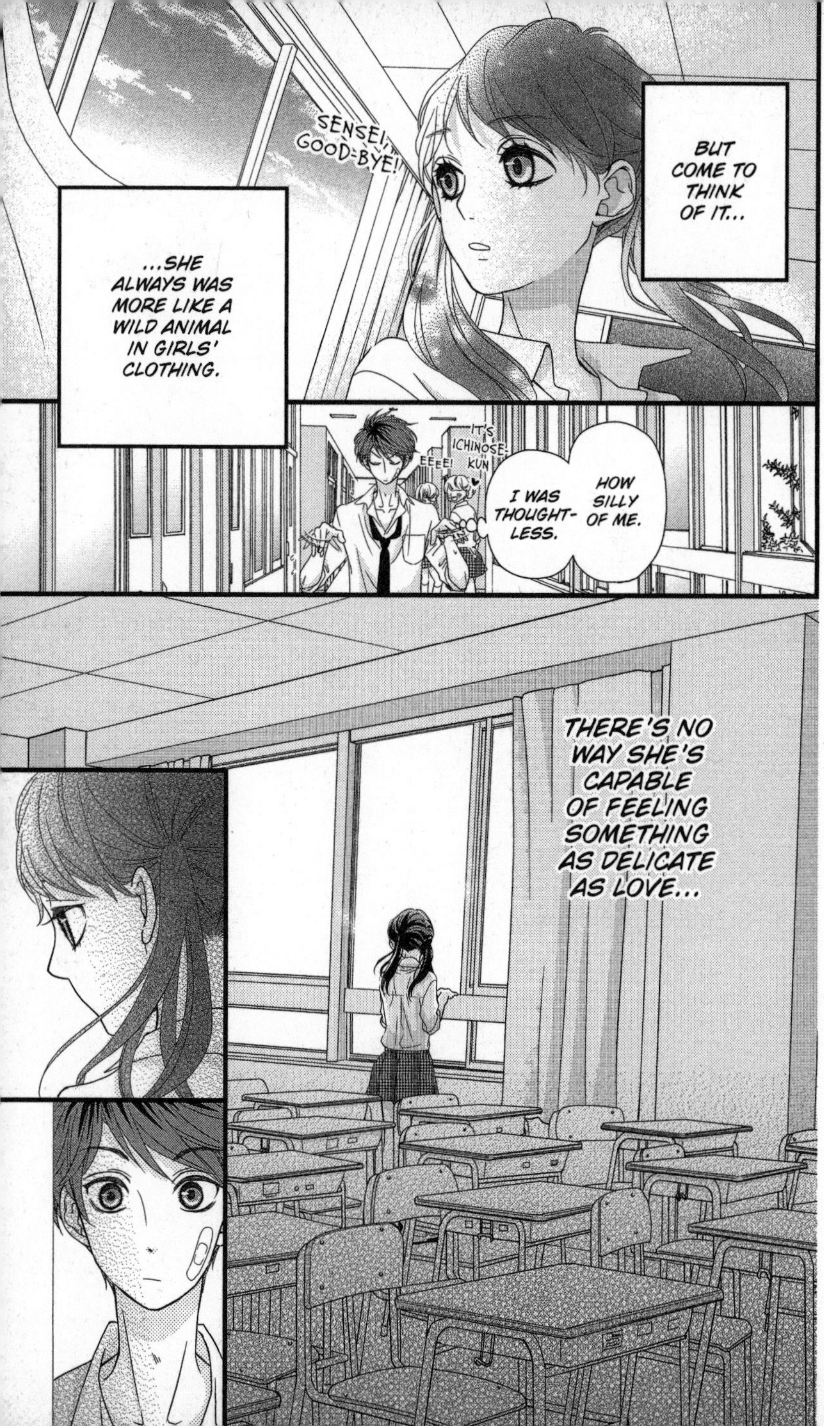
BUT COME TO THINK OF IT...
SENSEI, GOOD-BYE!
...SHE ALWAYS WAS MORE LIKE A WILD ANIMAL IN GIRLS' CLOTHING.
HOW SILLY OF ME.
I WAS THOUGHT-LESS.
IT'S ICHINOSE-KUN
EEEE!
THERE'S NO WAY SHE'S CAPABLE OF FEELING SOMETHING AS DELICATE AS LOVE...

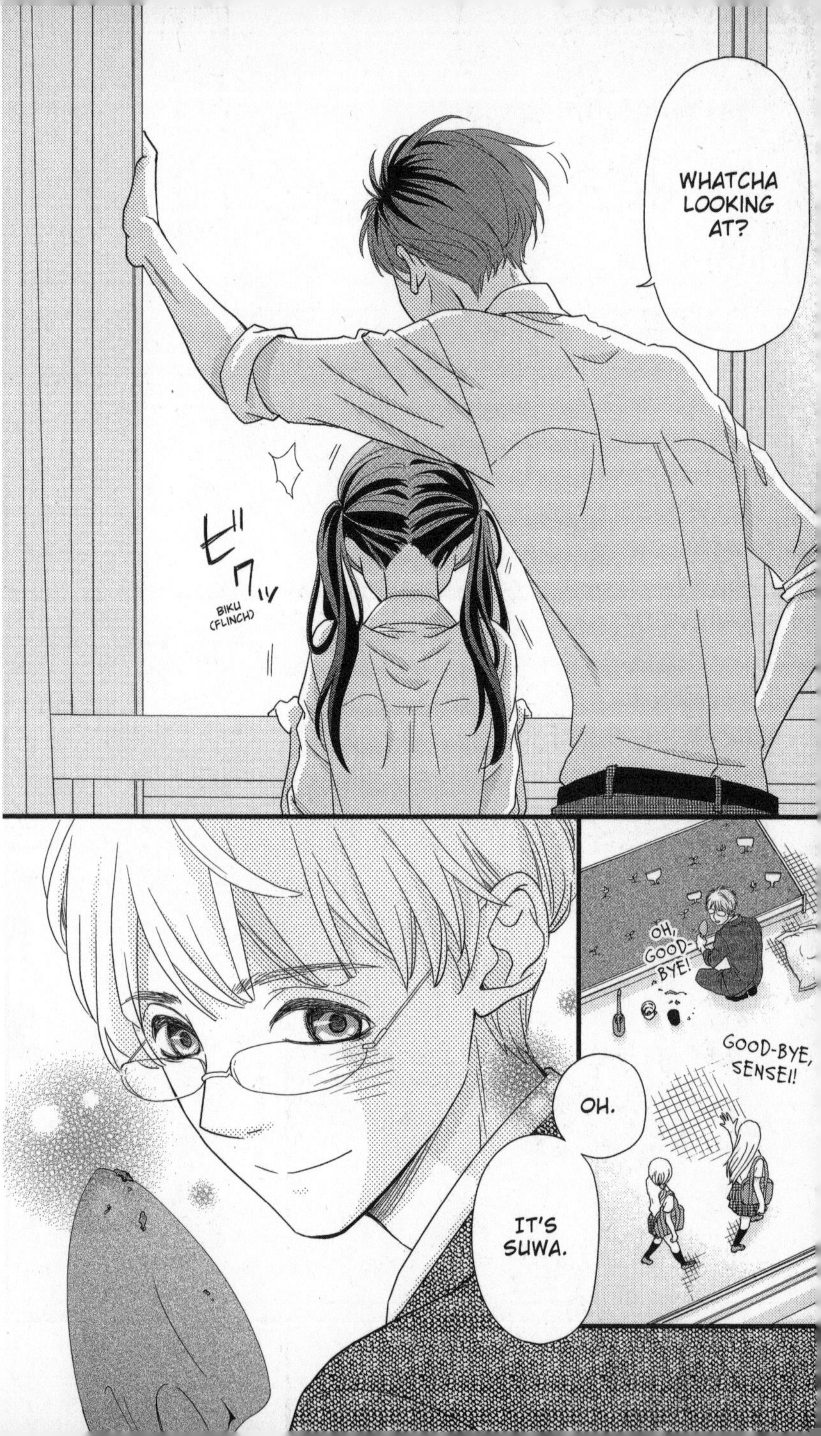
WHATCHA LOOKING AT?
ビクッ
BIKU (FLINCH)
OH, GOOD-BYE!
GOOD-BYE, SENSEI!
OH.
IT'S SUWA.

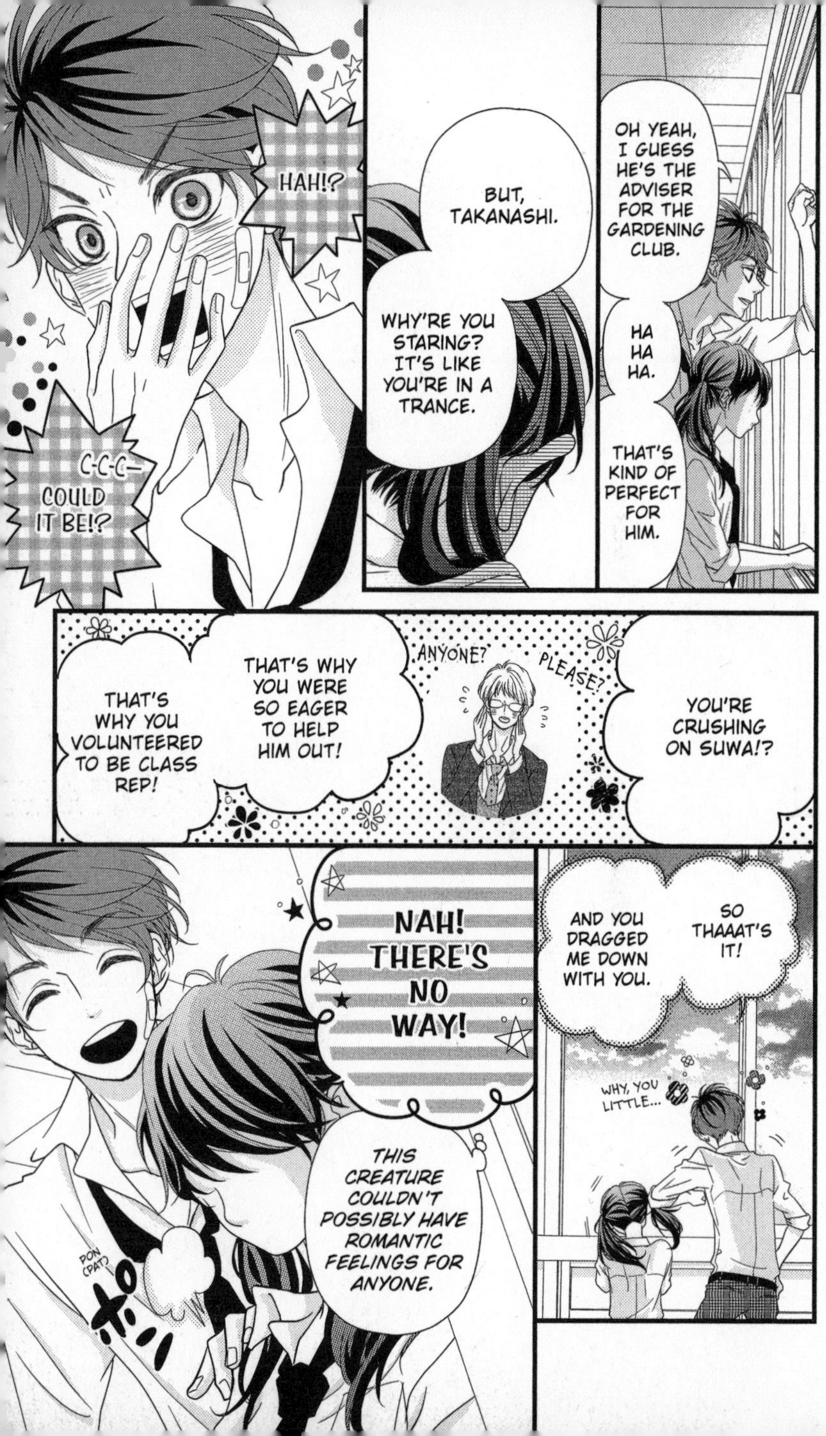
OH YEAH, I GUESS HE'S THE ADVISER FOR THE GARDENING CLUB.
HA HA HA.
THAT'S KIND OF PERFECT FOR HIM.
BUT, TAKANASHI.
WHY'RE YOU STARING? IT'S LIKE YOU'RE IN A TRANCE.
HAH!?
C-C-C— COULD IT BE!?
YOU'RE CRUSHING ON SUWA!?
PLEASE?
ANYONE?
THAT'S WHY YOU WERE SO EAGER TO HELP HIM OUT!
THAT'S WHY YOU VOLUNTEERED TO BE CLASS REP!
SO THAAAT'S IT!
AND YOU DRAGGED ME DOWN WITH YOU.
WHY, YOU LITTLE...
NAH! THERE'S NO WAY!
THIS CREATURE COULDN'T POSSIBLY HAVE ROMANTIC FEELINGS FOR ANYONE.
PON (PAT)

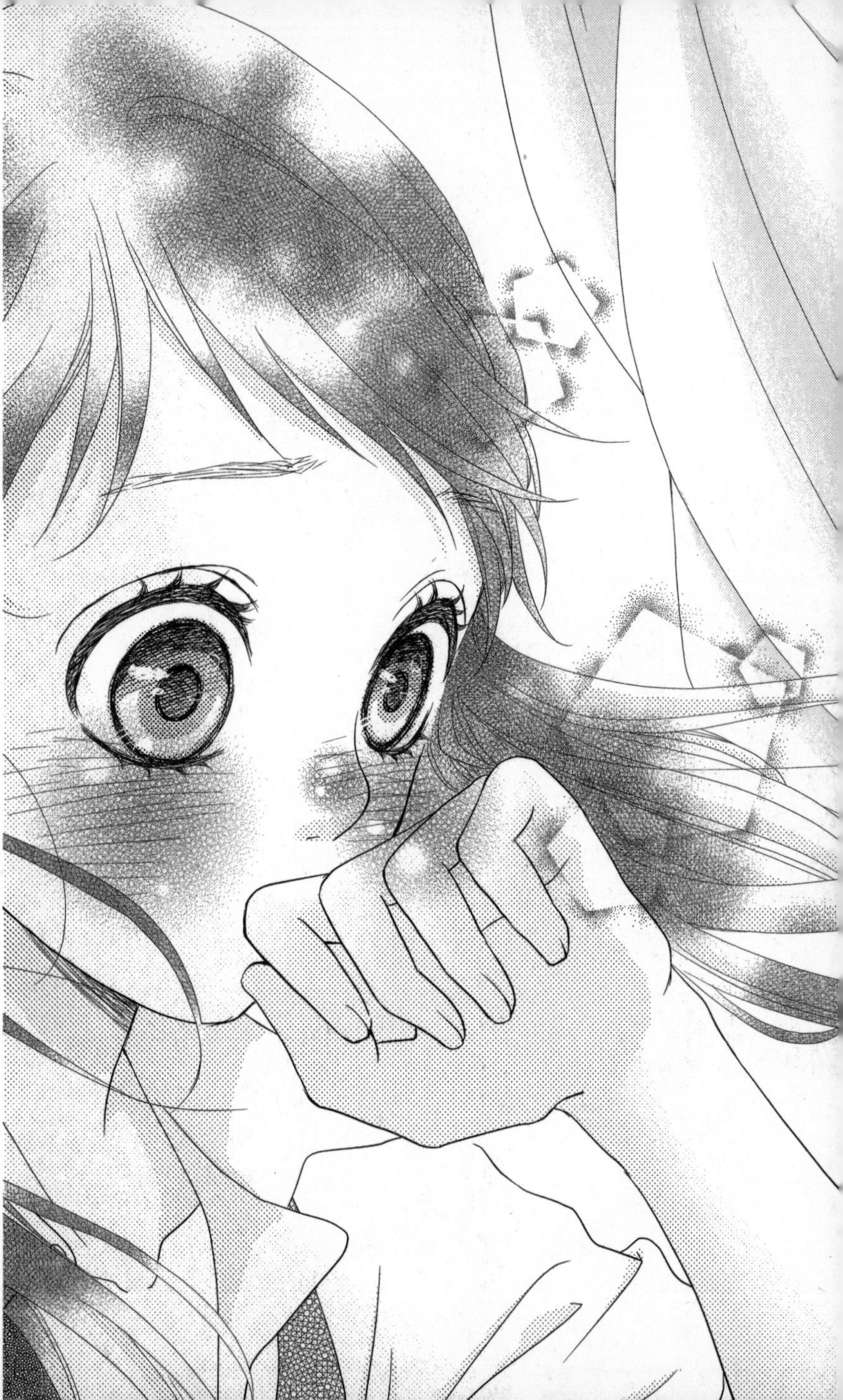

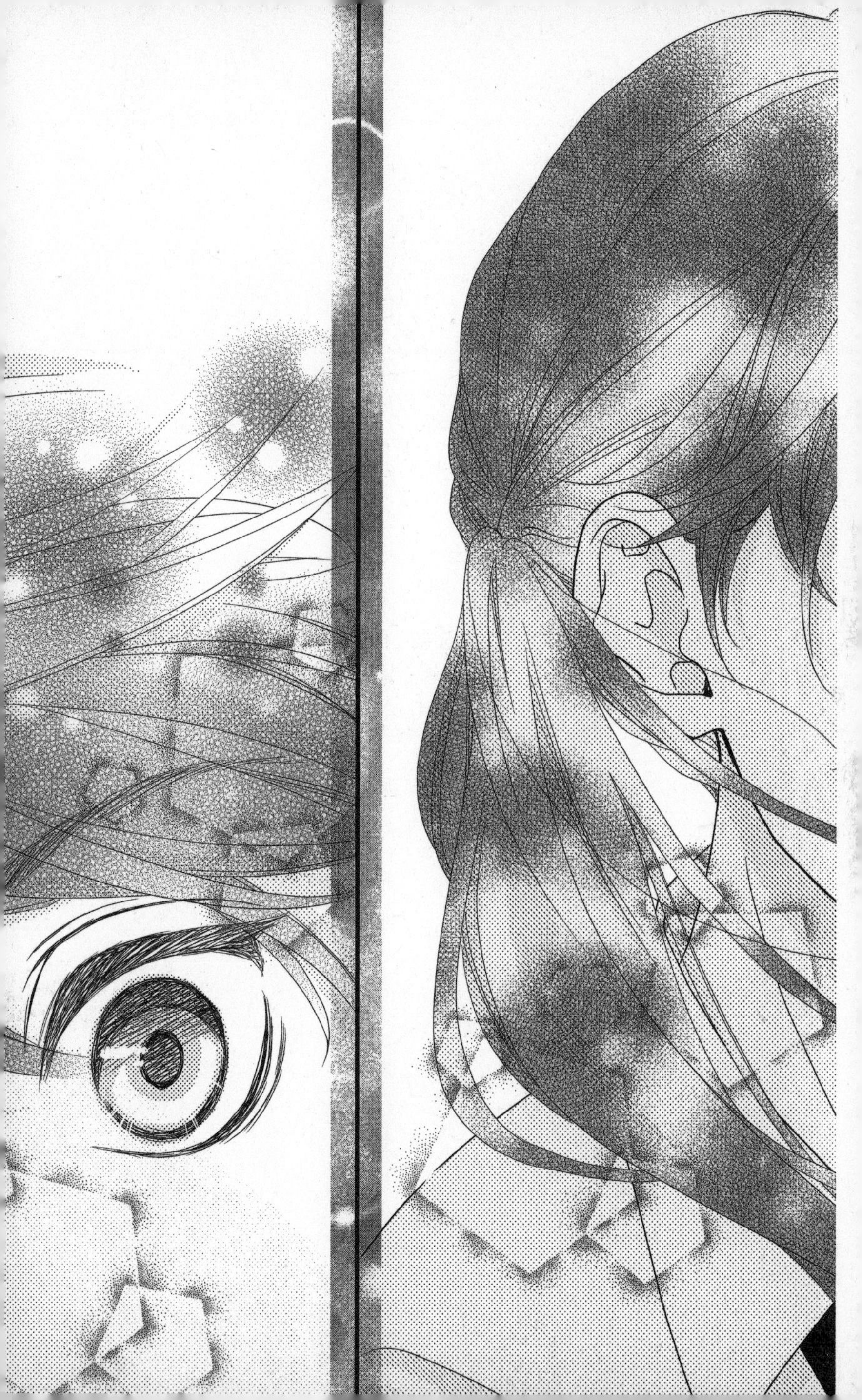

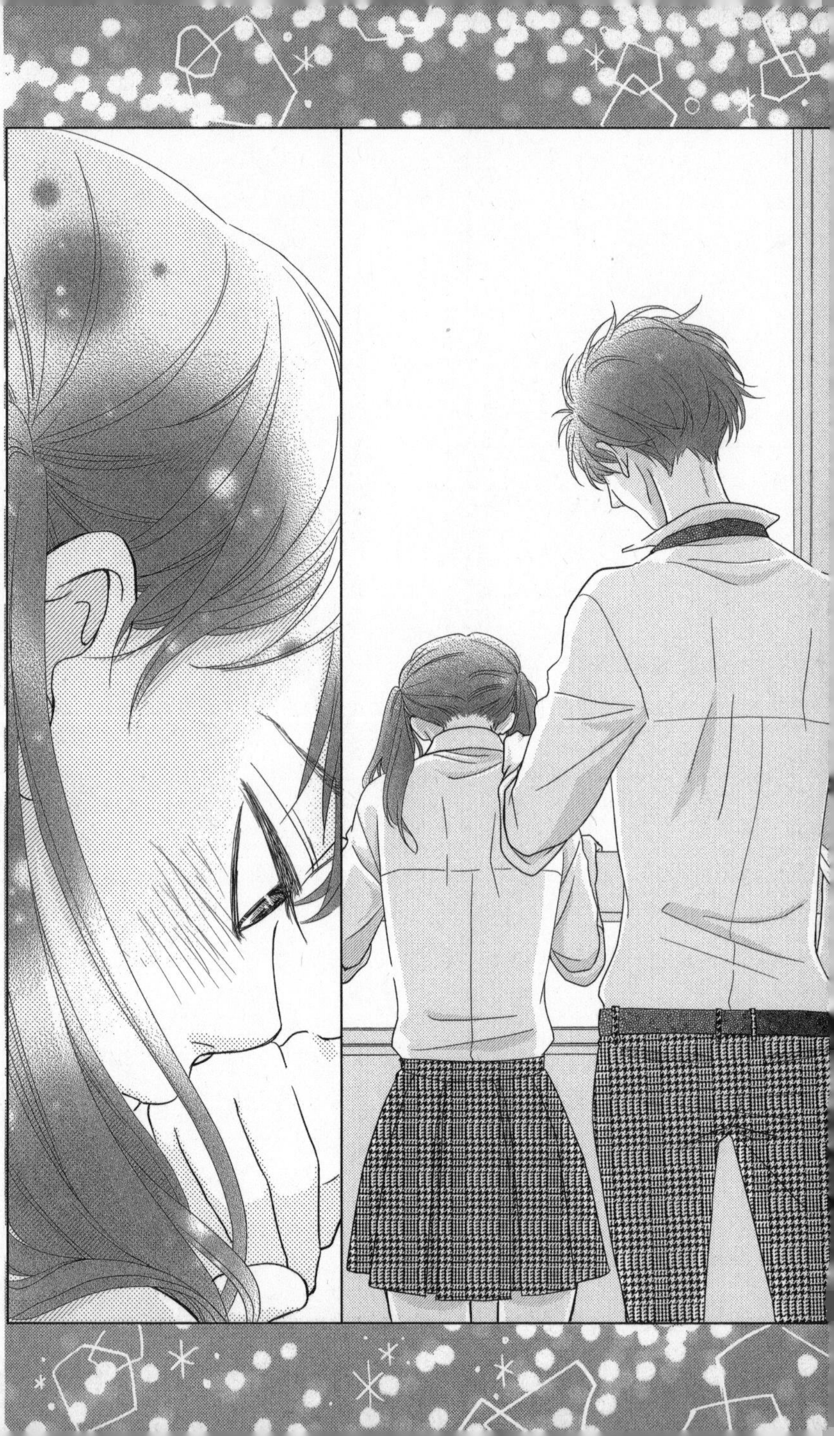

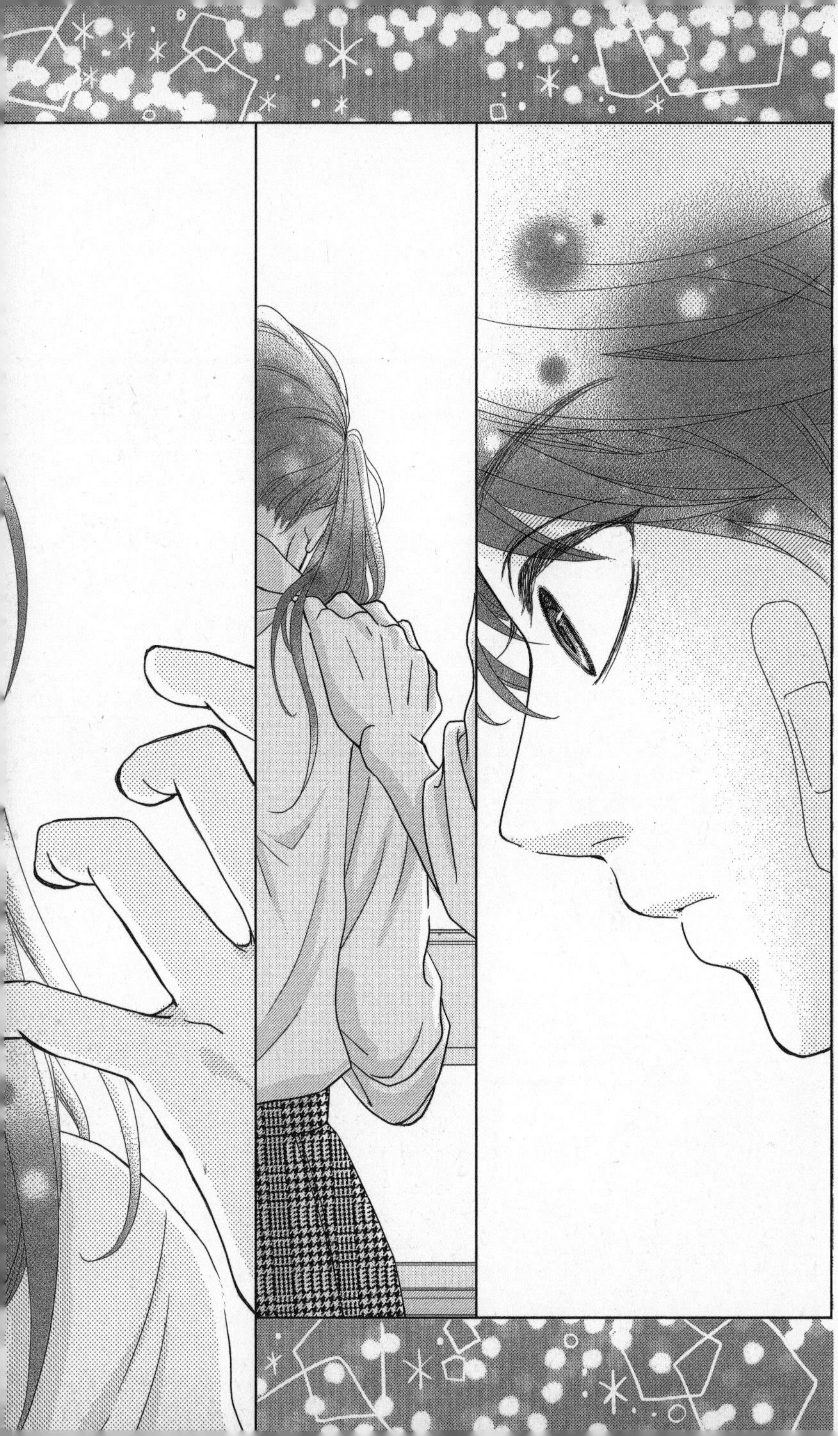

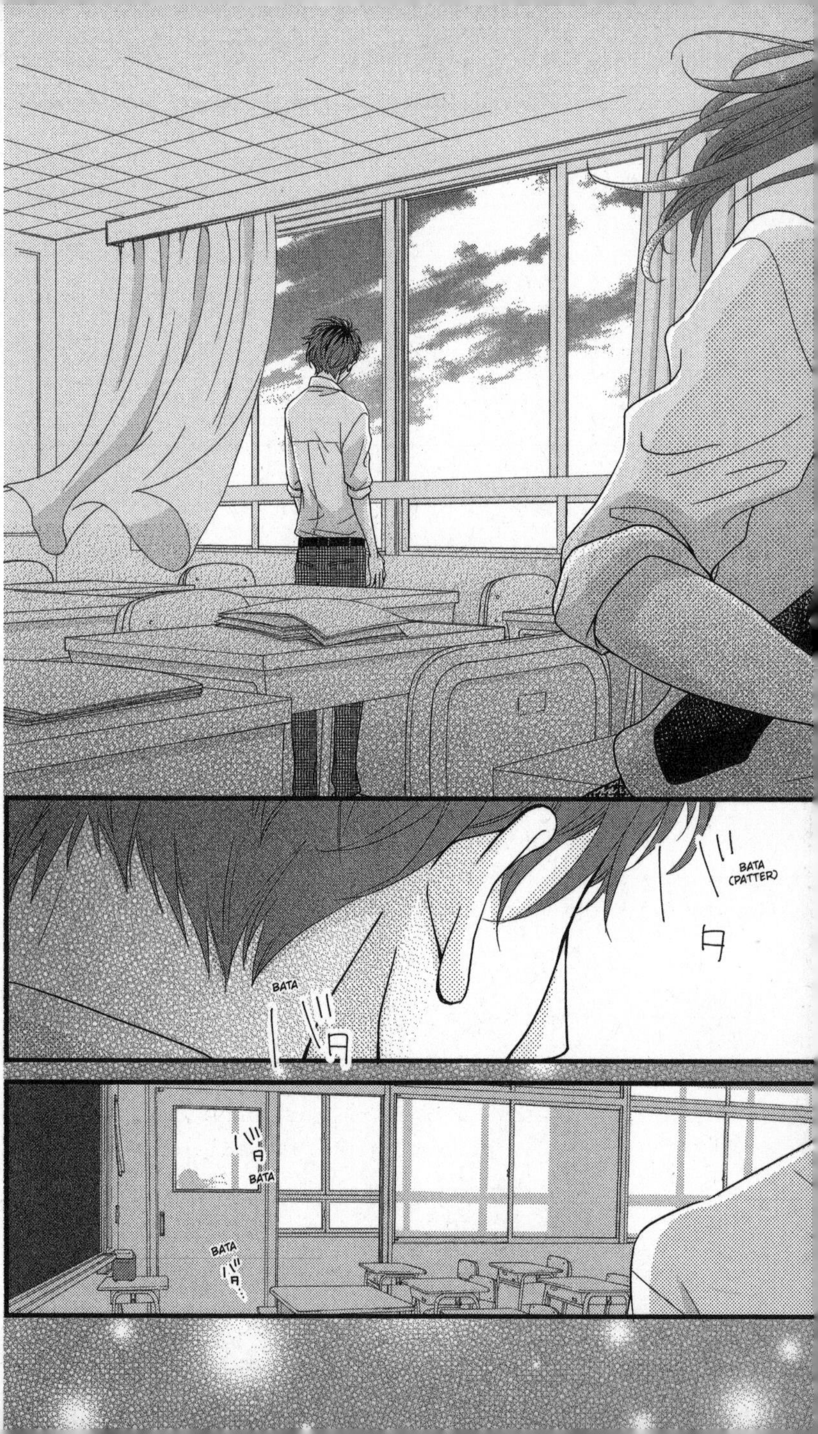
BATA (PATTER)
BATA
BATA
BATA

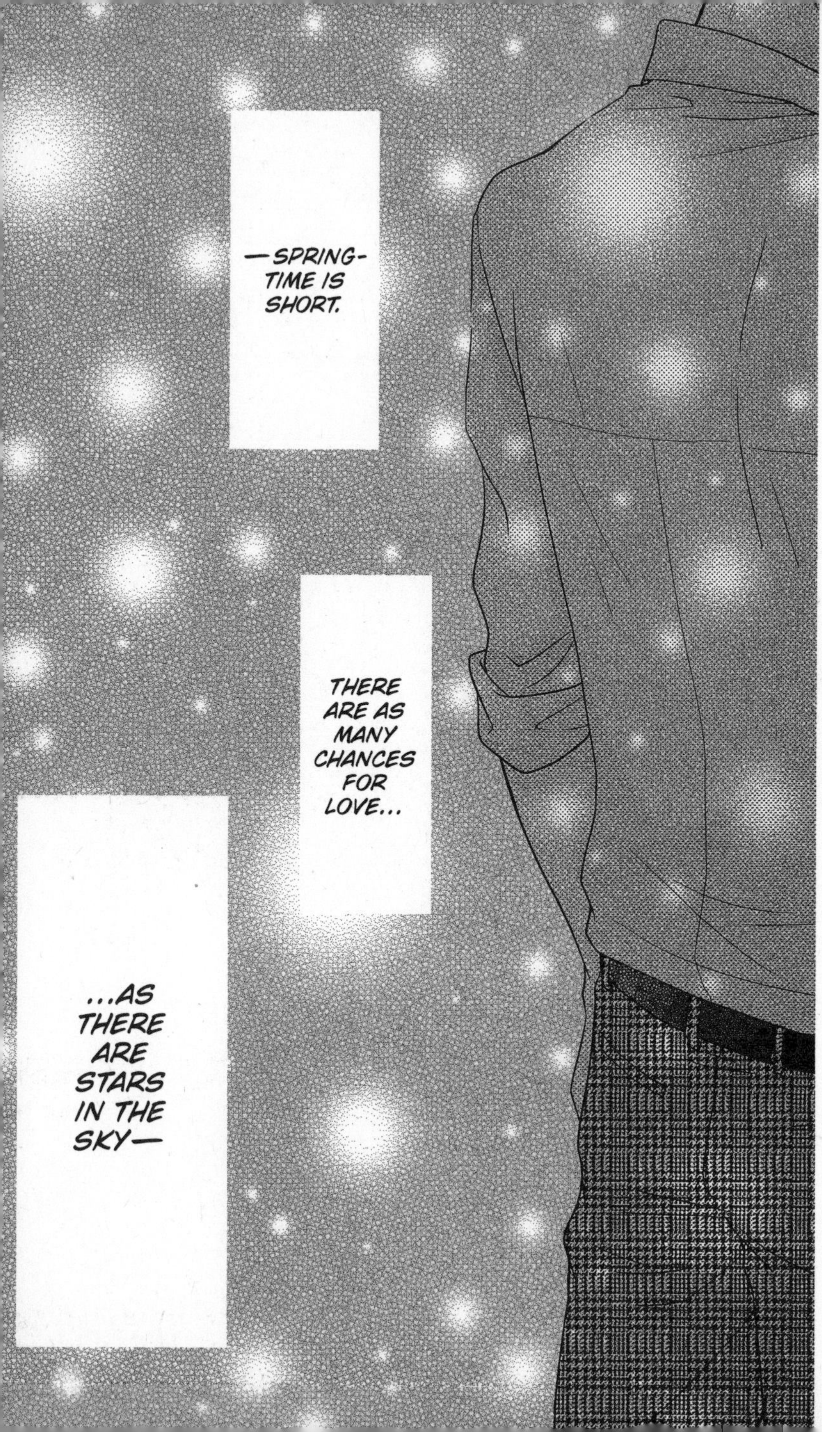
—SPRING-TIME IS SHORT.
THERE ARE AS MANY CHANCES FOR LOVE...
...AS THERE ARE STARS IN THE SKY—

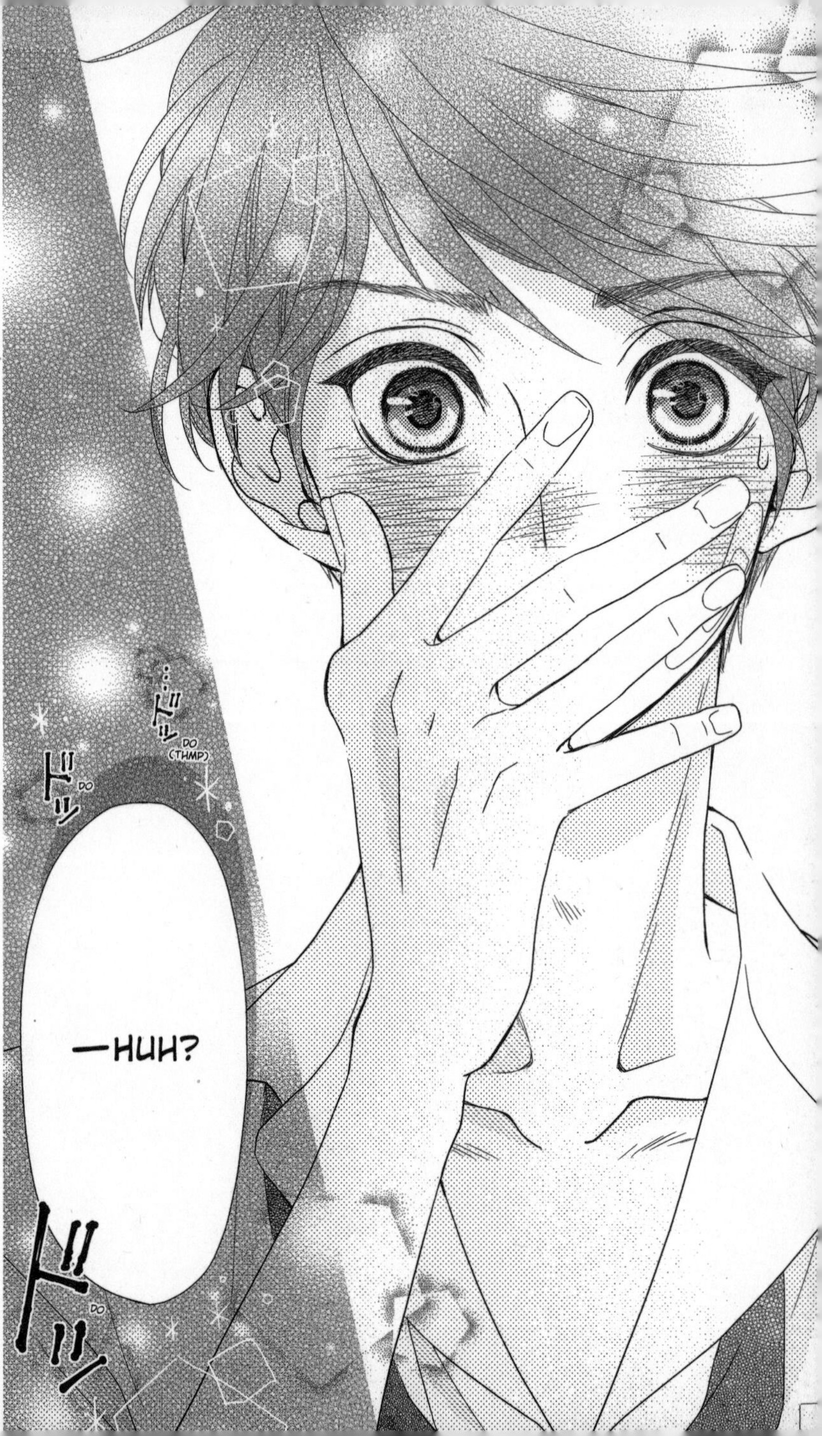
ドッ DO (THMP)
ドッ DO
—HUH?
ドッ DO

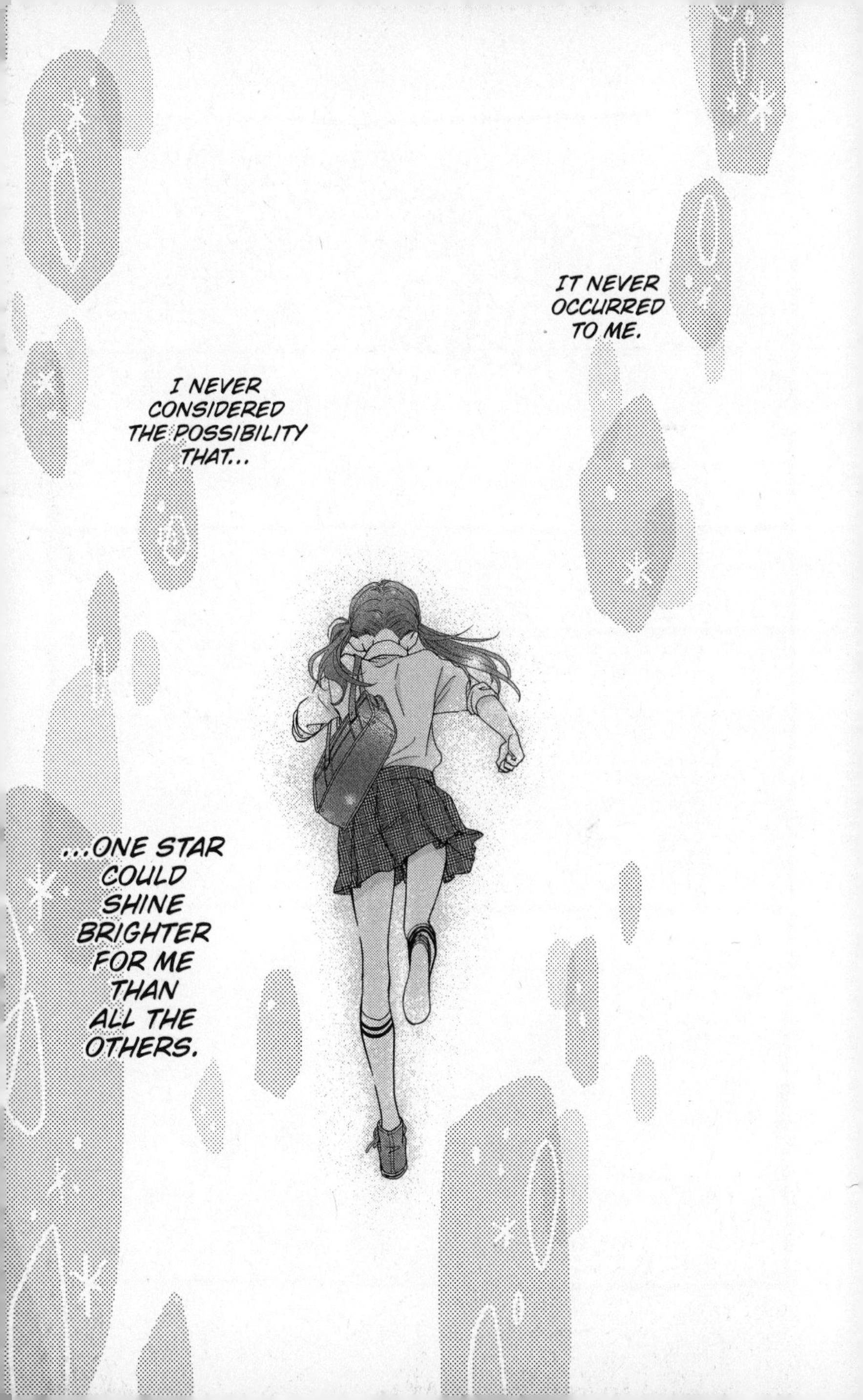
IT NEVER OCCURRED TO ME.
I NEVER CONSIDERED THE POSSIBILITY THAT...
...ONE STAR COULD SHINE BRIGHTER FOR ME THAN ALL THE OTHERS.

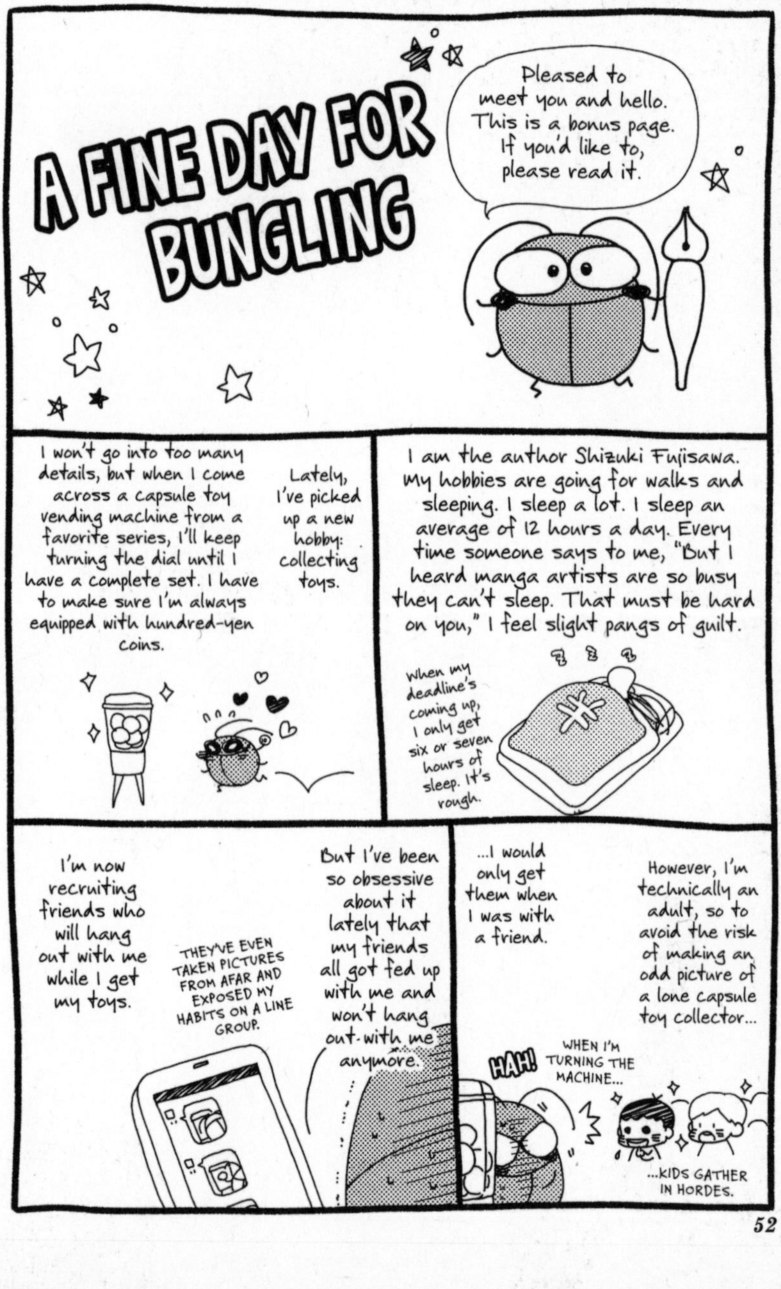
Pleased to meet you and hello. This is a bonus page. If you'd like to, please read it.
A FINE DAY FOR BUNGLING
I am the author Shizuki Fujisawa. My hobbies are going for walks and sleeping. I sleep a lot. I sleep an average of 12 hours a day. Every time someone says to me, "But I heard manga artists are so busy they can't sleep. That must be hard on you," I feel slight pangs of guilt.
When my deadline's coming up, I only get six or seven hours of sleep. It's rough.
Lately, I've picked up a new hobby: collecting toys.
I won't go into too many details, but when I come across a capsule toy vending machine from a favorite series, I'll keep turning the dial until I have a complete set. I have to make sure I'm always equipped with hundred-yen coins.
However, I'm technically an adult, so to avoid the risk of making an odd picture of a lone capsule toy collector...
...I would only get them when I was with a friend.
WHEN I'M TURNING THE MACHINE...
HAH!
...KIDS GATHER IN HORDES.
But I've been so obsessive about it lately that my friends all got fed up with me and won't hang out with me anymore.
THEY'VE EVEN TAKEN PICTURES FROM AFAR AND EXPOSED MY HABITS ON A LINE GROUP.
I'm now recruiting friends who will hang out with me while I get my toys.

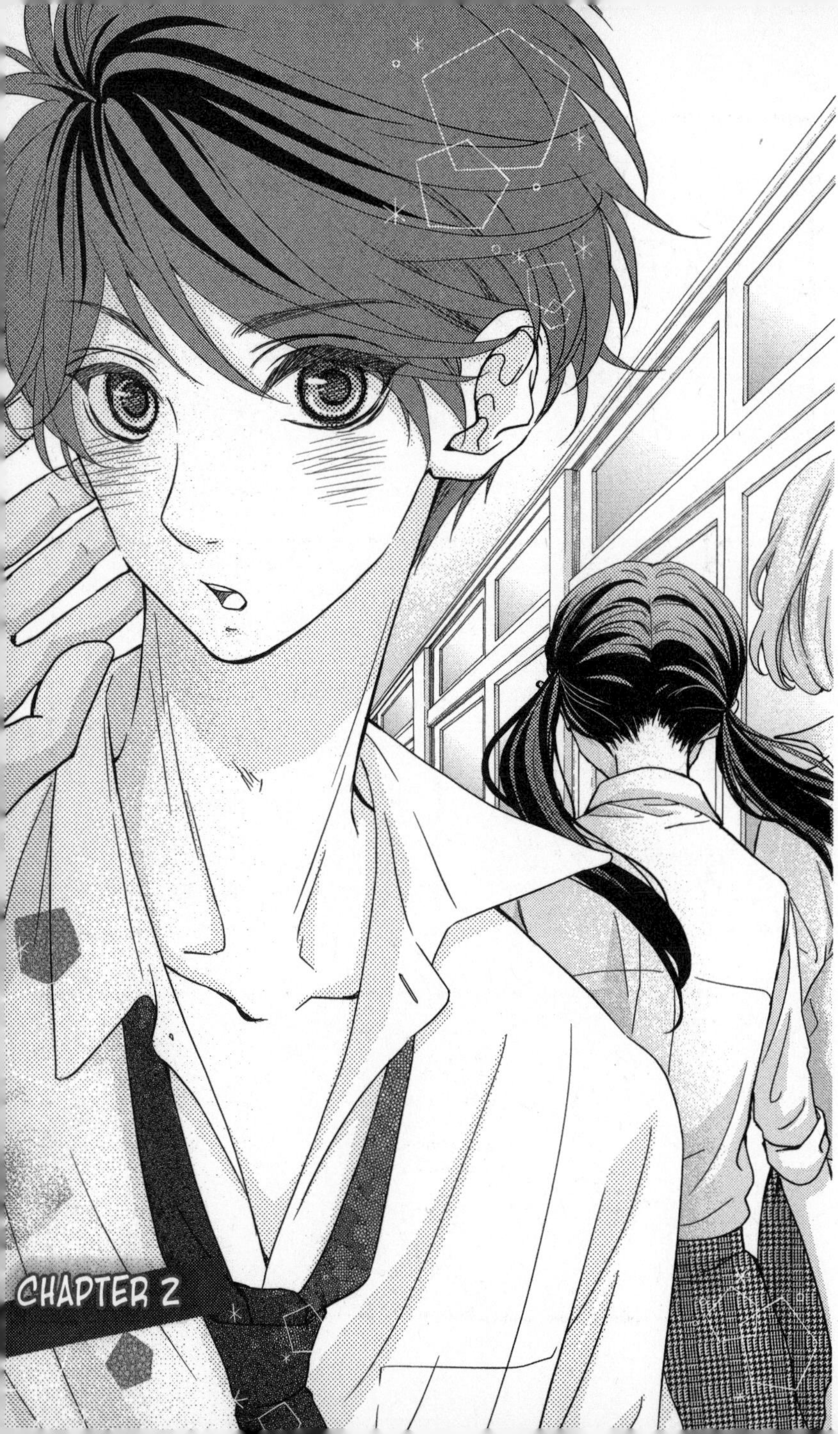
CHAPTER 2

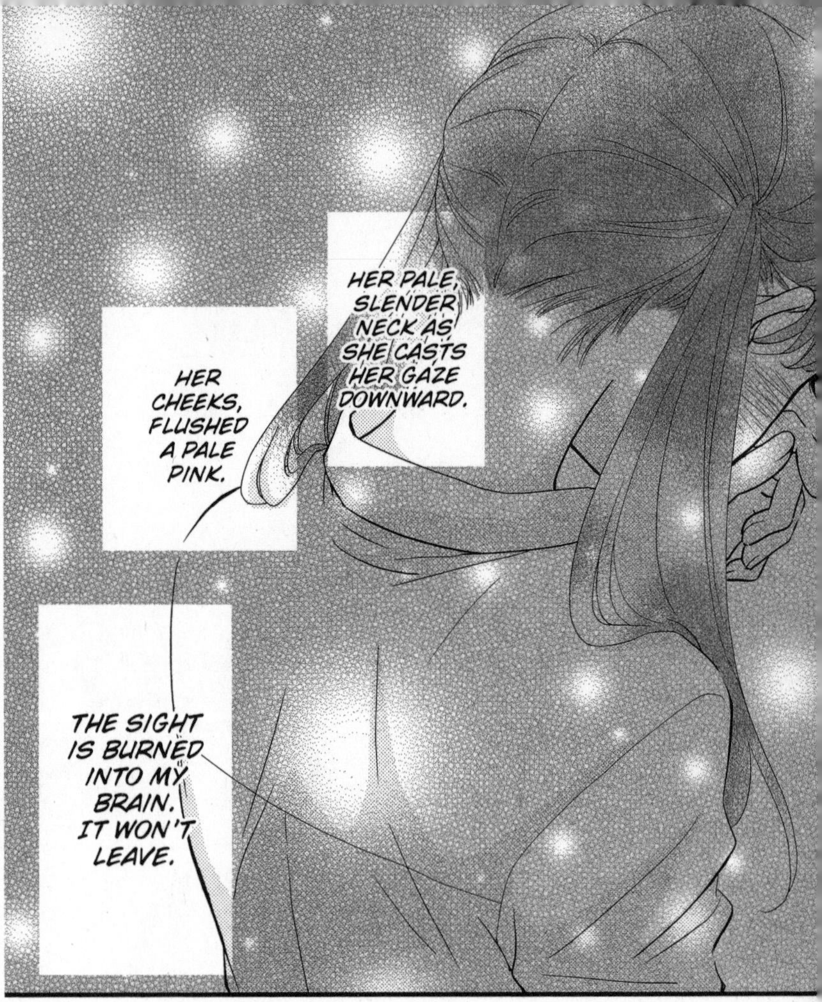
HER PALE, SLENDER NECK AS SHE CASTS HER GAZE DOWNWARD.
HER CHEEKS, FLUSHED A PALE PINK.
THE SIGHT IS BURNED INTO MY BRAIN. IT WON'T LEAVE.

hatsu haru

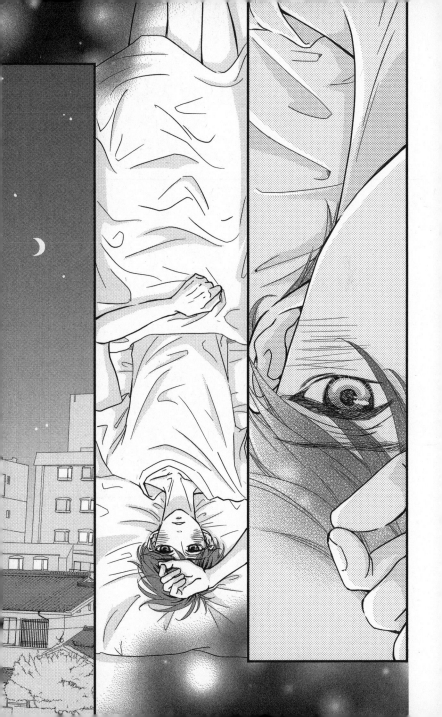

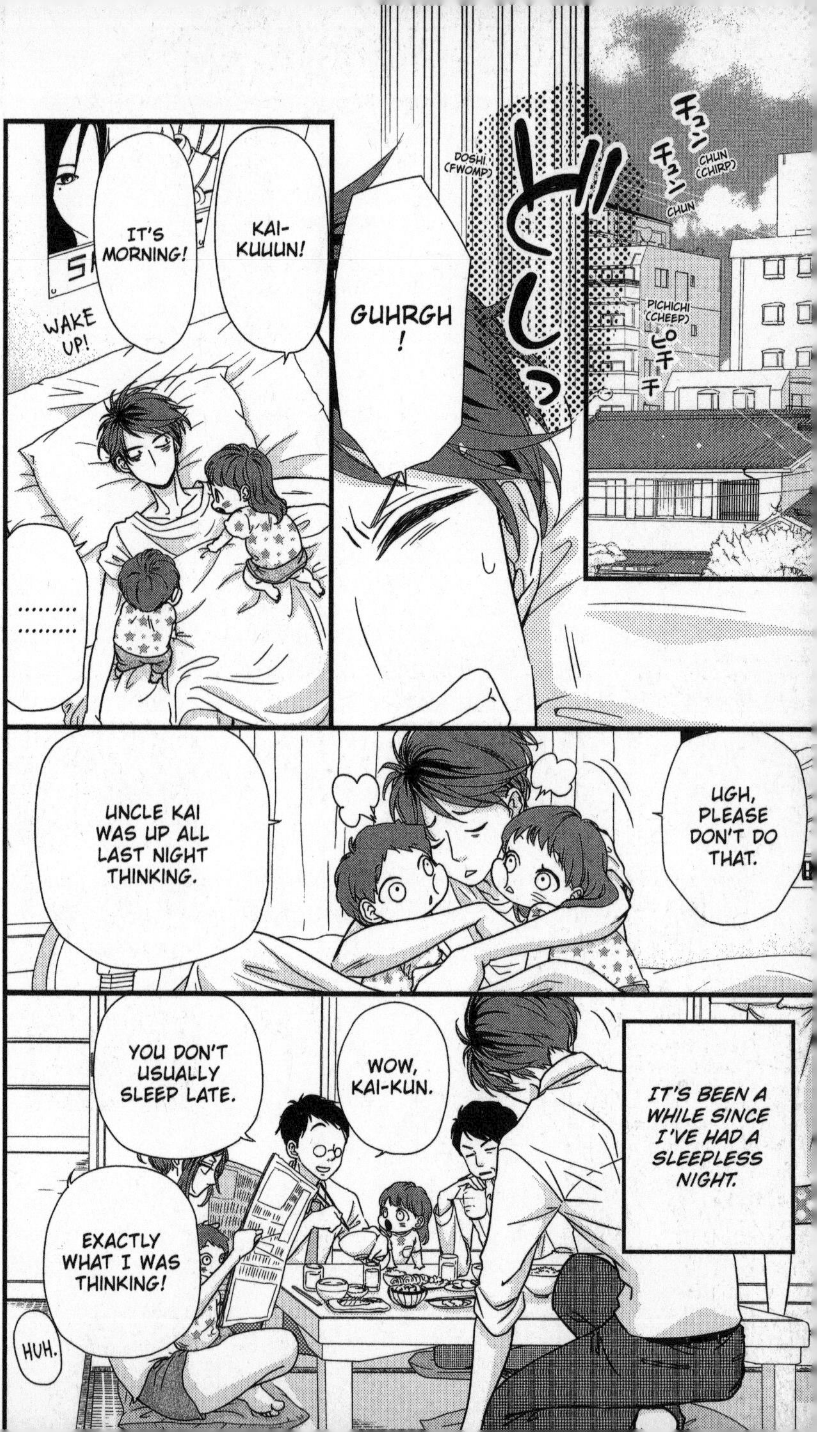
チュン
CHUN (CHIRP)
チュン
CHUN
ピチチ
PICHICHI (CHEEP)
どしっ
DOSHI (FWOMP)
GUHRGH!
KAI-KUUUN!
IT'S MORNING!
WAKE UP!
....
....
UGH, PLEASE DON'T DO THAT.
UNCLE KAI WAS UP ALL LAST NIGHT THINKING.
IT'S BEEN A WHILE SINCE I'VE HAD A SLEEPLESS NIGHT.
WOW, KAI-KUN.
YOU DON'T USUALLY SLEEP LATE.
EXACTLY WHAT I WAS THINKING!
HUH.

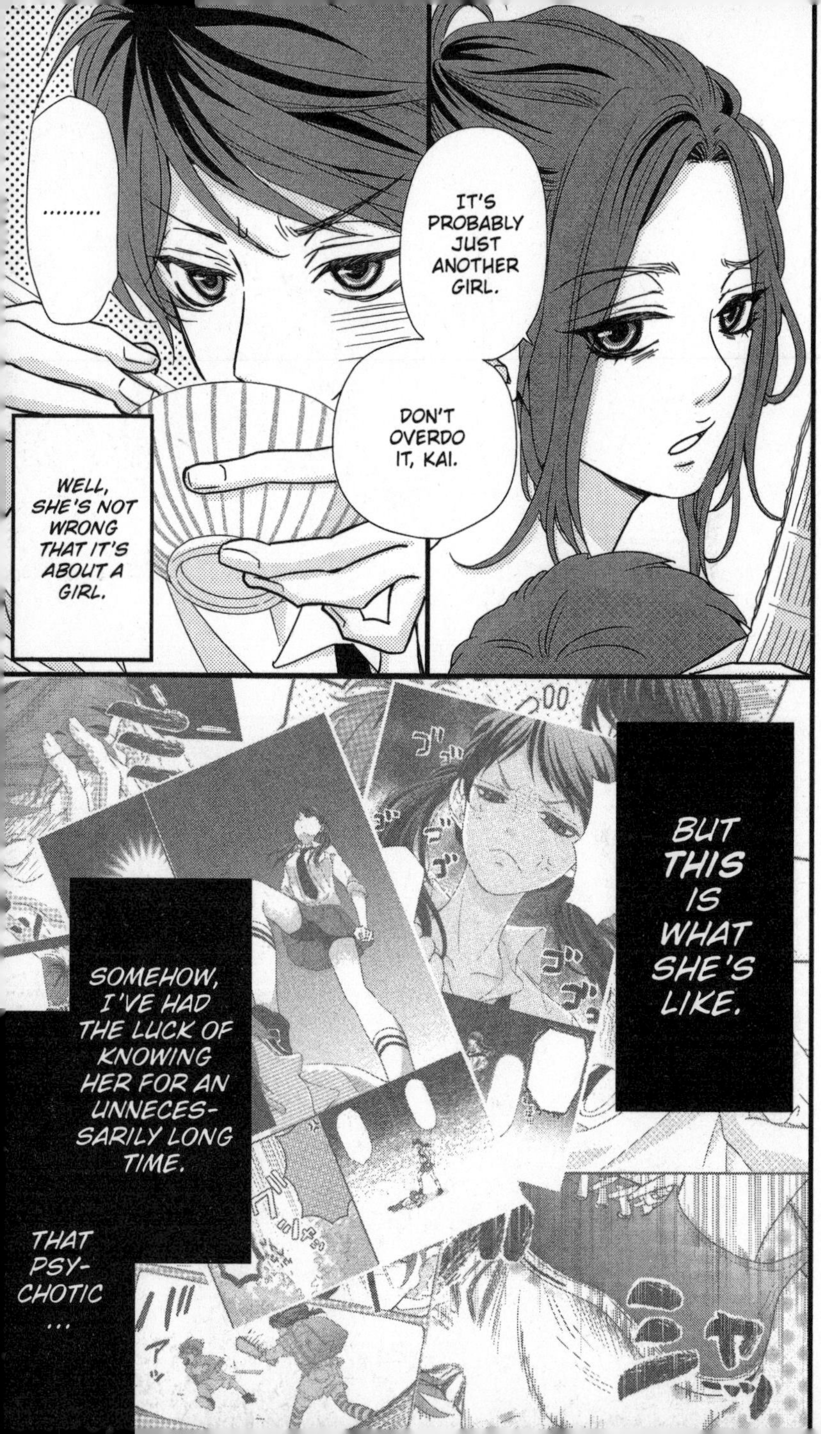
IT'S PROBABLY JUST ANOTHER GIRL.
DON'T OVERDO IT, KAI.
....
WELL, SHE'S NOT WRONG THAT IT'S ABOUT A GIRL.
BUT THIS IS WHAT SHE'S LIKE.
SOMEHOW, I'VE HAD THE LUCK OF KNOWING HER FOR AN UNNECES-SARILY LONG TIME.
THAT PSY-CHOTIC ...

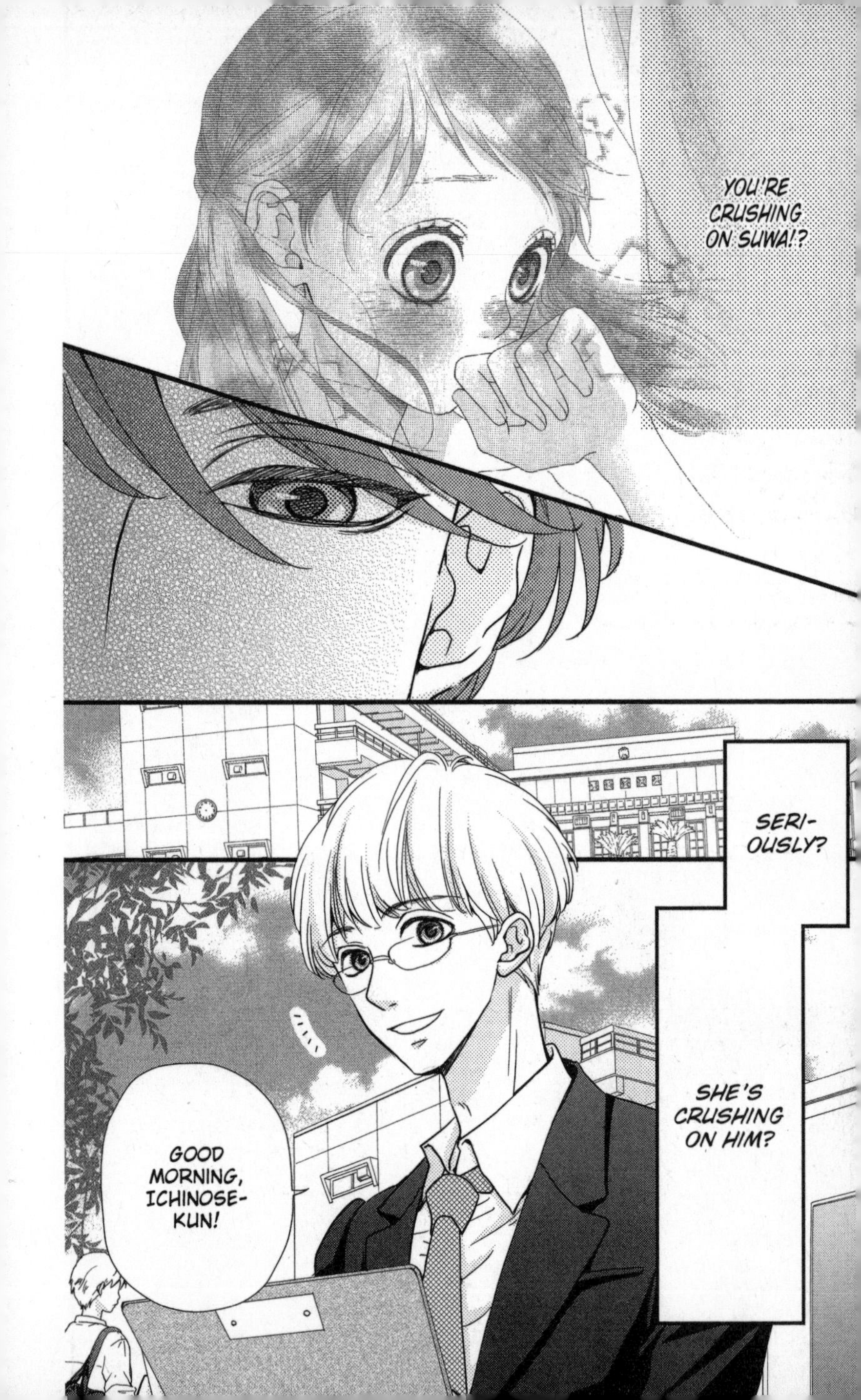
YOU'RE CRUSHING ON SUWA!?
SERI-OUSLY?
SHE'S CRUSHING ON HIM?
GOOD MORNING, ICHINOSE-KUN!

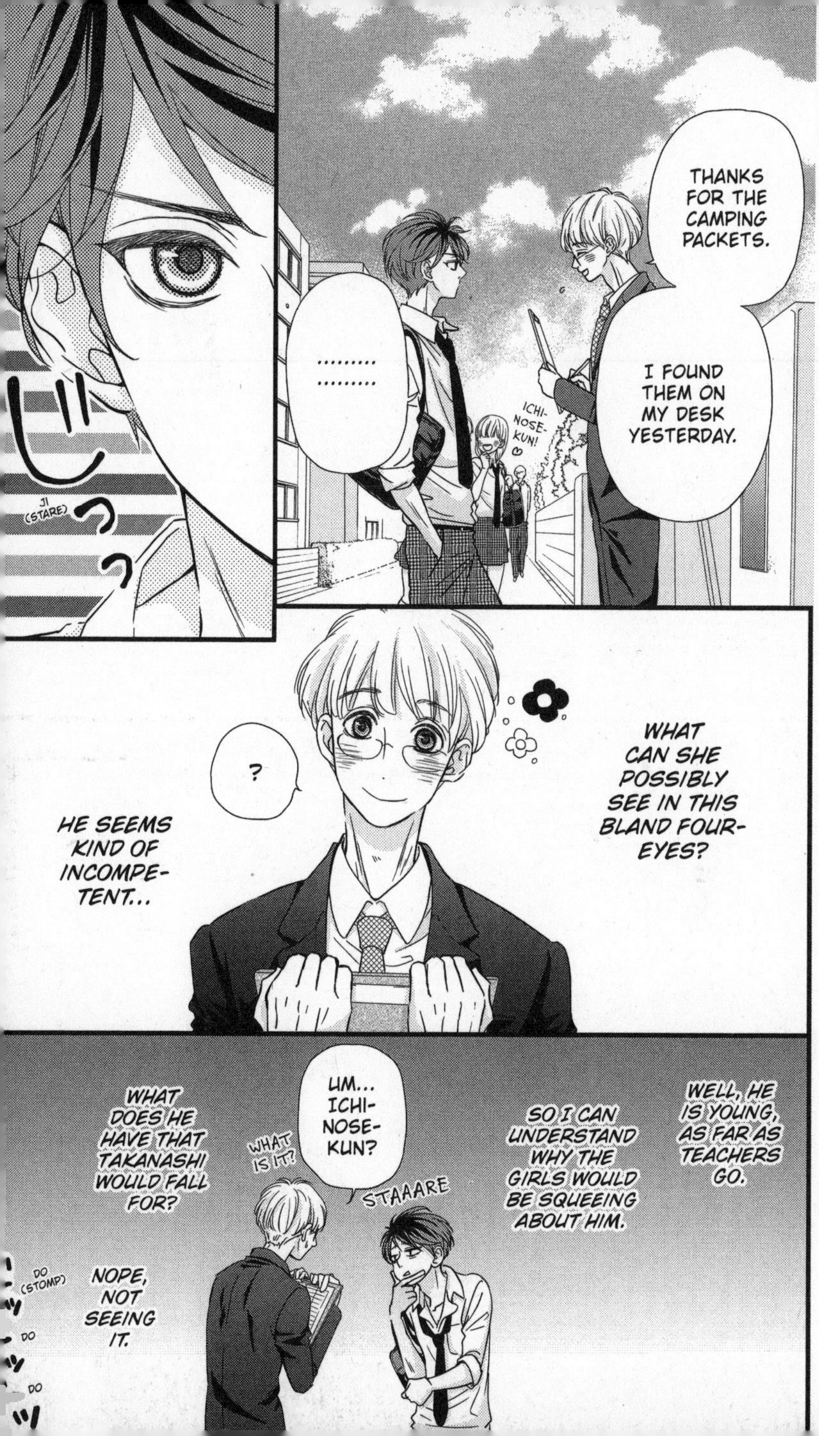

THANKS FOR THE CAMPING PACKETS.
I FOUND THEM ON MY DESK YESTERDAY.
ICHI-NOSE-KUN!
....
....
JI (STARE)
WHAT CAN SHE POSSIBLY SEE IN THIS BLAND FOUR-EYES?
?
HE SEEMS KIND OF INCOMPE-TENT...
WELL, HE IS YOUNG, AS FAR AS TEACHERS GO.
SO I CAN UNDERSTAND WHY THE GIRLS WOULD BE SQUEEING ABOUT HIM.
UM... ICHI-NOSE-KUN?
WHAT IS IT?
STAAARE
WHAT DOES HE HAVE THAT TAKANASHI WOULD FALL FOR?
NOPE, NOT SEEING IT.
DO (STOMP)
DO
DO

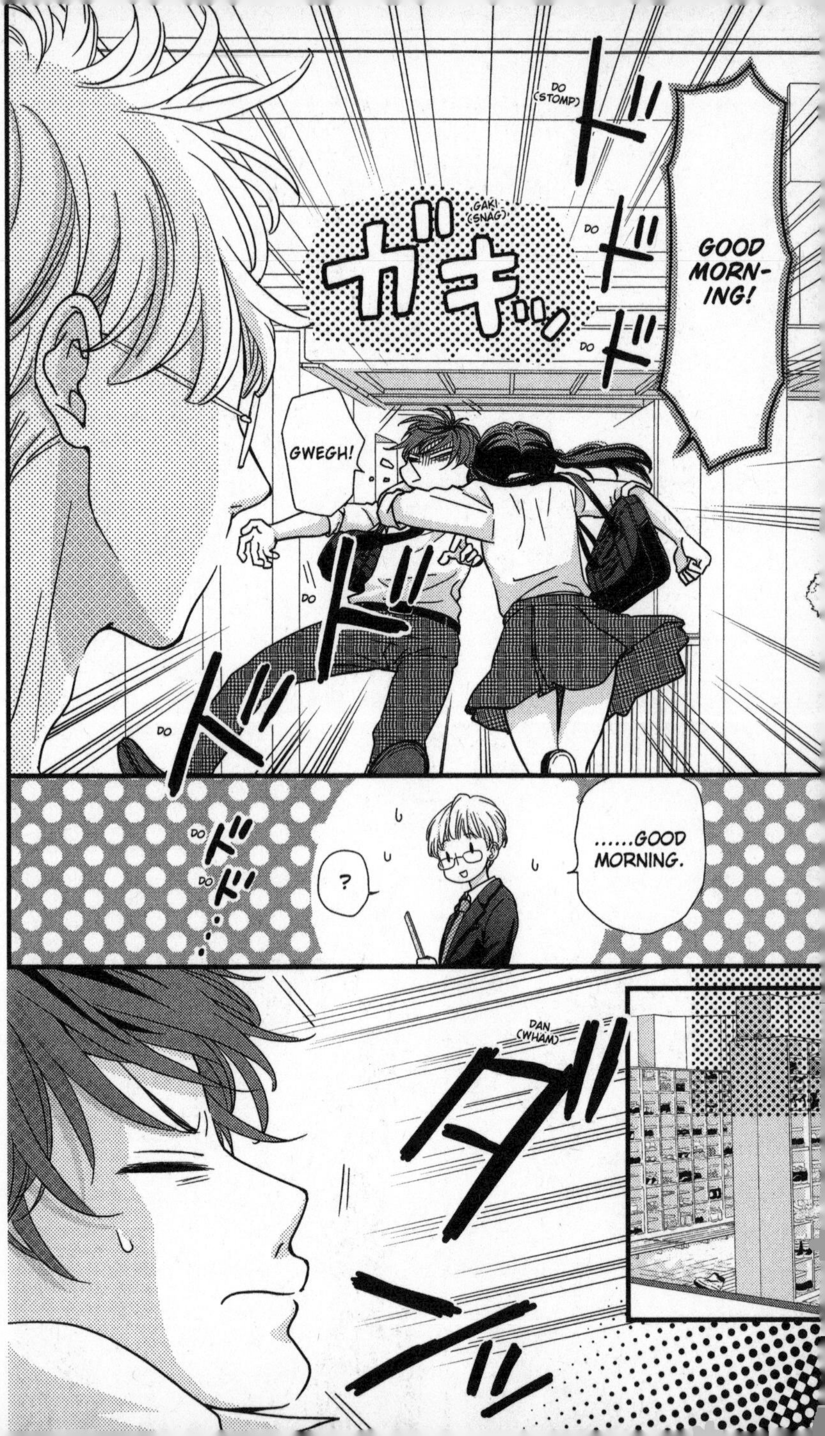
DO (STOMP)
GOOD MORNING!
GAKI (SNAG)
DO
DO
GWEGH!
DO
DO
......GOOD MORNING.
?
DO
DO
DAN (WHAM)

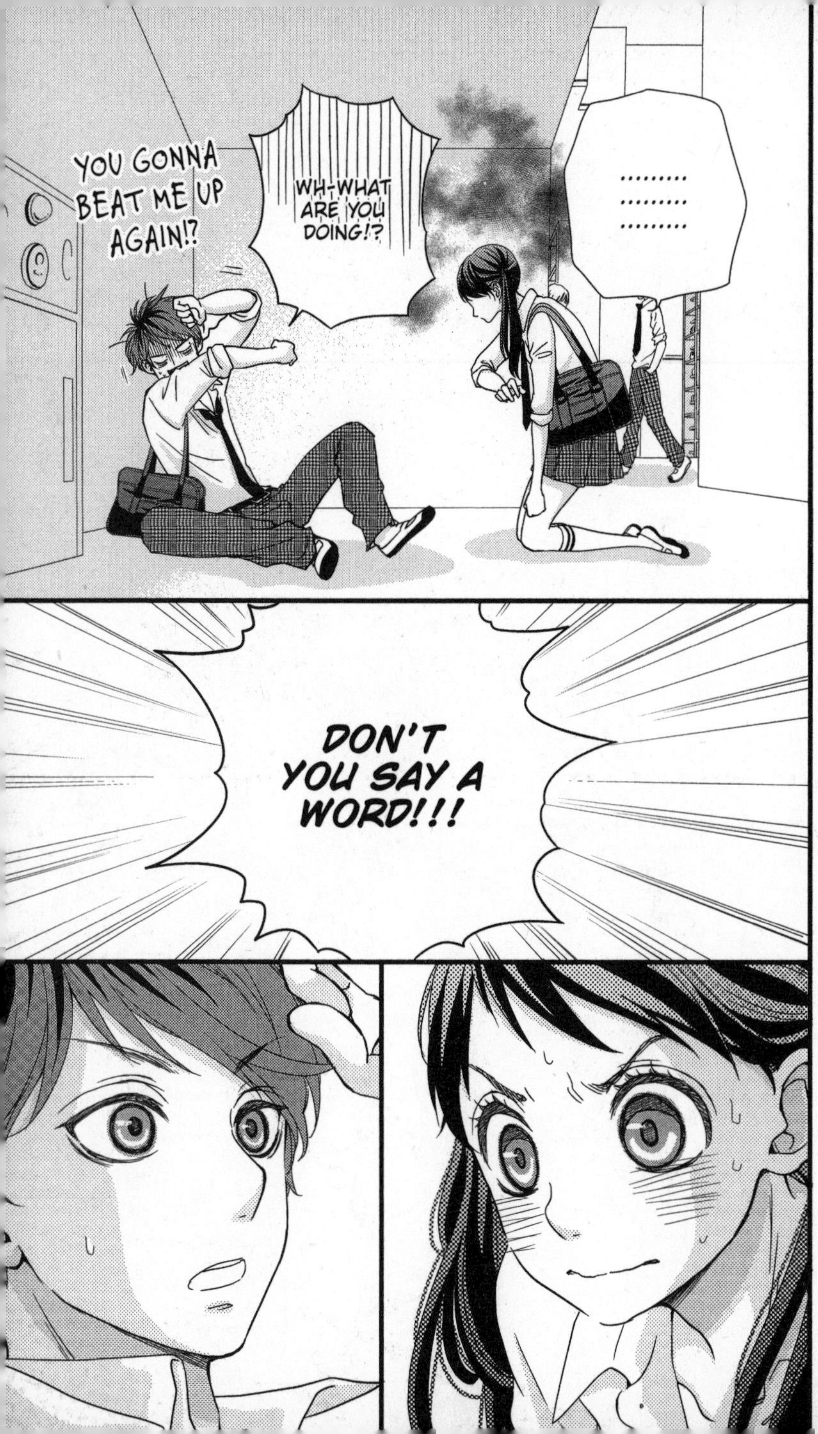
....
....
....
WH-WHAT ARE YOU DOING!?
YOU GONNA BEAT ME UP AGAIN!?
DON'T YOU SAY A WORD!!!

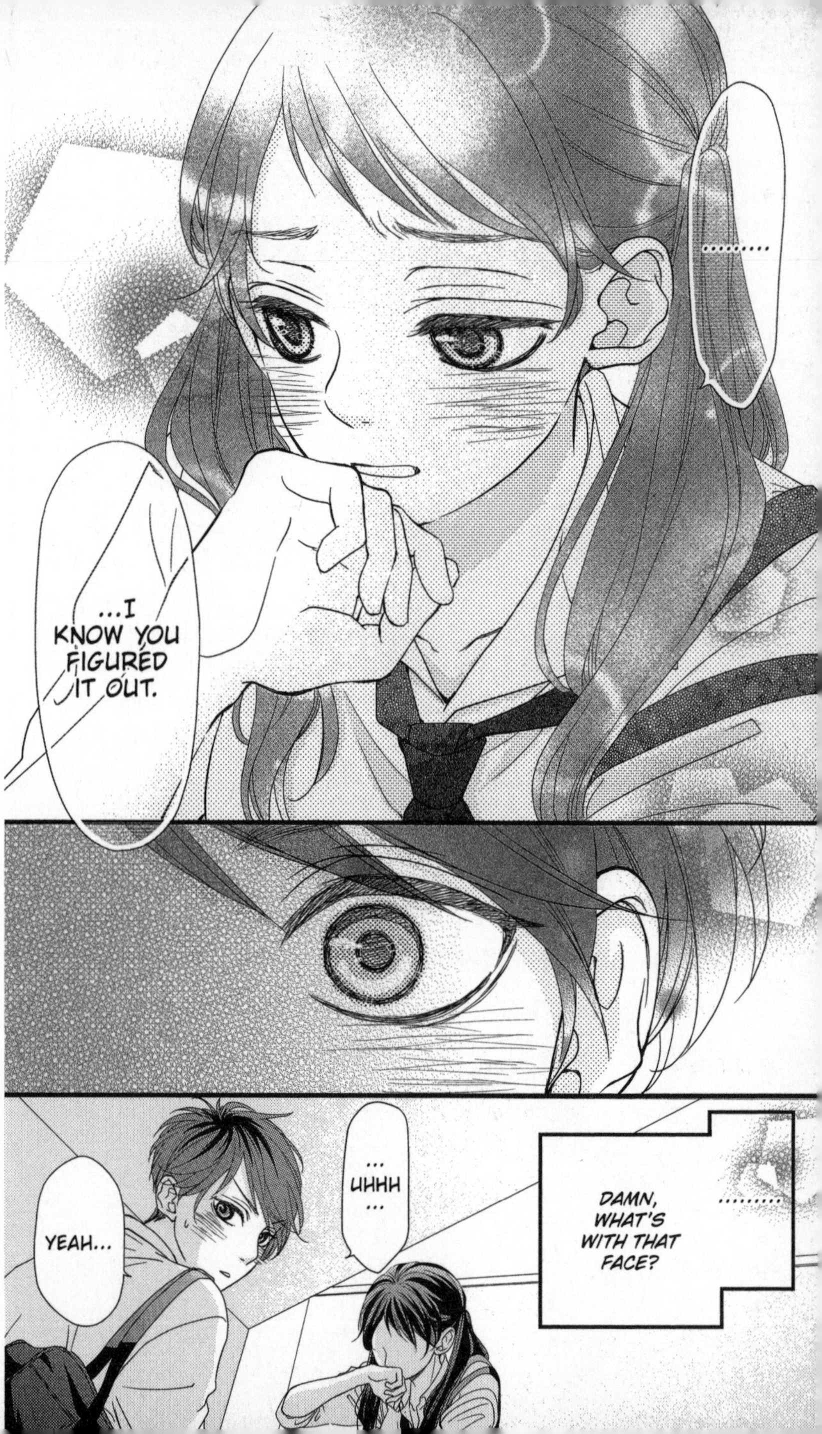
....
...I KNOW YOU FIGURED IT OUT.
....
DAMN, WHAT'S WITH THAT FACE?
... UHHH ...
YEAH...

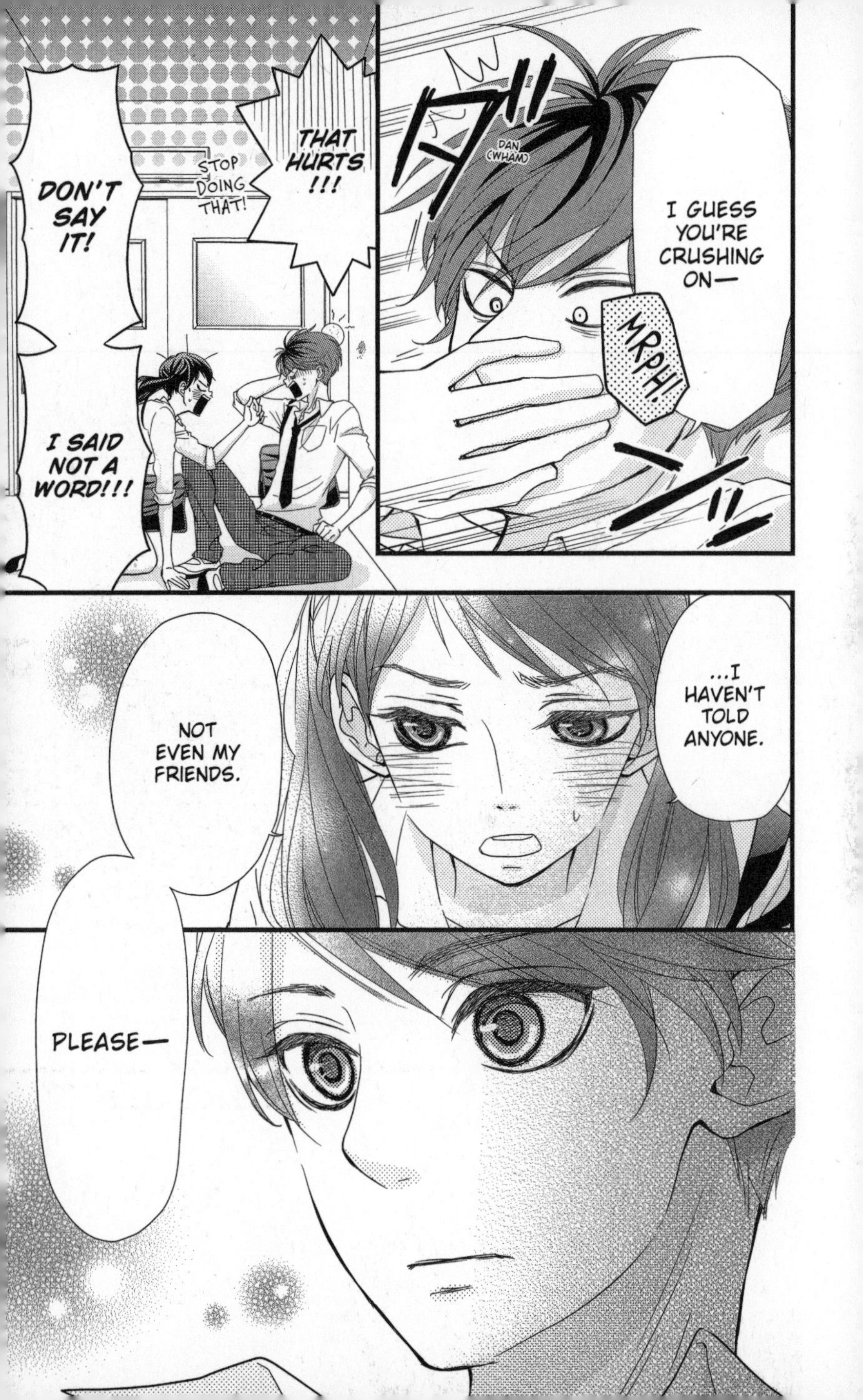
I GUESS YOU'RE CRUSHING ON—
DAN (WHAM)
MRPH!
THAT HURTS!!!
STOP DOING THAT!
DON'T SAY IT!
I SAID NOT A WORD!!!
...I HAVEN'T TOLD ANYONE.
NOT EVEN MY FRIENDS.
PLEASE—

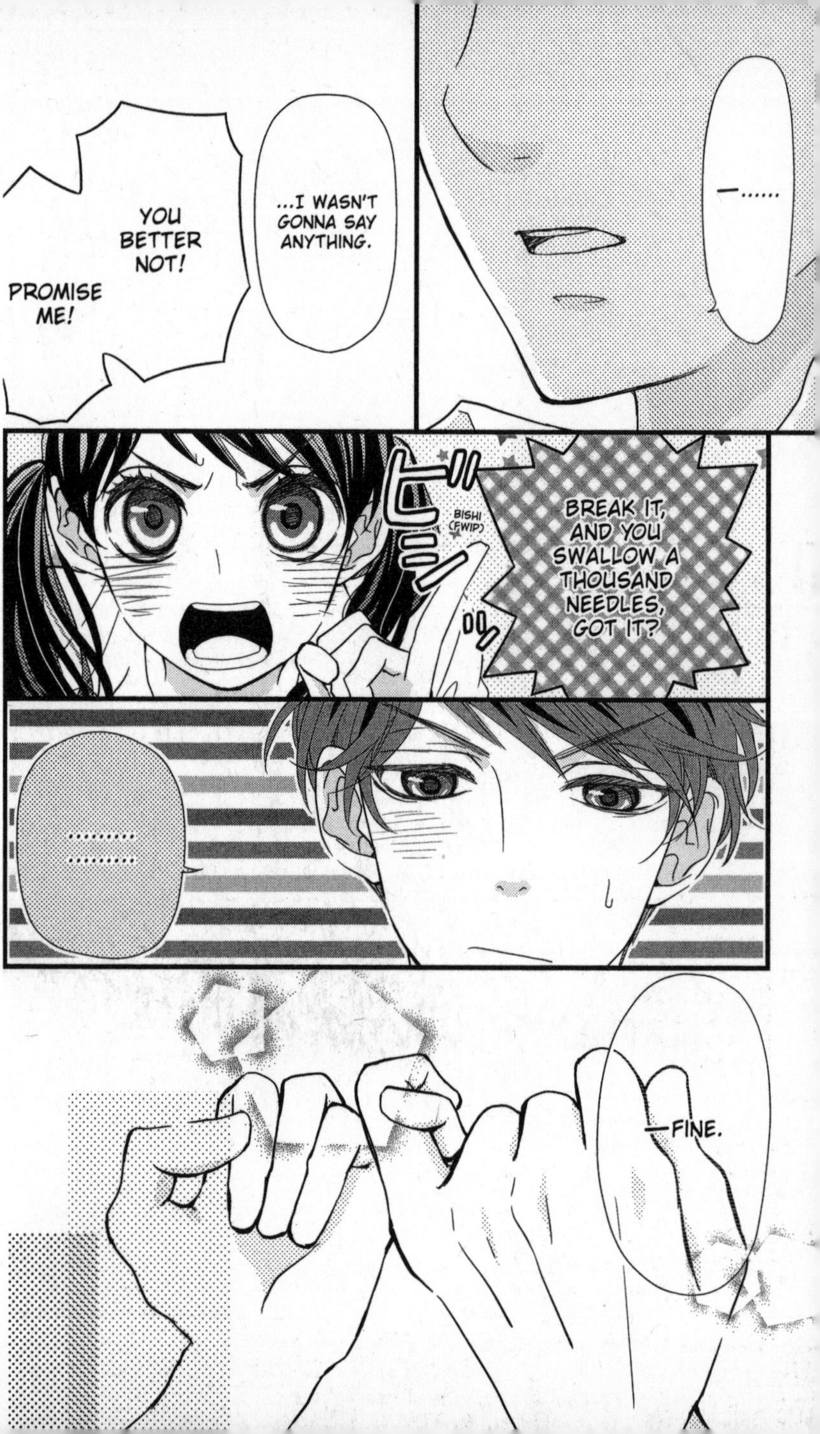
—......
...I WASN'T GONNA SAY ANYTHING.
YOU BETTER NOT!
PROMISE ME!
BREAK IT, AND YOU SWALLOW A THOUSAND NEEDLES, GOT IT?
BISHI (FWIP)
....
....
—FINE.

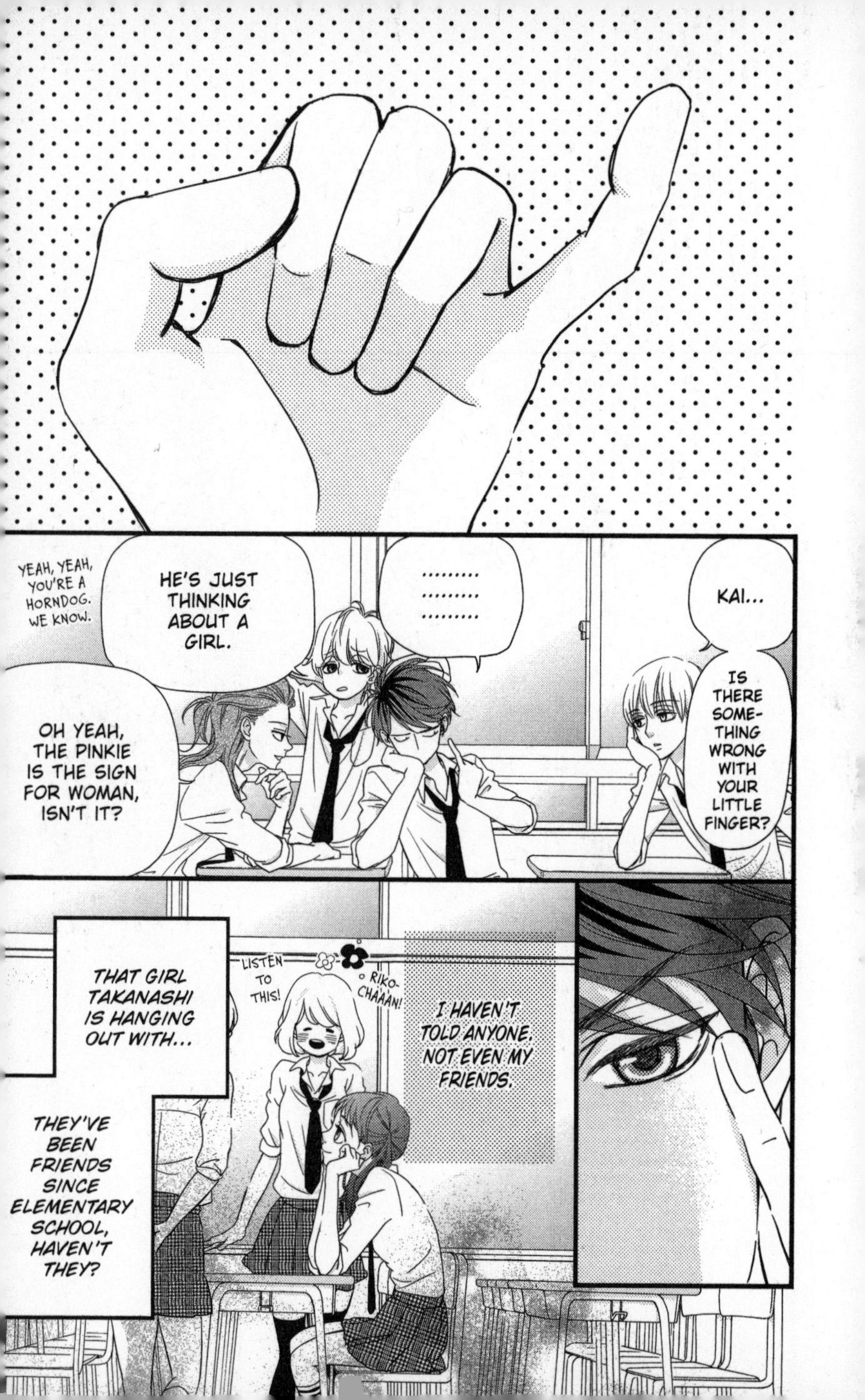
KAI...
IS THERE SOMETHING WRONG WITH YOUR LITTLE FINGER?
....
....
....
HE'S JUST THINKING ABOUT A GIRL.
YEAH, YEAH, YOU'RE A HORNDOG. WE KNOW.
OH YEAH, THE PINKIE IS THE SIGN FOR WOMAN, ISN'T IT?
I HAVEN'T TOLD ANYONE. NOT EVEN MY FRIENDS.
RIKO-CHAAAN!
LISTEN TO THIS!
THAT GIRL TAKANASHI IS HANGING OUT WITH...
THEY'VE BEEN FRIENDS SINCE ELEMENTARY SCHOOL, HAVEN'T THEY?

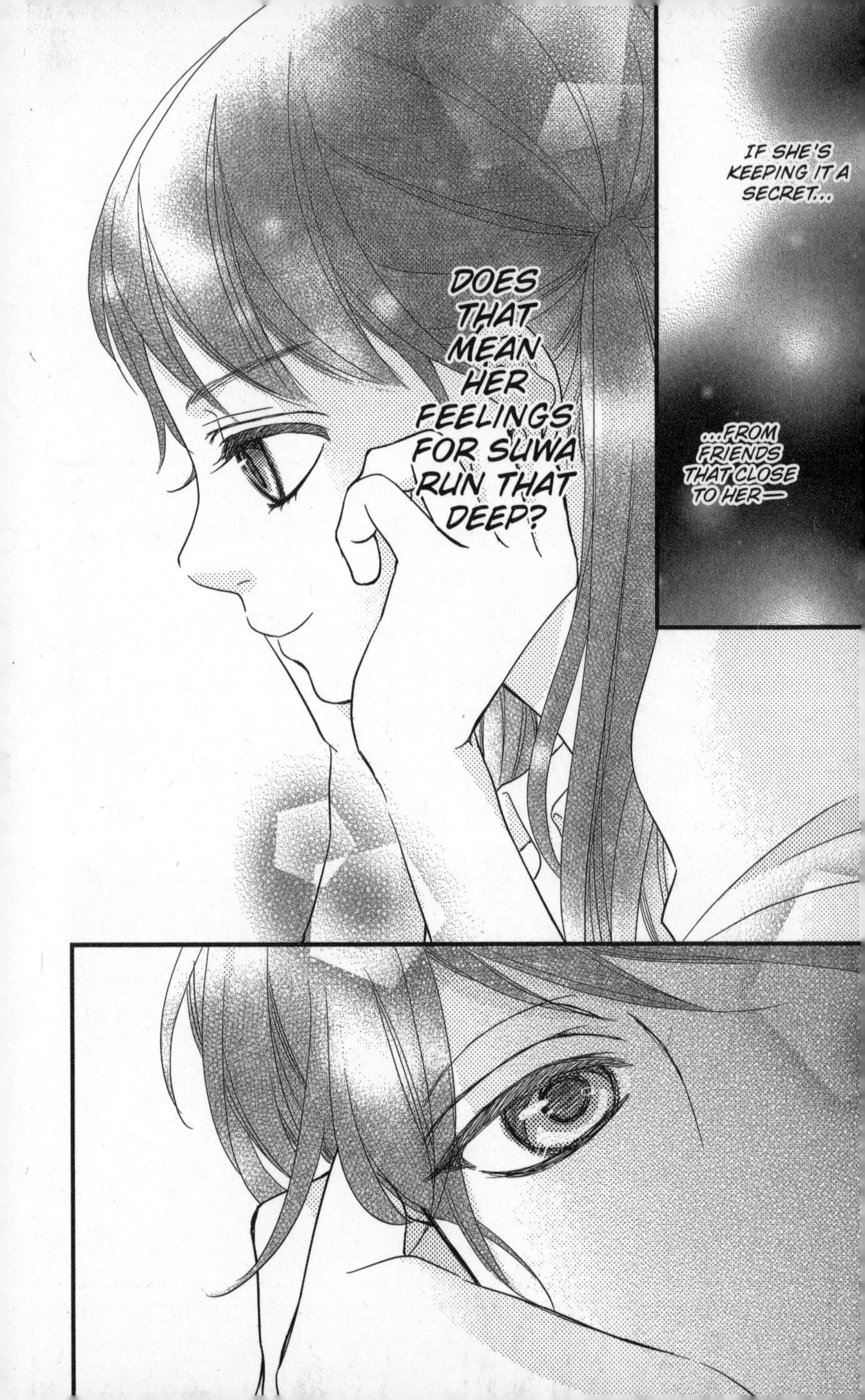
IF SHE'S KEEPING IT A SECRET...
...FROM FRIENDS THAT CLOSE TO HER—
DOES THAT MEAN HER FEELINGS FOR SUWA RUN THAT DEEP?

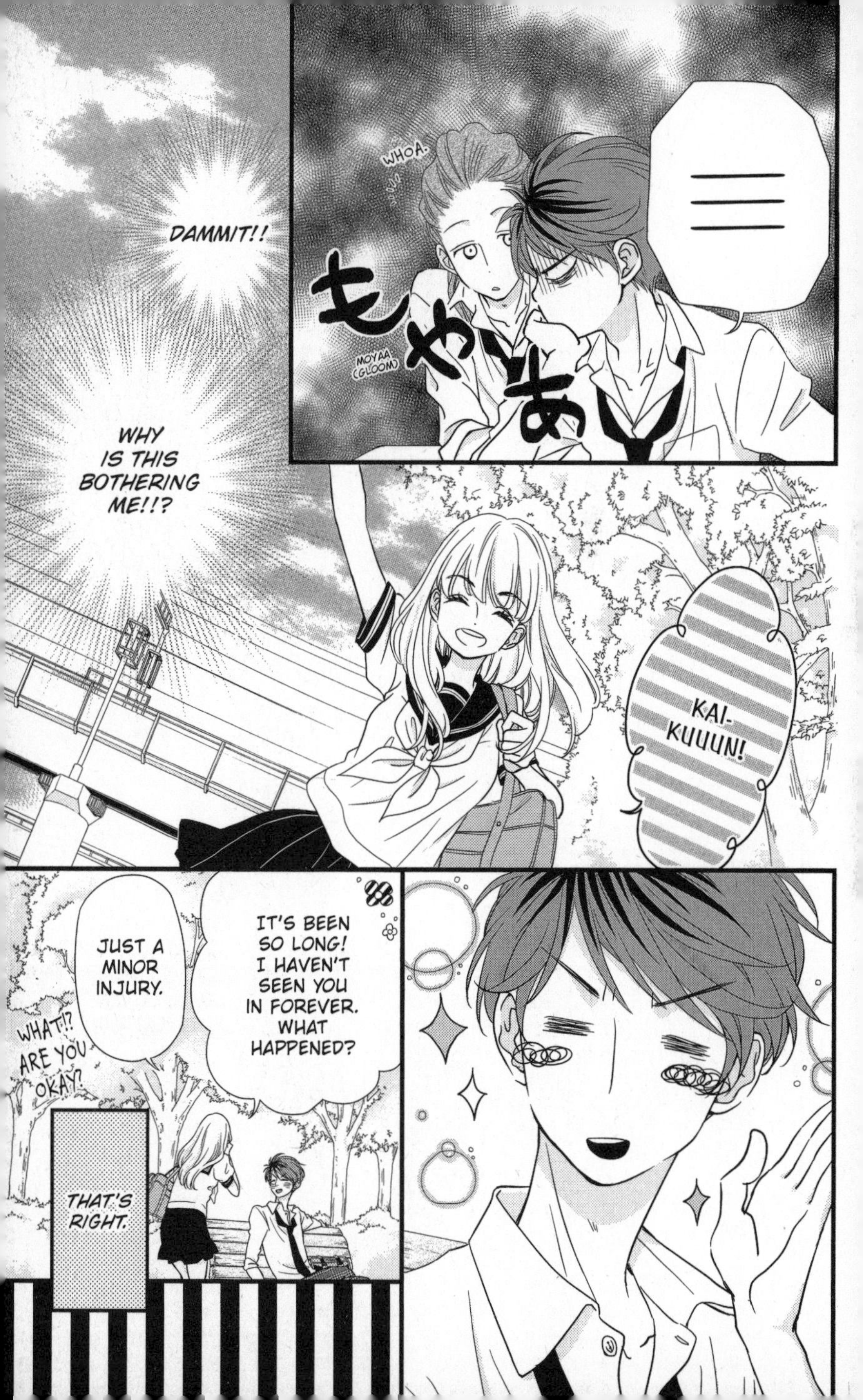
—
WHOA.
MOYAA (GLOOM)
DAMMIT!!
WHY IS THIS BOTHERING ME!!?
KAI-KUUUN!
IT'S BEEN SO LONG! I HAVEN'T SEEN YOU IN FOREVER. WHAT HAPPENED?
JUST A MINOR INJURY.
WHAT!? ARE YOU OKAY?
THAT'S RIGHT.

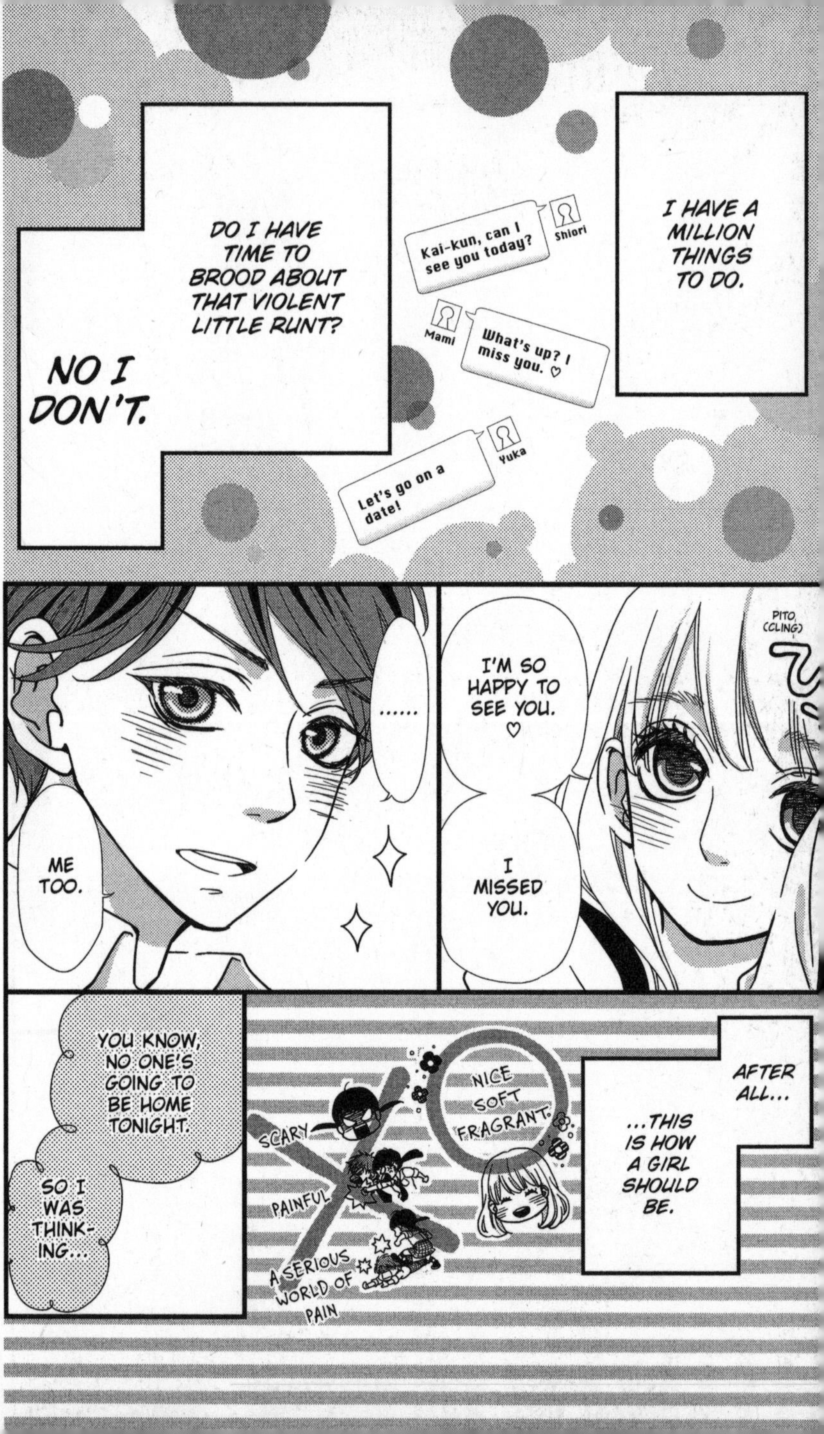
I HAVE A MILLION THINGS TO DO.
Shiori
Kai-kun, can I see you today?
Mami
What's up? I miss you. ♡
Yuka
Let's go on a date!
DO I HAVE TIME TO BROOD ABOUT THAT VIOLENT LITTLE RUNT?
NO I DON'T.
PITO (CLING)
I'M SO HAPPY TO SEE YOU. ♡
I MISSED YOU.
......
ME TOO.
AFTER ALL...
...THIS IS HOW A GIRL SHOULD BE.
NICE SOFT FRAGRANT
SCARY
PAINFUL
A SERIOUS WORLD OF PAIN
YOU KNOW, NO ONE'S GOING TO BE HOME TONIGHT.
SO I WAS THINKING-ING...

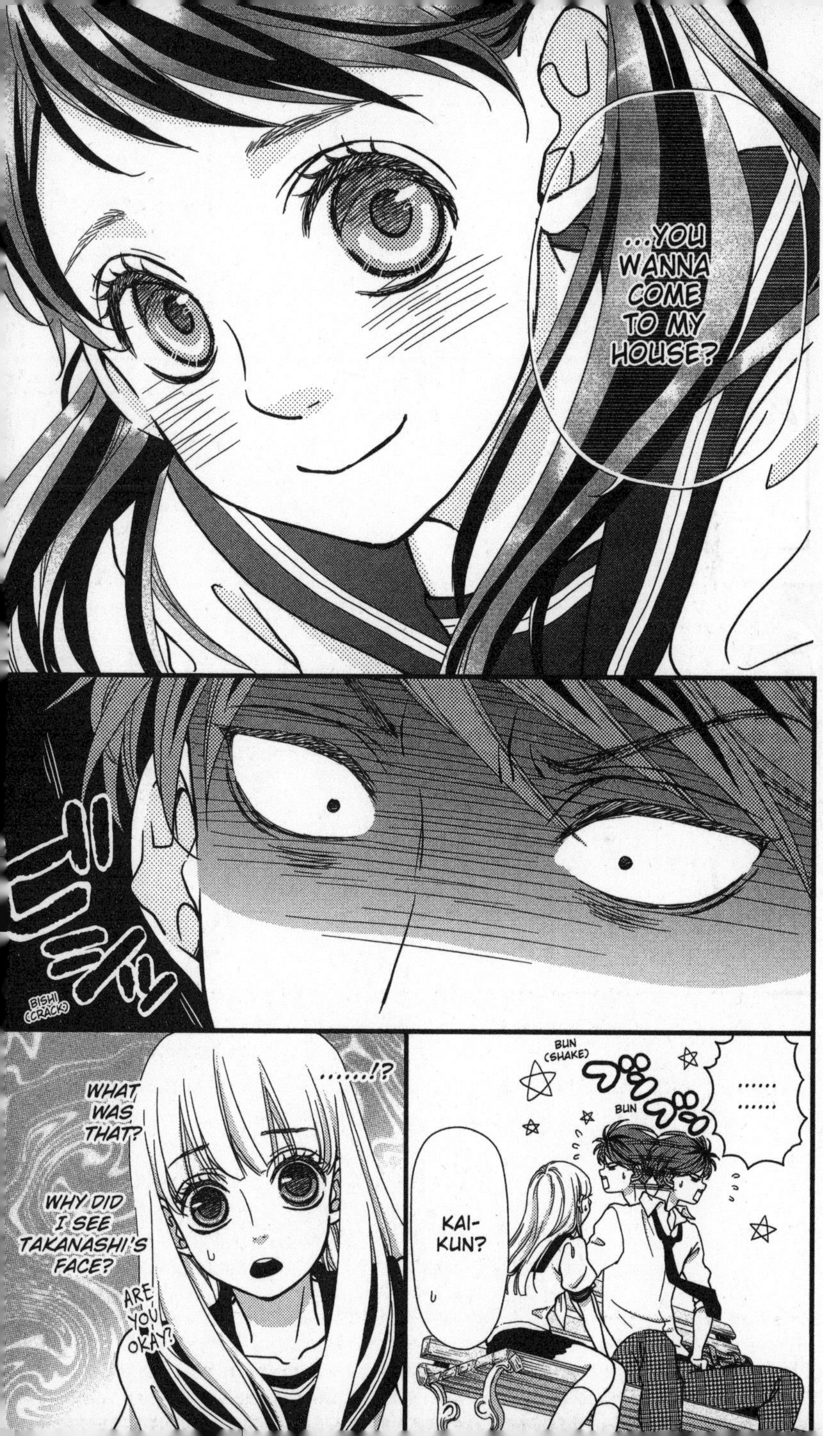
...YOU WANNA COME TO MY HOUSE?
BISHI (CRACK)
......
......
BUN (SHAKE)
BUN
KAI-KUN?
......!?
WHAT WAS THAT?
WHY DID I SEE TAKANASHI'S FACE?
ARE YOU OKAY?

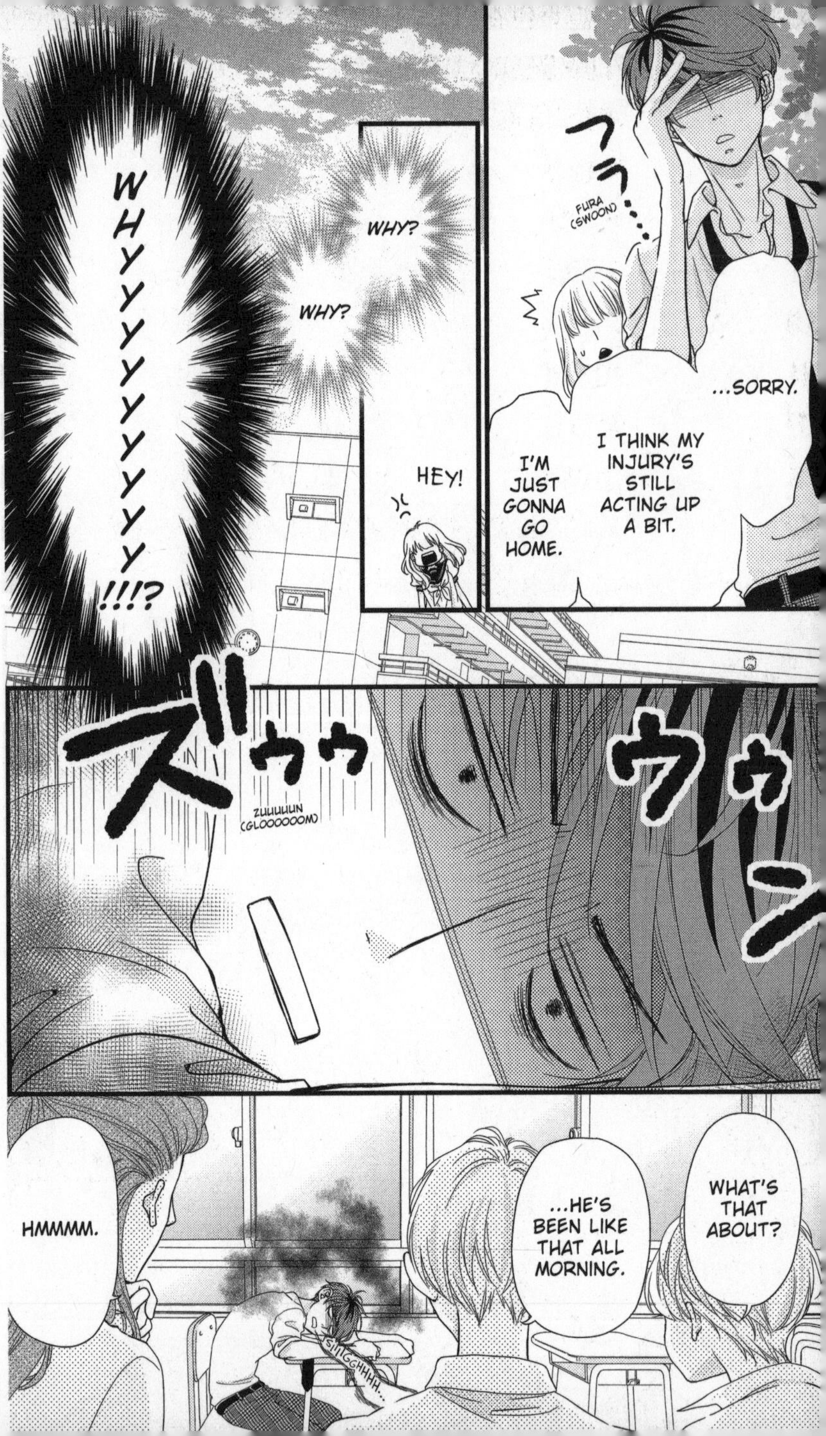

フラ…
FURA (SWOON)
...SORRY.
I THINK MY INJURY'S STILL ACTING UP A BIT.
I'M JUST GONNA GO HOME.
HEY!
WHY?
WHY?
WHYYYYYYYYYYYY!!!?
ズゥゥ ウゥン
ZUUUUUN (GLOOOOOOM)
WHAT'S THAT ABOUT?
...HE'S BEEN LIKE THAT ALL MORNING.
HMMMM.
SIIIGGHHHH...

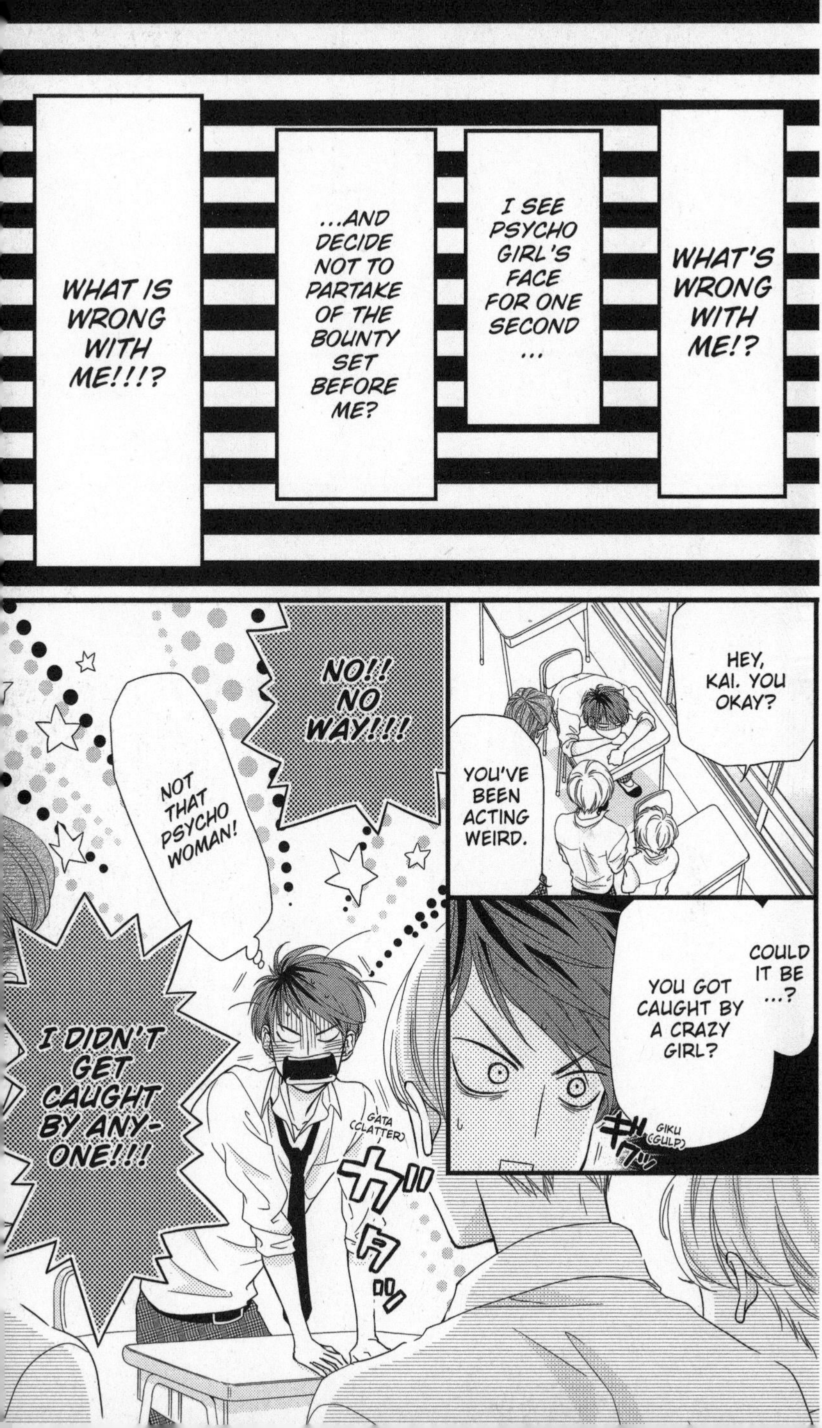
WHAT'S WRONG WITH ME!?
I SEE PSYCHO GIRL'S FACE FOR ONE SECOND ...
...AND DECIDE NOT TO PARTAKE OF THE BOUNTY SET BEFORE ME?
WHAT IS WRONG WITH ME!!!?
HEY, KAI. YOU OKAY?
YOU'VE BEEN ACTING WEIRD.
COULD IT BE ...?
YOU GOT CAUGHT BY A CRAZY GIRL?
GIKU (GULP)
NO!! NO WAY!!!
NOT THAT PSYCHO WOMAN!
I DIDN'T GET CAUGHT BY ANY-ONE!!!
GATA (CLATTER)

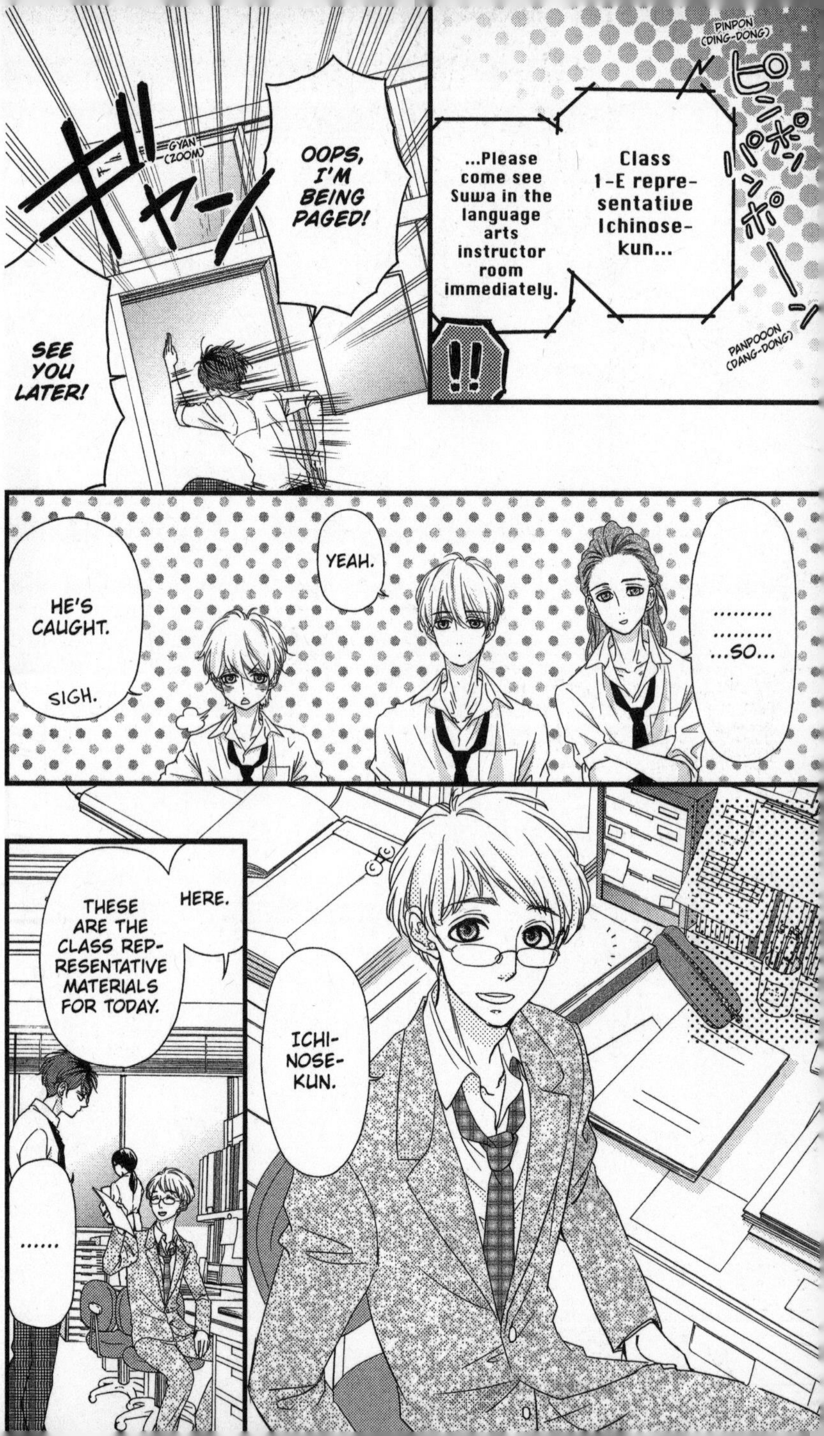
PINPON (DING-DONG)
Class 1-E representative Ichinose-kun...
...Please come see Suwa in the language arts instructor room immediately.
PANPOOON (DANG-DONG)
!!
OOPS, I'M BEING PAGED!
GYAN (ZOOM)
SEE YOU LATER!
....SO...
YEAH.
HE'S CAUGHT.
SIGH.
ICHINOSE-KUN.
HERE.
THESE ARE THE CLASS REPRESENTATIVE MATERIALS FOR TODAY.
......

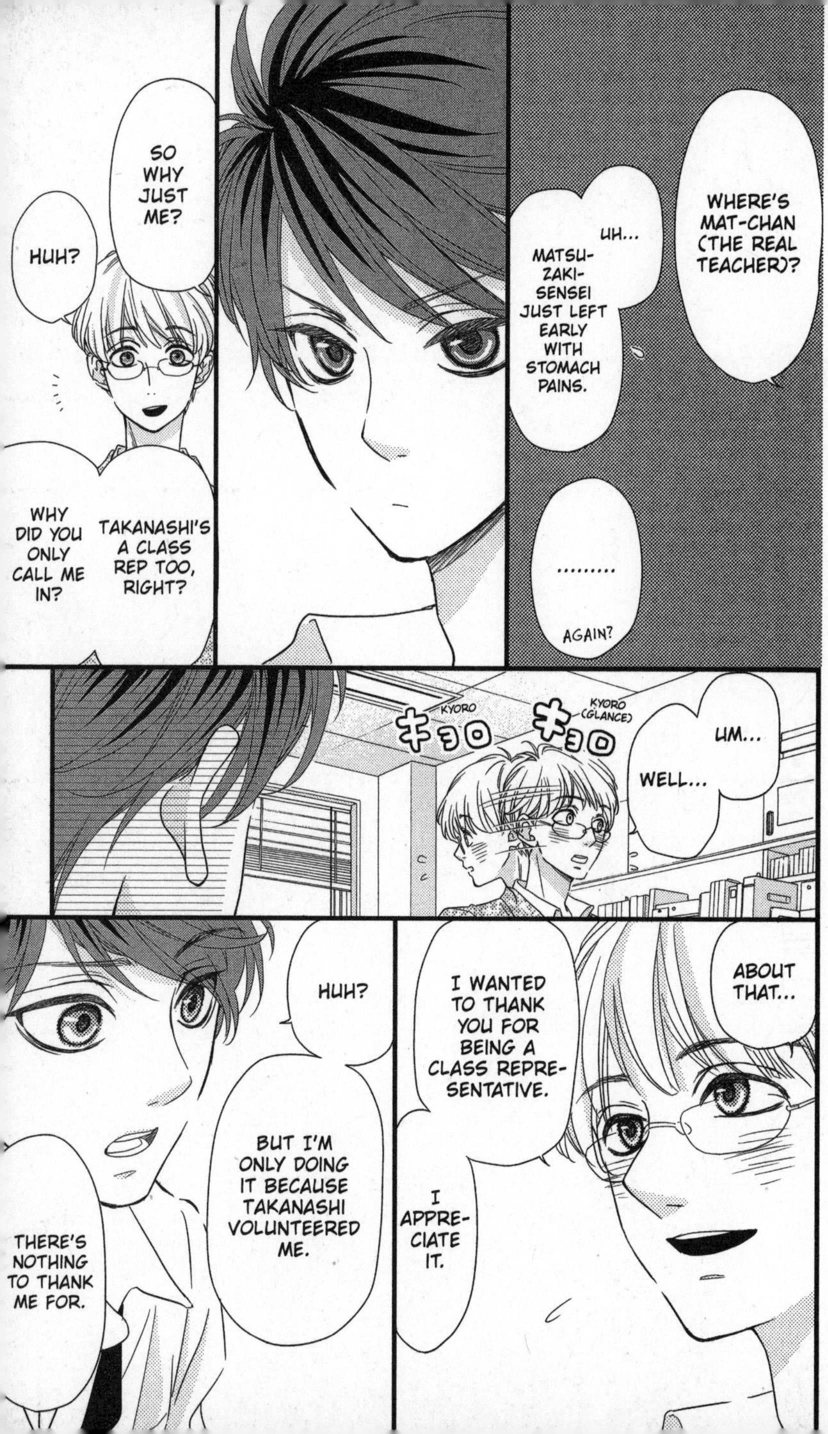
WHERE'S MAT-CHAN (THE REAL TEACHER)?
UH... MATSU-ZAKI-SENSEI JUST LEFT EARLY WITH STOMACH PAINS.
....
AGAIN?
SO WHY JUST ME?
HUH?
TAKANASHI'S A CLASS REP TOO, RIGHT?
WHY DID YOU ONLY CALL ME IN?
UM...
WELL...
キョロ KYORO (GLANCE)
キョロ KYORO
ABOUT THAT...
I WANTED TO THANK YOU FOR BEING A CLASS REPRESENTATIVE.
I APPRECIATE IT.
HUH?
BUT I'M ONLY DOING IT BECAUSE TAKANASHI VOLUNTEERED ME.
THERE'S NOTHING TO THANK ME FOR.

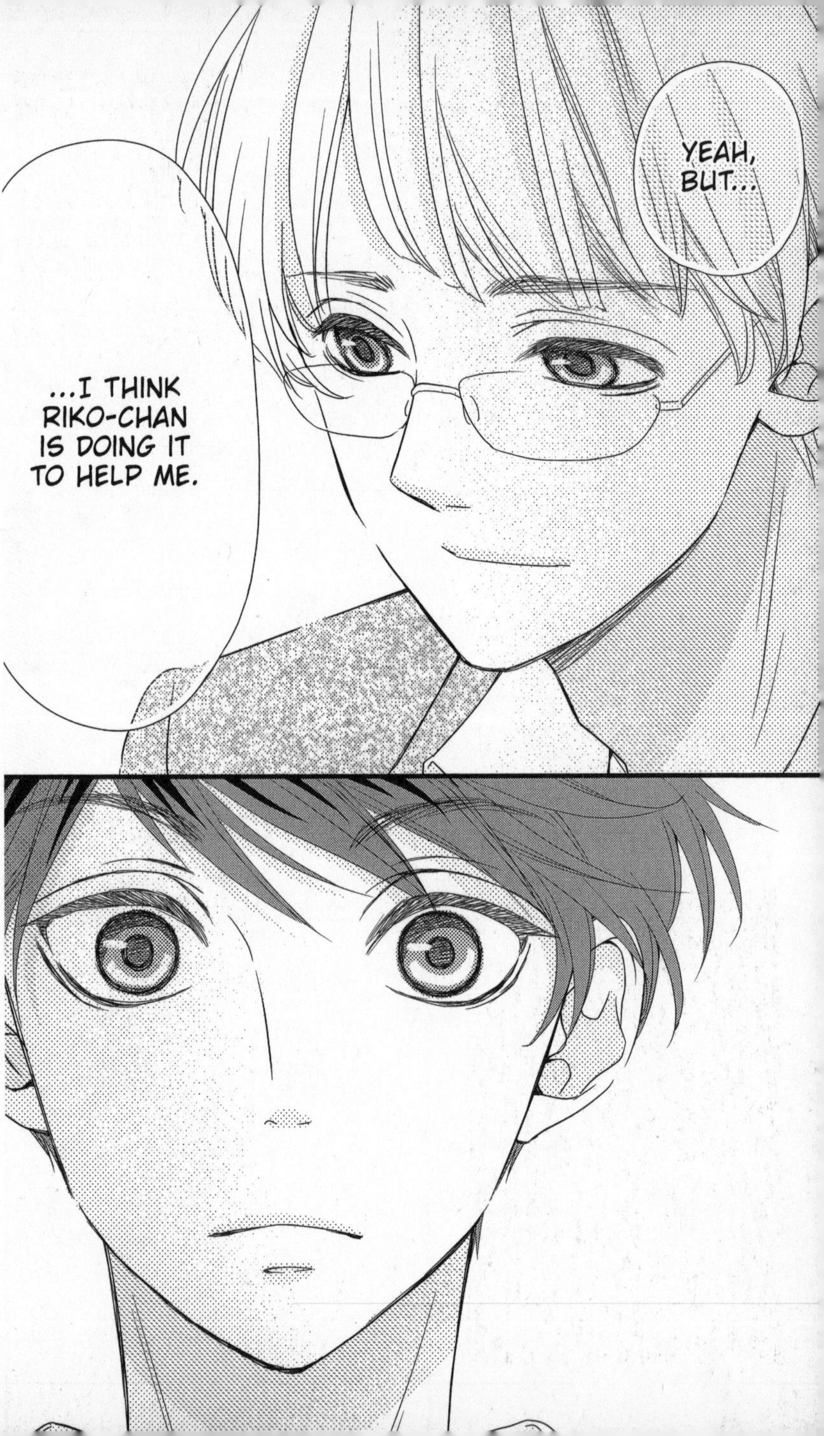
YEAH, BUT...
...I THINK RIKO-CHAN IS DOING IT TO HELP ME.

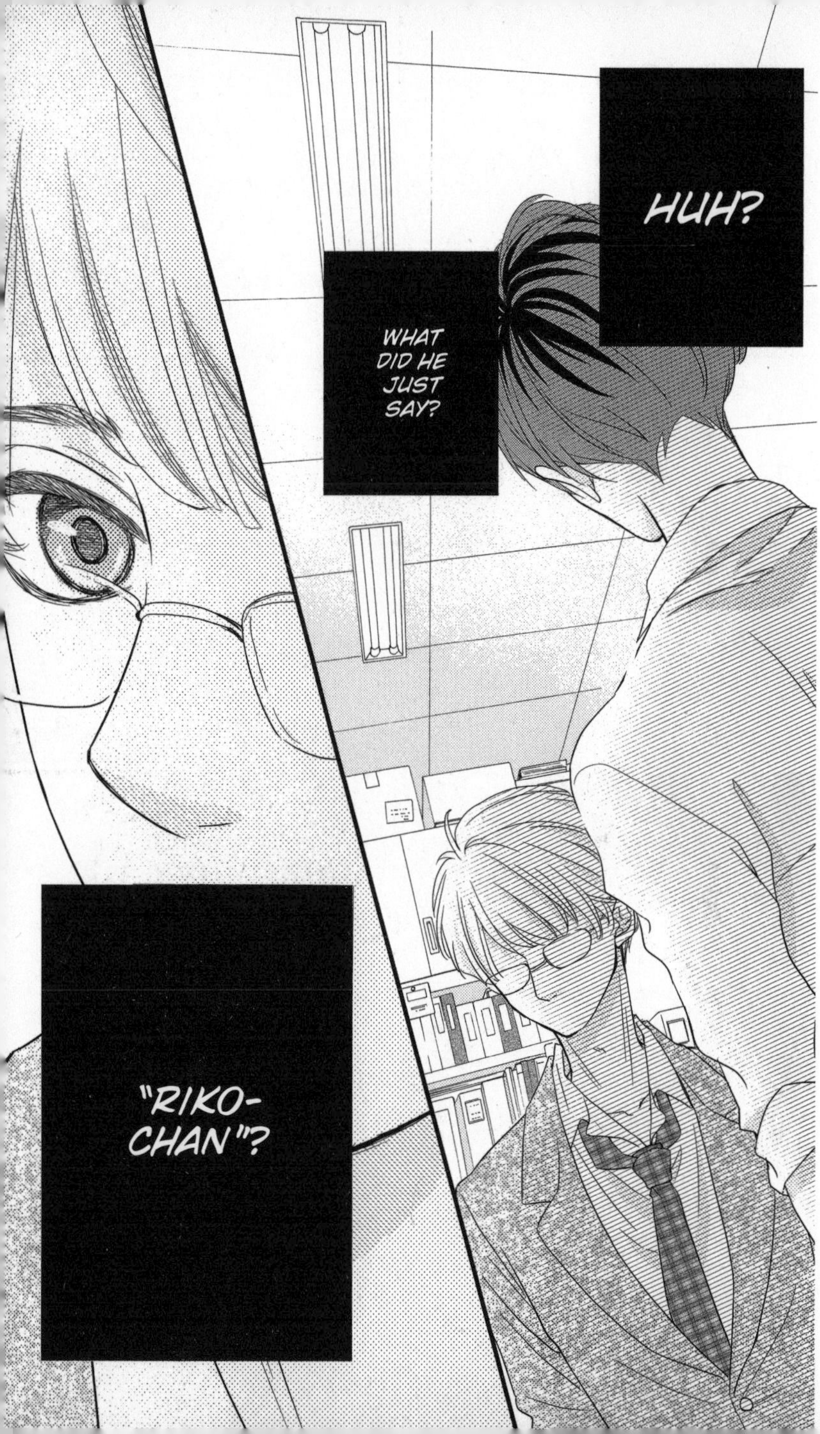
HUH?
WHAT DID HE JUST SAY?
"RIKO-CHAN"?

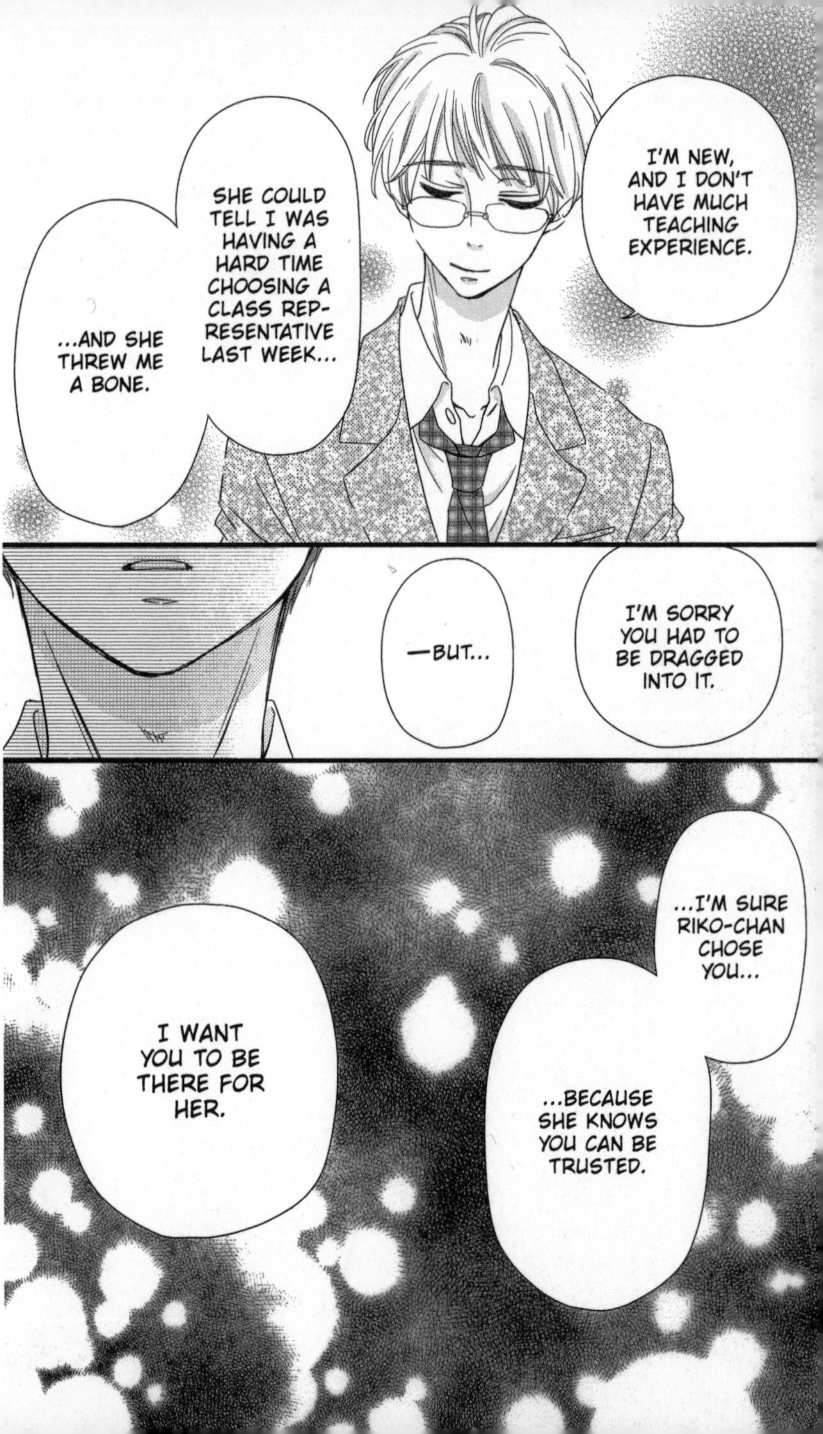
I'M NEW, AND I DON'T HAVE MUCH TEACHING EXPERIENCE.
SHE COULD TELL I WAS HAVING A HARD TIME CHOOSING A CLASS REP-RESENTATIVE LAST WEEK...
...AND SHE THREW ME A BONE.
I'M SORRY YOU HAD TO BE DRAGGED INTO IT.
—BUT...
...I'M SURE RIKO-CHAN CHOSE YOU...
...BECAUSE SHE KNOWS YOU CAN BE TRUSTED.
I WANT YOU TO BE THERE FOR HER.

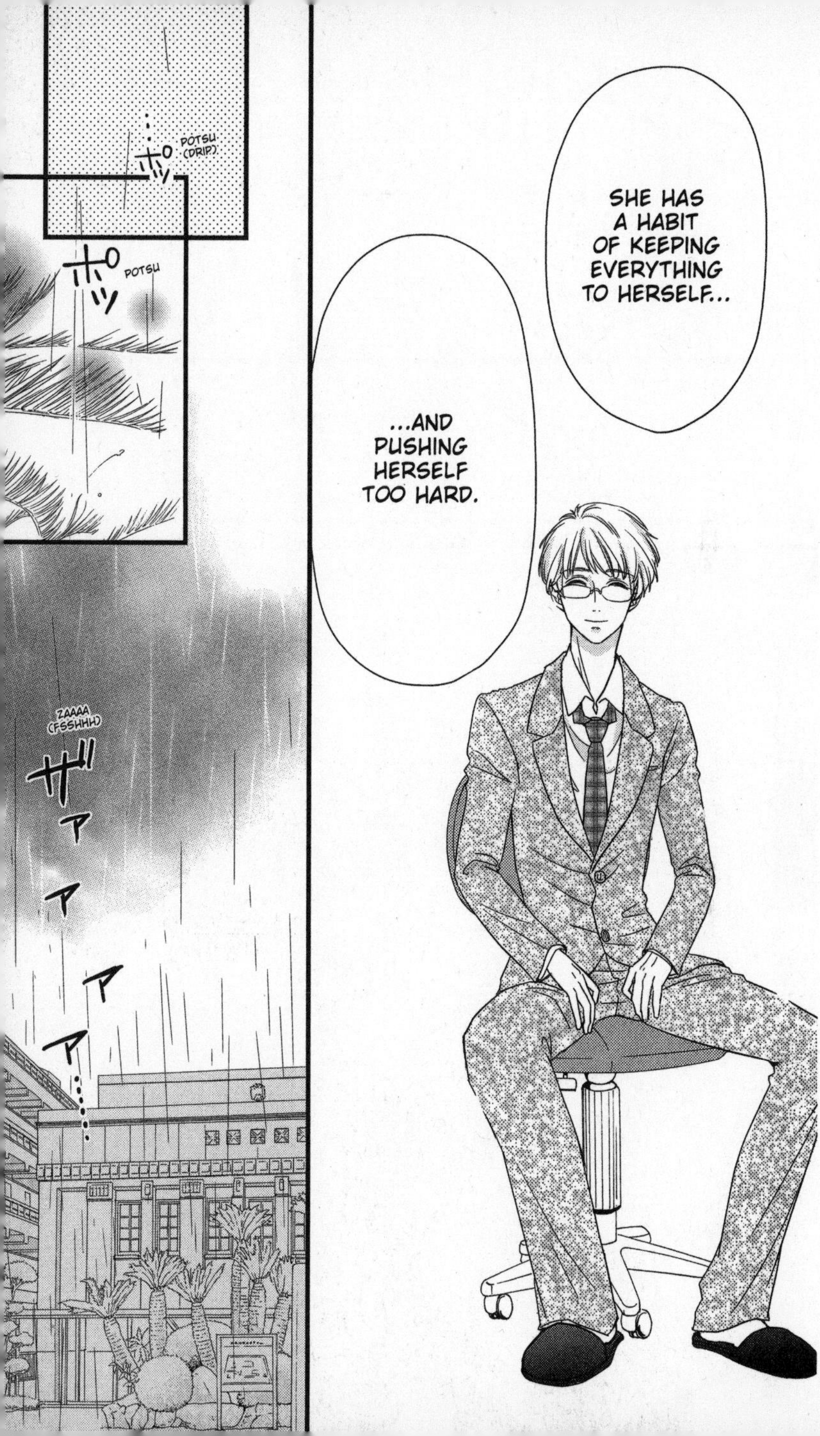
SHE HAS A HABIT OF KEEPING EVERYTHING TO HERSELF...
...AND PUSHING HERSELF TOO HARD.
POTSU (DRIP)
POTSU
ZAAAA (FSSHHH)

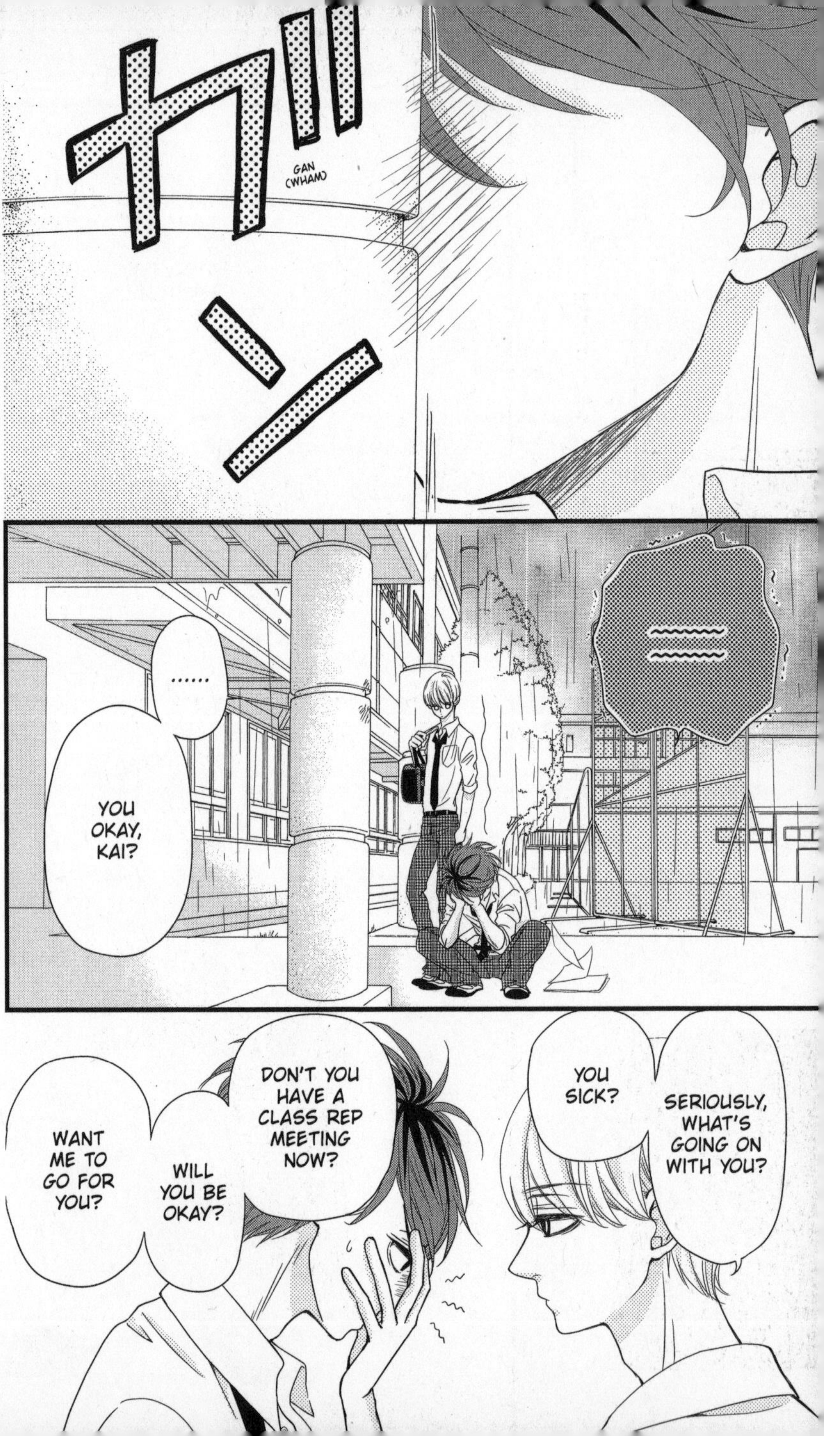
ガン
GAN (WHAM)
......
YOU OKAY, KAI?
SERIOUSLY, WHAT'S GOING ON WITH YOU?
YOU SICK?
DON'T YOU HAVE A CLASS REP MEETING NOW?
WILL YOU BE OKAY?
WANT ME TO GO FOR YOU?

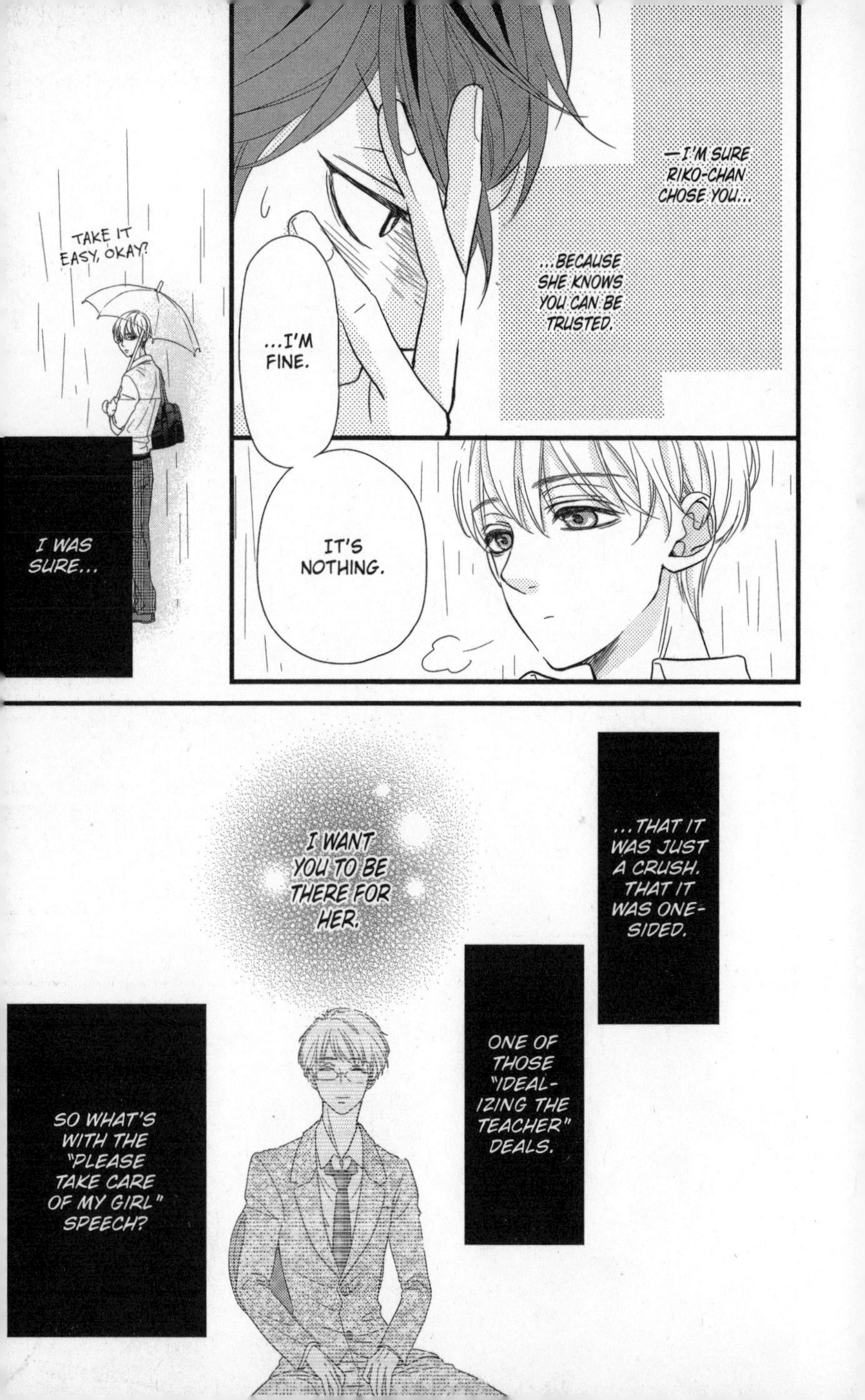
—I'M SURE RIKO-CHAN CHOSE YOU...
...BECAUSE SHE KNOWS YOU CAN BE TRUSTED.
...I'M FINE.
IT'S NOTHING.
TAKE IT EASY, OKAY?
I WAS SURE...
...THAT IT WAS JUST A CRUSH. THAT IT WAS ONE-SIDED.
I WANT YOU TO BE THERE FOR HER.
ONE OF THOSE "IDEAL-IZING THE TEACHER" DEALS.
SO WHAT'S WITH THE "PLEASE TAKE CARE OF MY GIRL" SPEECH?

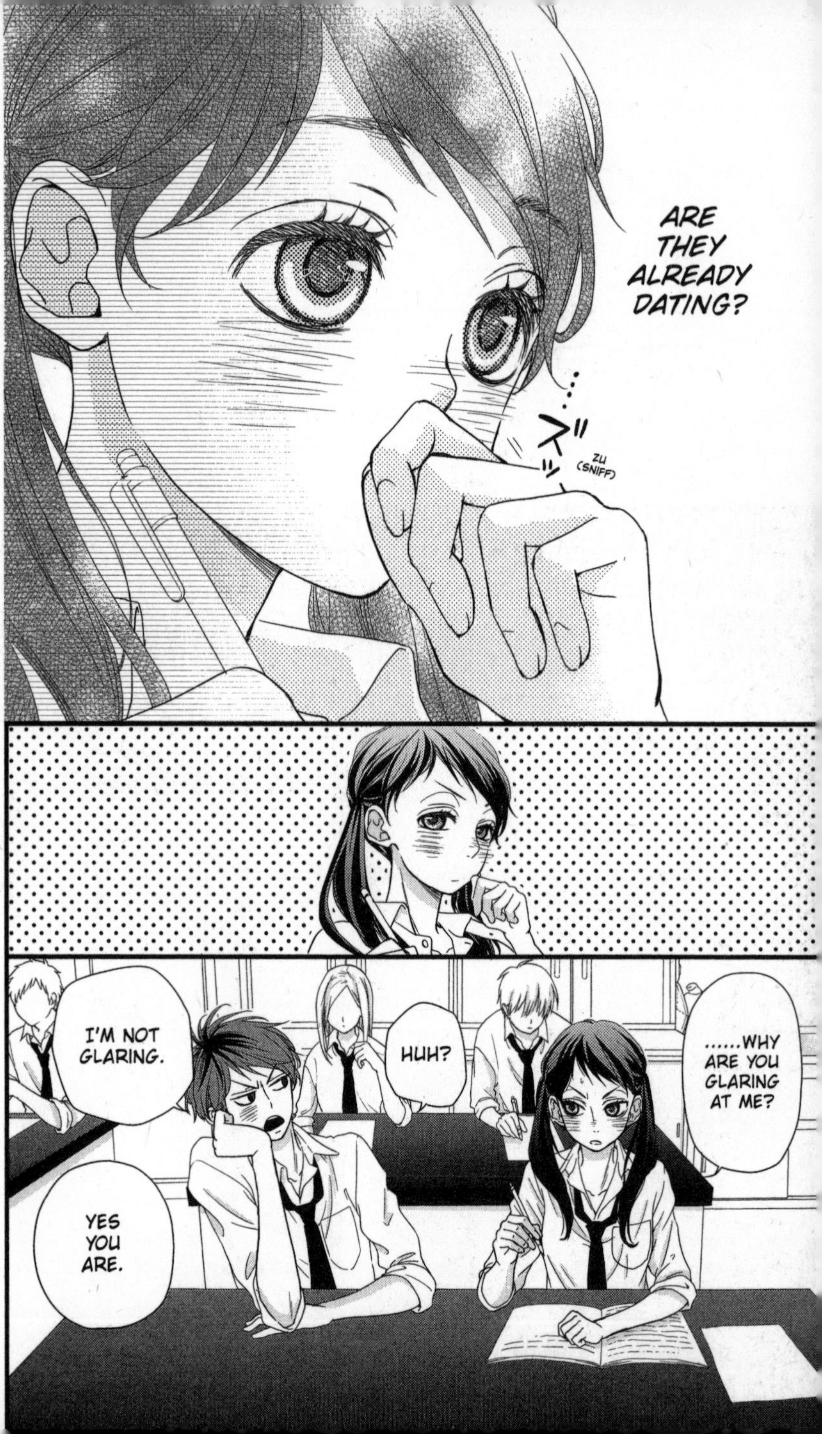
ARE THEY ALREADY DATING?
...
ズッ
ZU (SNIFF)
......WHY ARE YOU GLARING AT ME?
HUH?
I'M NOT GLARING.
YES YOU ARE.

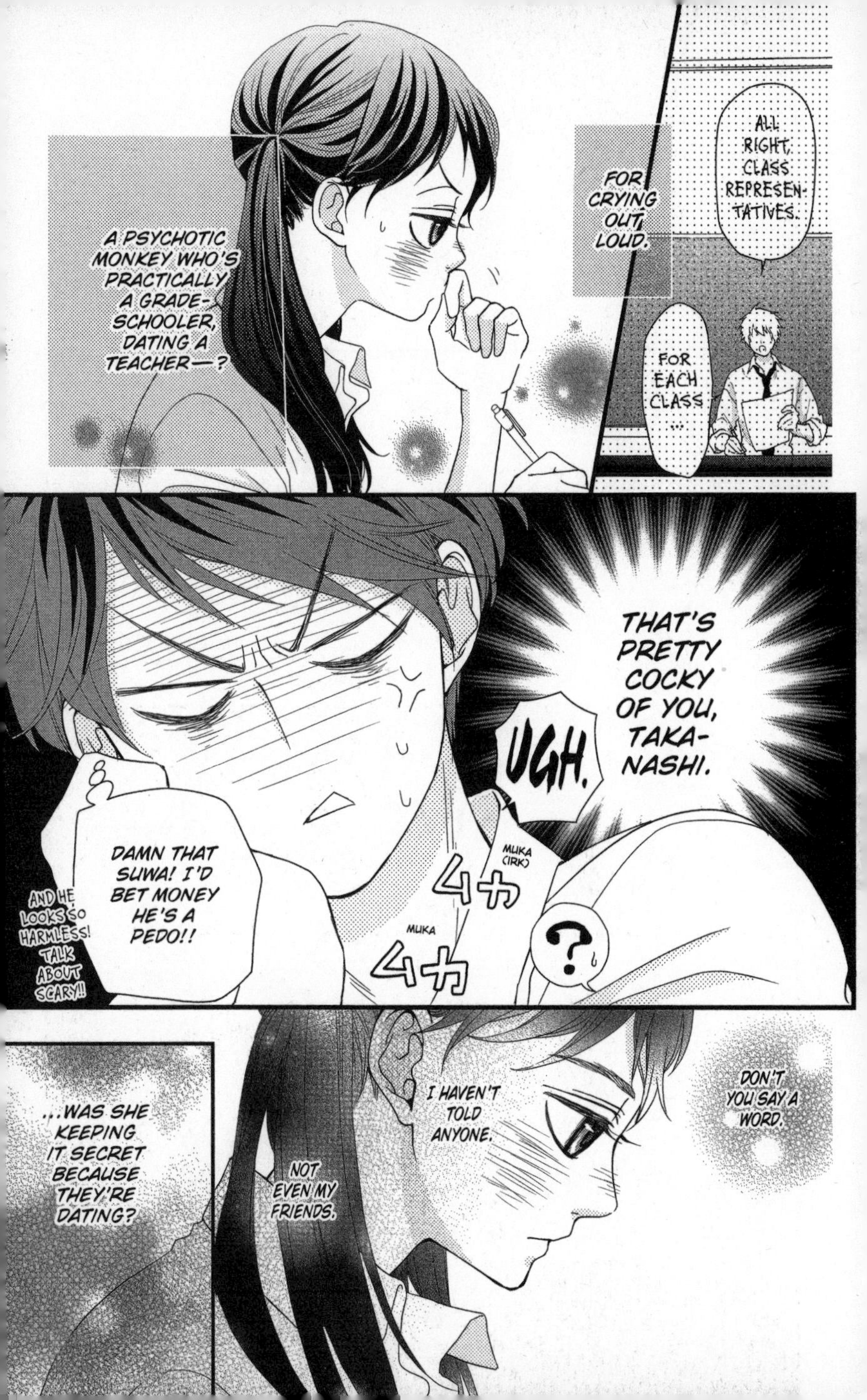
ALL RIGHT, CLASS REPRESEN-TATIVES.
FOR EACH CLASS...
FOR CRYING OUT LOUD.
A PSYCHOTIC MONKEY WHO'S PRACTICALLY A GRADE-SCHOOLER, DATING A TEACHER—?
THAT'S PRETTY COCKY OF YOU, TAKA-NASHI.
UGH.
ムカ
MUKA (IRK)
ムカ
MUKA
?
DAMN THAT SUWA! I'D BET MONEY HE'S A PEDO!!
AND HE LOOKS SO HARMLESS! TALK ABOUT SCARY!!
DON'T YOU SAY A WORD.
I HAVEN'T TOLD ANYONE.
NOT EVEN MY FRIENDS.
...WAS SHE KEEPING IT SECRET BECAUSE THEY'RE DATING?

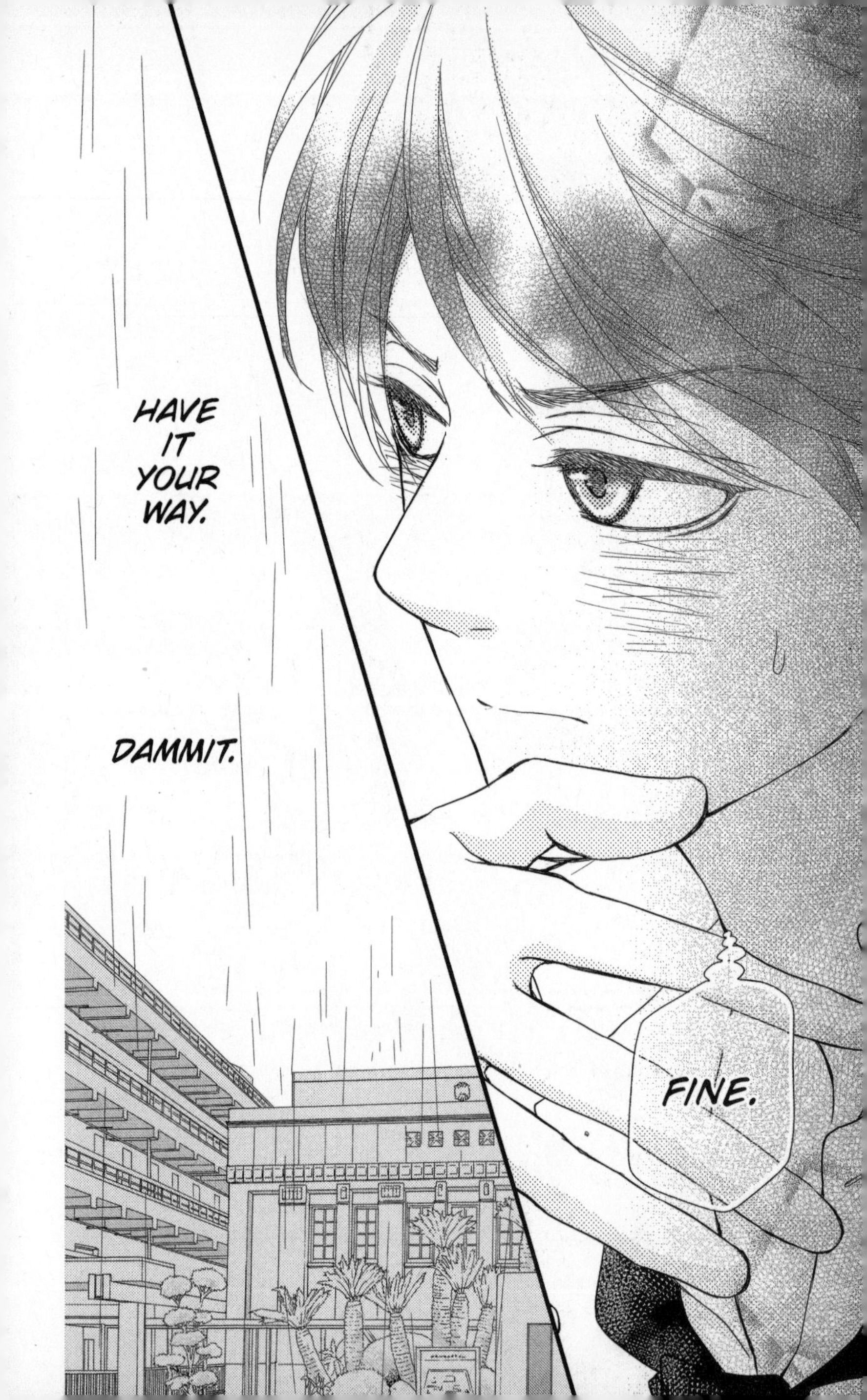
FINE.
HAVE IT YOUR WAY.
DAMMIT.

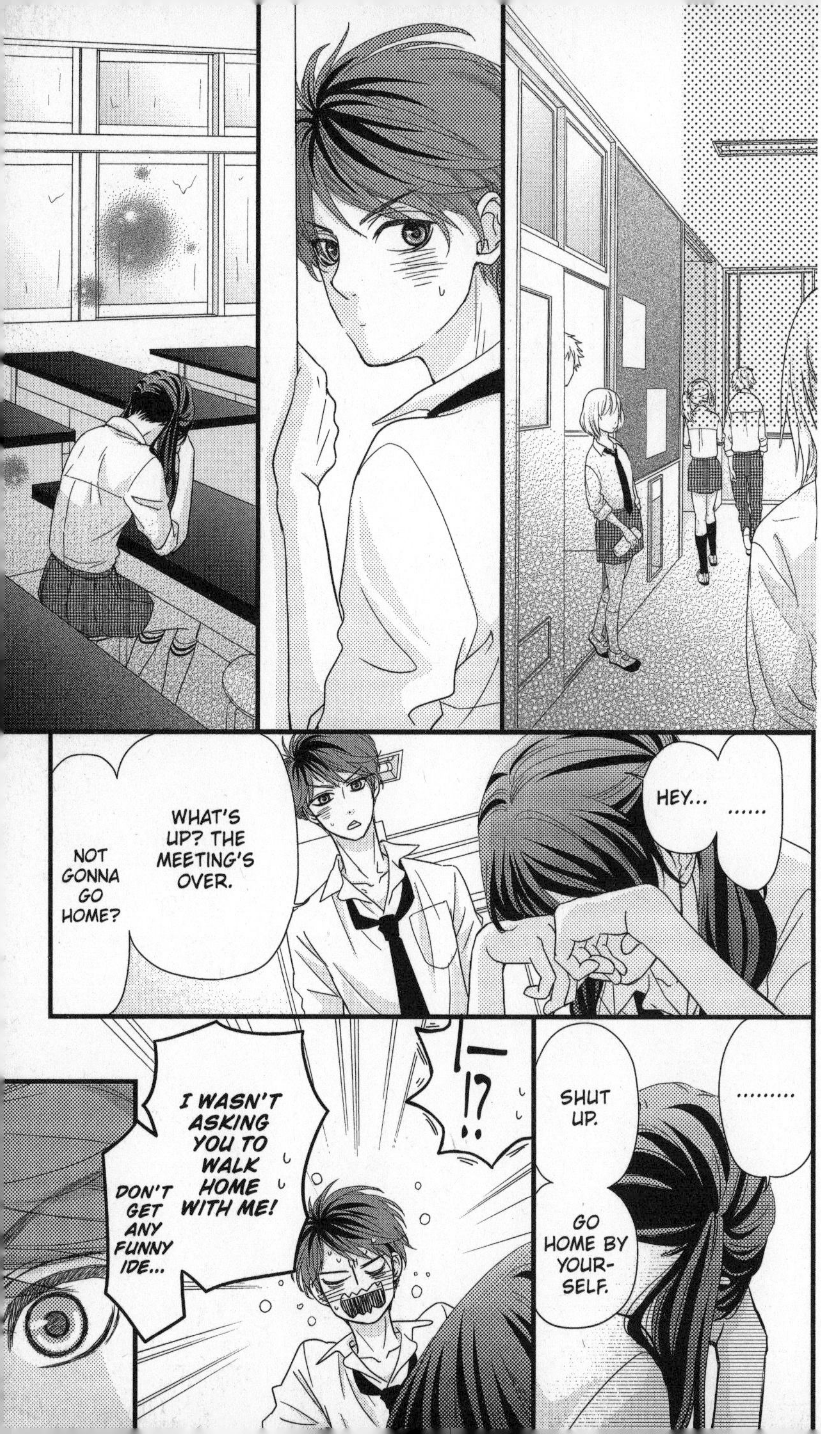
HEY... ......
WHAT'S UP? THE MEETING'S OVER.
NOT GONNA GO HOME?
....
SHUT UP.
GO HOME BY YOURSELF.
!—!?
I WASN'T ASKING YOU TO WALK HOME WITH ME!
DON'T GET ANY FUNNY IDE...

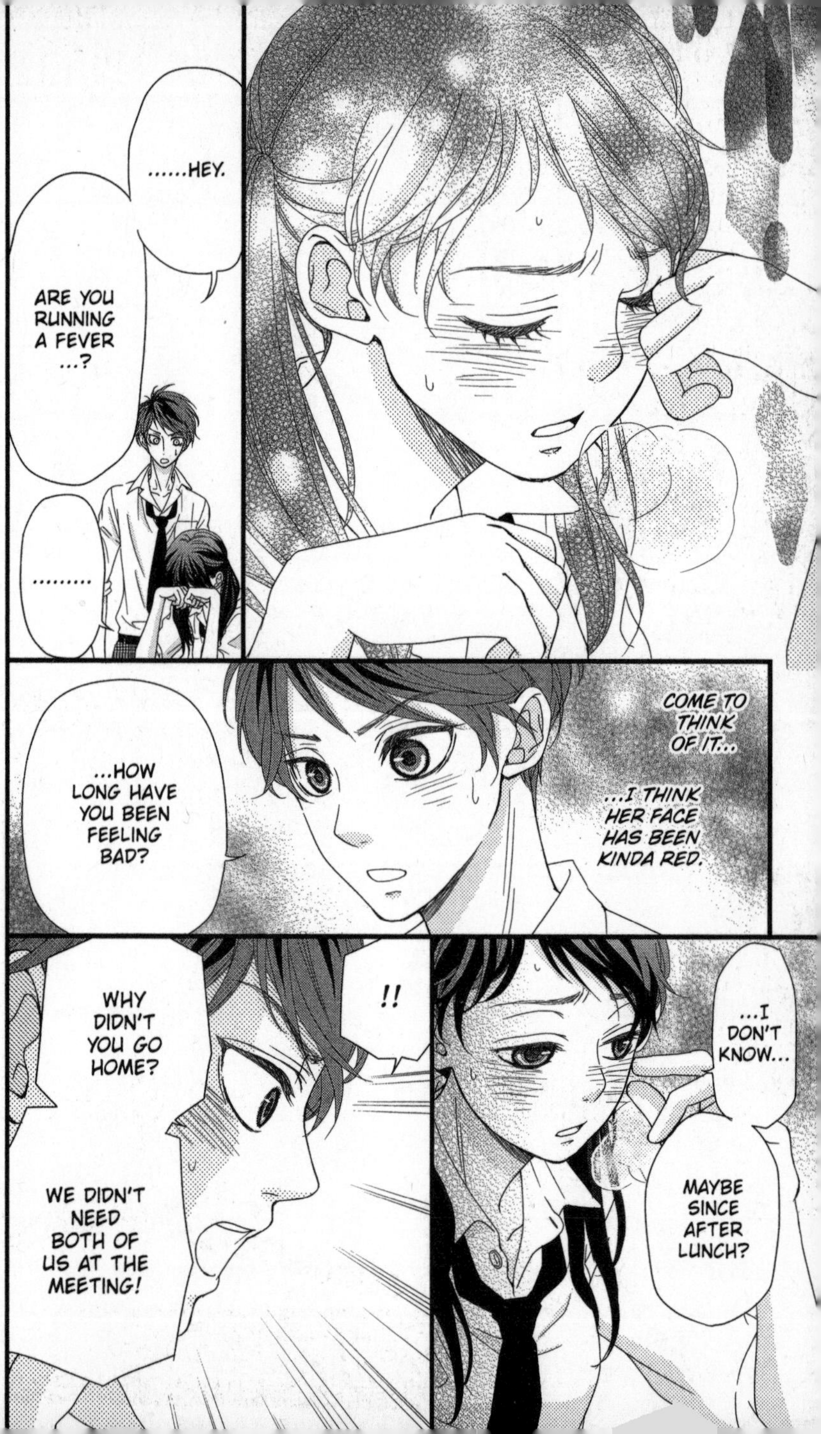
......HEY.
ARE YOU RUNNING A FEVER ...?
....
COME TO THINK OF IT...
...I THINK HER FACE HAS BEEN KINDA RED.
...HOW LONG HAVE YOU BEEN FEELING BAD?
...I DON'T KNOW...
MAYBE SINCE AFTER LUNCH?
!!
WHY DIDN'T YOU GO HOME?
WE DIDN'T NEED BOTH OF US AT THE MEETING!

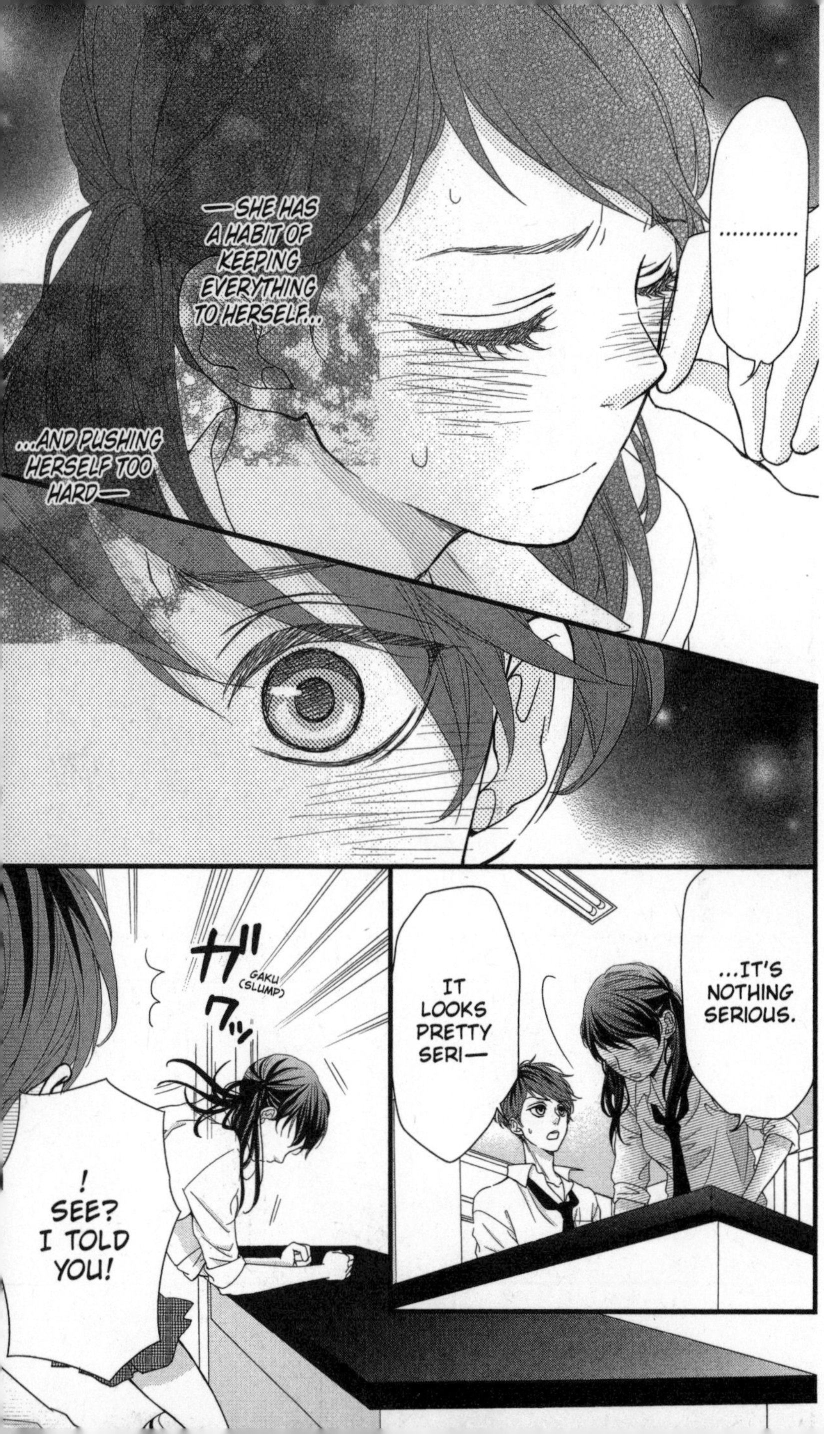
....
—SHE HAS A HABIT OF KEEPING EVERYTHING TO HERSELF...
...AND PUSHING HERSELF TOO HARD—
...IT'S NOTHING SERIOUS.
IT LOOKS PRETTY SERI—
ガクッ
GAKU (SLUMP)
!
SEE? I TOLD YOU!

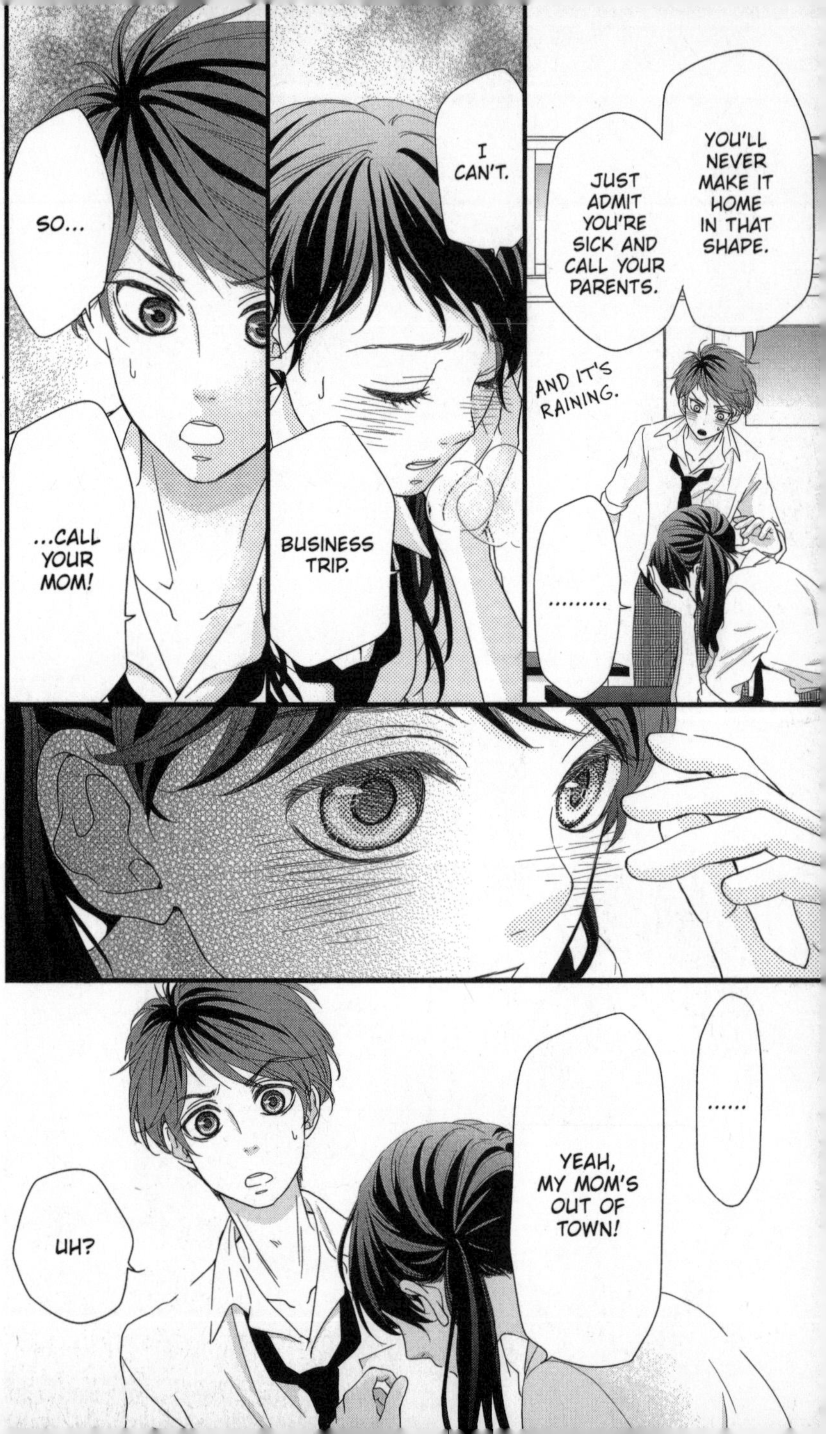
YOU'LL NEVER MAKE IT HOME IN THAT SHAPE.
JUST ADMIT YOU'RE SICK AND CALL YOUR PARENTS.
AND IT'S RAINING.
....
I CAN'T.
BUSINESS TRIP.
SO...
...CALL YOUR MOM!
......
YEAH, MY MOM'S OUT OF TOWN!
UH?

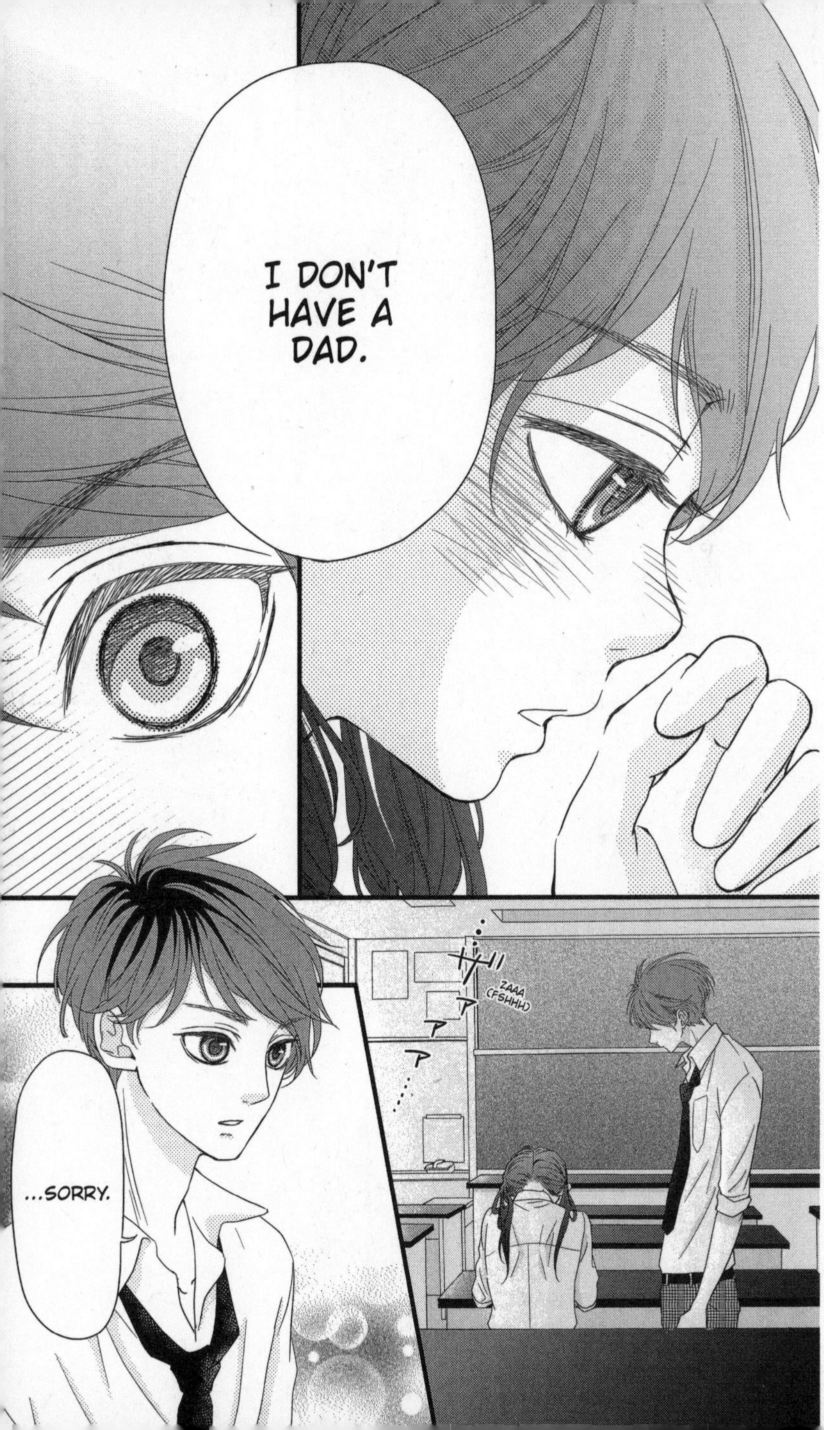
I DON'T HAVE A DAD.
ZAAA (FSHHH)
...SORRY.

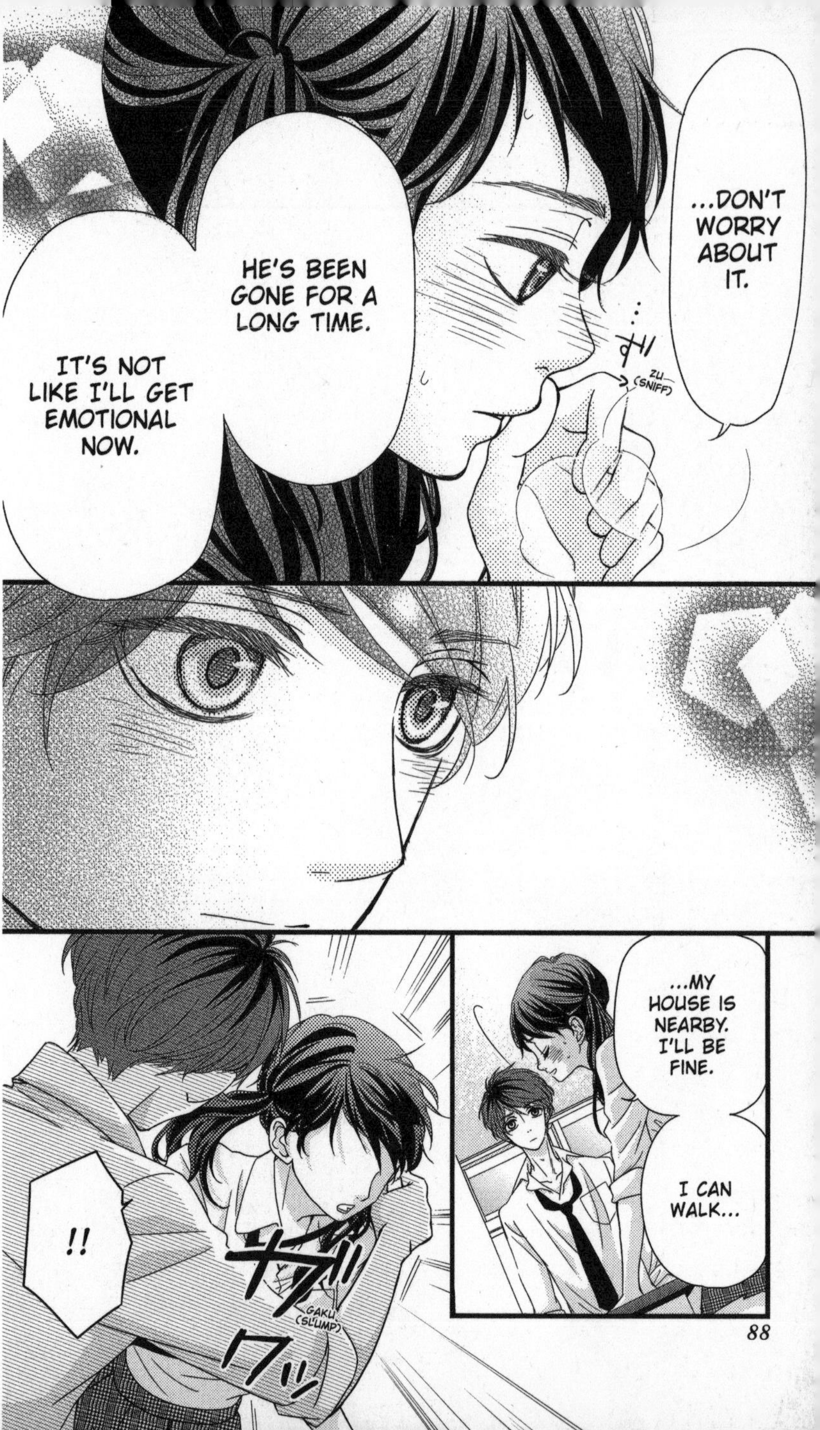
...DON'T WORRY ABOUT IT.
ZU (SNIFF)
HE'S BEEN GONE FOR A LONG TIME.
IT'S NOT LIKE I'LL GET EMOTIONAL NOW.
...MY HOUSE IS NEARBY. I'LL BE FINE.
I CAN WALK...
!!
GAKU (SLUMP)

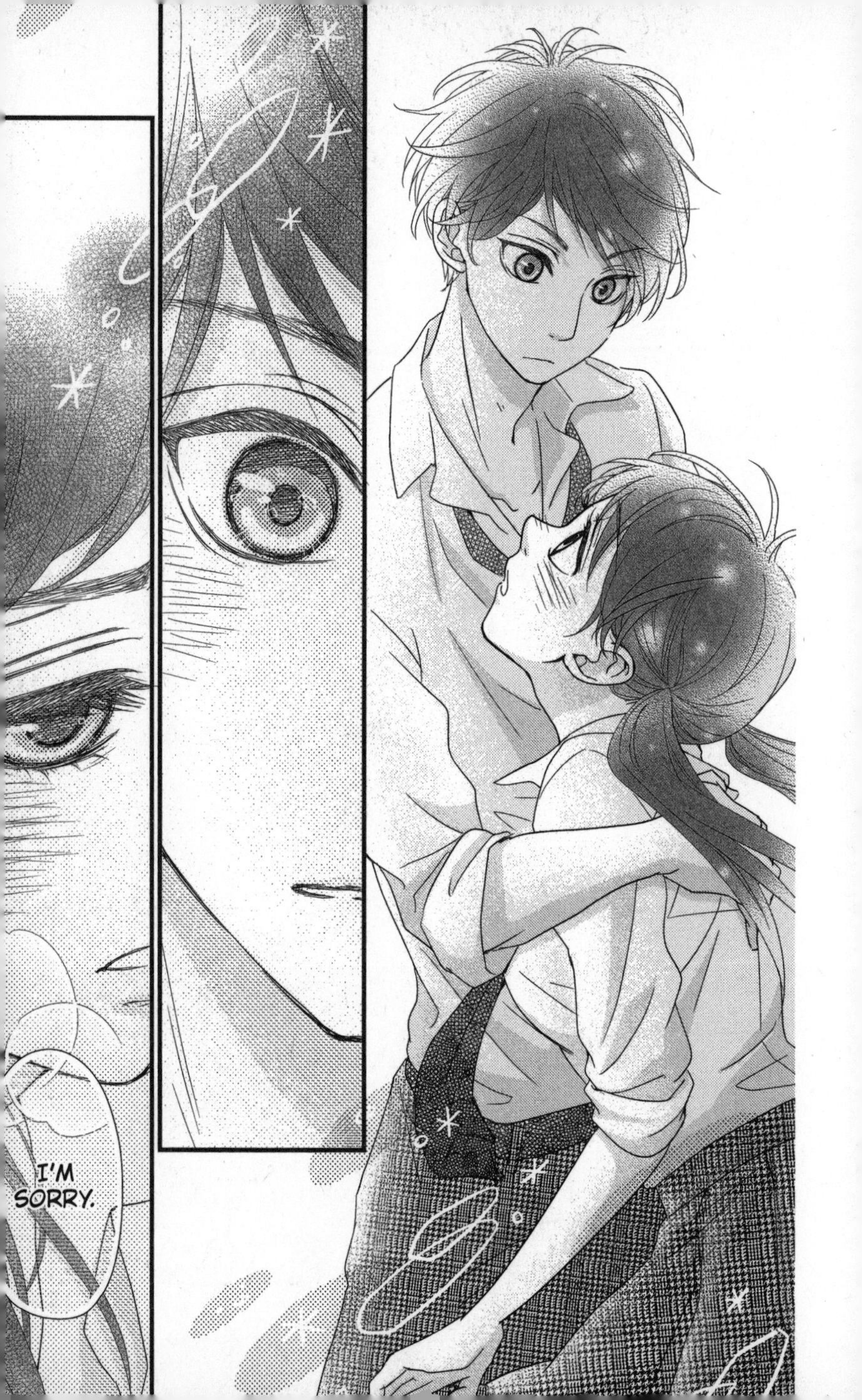
I'M SORRY.

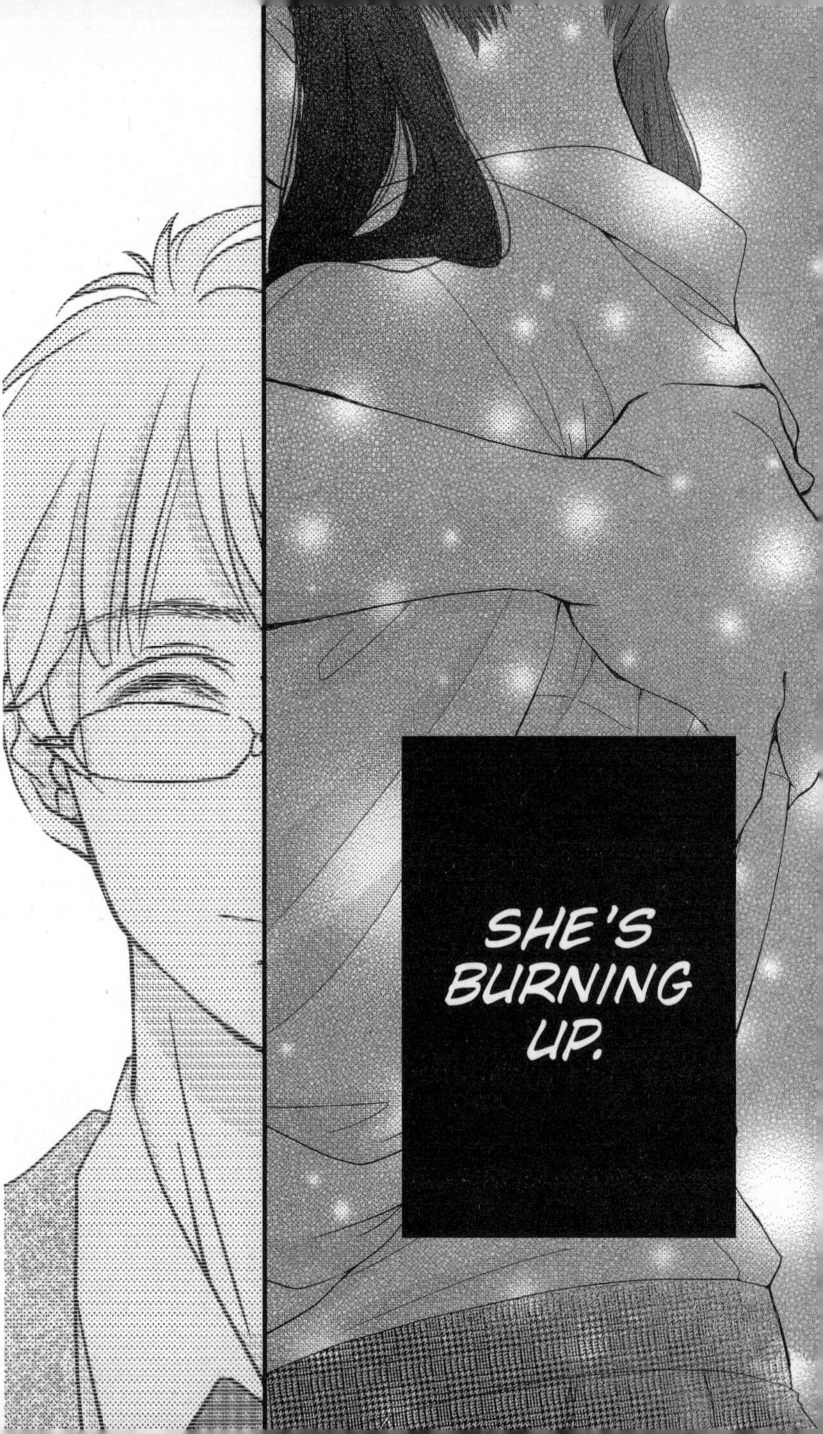
SHE'S BURNING UP.

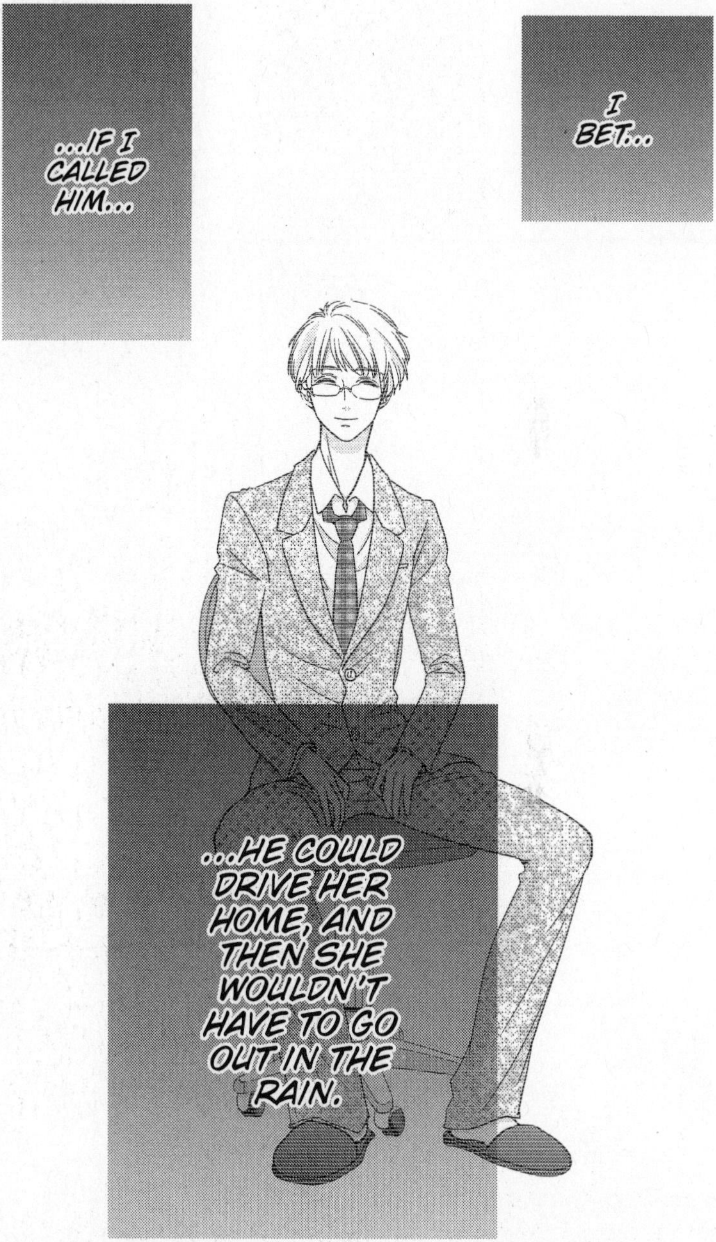
I BET...
...IF I CALLED HIM...
...HE COULD DRIVE HER HOME, AND THEN SHE WOULDN'T HAVE TO GO OUT IN THE RAIN.

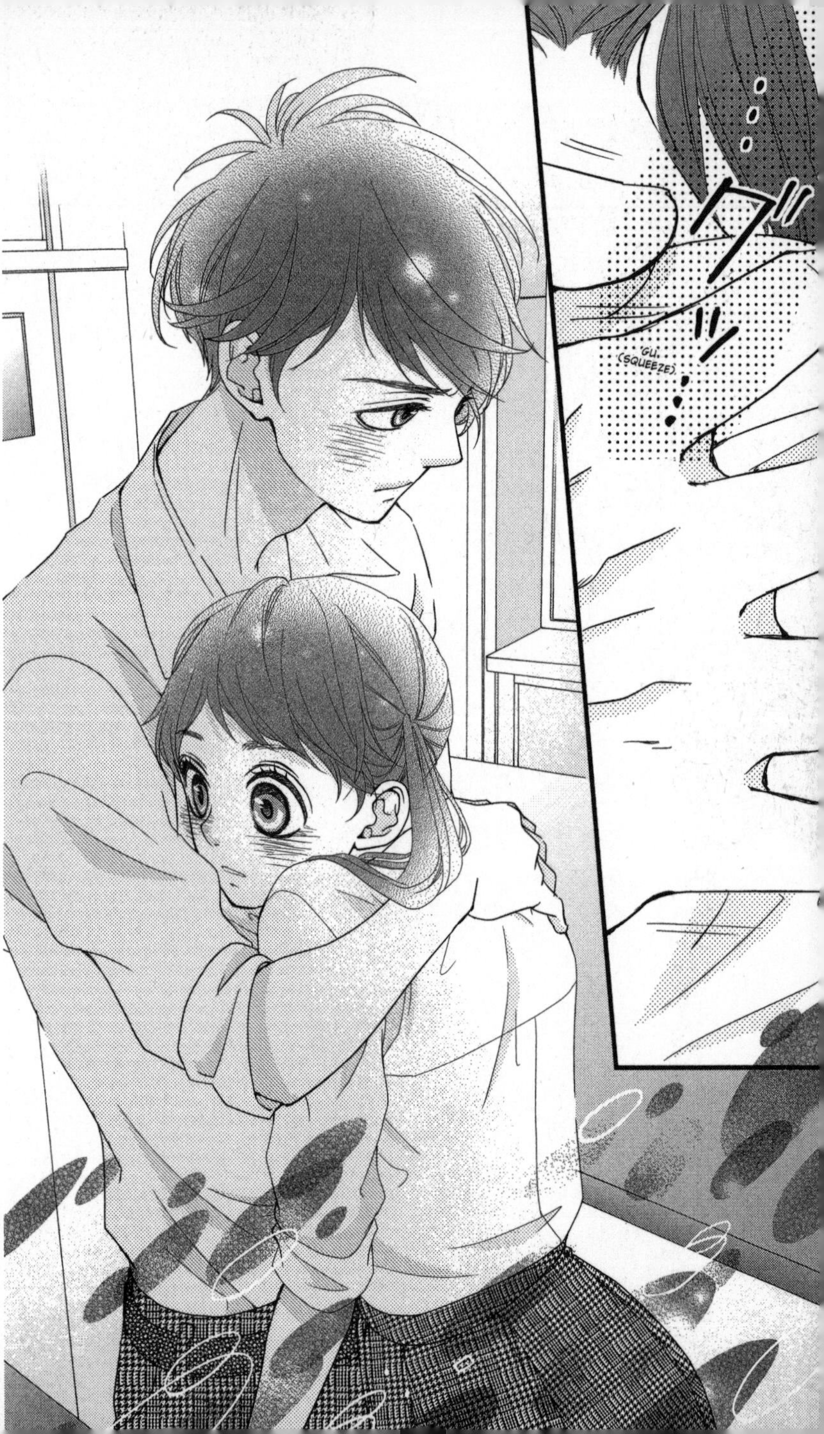
....
グッ
GU (SQUEEZE)

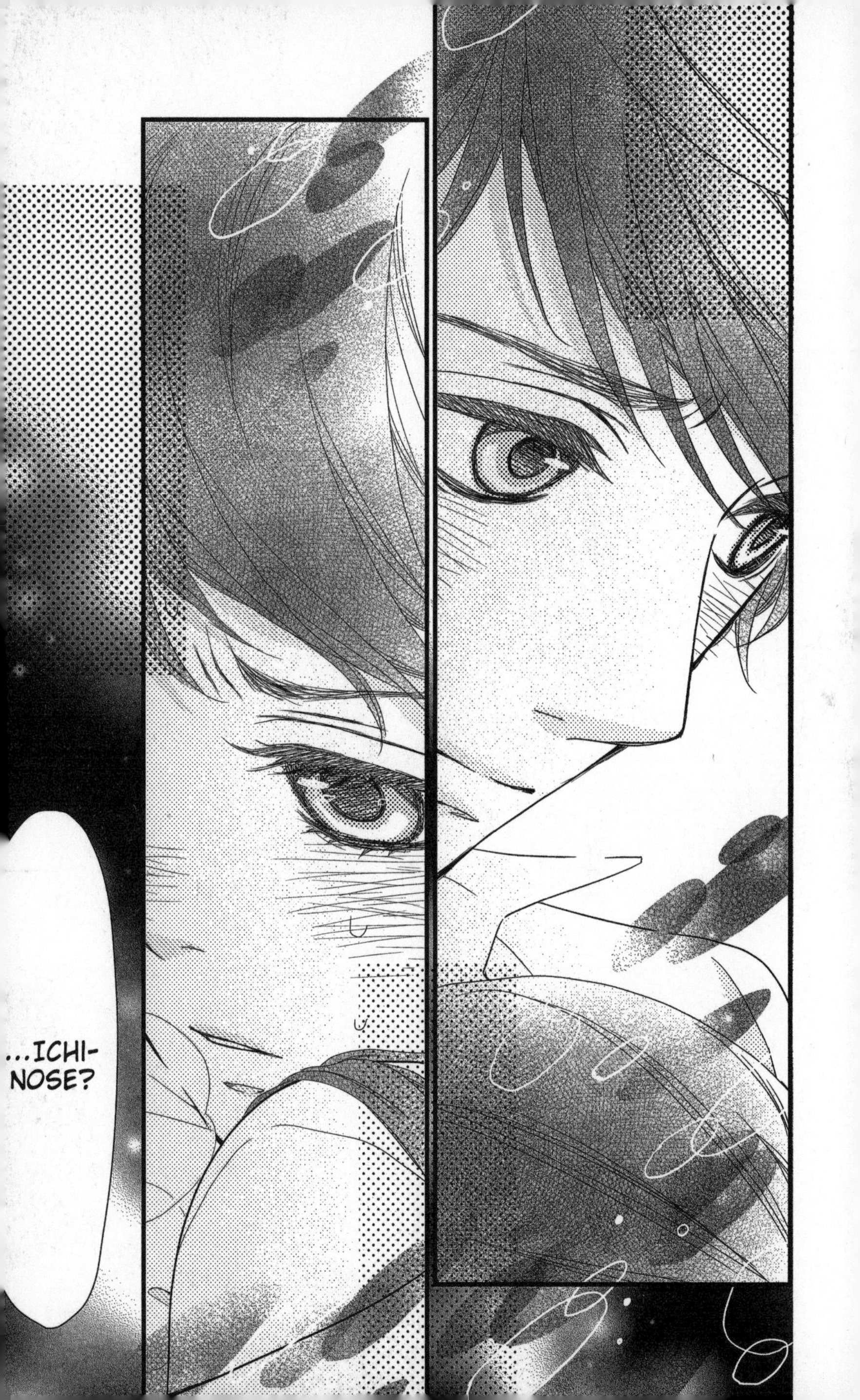
...ICHI-NOSE?

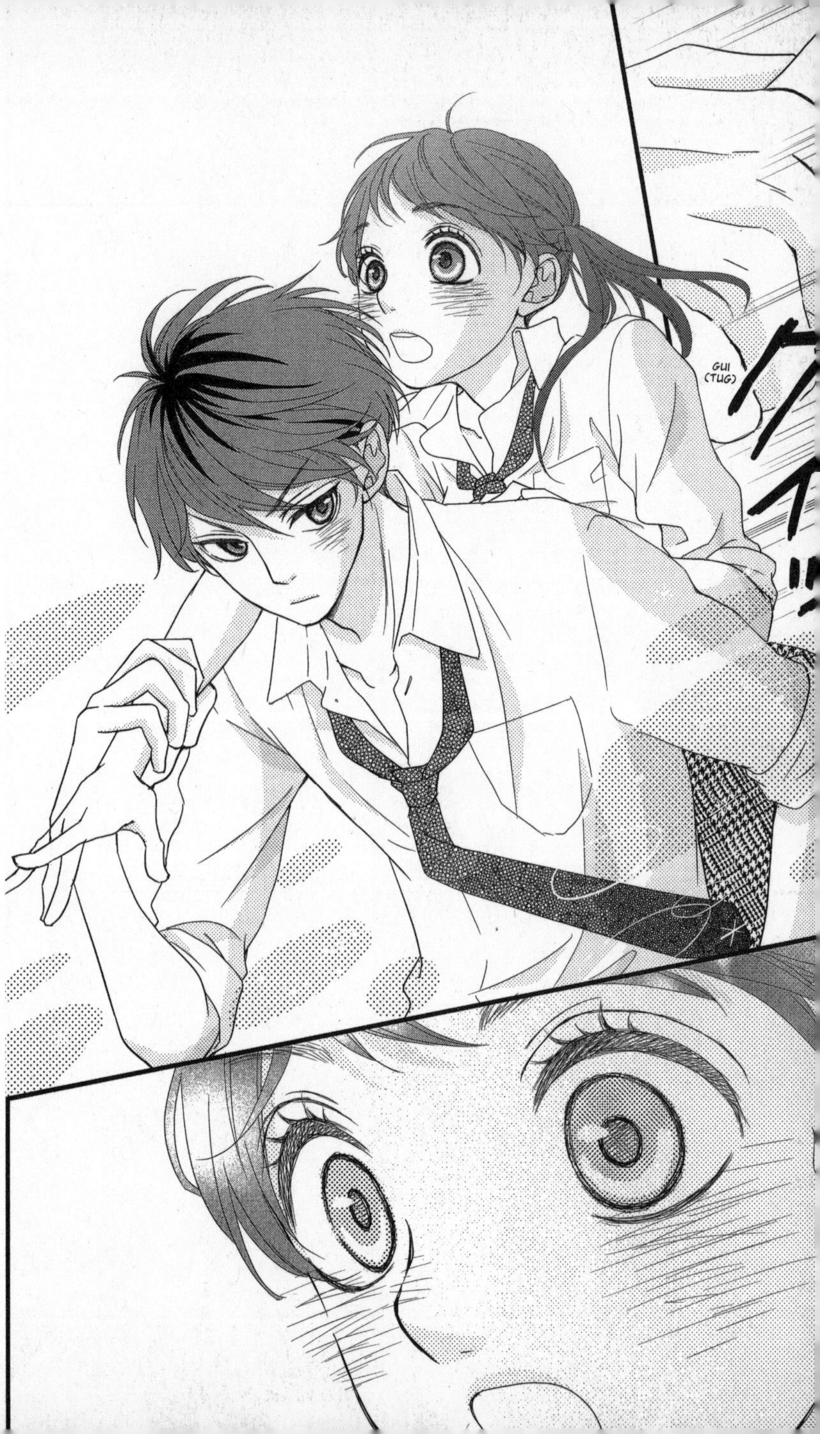
GUI
(TUG)

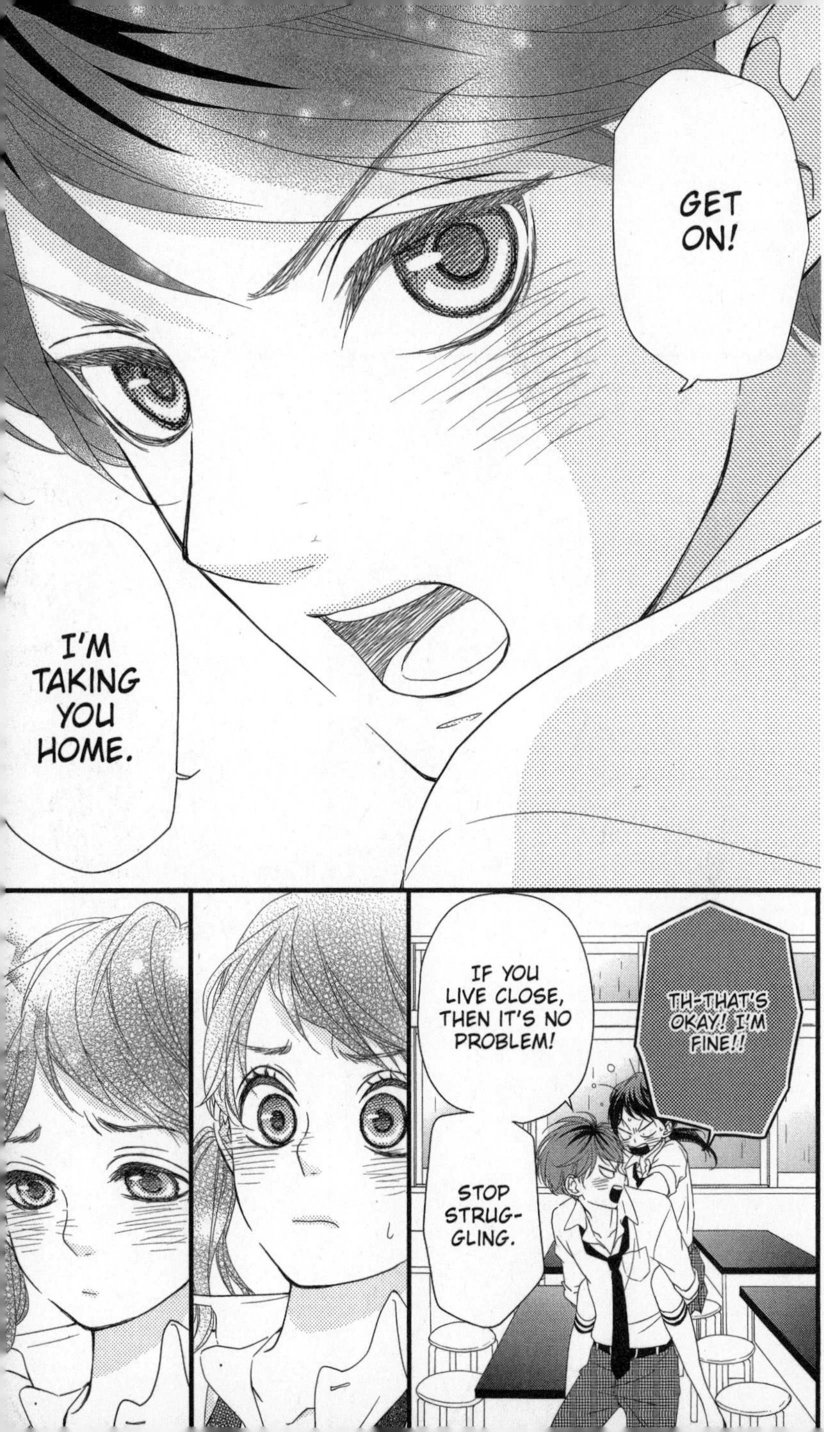
GET ON!
I'M TAKING YOU HOME.
TH-THAT'S OKAY! I'M FINE!!
IF YOU LIVE CLOSE, THEN IT'S NO PROBLEM!
STOP STRUG-GLING.

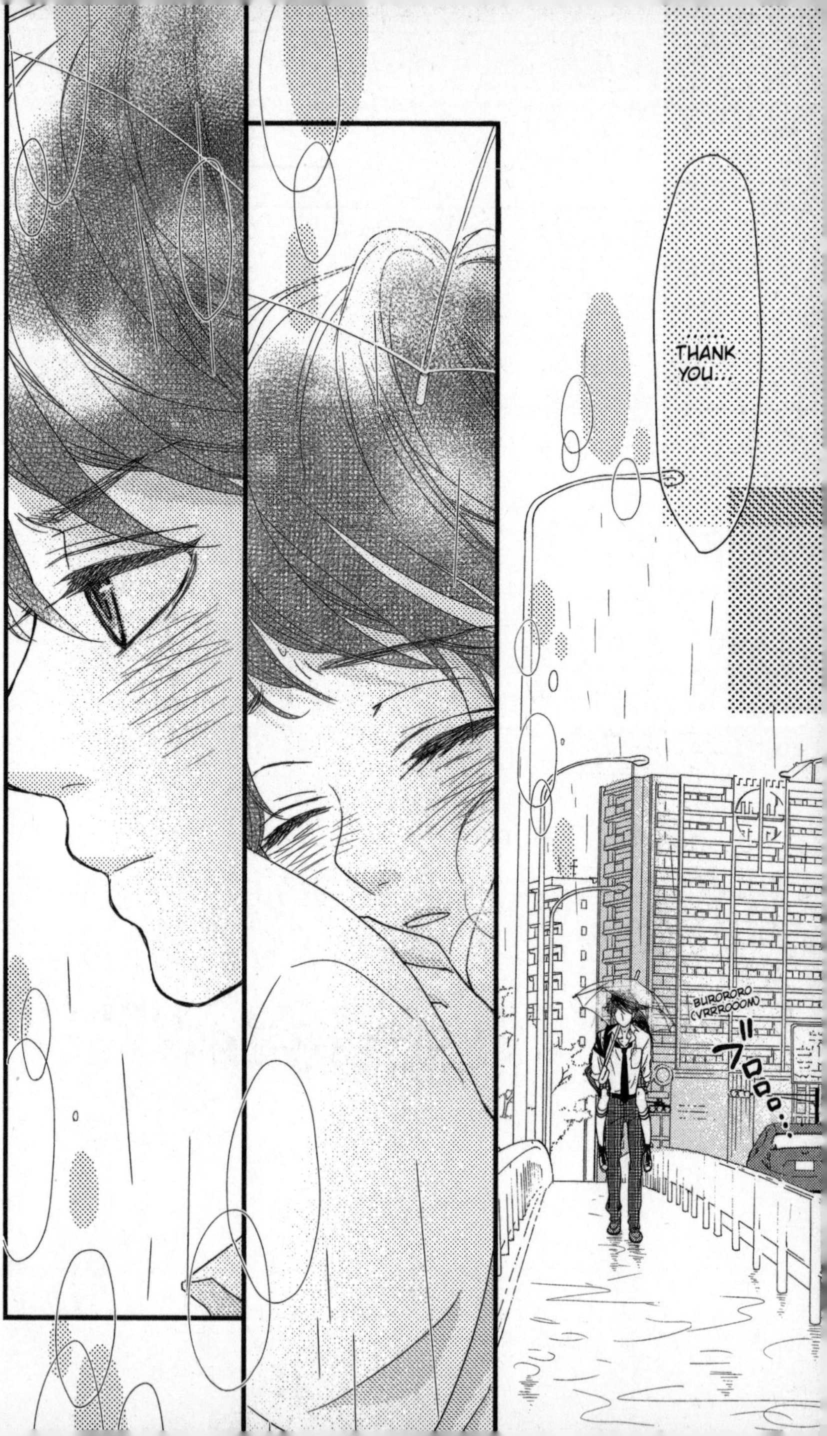
THANK YOU...
BURORORO (VRRROOOM)
ブロロロ...

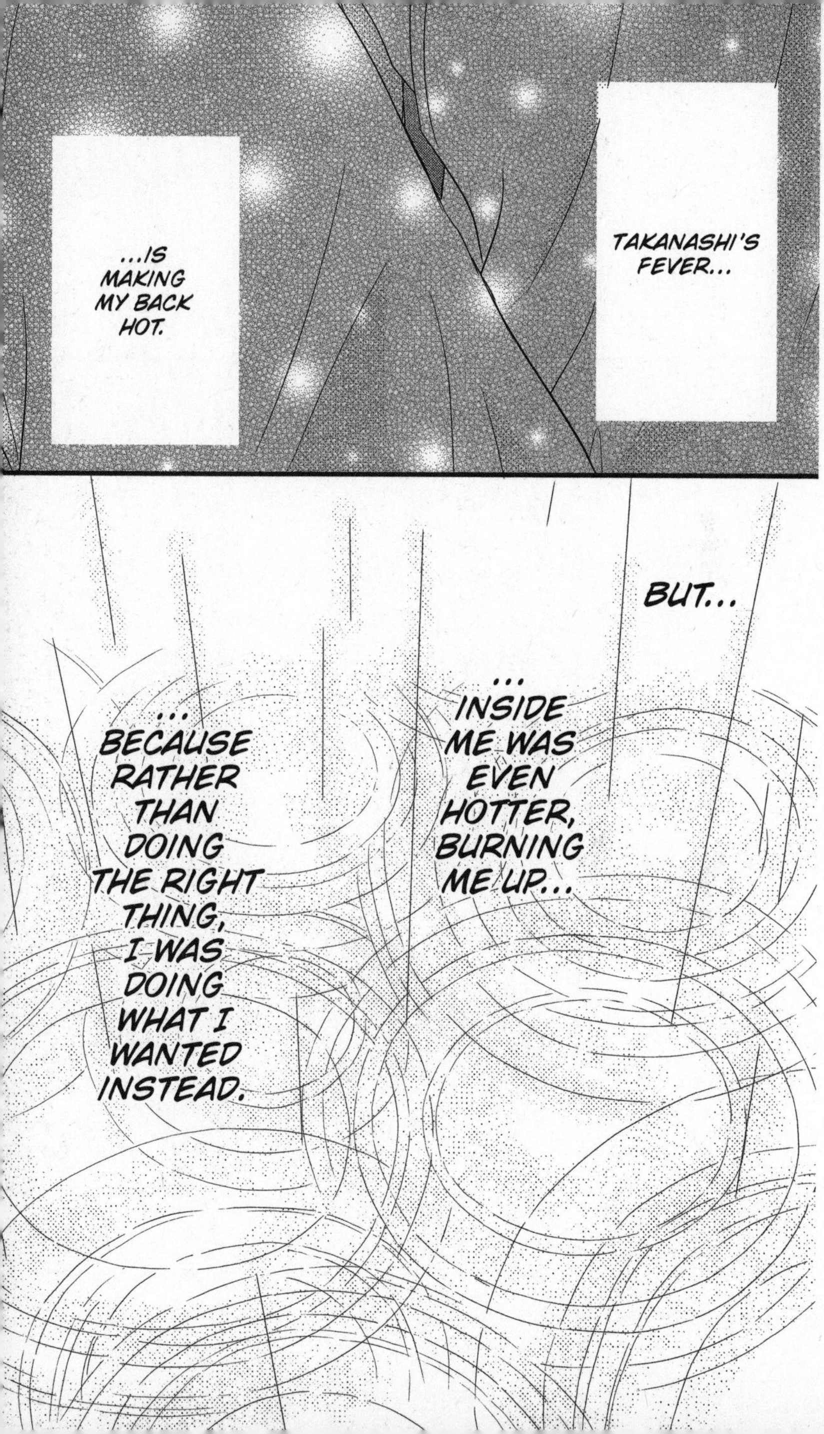
TAKANASHI'S FEVER...
...IS MAKING MY BACK HOT.
BUT...
...INSIDE ME WAS EVEN HOTTER, BURNING ME UP...
...BECAUSE RATHER THAN DOING THE RIGHT THING, I WAS DOING WHAT I WANTED INSTEAD.

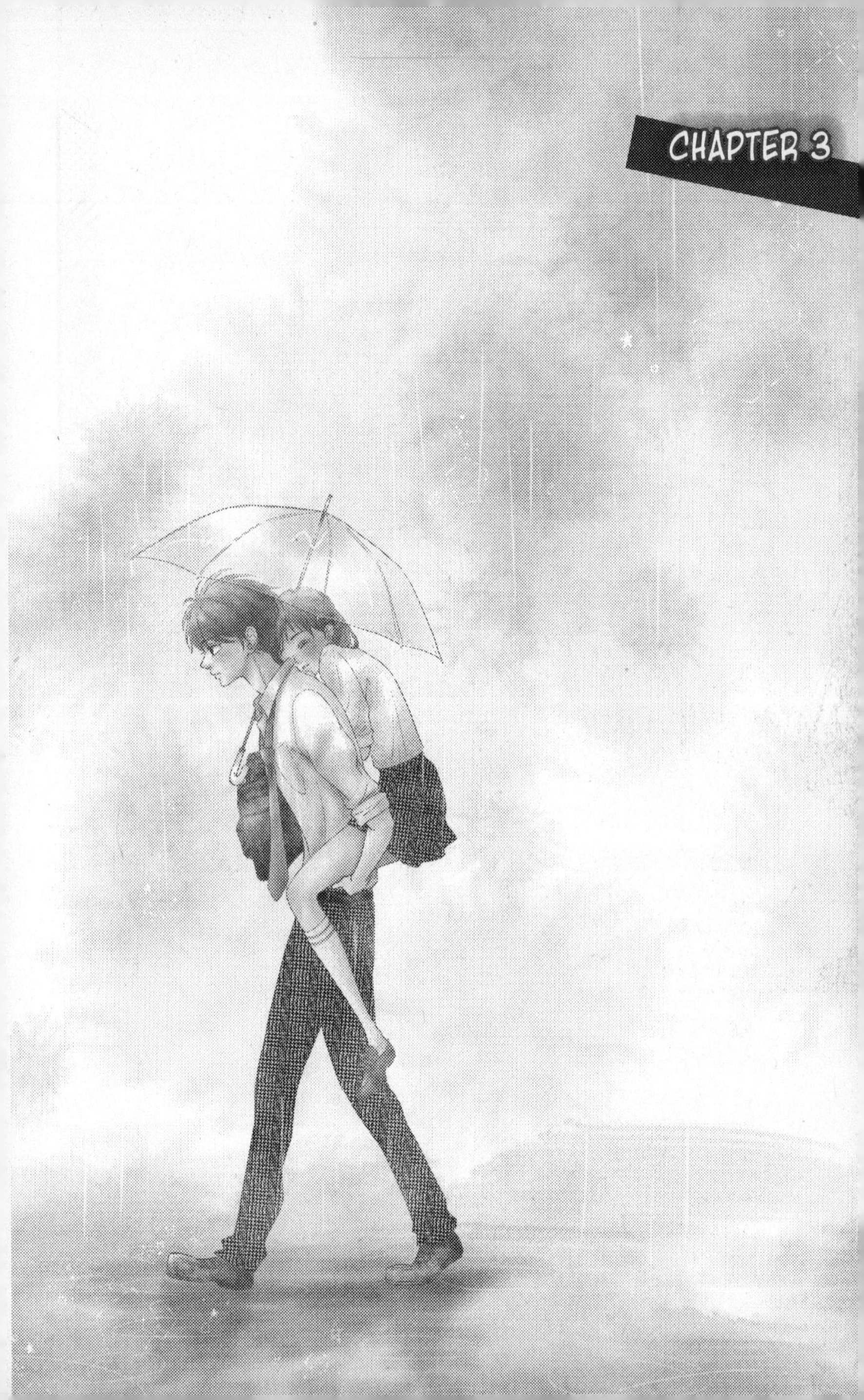
CHAPTER 3

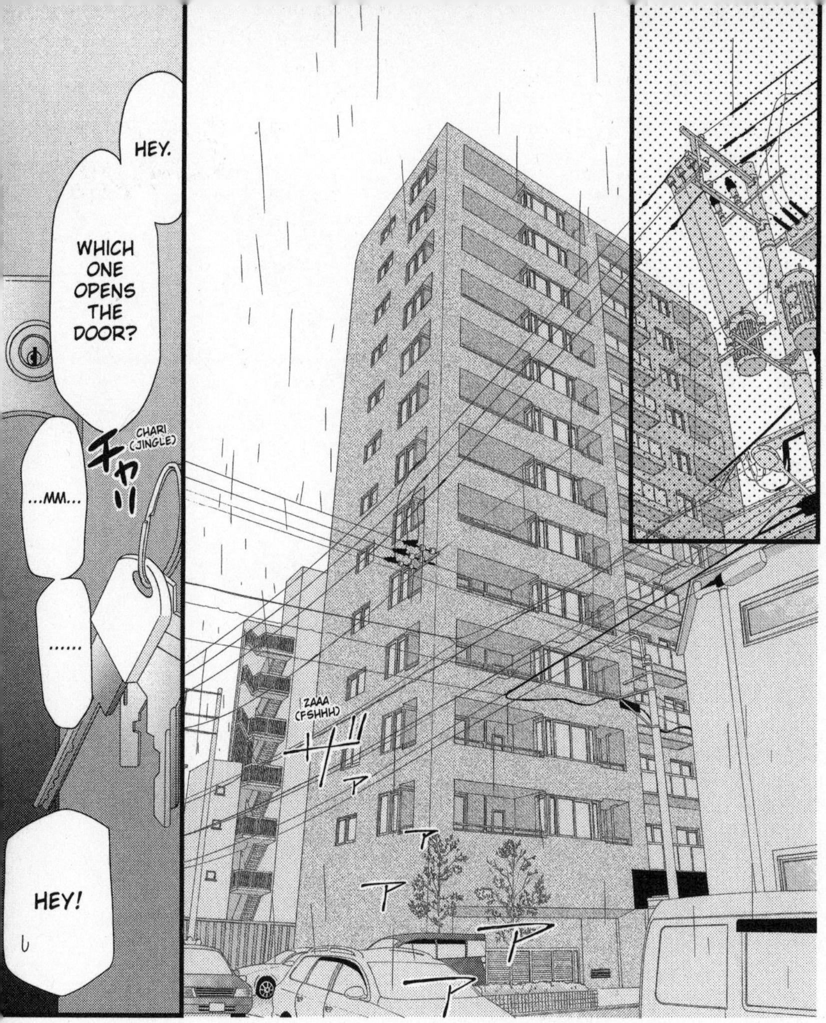
ZAAA (FSHHH)
ザァァァァ
HEY.
WHICH ONE OPENS THE DOOR?
CHARI (JINGLE)
チャリ
...MM...
......
HEY!

hatsu haru

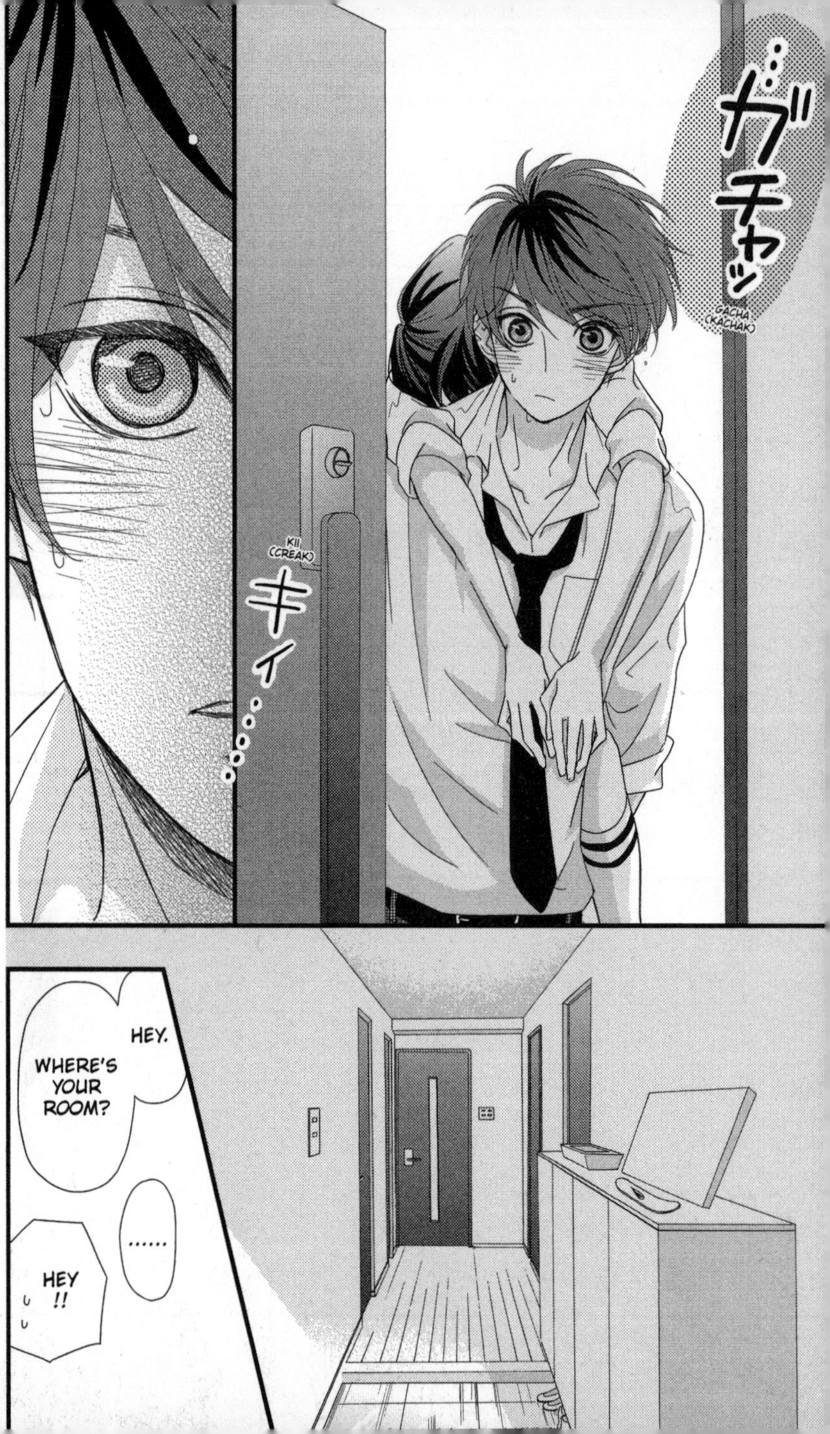
ガチャッ
GACHA (KACHAK)
KII (CREAK)
キイ……
HEY.
WHERE'S YOUR ROOM?
……
HEY !!

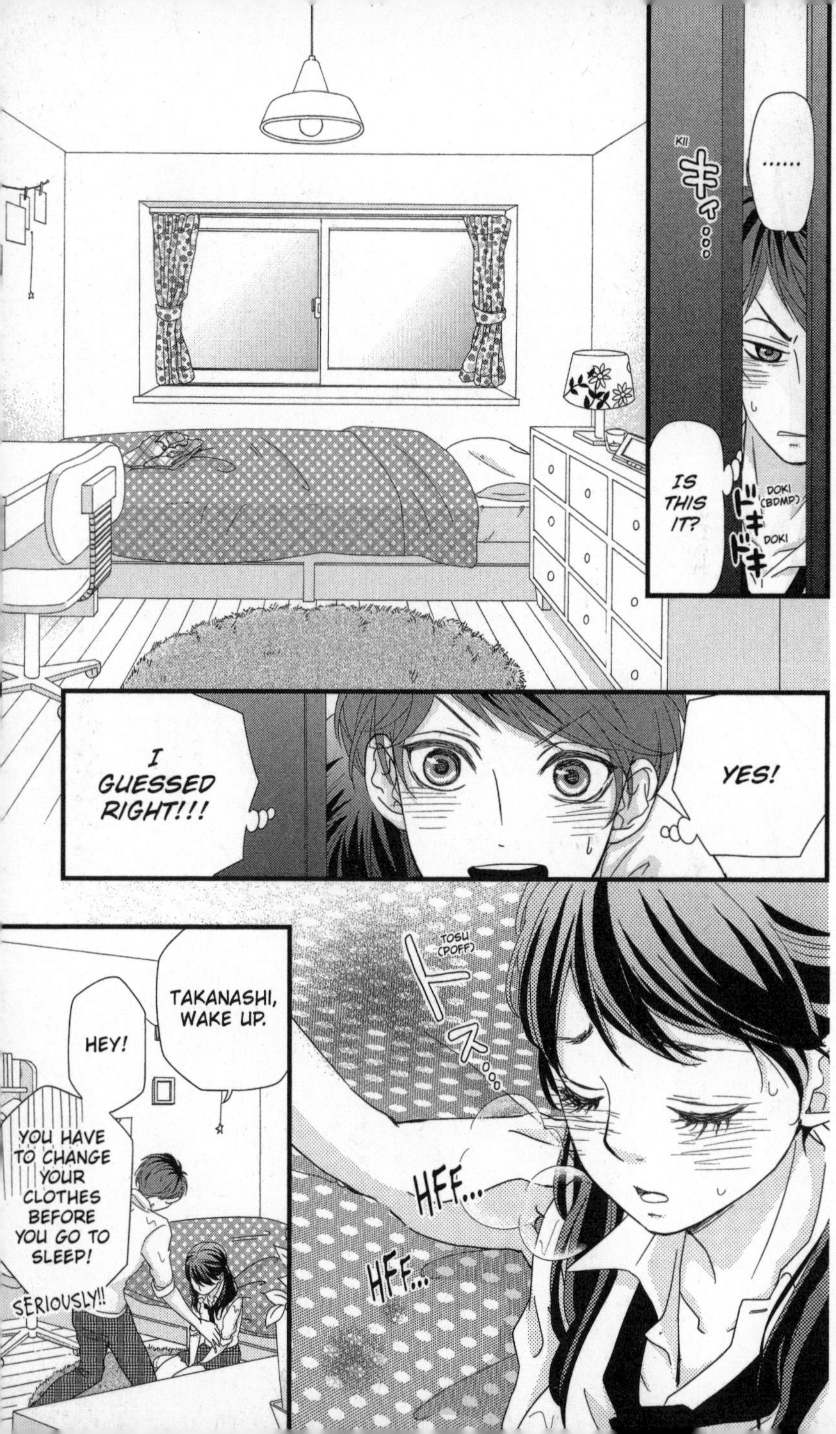
......
KII
キィ...
IS THIS IT?
DOKI (BDMP) DOKI
ドキドキ
YES!
I GUESSED RIGHT!!!
TOSU (POFF)
トス...
HFF...
HFF...
TAKANASHI, WAKE UP.
HEY!
YOU HAVE TO CHANGE YOUR CLOTHES BEFORE YOU GO TO SLEEP!
SERIOUSLY!!

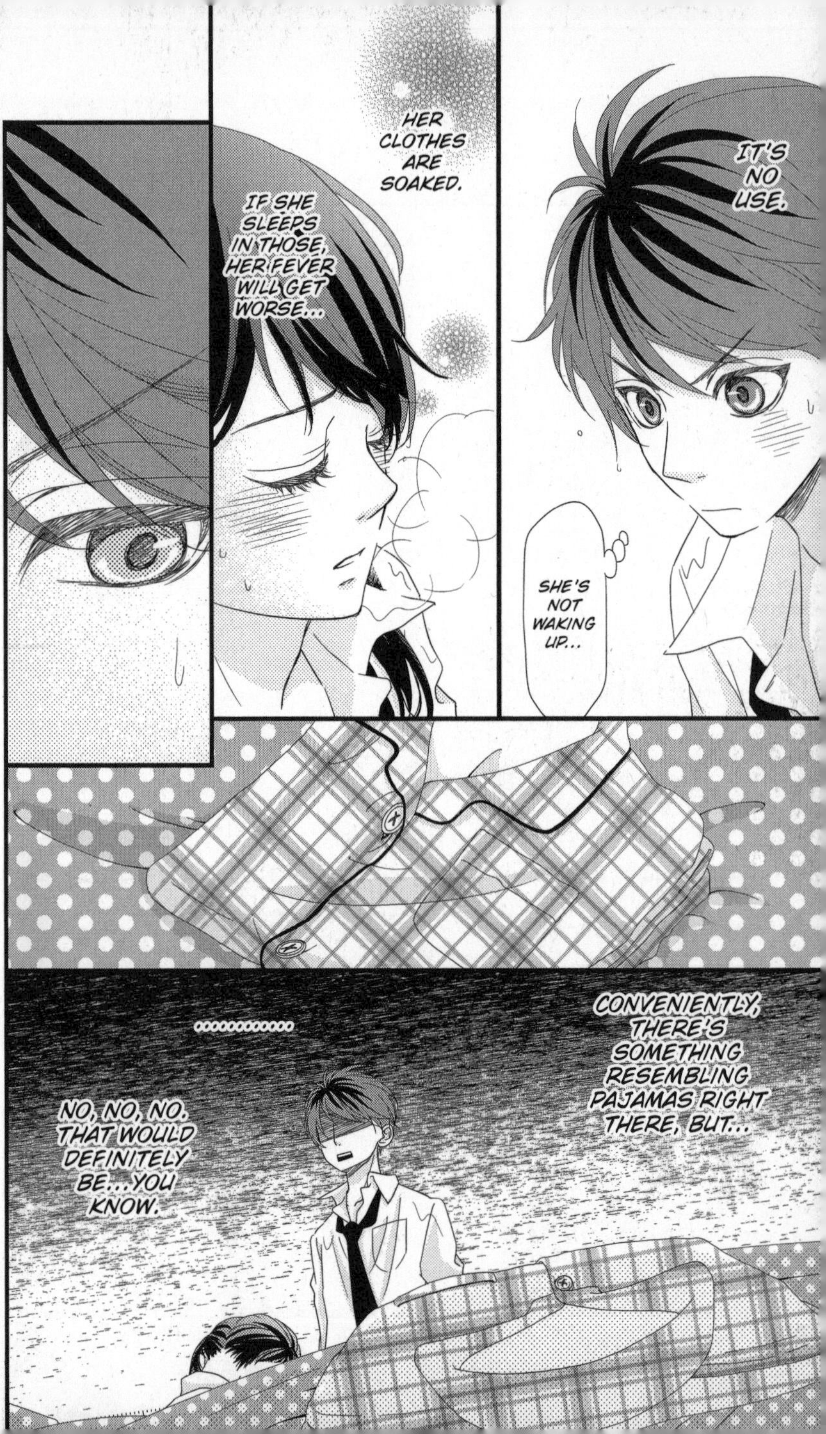
IT'S NO USE.
SHE'S NOT WAKING UP...
HER CLOTHES ARE SOAKED.
IF SHE SLEEPS IN THOSE, HER FEVER WILL GET WORSE...
CONVENIENTLY, THERE'S SOMETHING RESEMBLING PAJAMAS RIGHT THERE, BUT...
....
NO, NO, NO. THAT WOULD DEFINITELY BE...YOU KNOW.

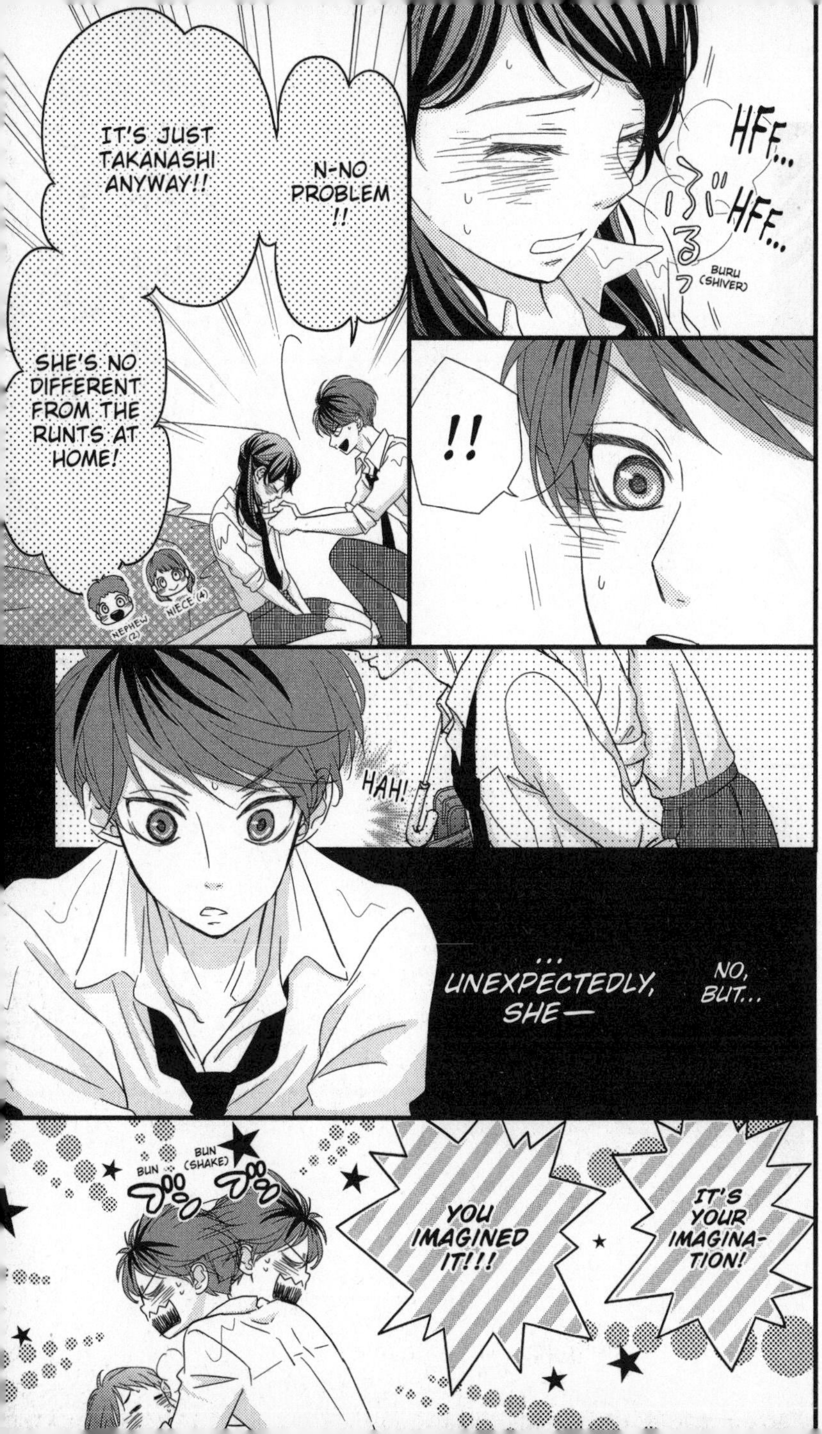
HFF... HFF...
BURU (SHIVER)
!!
N-NO PROBLEM!!
IT'S JUST TAKANASHI ANYWAY!!
SHE'S NO DIFFERENT FROM THE RUNTS AT HOME!
NIECE (4)
NEPHEW (2)
HAH!
NO, BUT...
...UNEXPECTEDLY, SHE—
IT'S YOUR IMAGINATION!
YOU IMAGINED IT!!!
BUN (SHAKE)
BUN

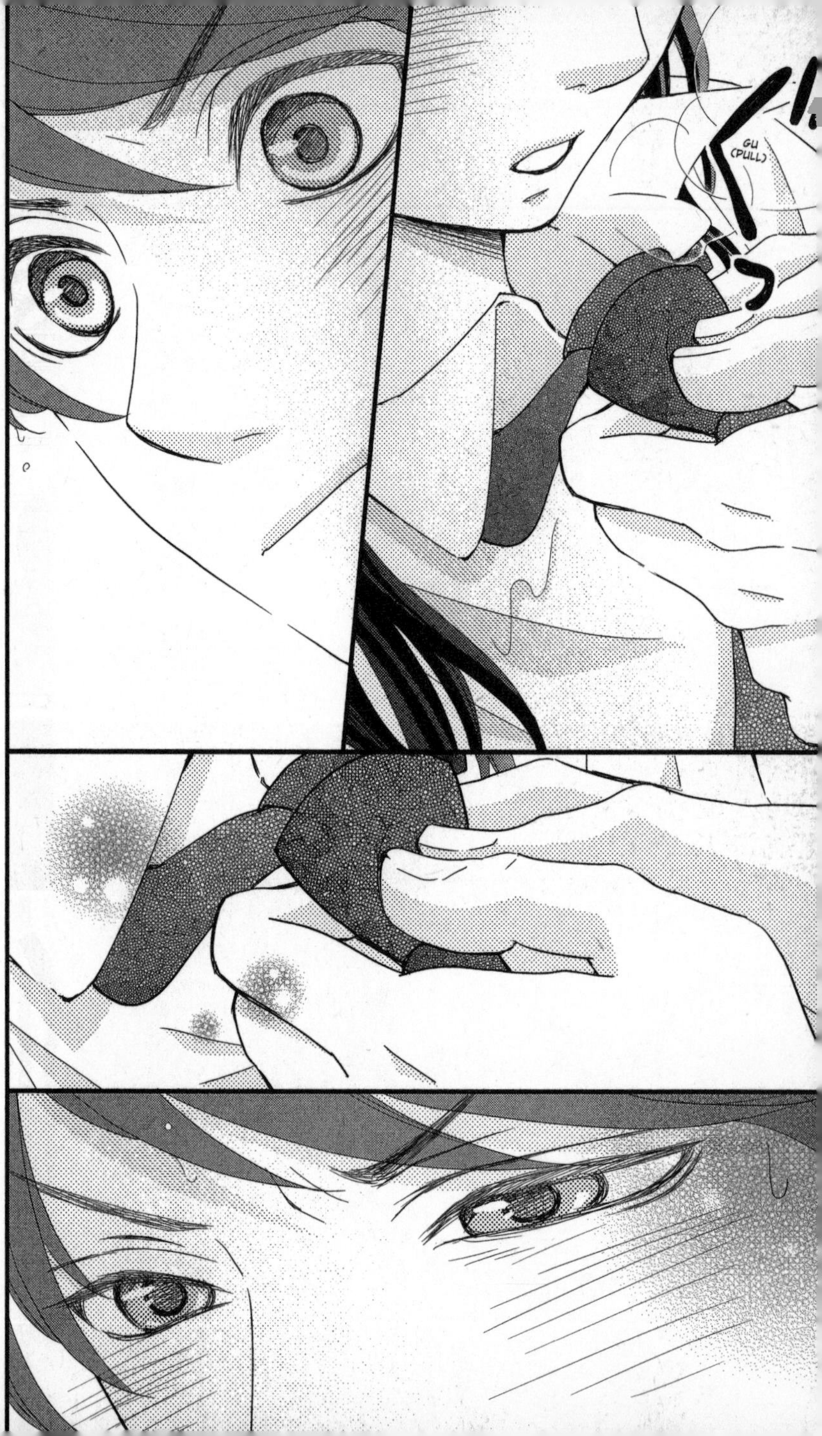
GU (PULL)

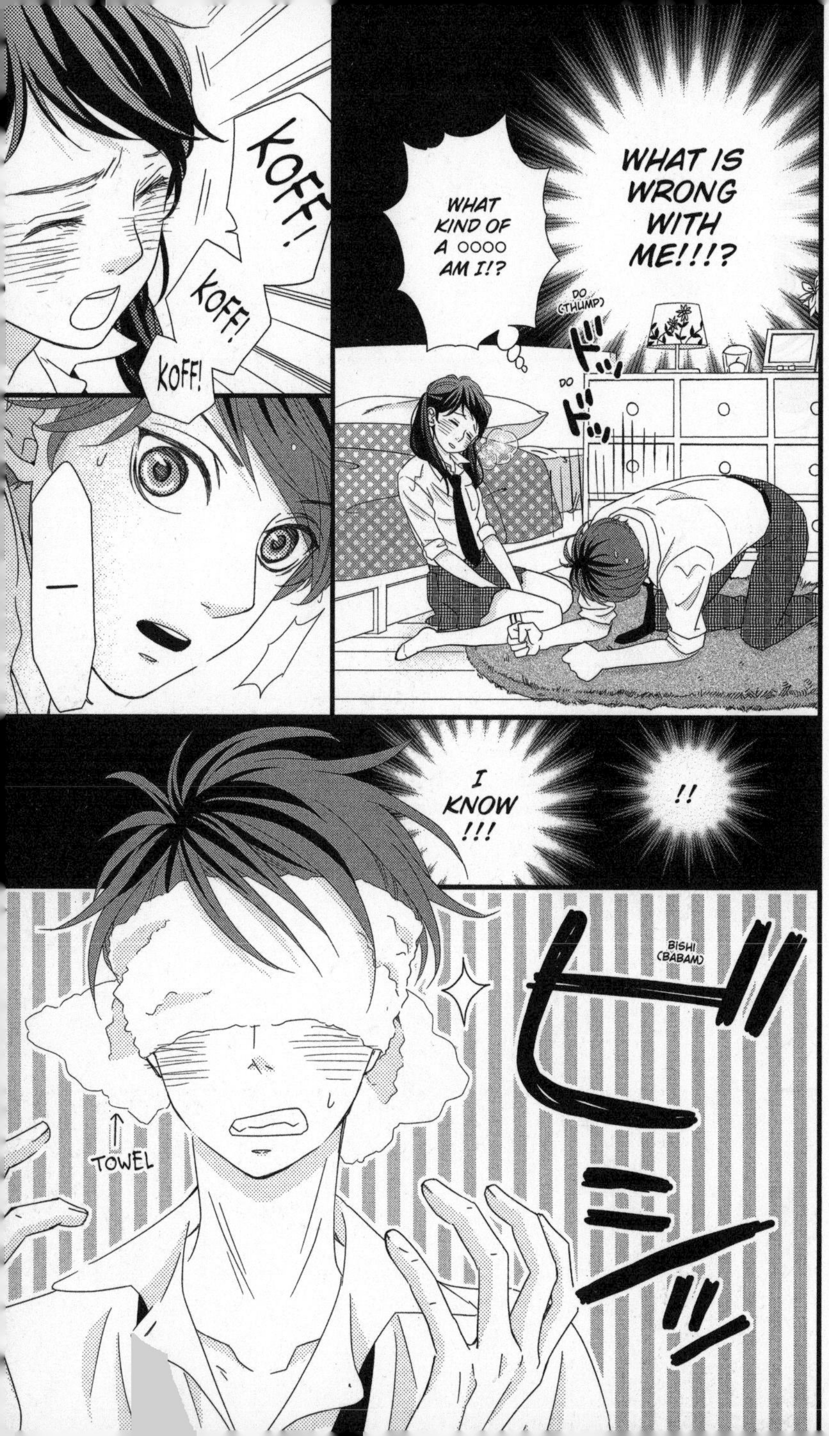

WHAT IS WRONG WITH ME!!!?
WHAT KIND OF A OOOO AM I!?
DO (THUMP)
DO
KOFF!
KOFF!
KOFF!
—
!!
I KNOW!!!
BISHI (BABAM)
TOWEL

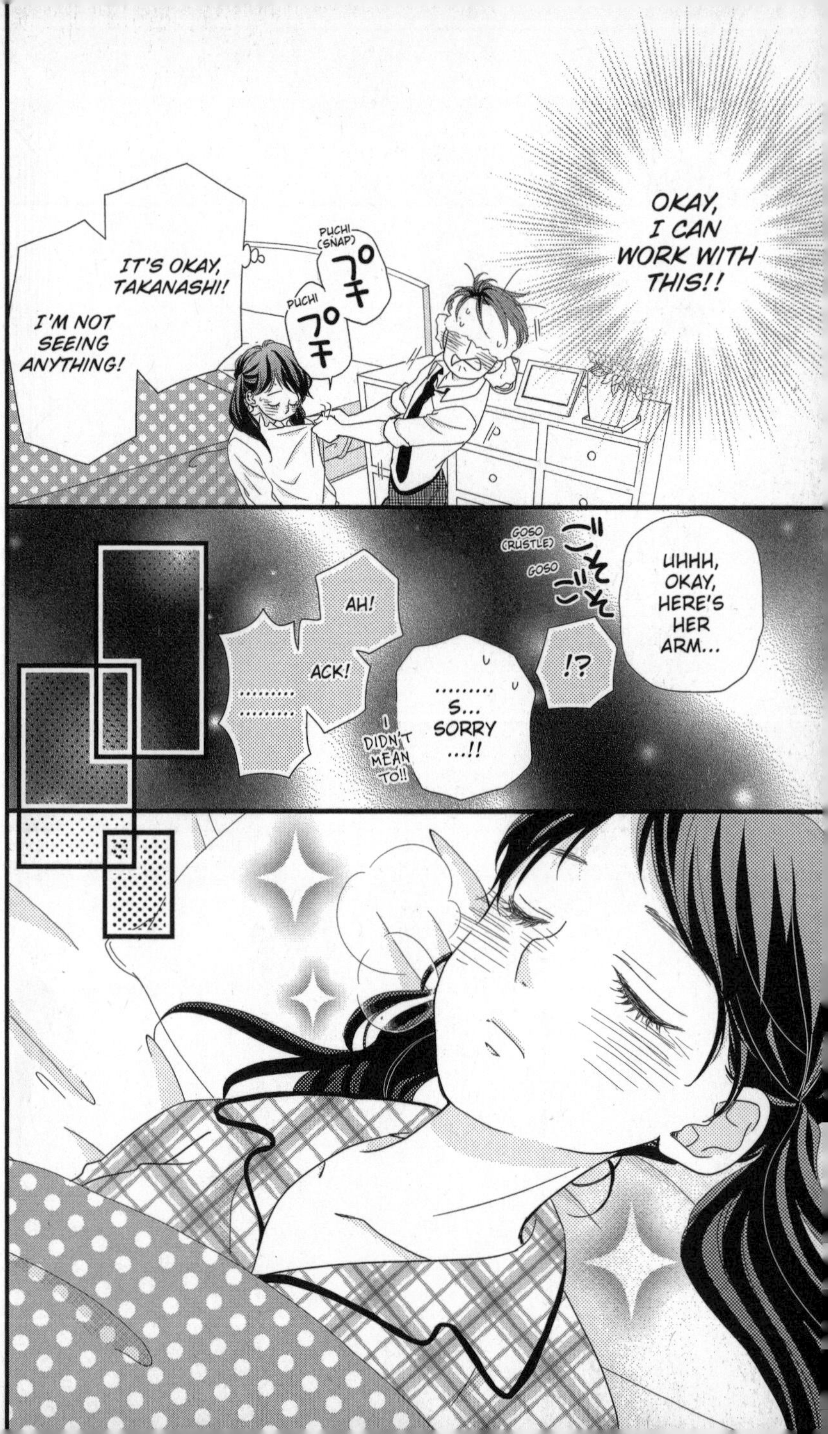
OKAY, I CAN WORK WITH THIS!!
PUCHI (SNAP)
プチ
PUCHI
プチ
IT'S OKAY, TAKANASHI!
I'M NOT SEEING ANYTHING!
UHHH, OKAY, HERE'S HER ARM...
GOSO (RUSTLE)
ごそ
GOSO
ごそ
!?
.... S... SORRY ...!!
I DIDN'T MEAN TO!!
AH!
ACK!
....
....

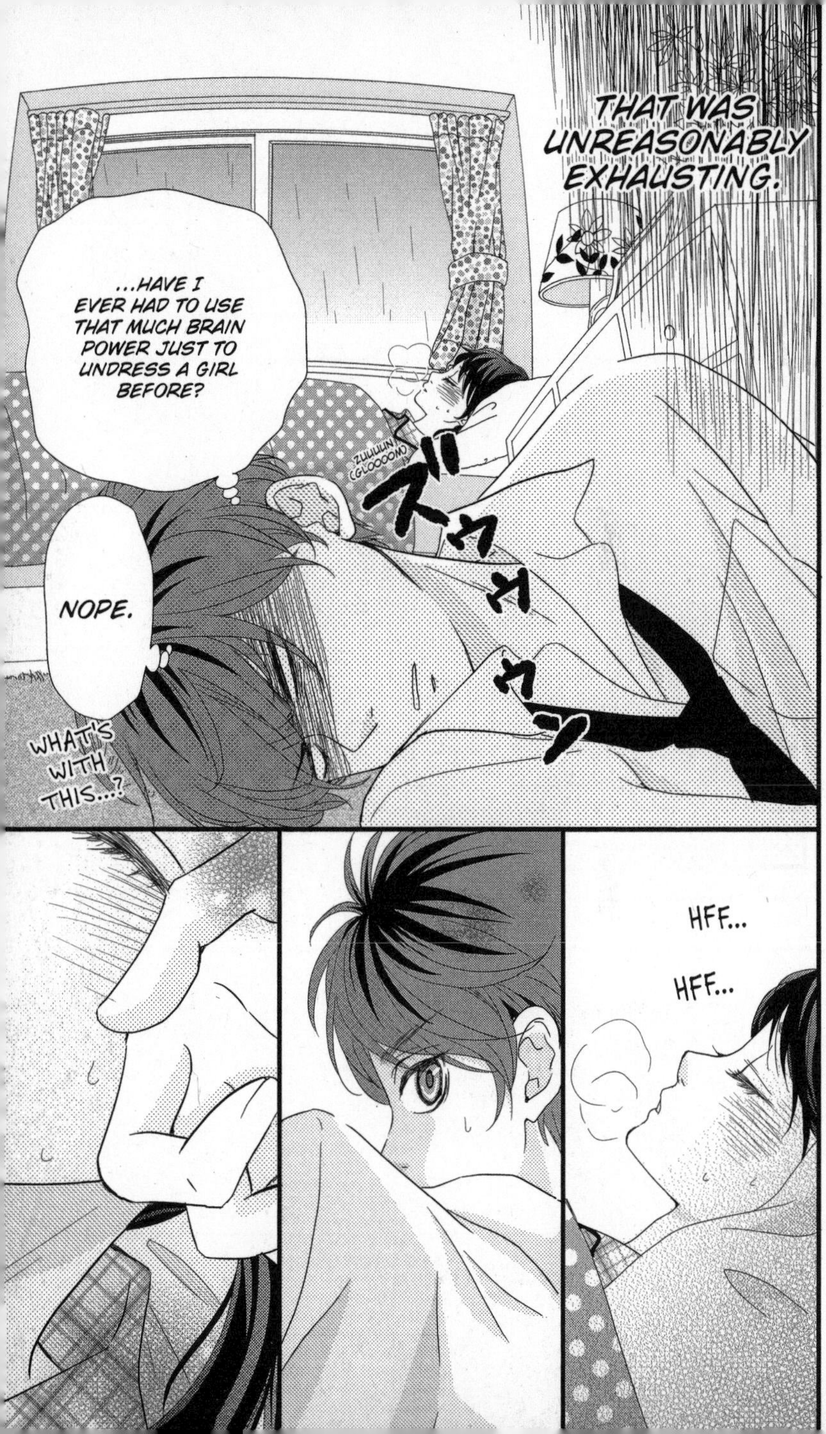
THAT WAS UNREASONABLY EXHAUSTING.
ZUUUUN (GLOOOOM)
...HAVE I EVER HAD TO USE THAT MUCH BRAIN POWER JUST TO UNDRESS A GIRL BEFORE?
NOPE.
WHAT'S WITH THIS...?
HFF...
HFF...

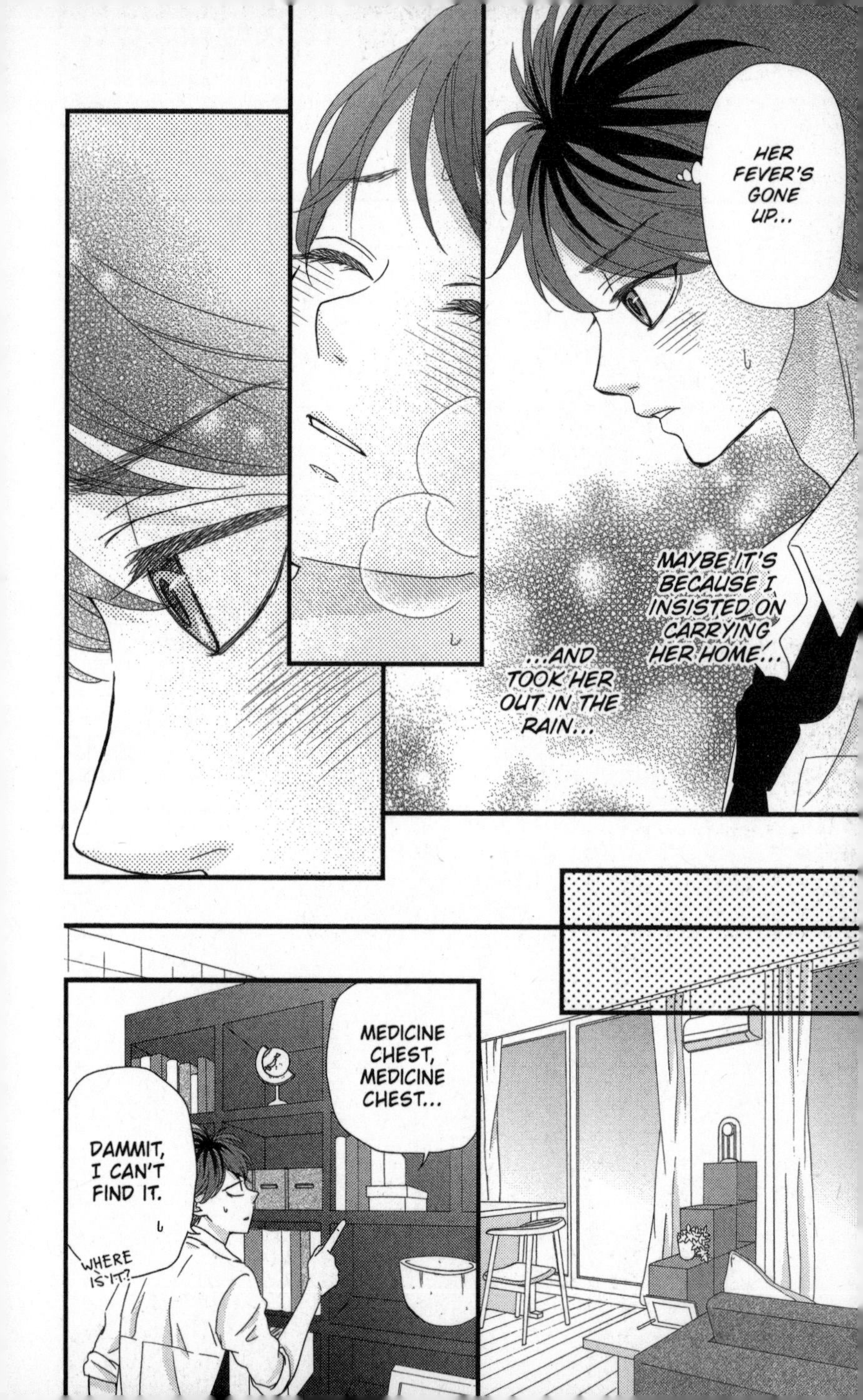
HER FEVER'S GONE UP...
MAYBE IT'S BECAUSE I INSISTED ON CARRYING HER HOME...
...AND TOOK HER OUT IN THE RAIN...
MEDICINE CHEST, MEDICINE CHEST...
DAMMIT, I CAN'T FIND IT.
WHERE IS IT?

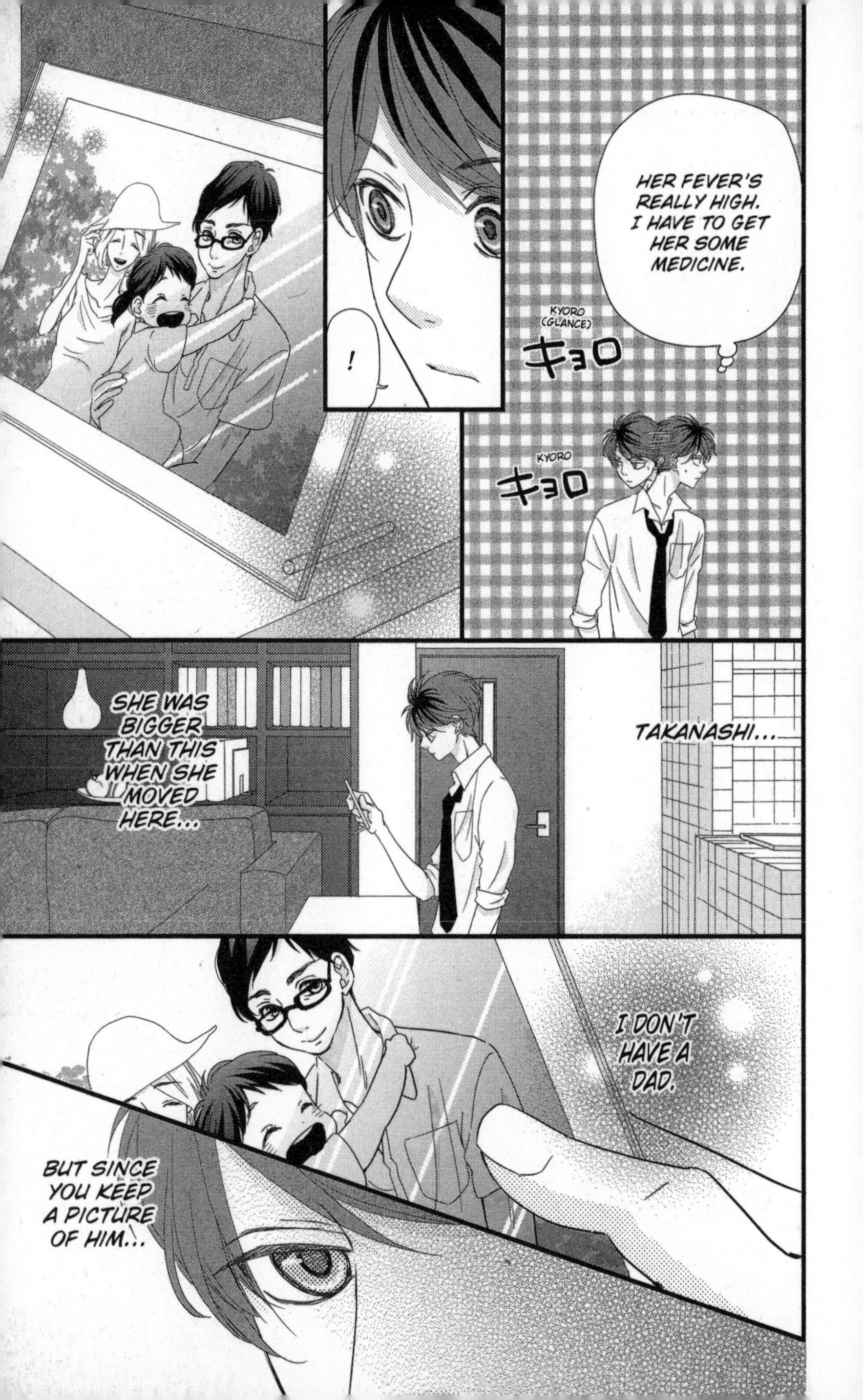
HER FEVER'S REALLY HIGH. I HAVE TO GET HER SOME MEDICINE.
KYORO (GLANCE)
キョロ
KYORO
キョロ
!
TAKANASHI...
SHE WAS BIGGER THAN THIS WHEN SHE MOVED HERE...
I DON'T HAVE A DAD.
BUT SINCE YOU KEEP A PICTURE OF HIM...

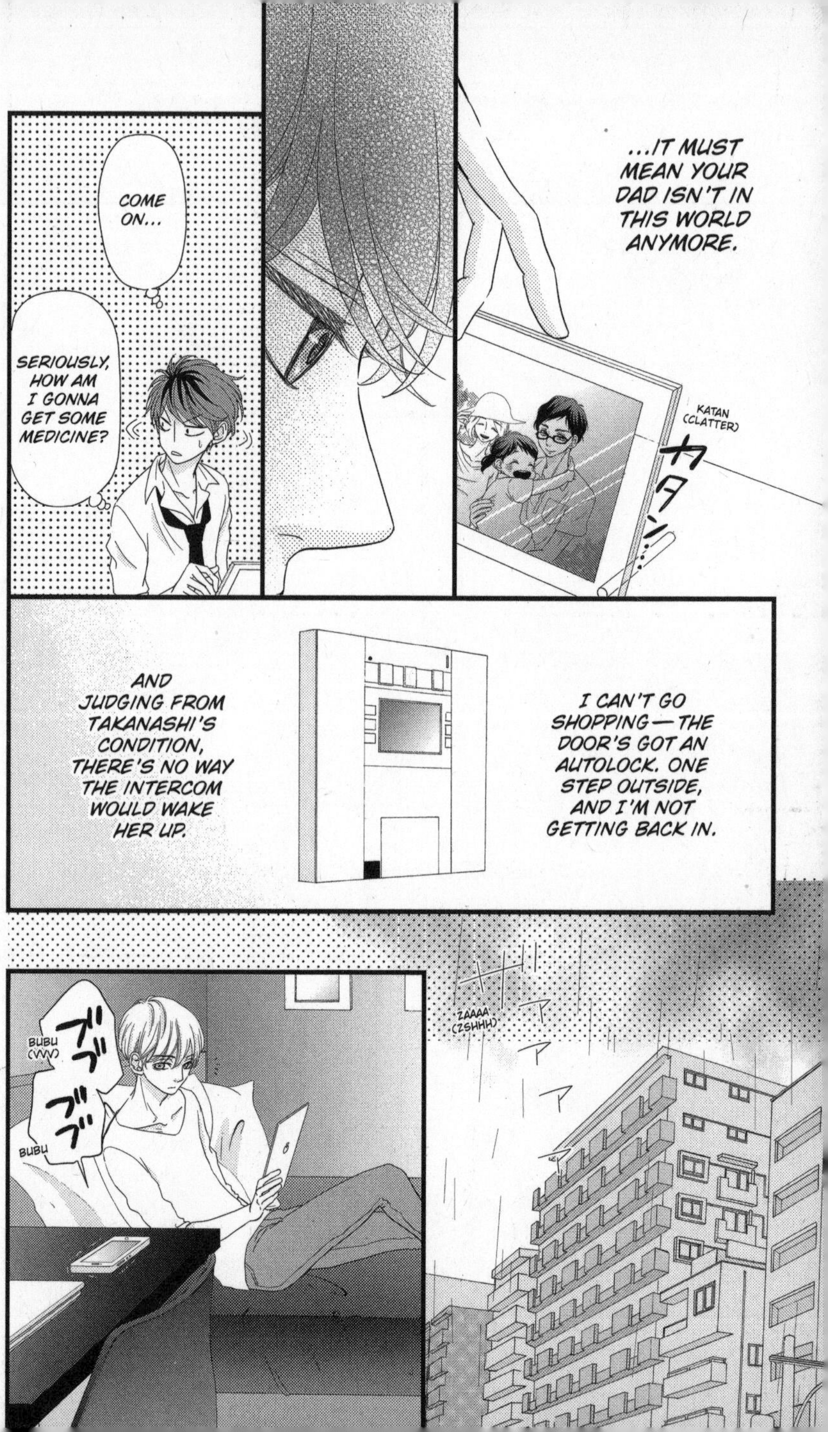
...IT MUST MEAN YOUR DAD ISN'T IN THIS WORLD ANYMORE.
KATAN (CLATTER)
カタン…
COME ON...
SERIOUSLY, HOW AM I GONNA GET SOME MEDICINE?
I CAN'T GO SHOPPING—THE DOOR'S GOT AN AUTOLOCK. ONE STEP OUTSIDE, AND I'M NOT GETTING BACK IN.
AND JUDGING FROM TAKANASHI'S CONDITION, THERE'S NO WAY THE INTERCOM WOULD WAKE HER UP.
ZAAAA (ZSHHH)
ザアアア
BUBU (VVV)
ブブ
BUBU
ブブ

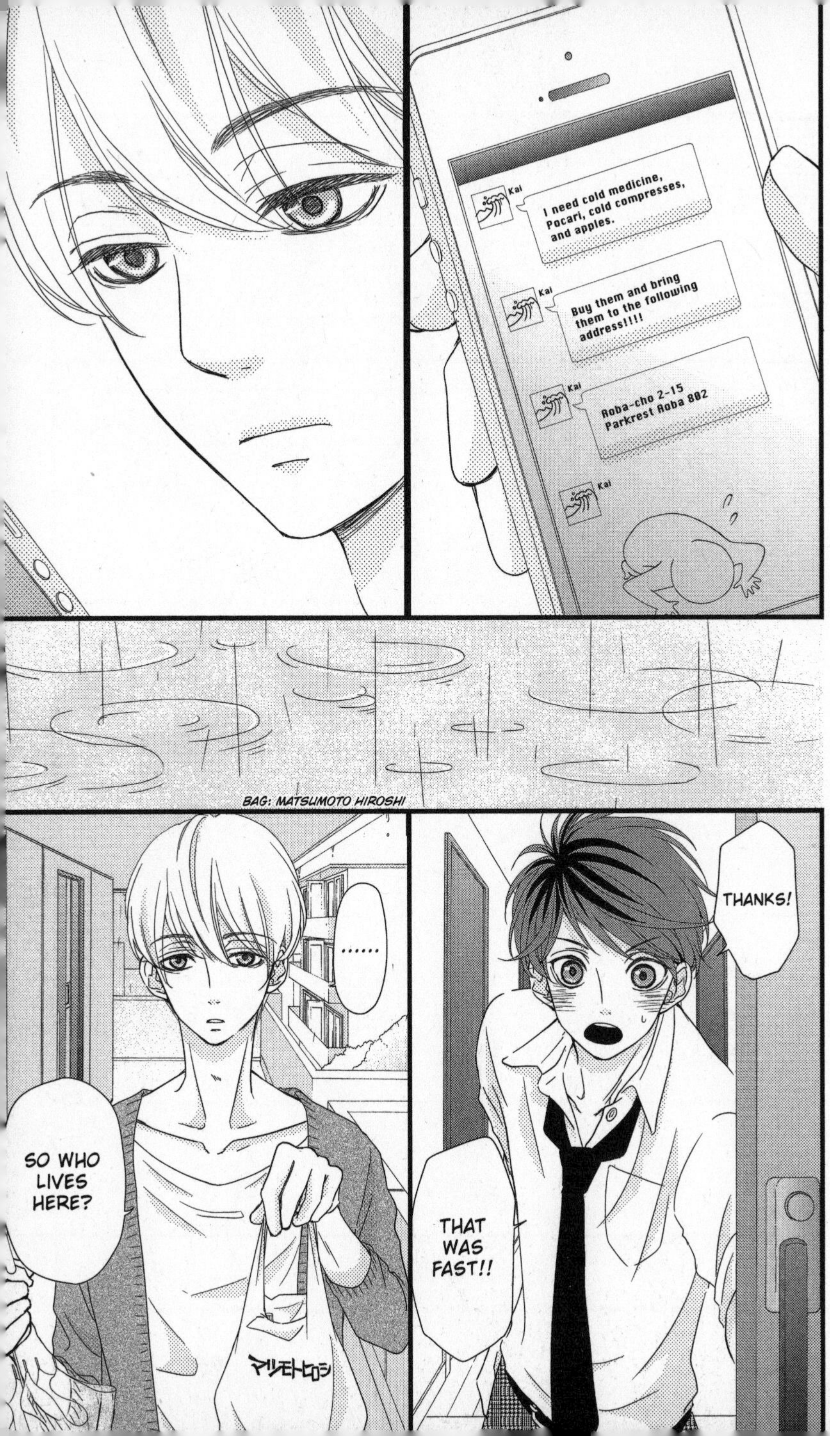
Kai
I need cold medicine, Pocari, cold compresses, and apples.
Kai
Buy them and bring them to the following address!!!!
Kai
Aoba-cho 2-15 Parkrest Aoba 802
Kai
BAG: MATSUMOTO HIROSHI
THANKS!
THAT WAS FAST!!
......
SO WHO LIVES HERE?
マツモトヒロシ

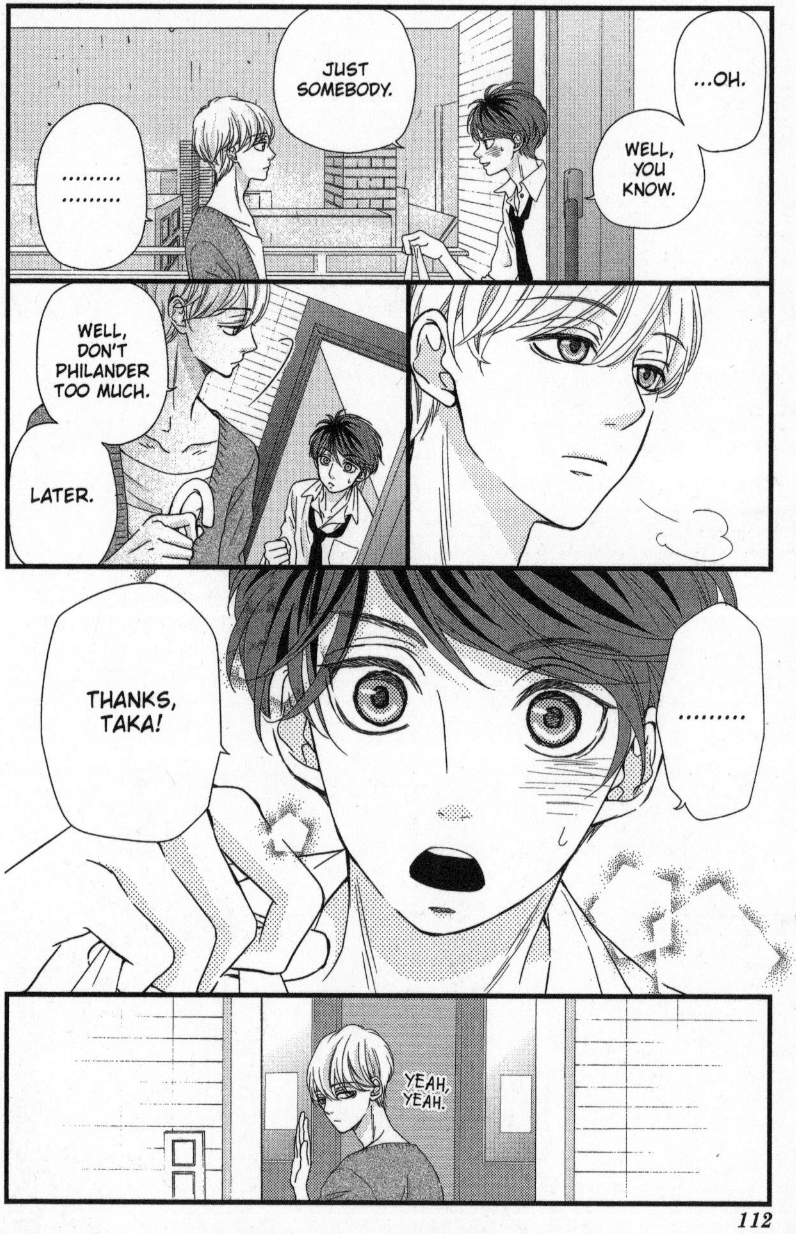
...OH.
WELL, YOU KNOW.
JUST SOMEBODY.
....
....
WELL, DON'T PHILANDER TOO MUCH.
LATER.
....
THANKS, TAKA!
YEAH, YEAH.

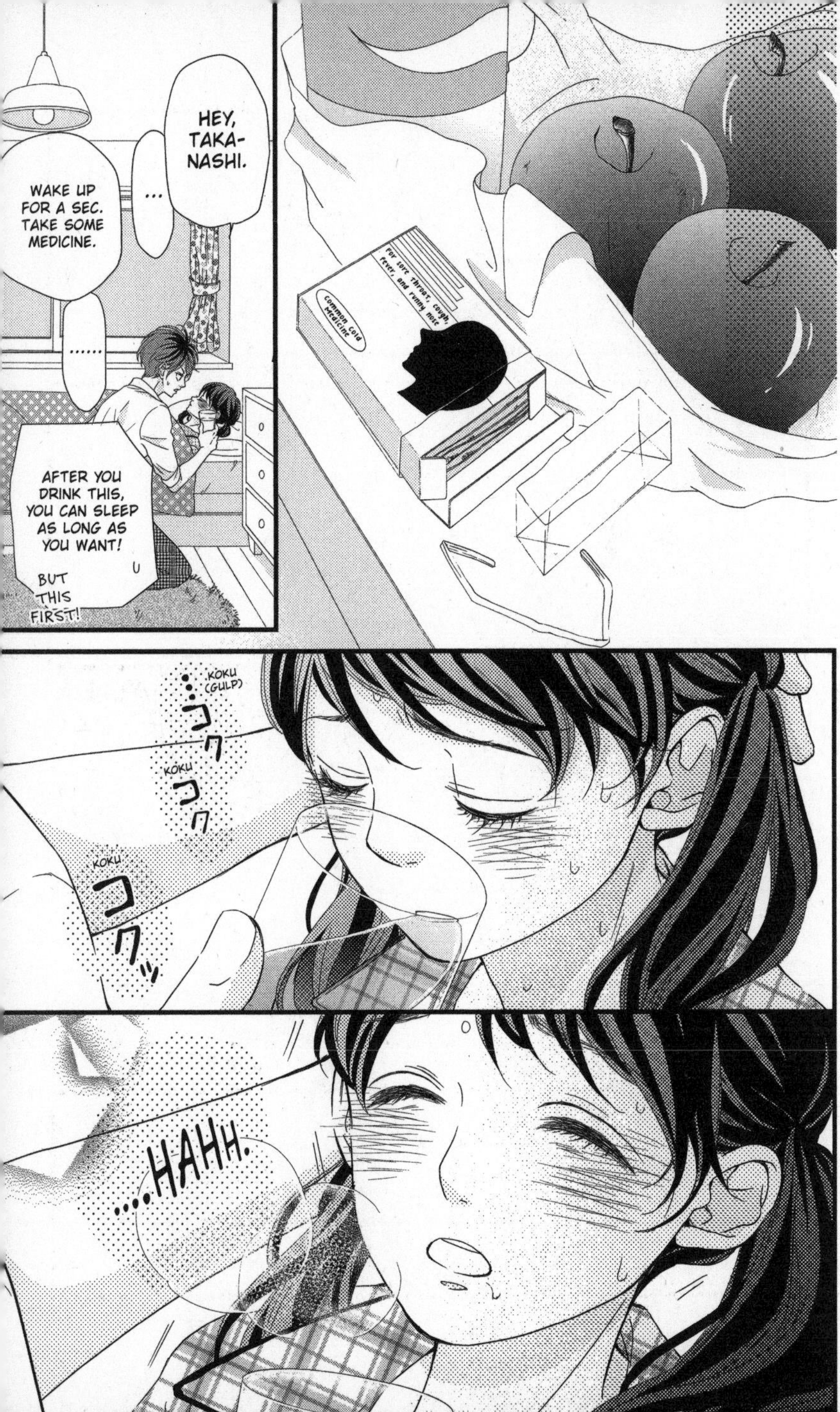
For sore throat, cough, fever, and runny nose
Common Cold Medicine
HEY, TAKA-NASHI.
...
WAKE UP FOR A SEC. TAKE SOME MEDICINE.
......
AFTER YOU DRINK THIS, YOU CAN SLEEP AS LONG AS YOU WANT!
BUT THIS FIRST!
KOKU (GULP)
KOKU
KOKU
....HAHH.

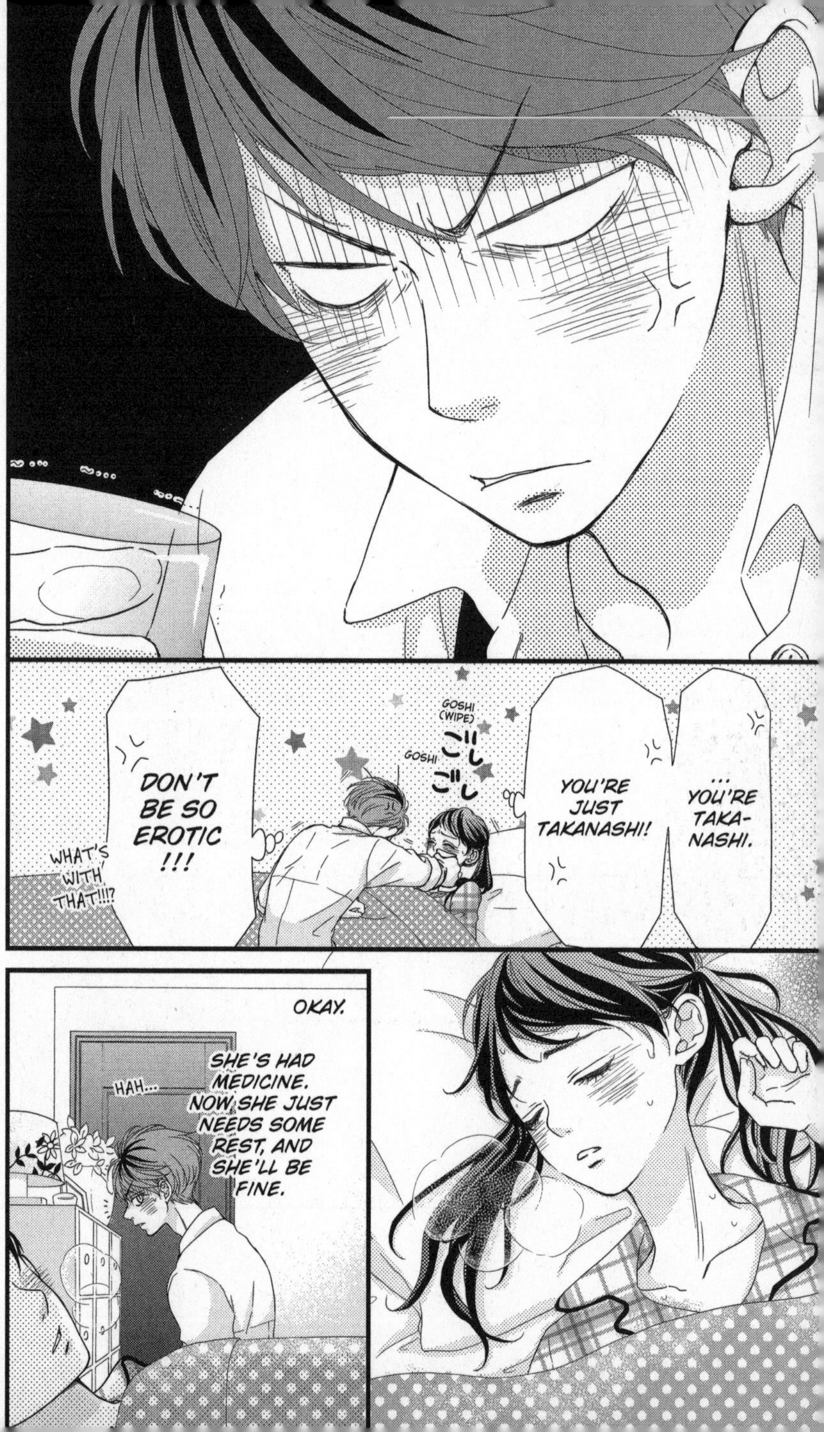
...YOU'RE TAKANASHI.
YOU'RE JUST TAKANASHI!
GOSHI (WIPE)
ごし
GOSHI
ごし
DON'T BE SO EROTIC!!!
WHAT'S WITH THAT!!!?
OKAY.
SHE'S HAD MEDICINE. NOW SHE JUST NEEDS SOME REST, AND SHE'LL BE FINE.
HAH...

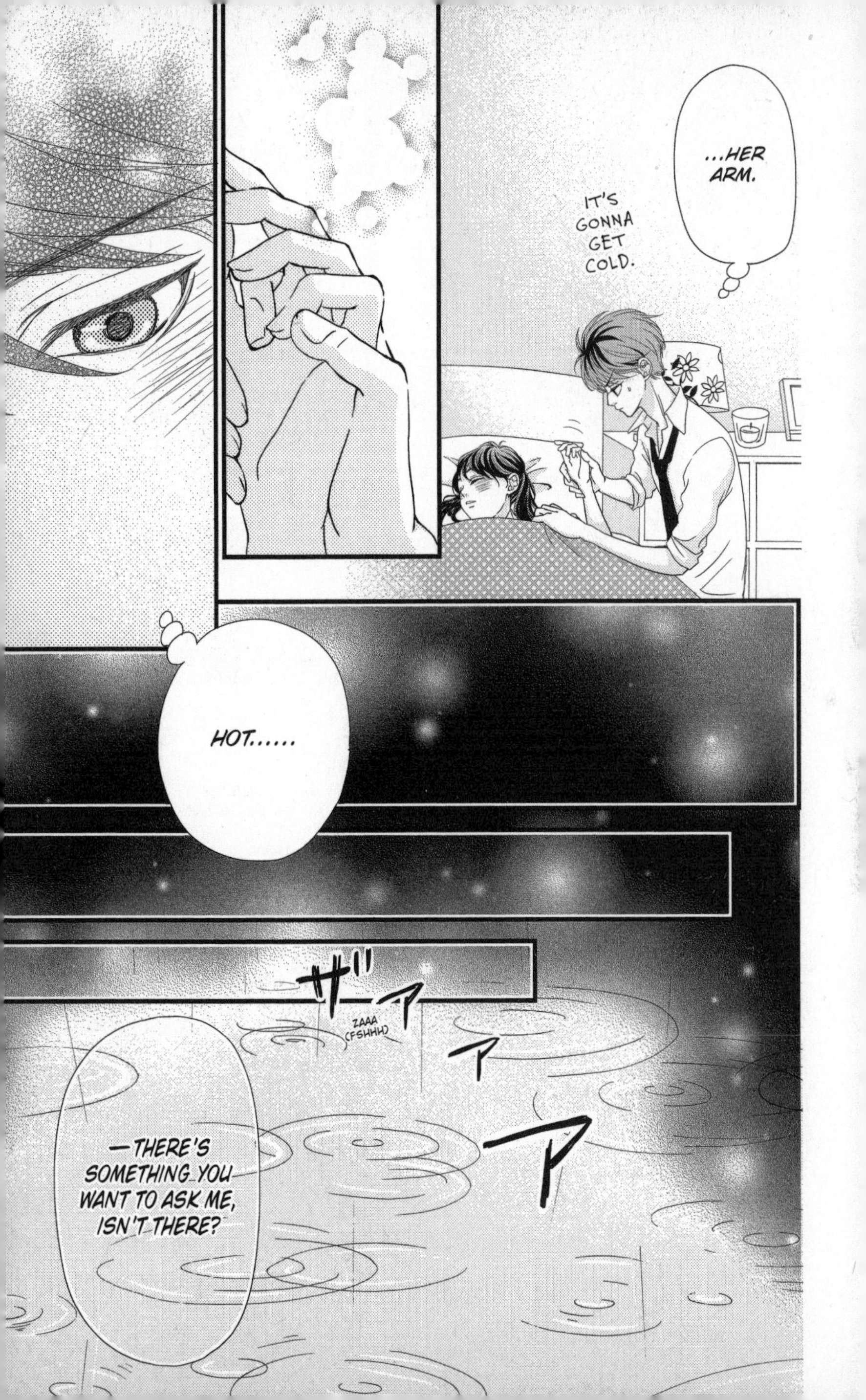
...HER ARM.
IT'S GONNA GET COLD.
HOT......
ザァァァ
ZAAA (FSHHH)
—THERE'S SOMETHING YOU WANT TO ASK ME, ISN'T THERE?

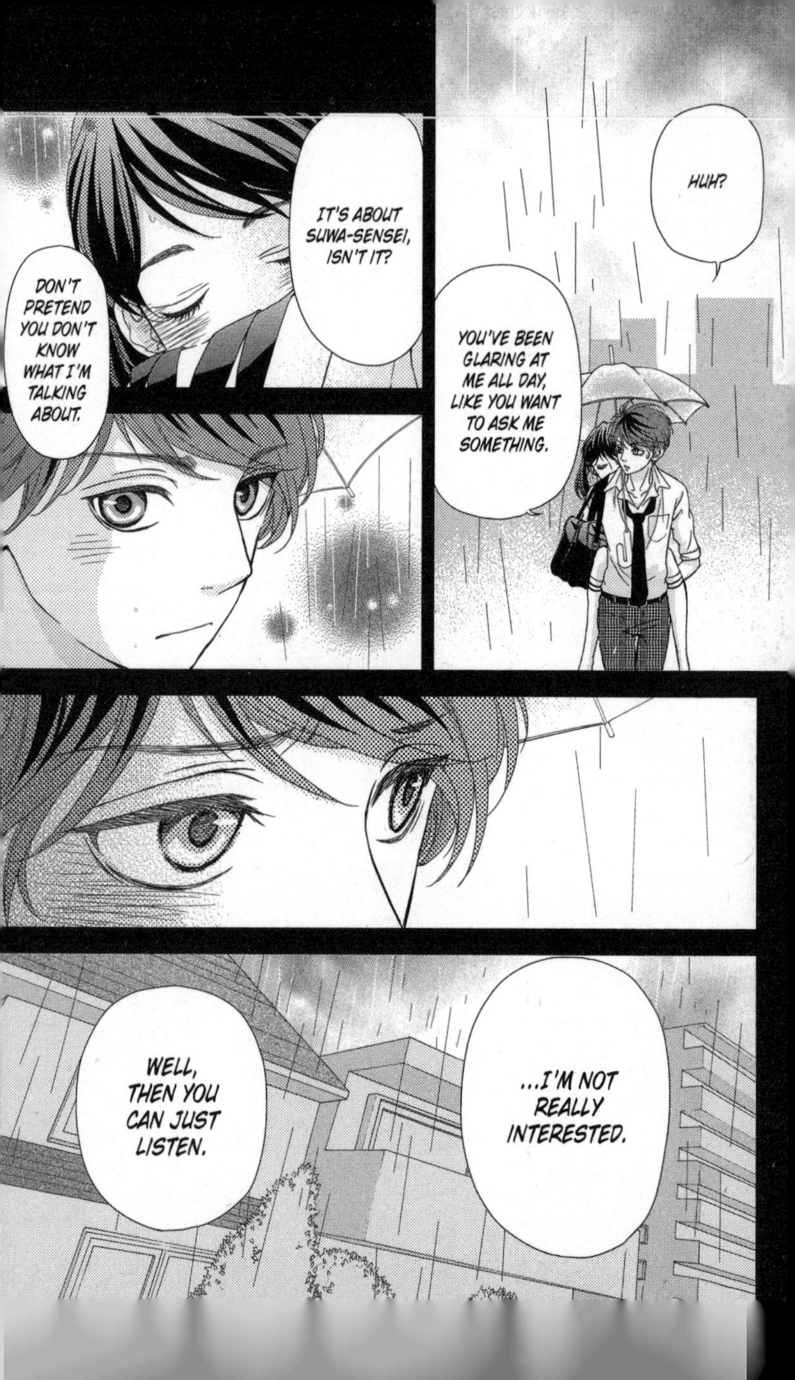
HUH?
YOU'VE BEEN GLARING AT ME ALL DAY, LIKE YOU WANT TO ASK ME SOMETHING.
IT'S ABOUT SUWA-SENSEI, ISN'T IT?
DON'T PRETEND YOU DON'T KNOW WHAT I'M TALKING ABOUT.
...I'M NOT REALLY INTERESTED.
WELL, THEN YOU CAN JUST LISTEN.

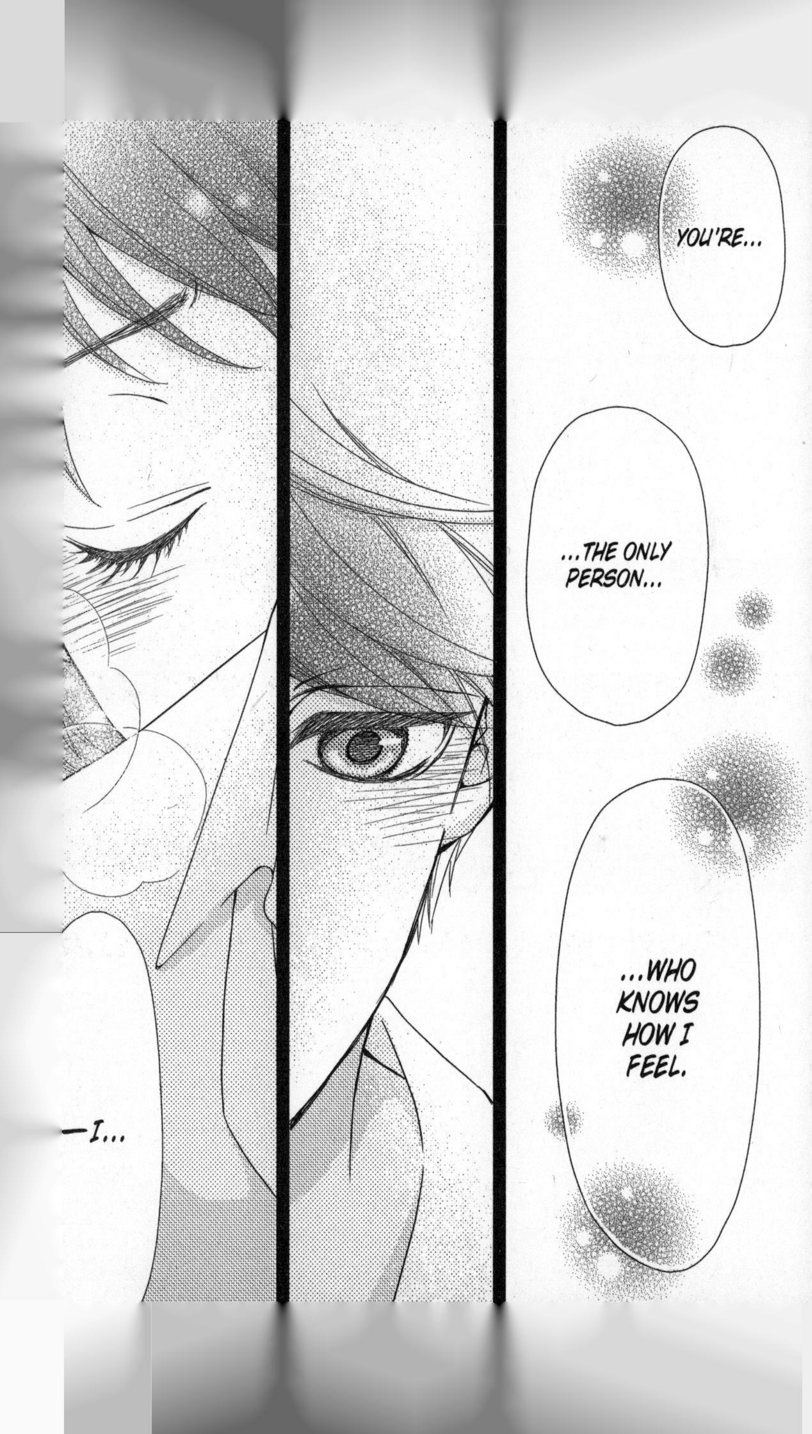
YOU'RE...
...THE ONLY PERSON...
...WHO KNOWS HOW I FEEL.
—I...

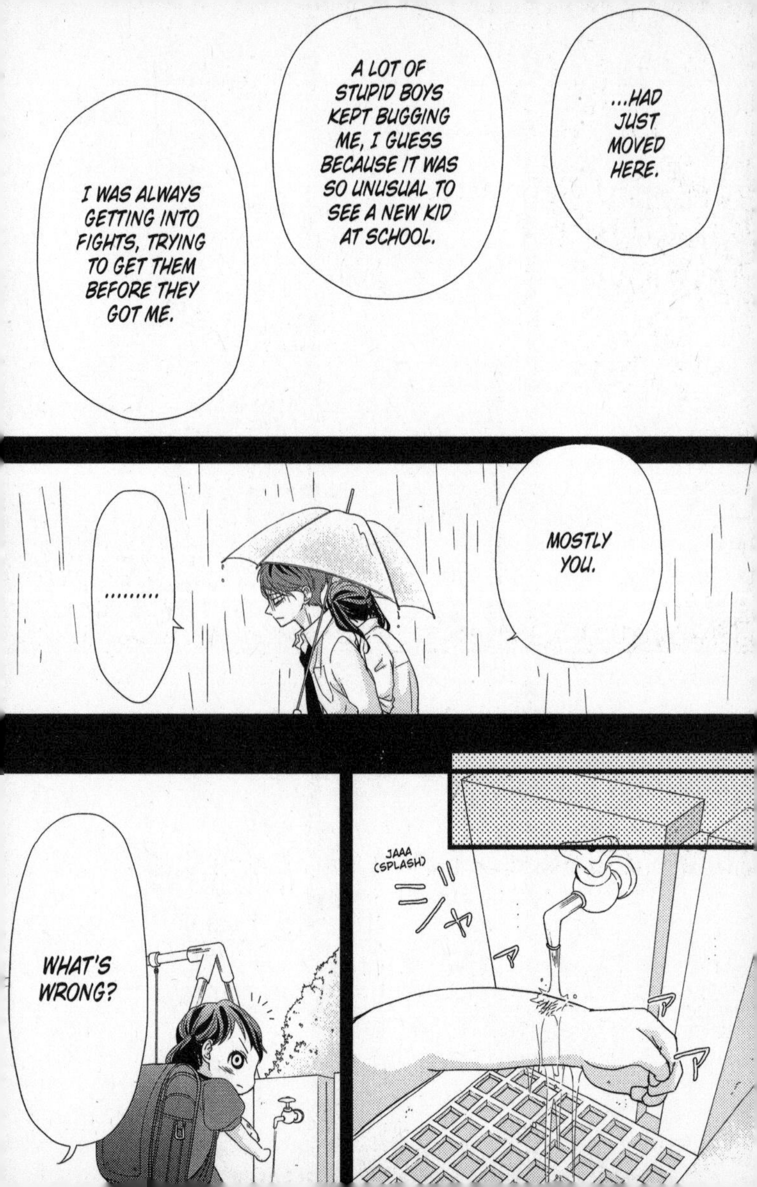
...HAD JUST MOVED HERE.
A LOT OF STUPID BOYS KEPT BUGGING ME, I GUESS BECAUSE IT WAS SO UNUSUAL TO SEE A NEW KID AT SCHOOL.
I WAS ALWAYS GETTING INTO FIGHTS, TRYING TO GET THEM BEFORE THEY GOT ME.
MOSTLY YOU.
....
JAAA (SPLASH)
WHAT'S WRONG?

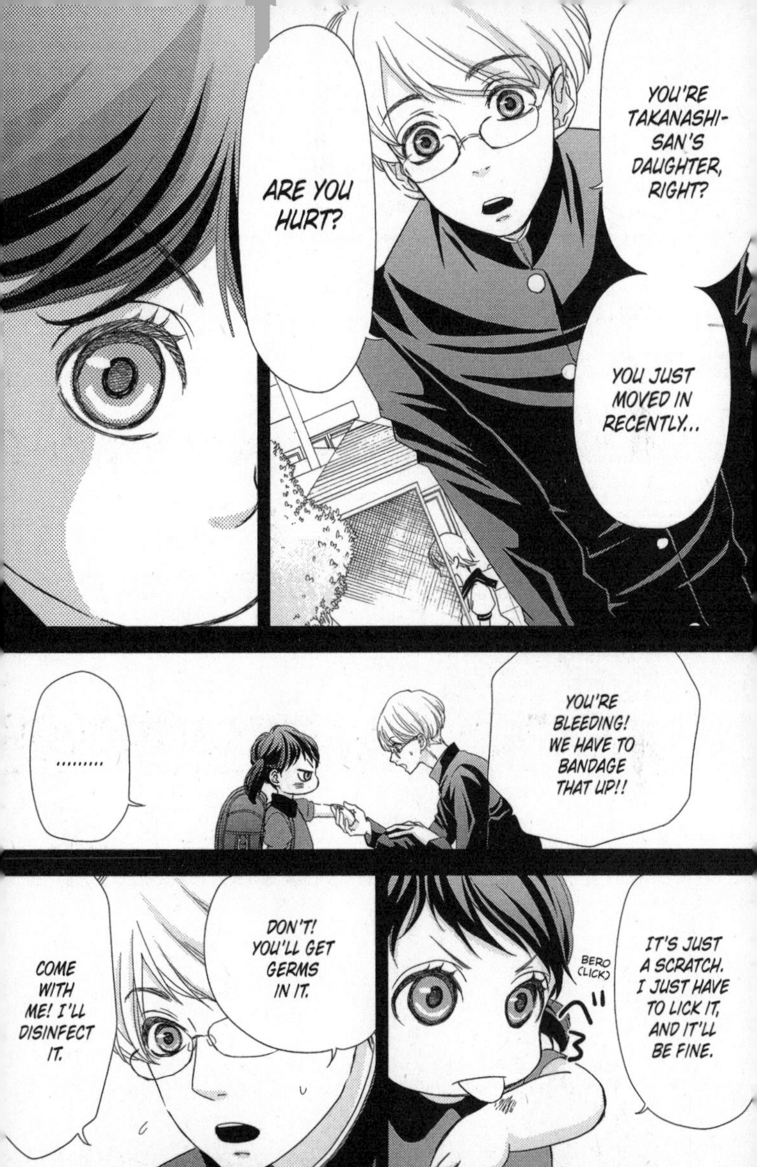
YOU'RE TAKANASHI-SAN'S DAUGHTER, RIGHT?
YOU JUST MOVED IN RECENTLY...
ARE YOU HURT?
YOU'RE BLEEDING! WE HAVE TO BANDAGE THAT UP!!
....
IT'S JUST A SCRATCH. I JUST HAVE TO LICK IT, AND IT'LL BE FINE.
BERO (LICK)
DON'T! YOU'LL GET GERMS IN IT.
COME WITH ME! I'LL DISINFECT IT.

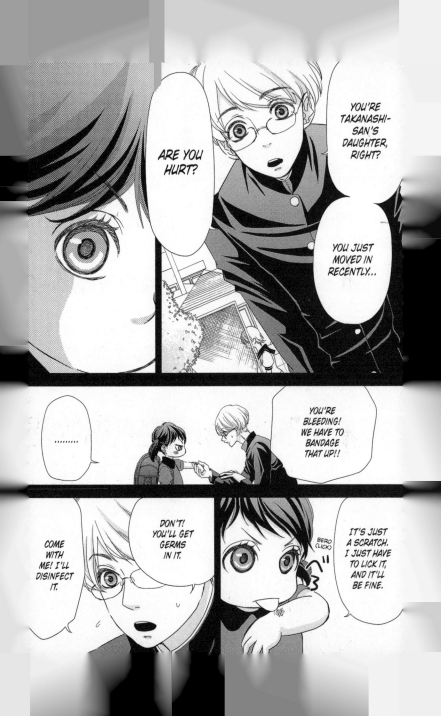

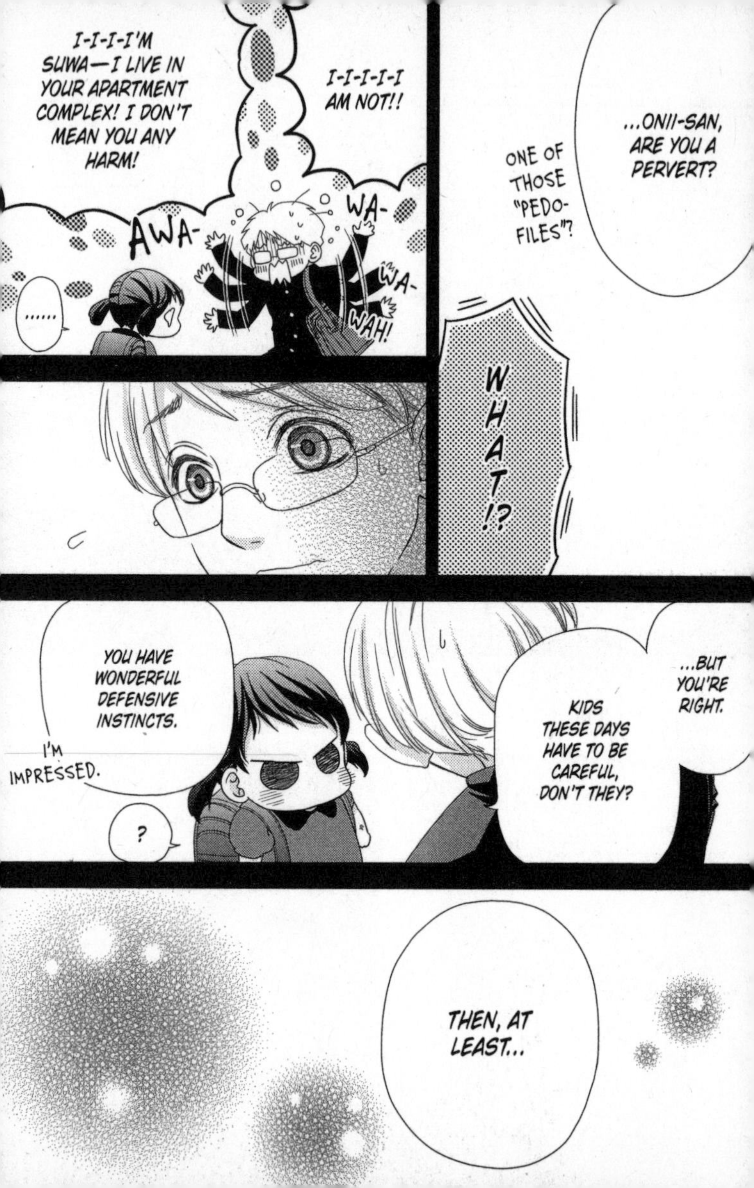
...ONII-SAN, ARE YOU A PERVERT?
ONE OF THOSE "PEDO-FILES"?
WHAT!?
I-I-I-I-I AM NOT!!
I-I-I-I'M SUWA—I LIVE IN YOUR APARTMENT COMPLEX! I DON'T MEAN YOU ANY HARM!
AWA-
WA-
WA-
WAH!
......
...BUT YOU'RE RIGHT.
KIDS THESE DAYS HAVE TO BE CAREFUL, DON'T THEY?
YOU HAVE WONDERFUL DEFENSIVE INSTINCTS.
I'M IMPRESSED.
?
THEN, AT LEAST...

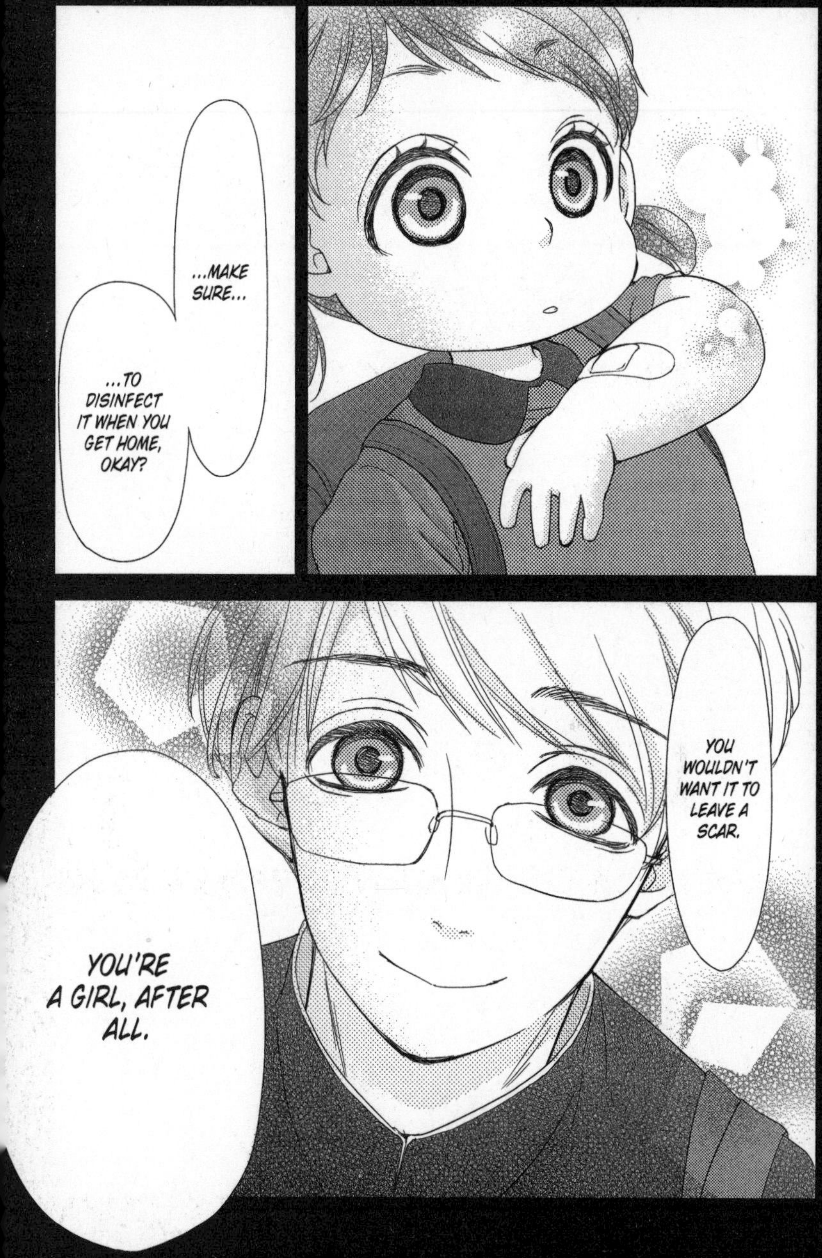
...MAKE SURE...
...TO DISINFECT IT WHEN YOU GET HOME, OKAY?
YOU WOULDN'T WANT IT TO LEAVE A SCAR.
YOU'RE A GIRL, AFTER ALL.

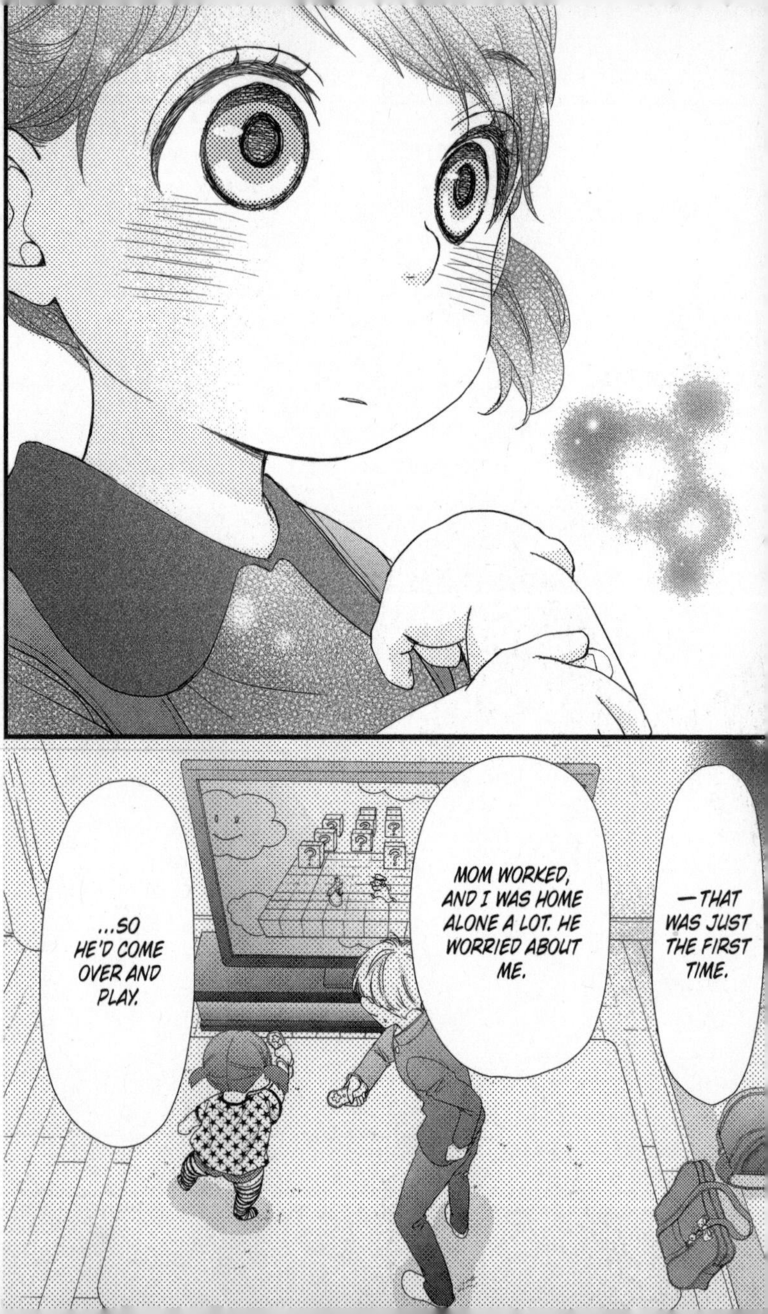
—THAT WAS JUST THE FIRST TIME.
MOM WORKED, AND I WAS HOME ALONE A LOT. HE WORRIED ABOUT ME.
...SO HE'D COME OVER AND PLAY.

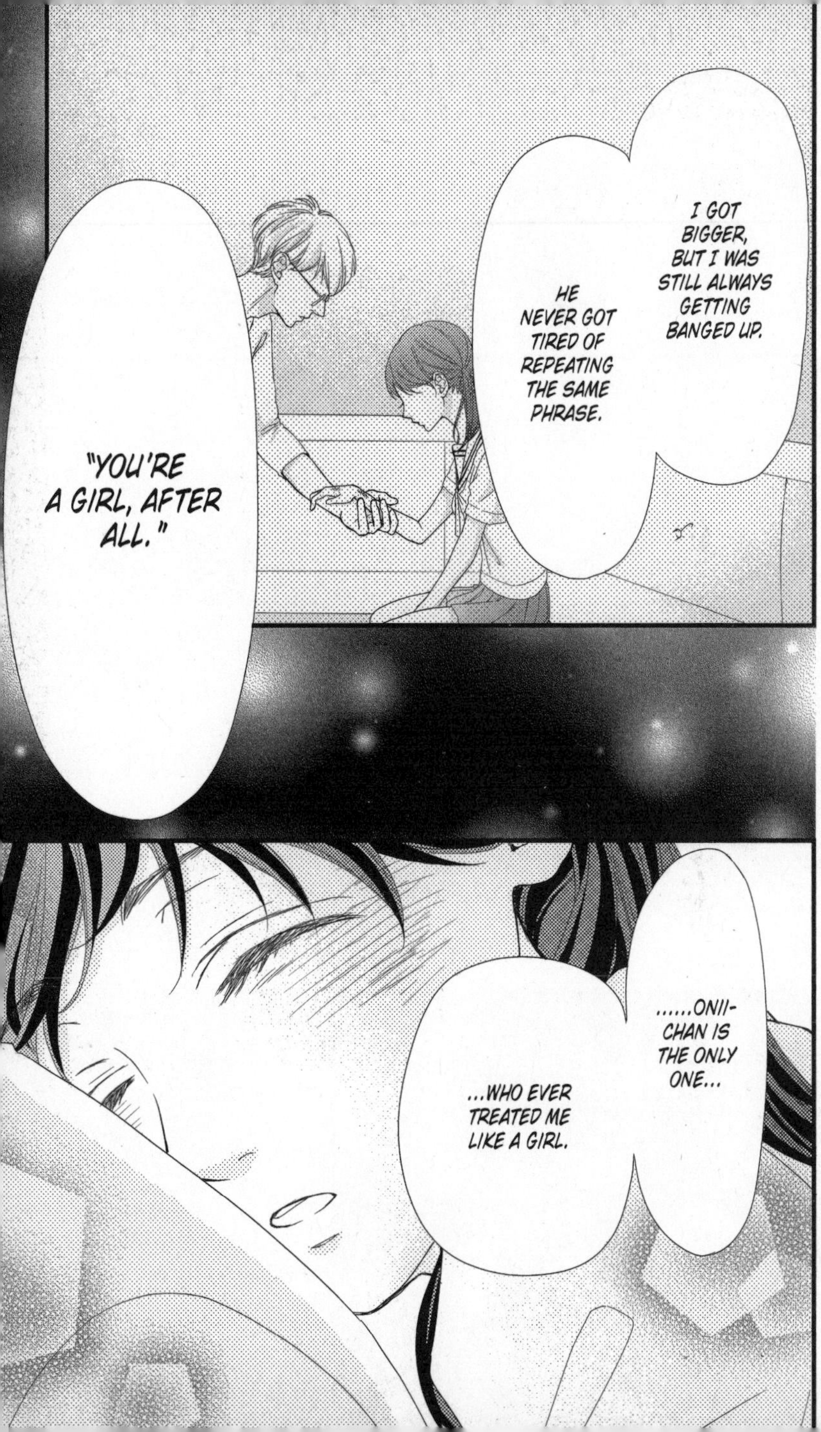
I GOT BIGGER, BUT I WAS STILL ALWAYS GETTING BANGED UP.
HE NEVER GOT TIRED OF REPEATING THE SAME PHRASE.
"YOU'RE A GIRL, AFTER ALL."
......ONII-CHAN IS THE ONLY ONE...
...WHO EVER TREATED ME LIKE A GIRL.

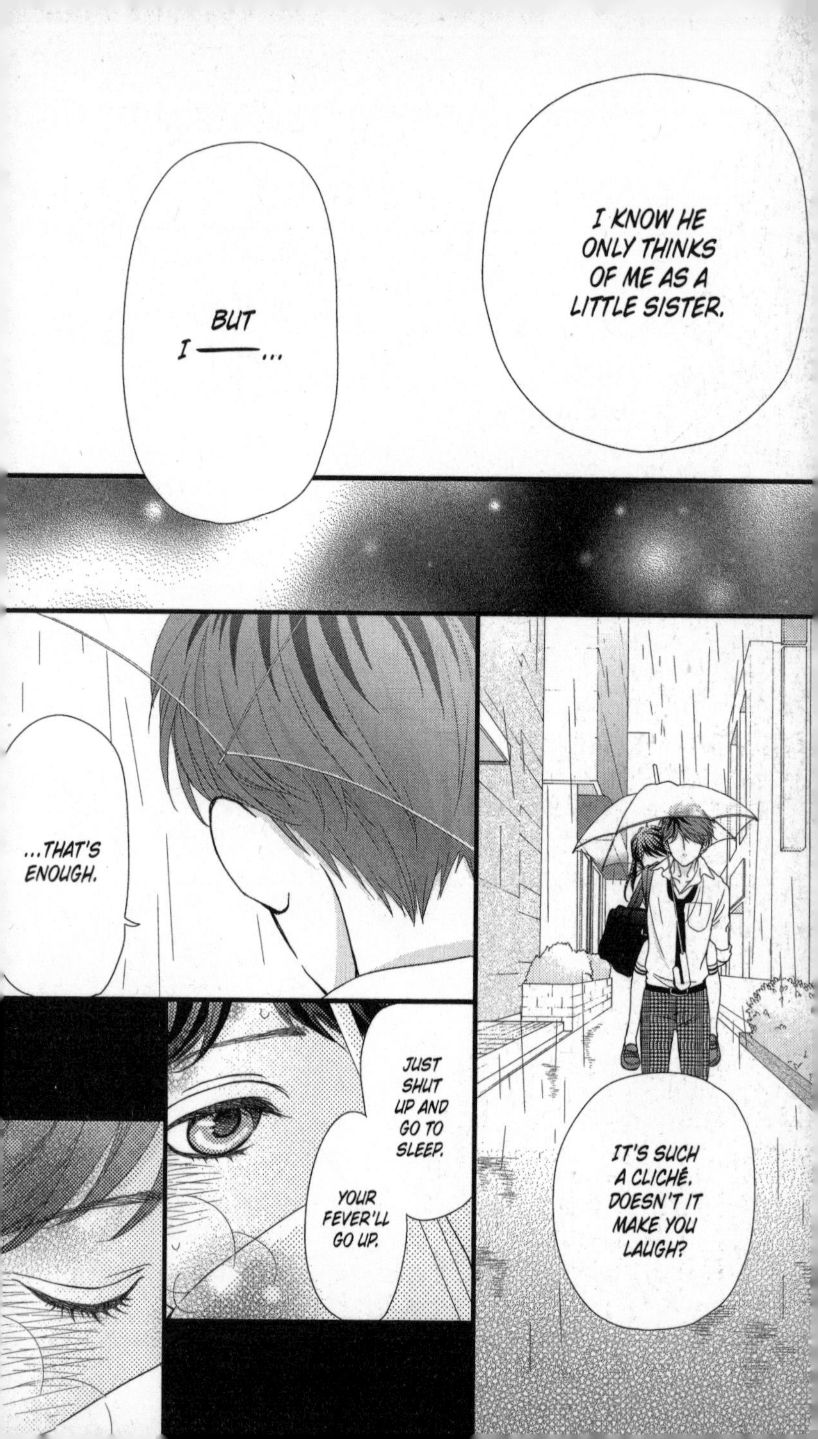
I KNOW HE ONLY THINKS OF ME AS A LITTLE SISTER.
BUT I——...
IT'S SUCH A CLICHÉ. DOESN'T IT MAKE YOU LAUGH?
...THAT'S ENOUGH.
JUST SHUT UP AND GO TO SLEEP.
YOUR FEVER'LL GO UP.

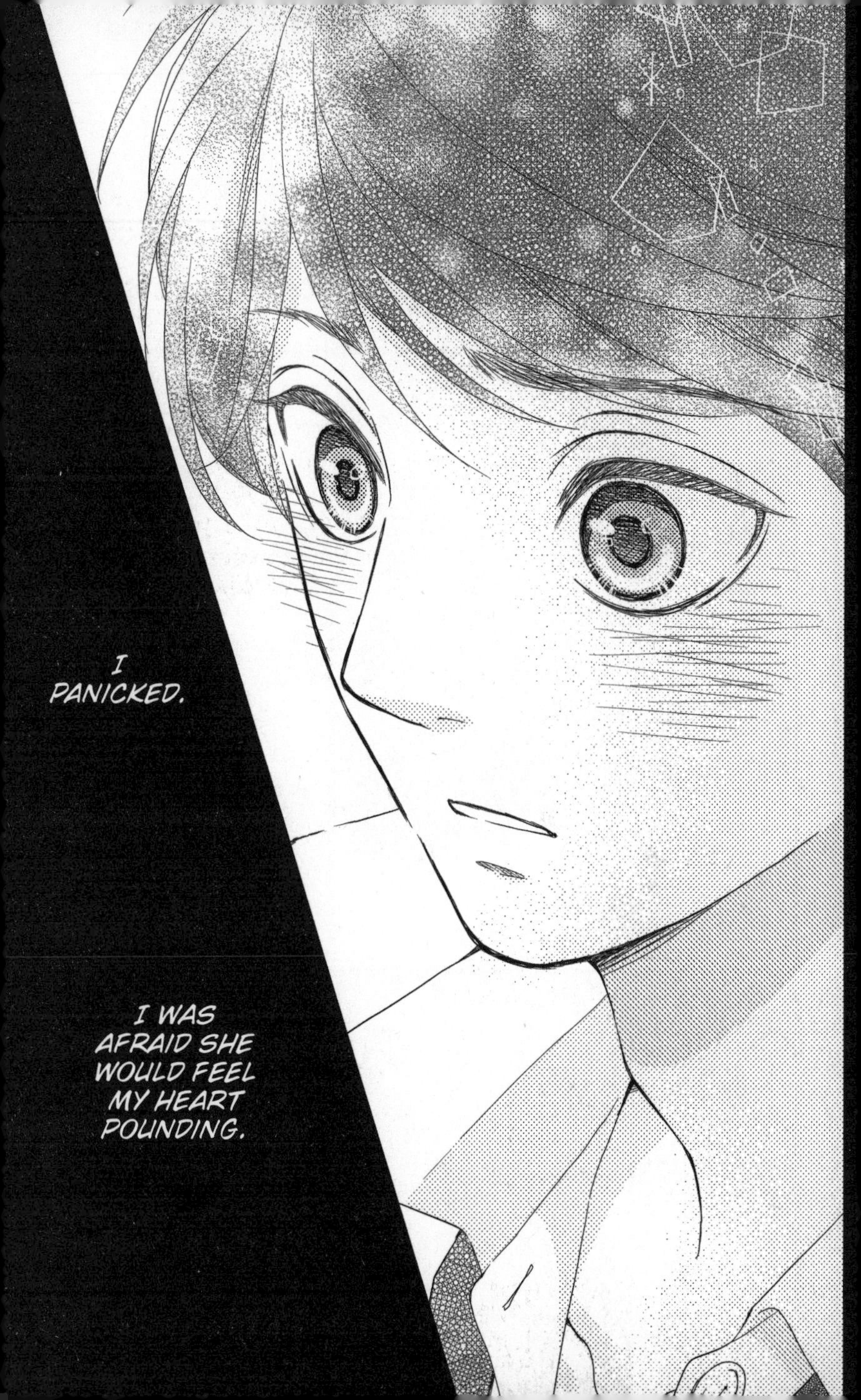
I PANICKED.
I WAS AFRAID SHE WOULD FEEL MY HEART POUNDING.

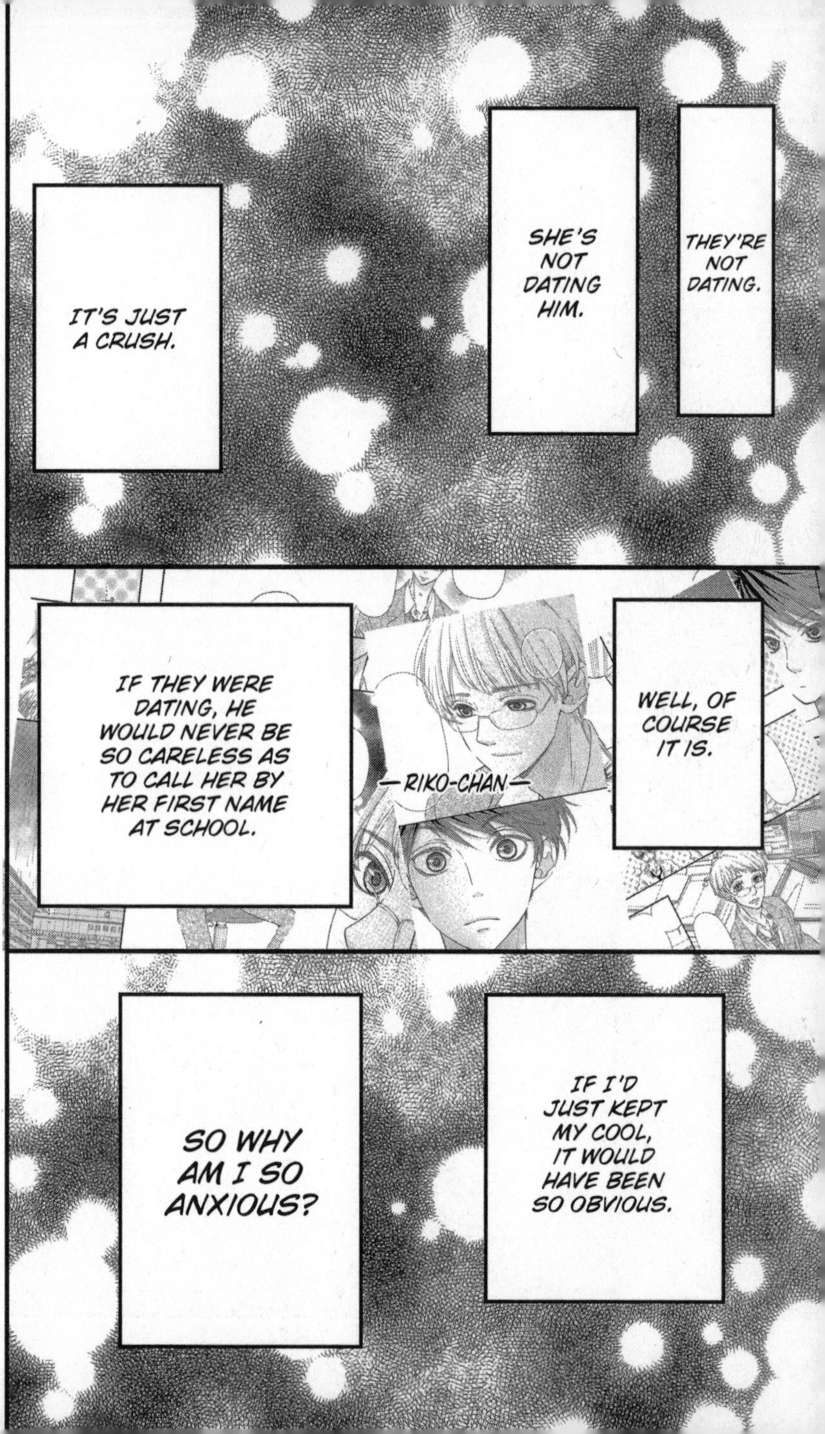
THEY'RE NOT DATING.
SHE'S NOT DATING HIM.
IT'S JUST A CRUSH.
WELL, OF COURSE IT IS.
—RIKO-CHAN—
IF THEY WERE DATING, HE WOULD NEVER BE SO CARELESS AS TO CALL HER BY HER FIRST NAME AT SCHOOL.
IF I'D JUST KEPT MY COOL, IT WOULD HAVE BEEN SO OBVIOUS.
SO WHY AM I SO ANXIOUS?

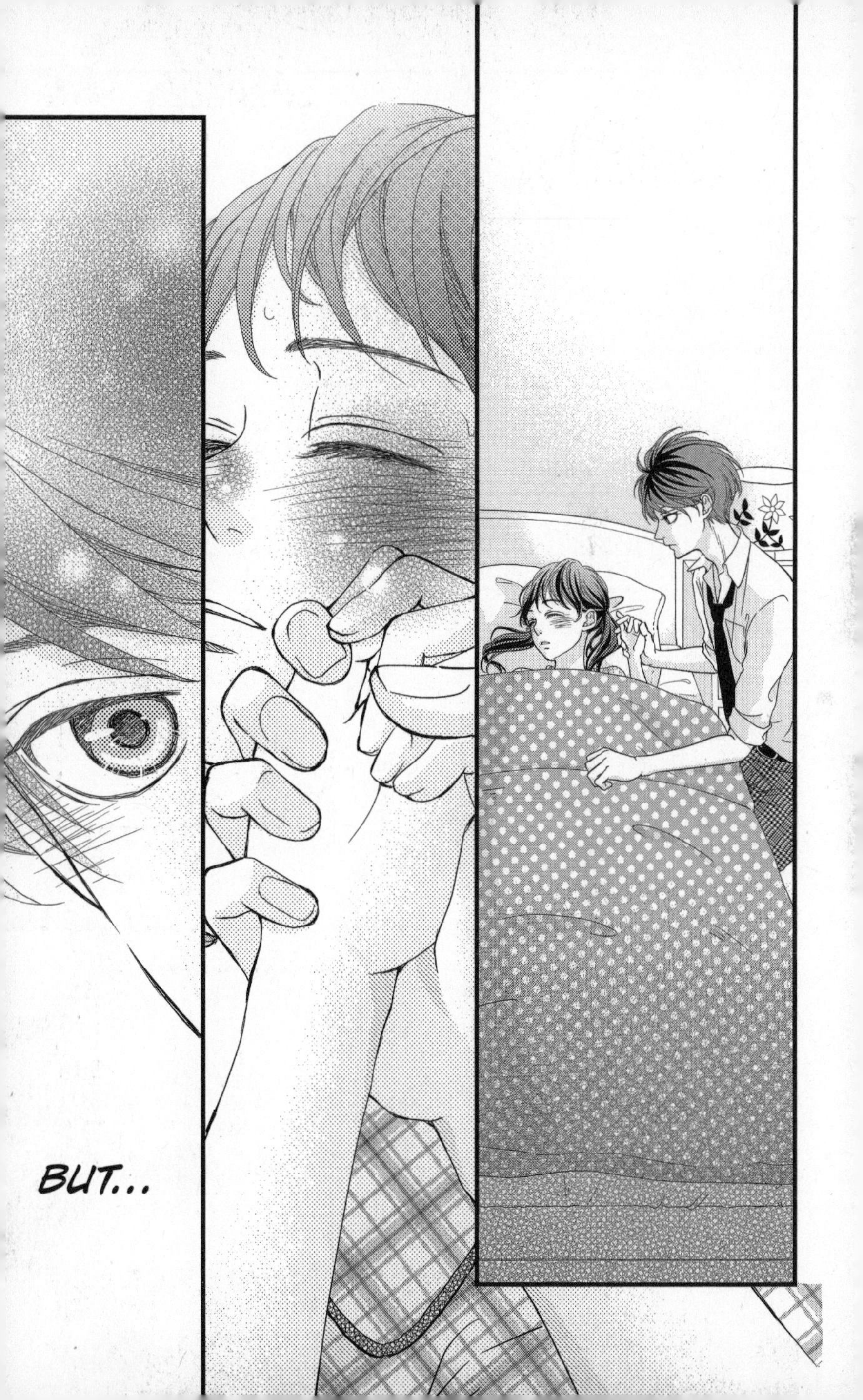
BUT...

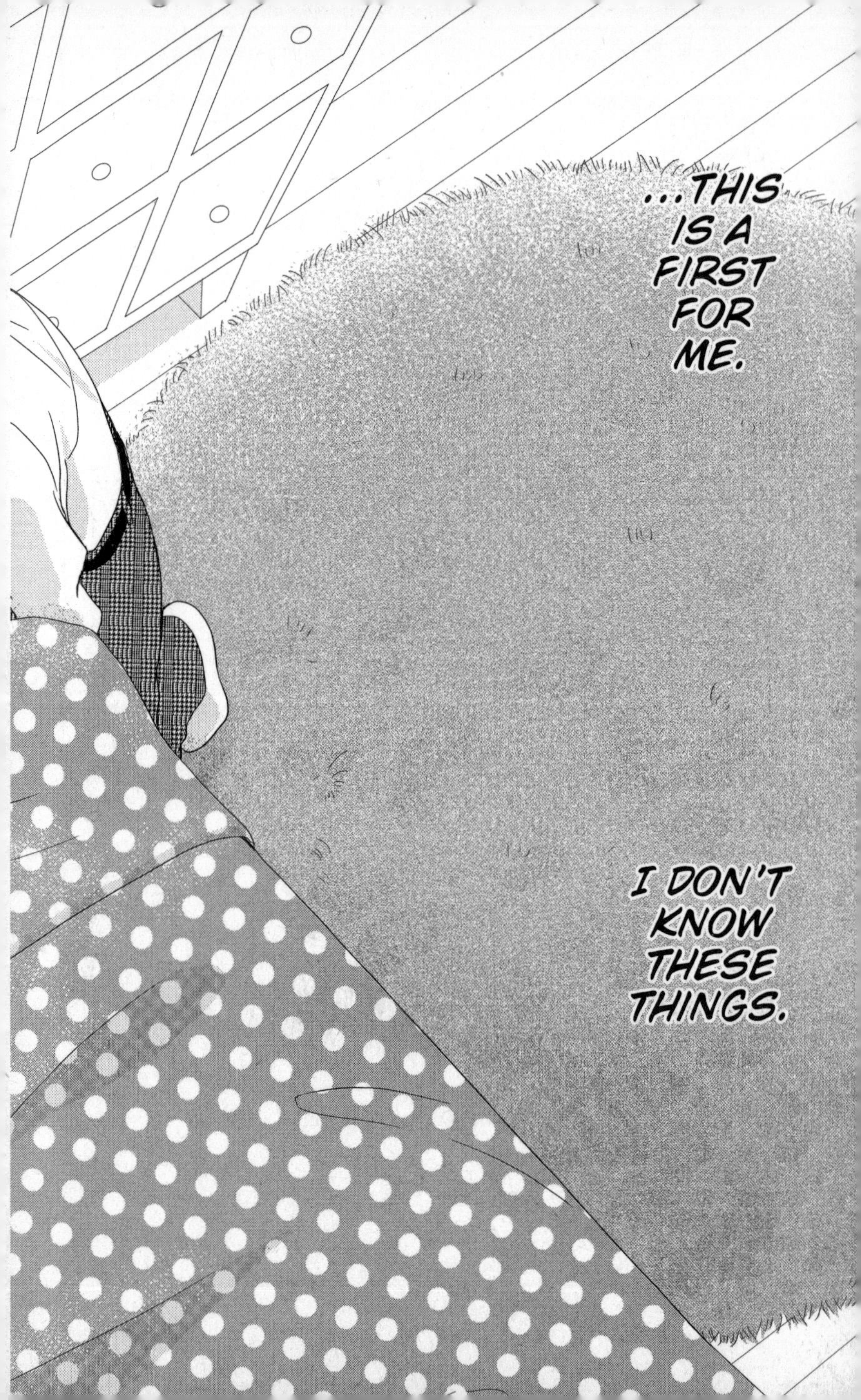
...THIS IS A FIRST FOR ME.
I DON'T KNOW THESE THINGS.

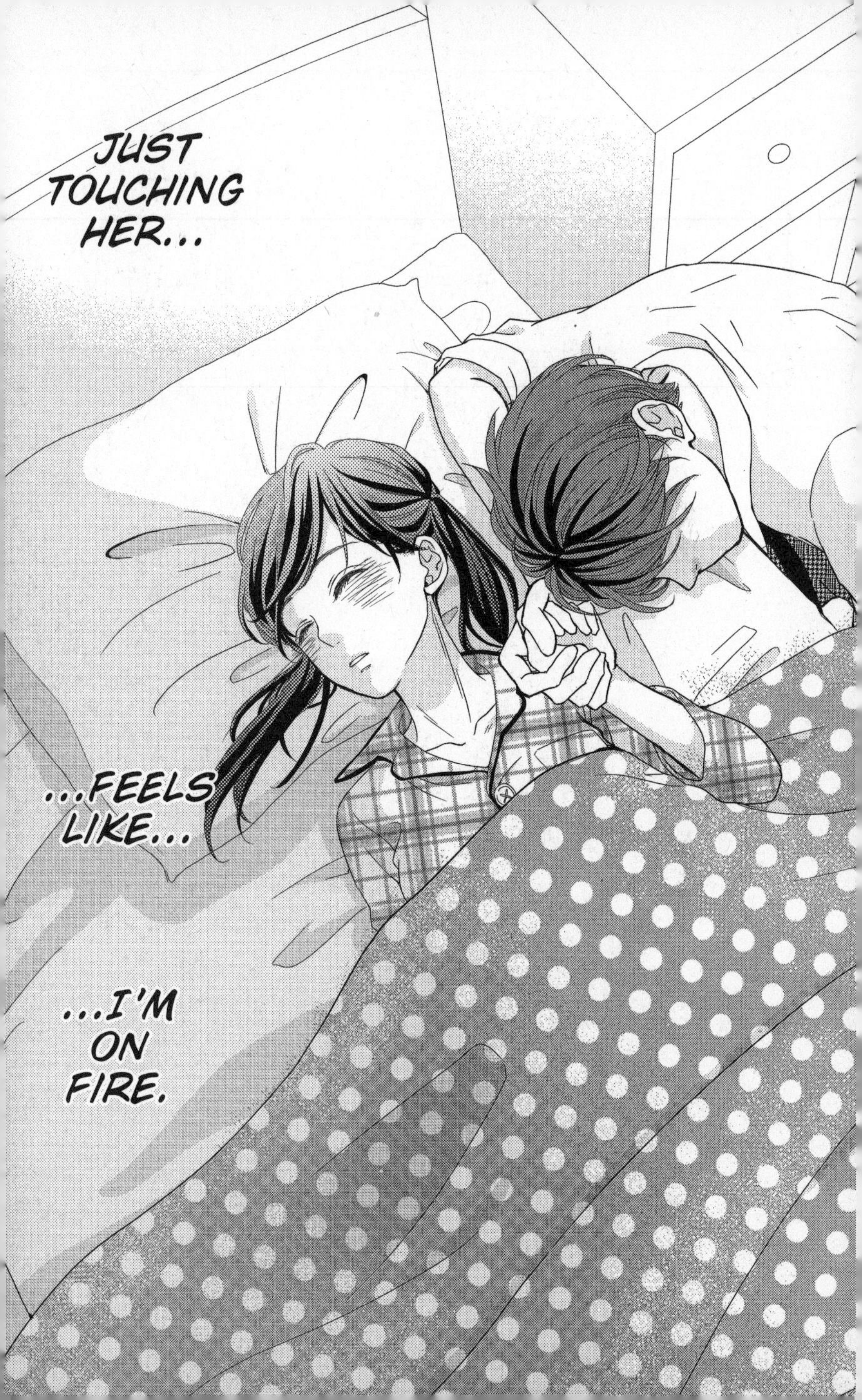
JUST TOUCHING HER...
...FEELS LIKE...
...I'M ON FIRE.

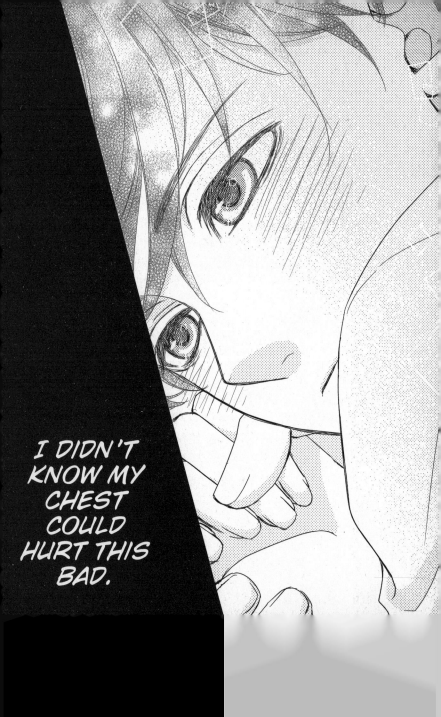

I DIDN'T KNOW MY CHEST COULD HURT THIS BAD.

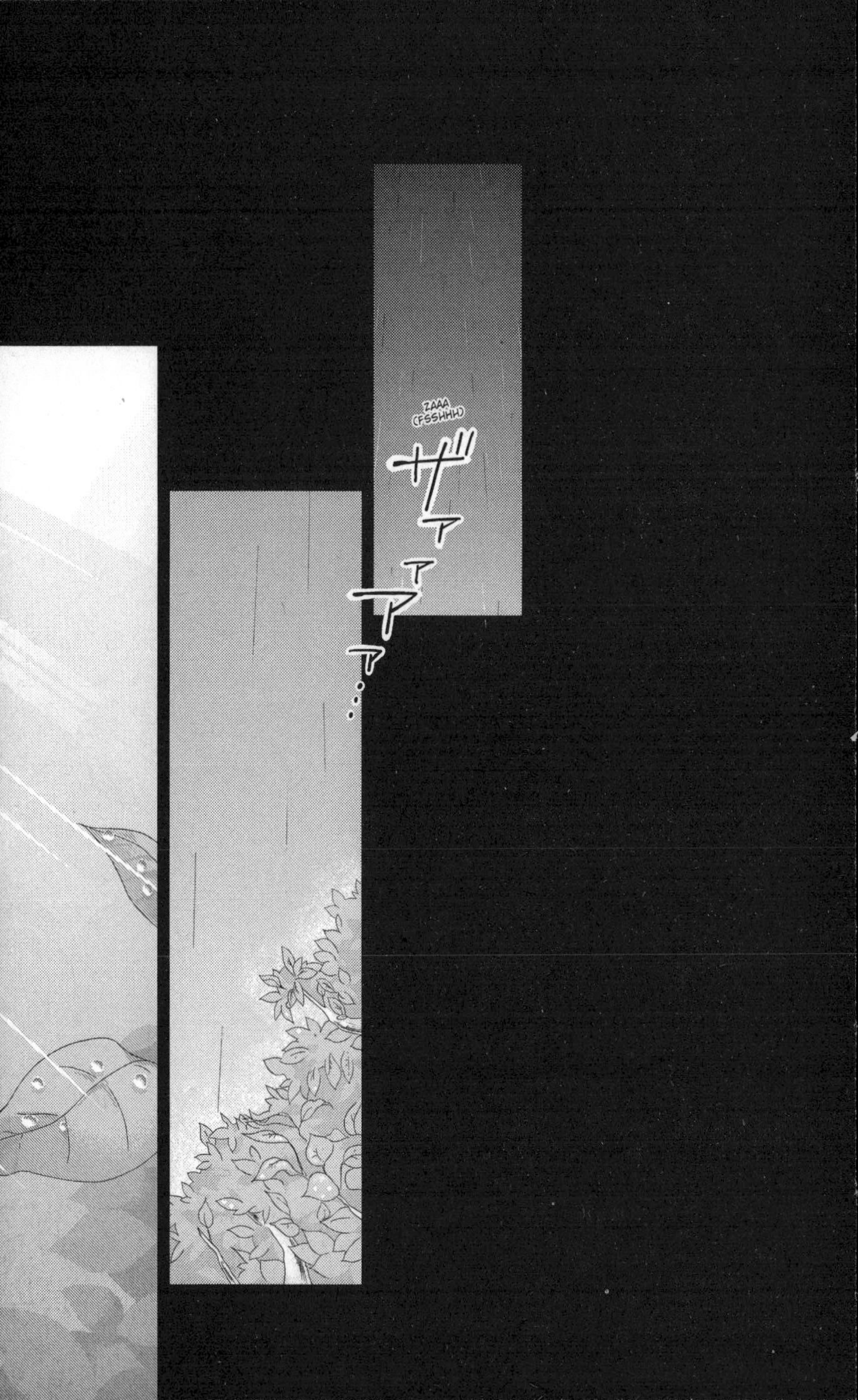
ZAAA (FSSHHH)
ザァァァァ…

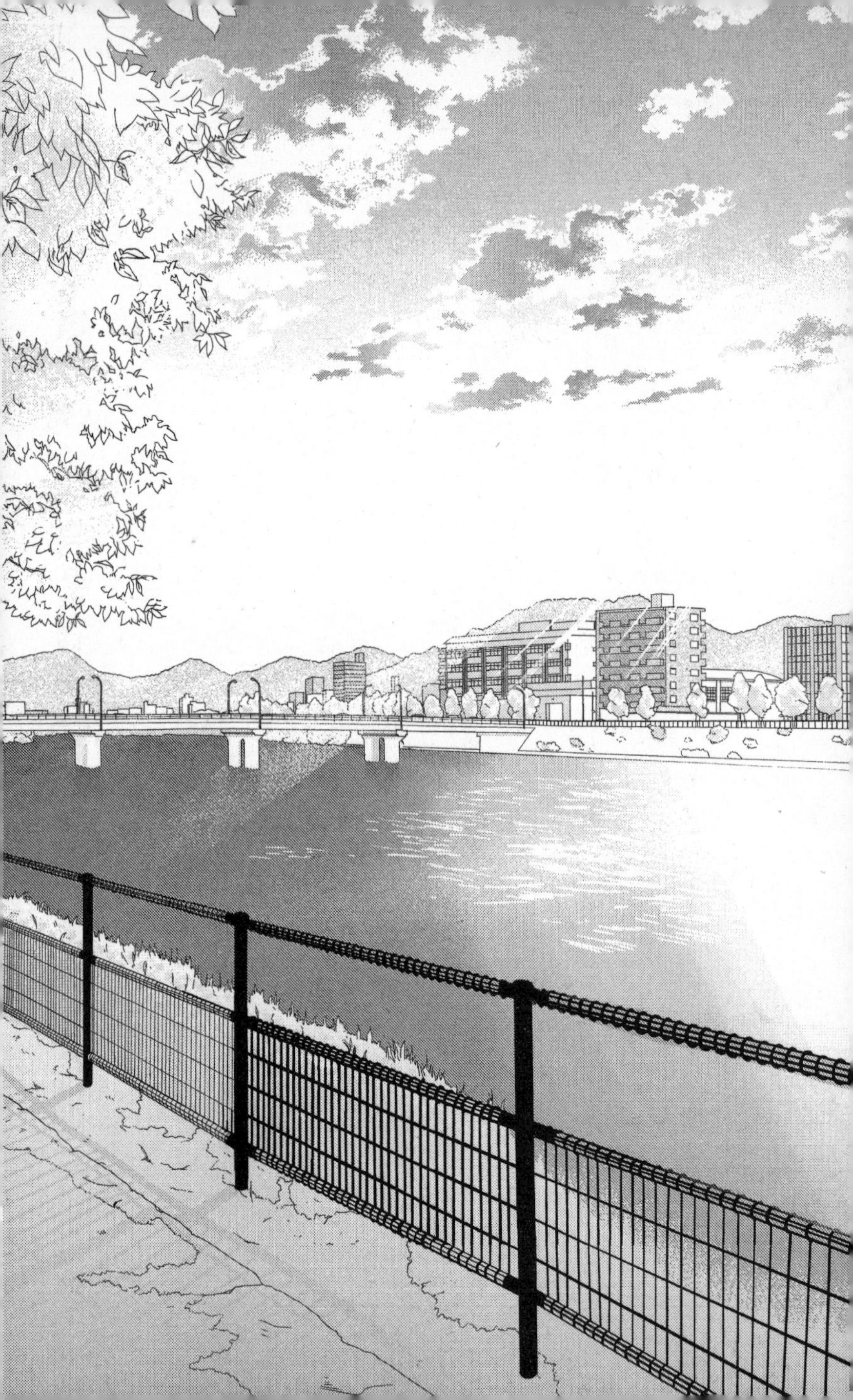

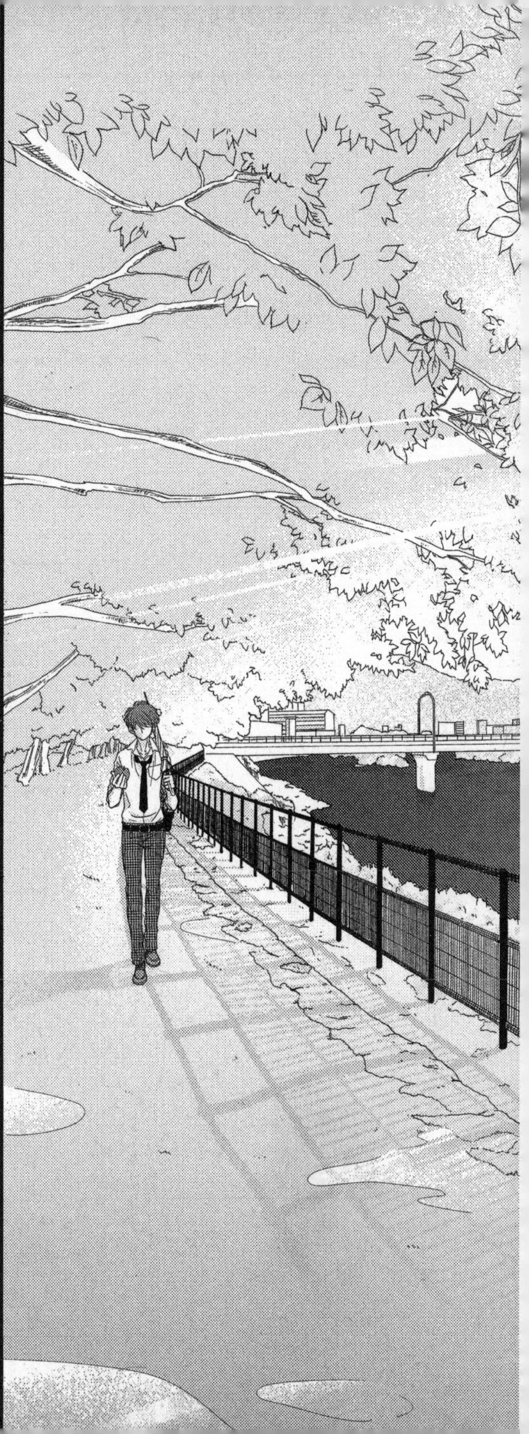
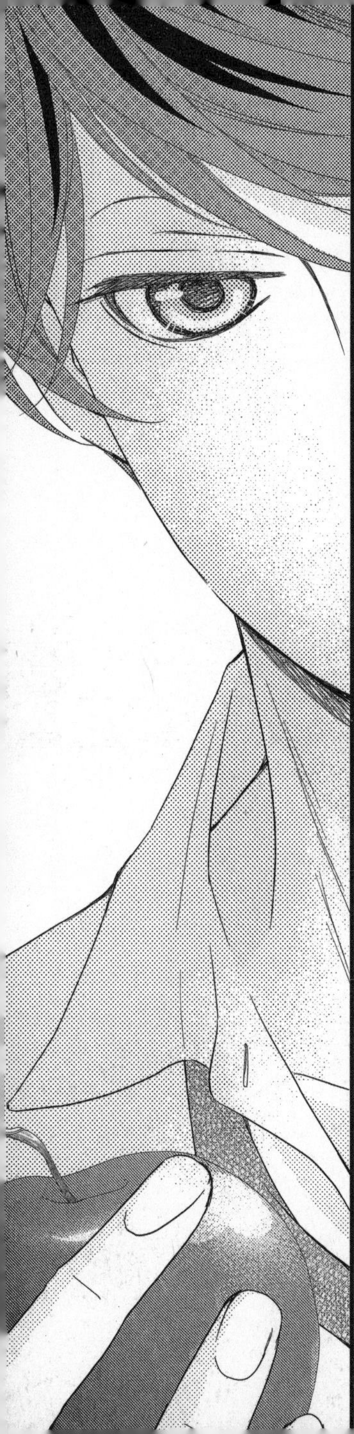

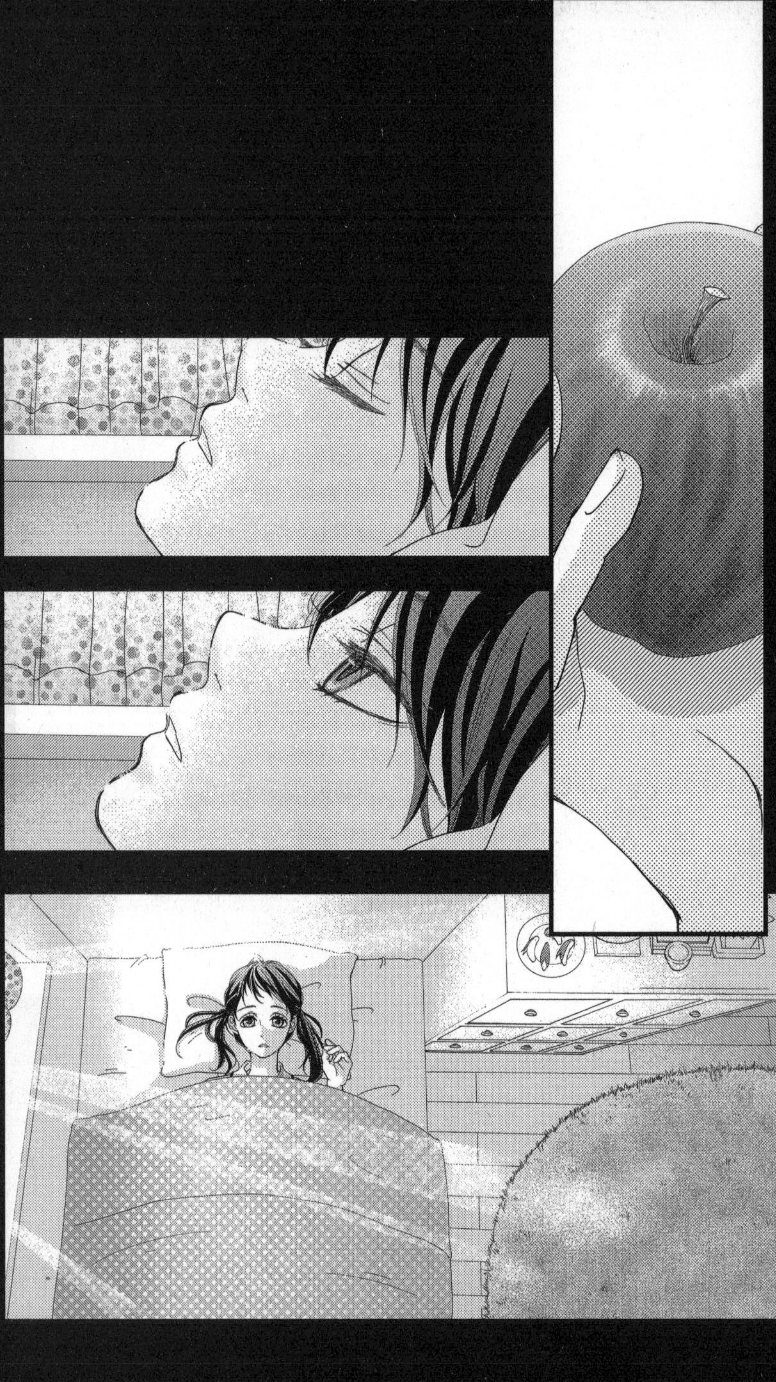

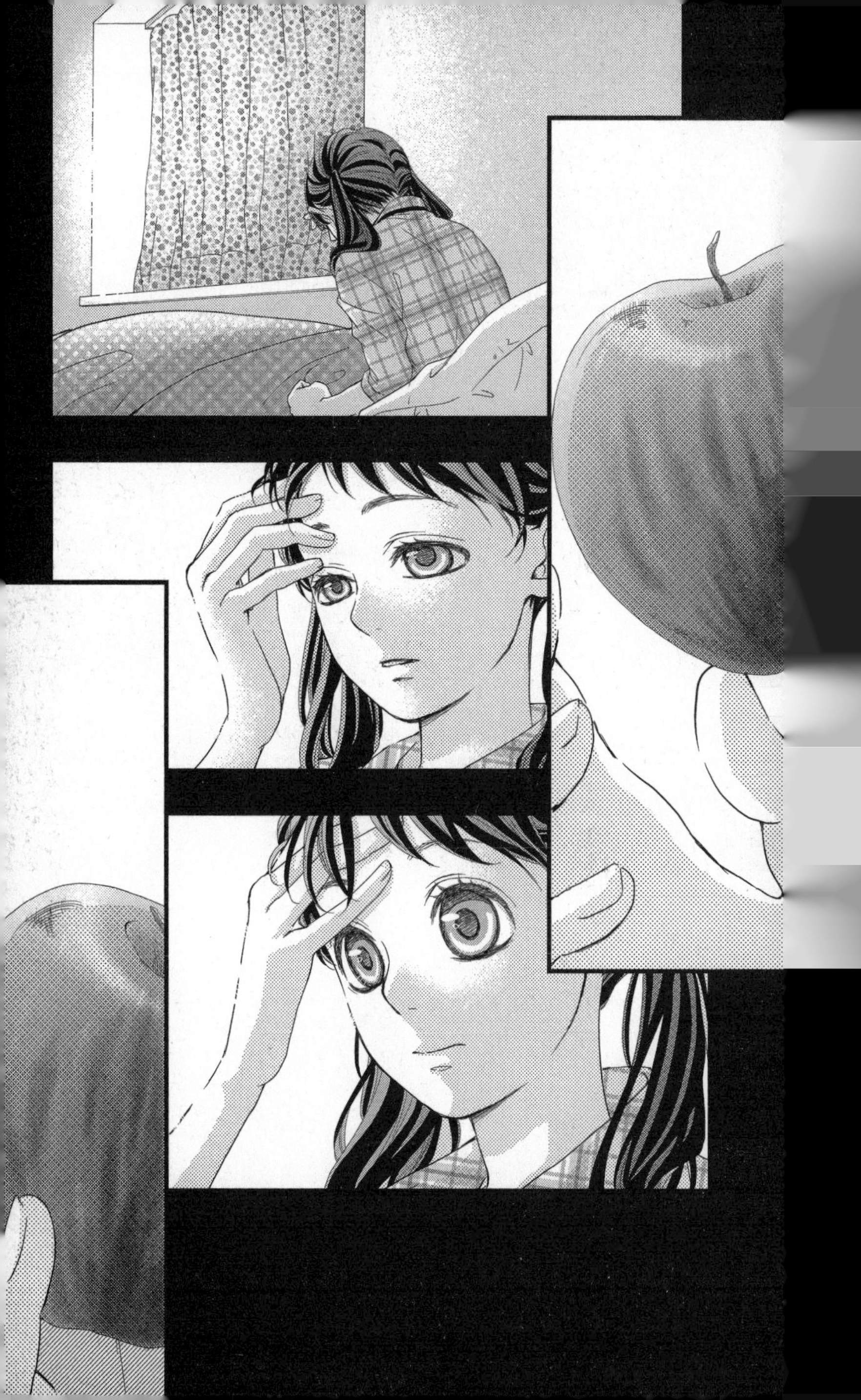

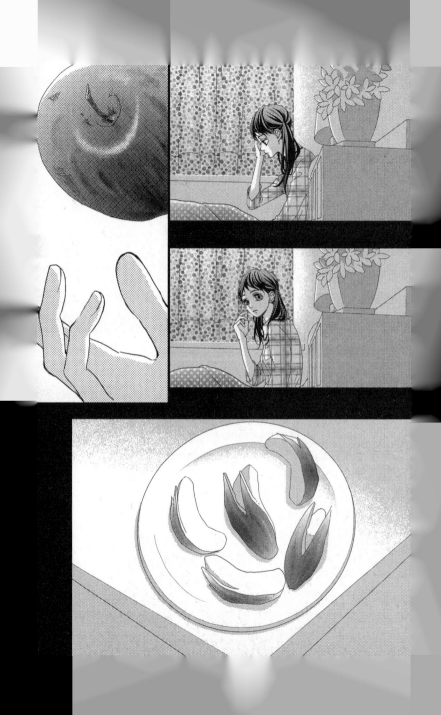

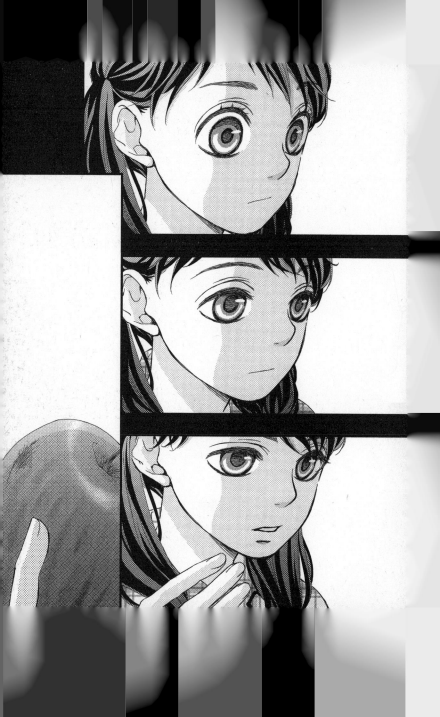

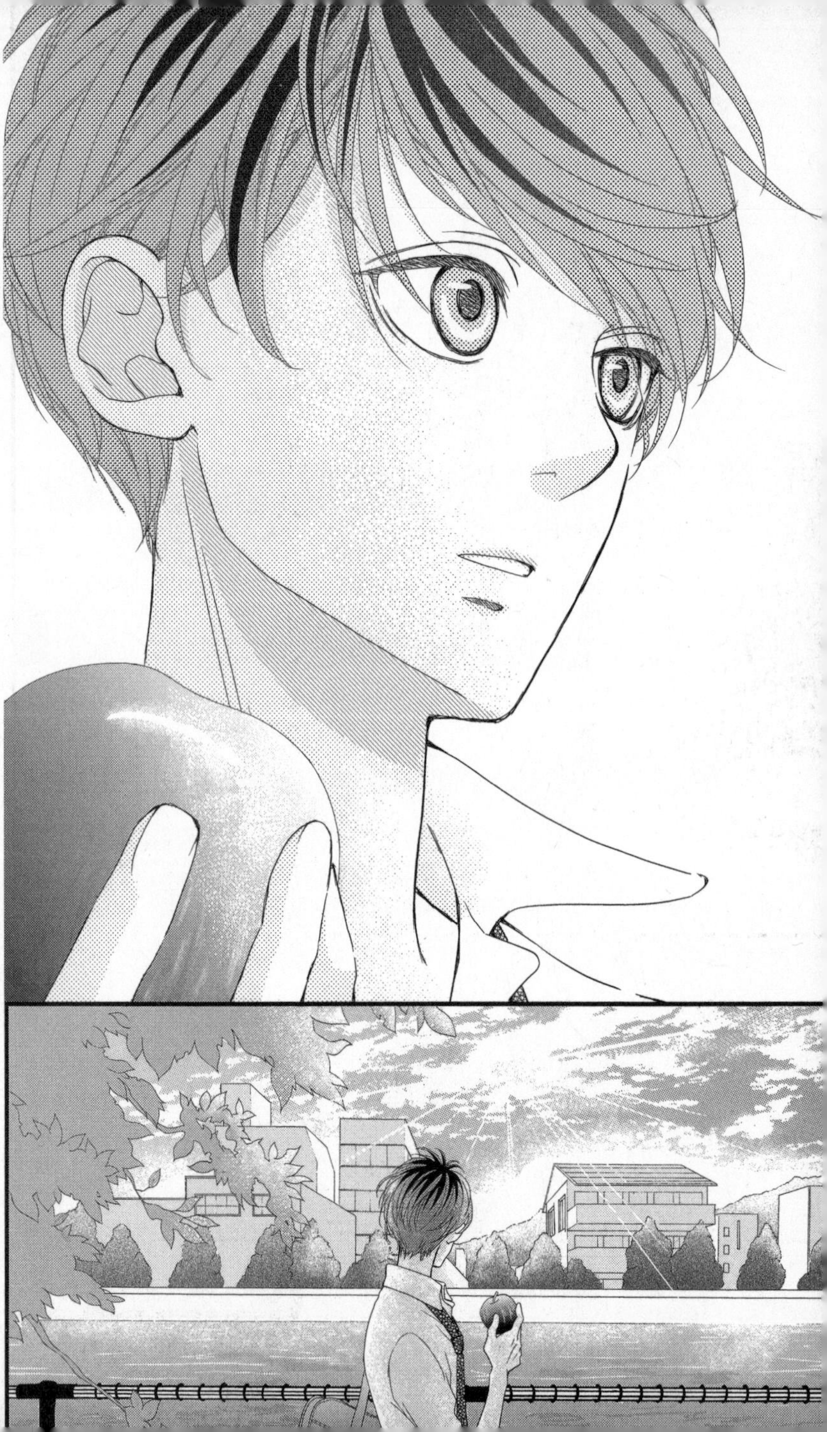

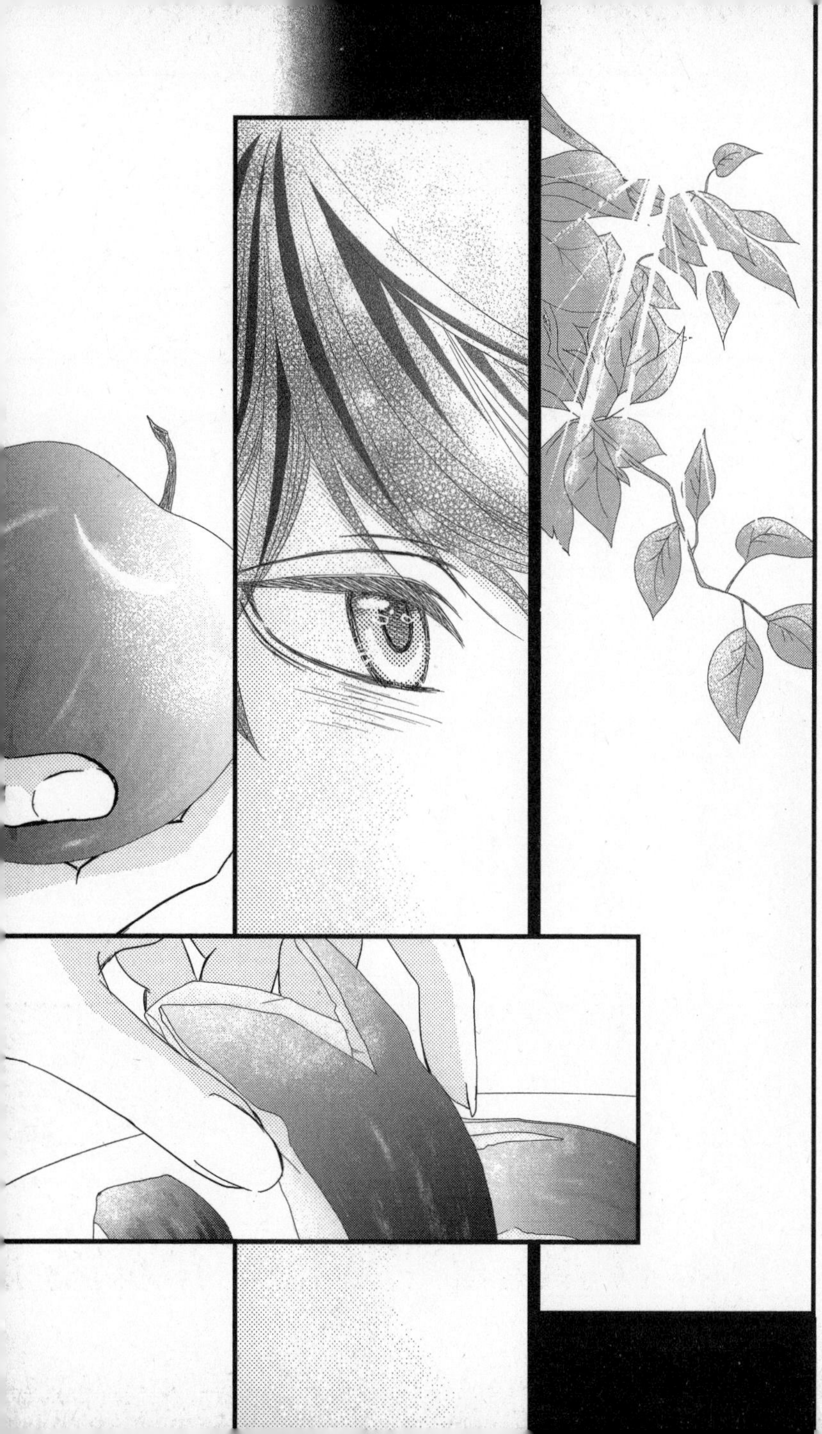

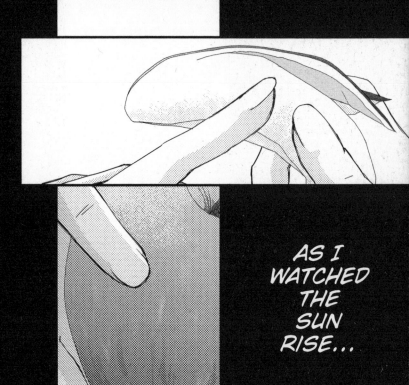

AS I
WATCHED
THE
SUN
RISE...

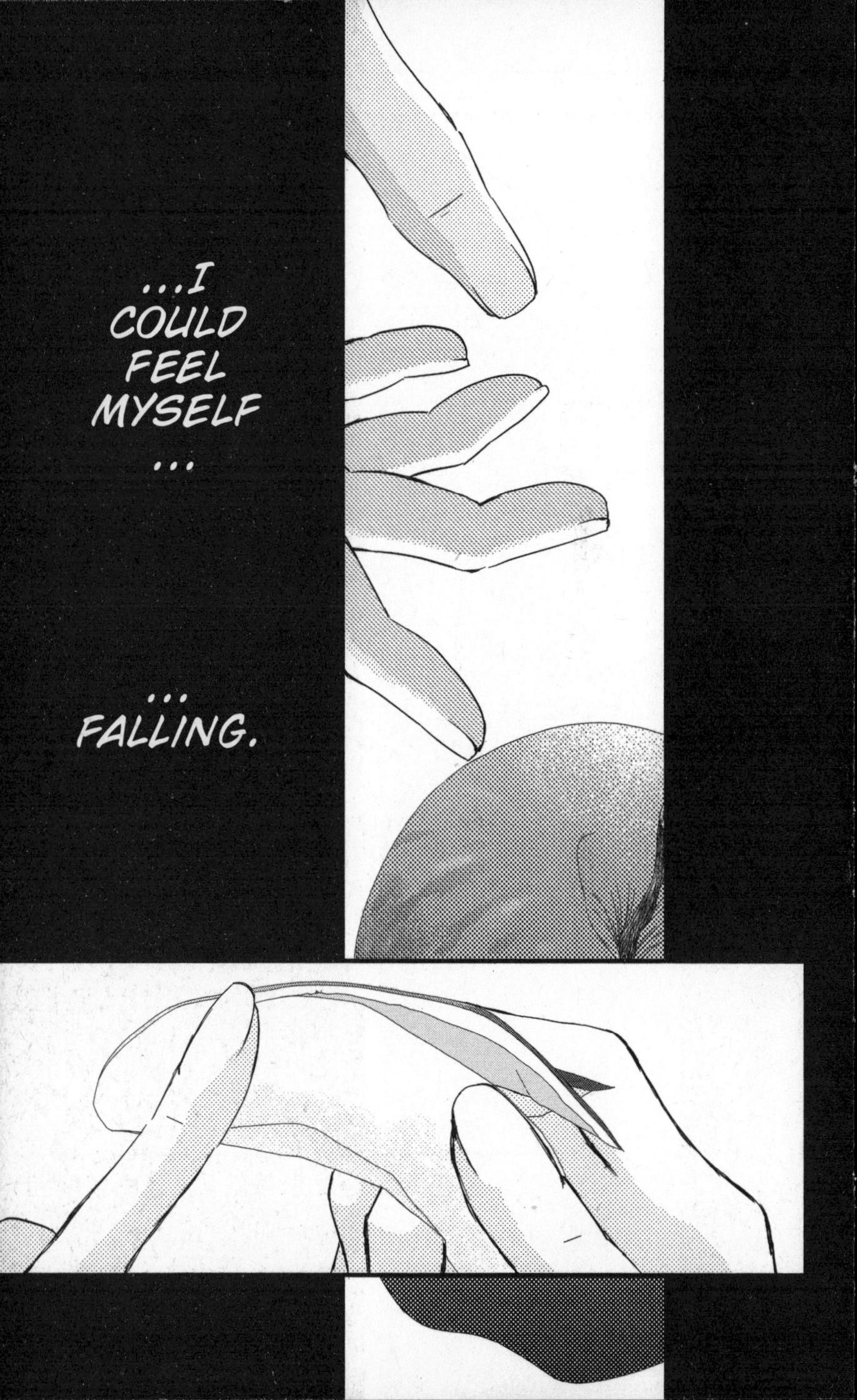

...I
COULD
FEEL
MYSELF
...

FALLING.

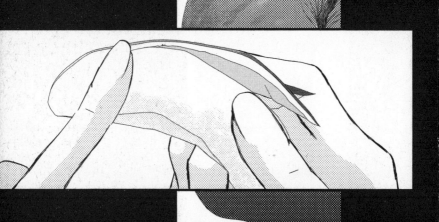

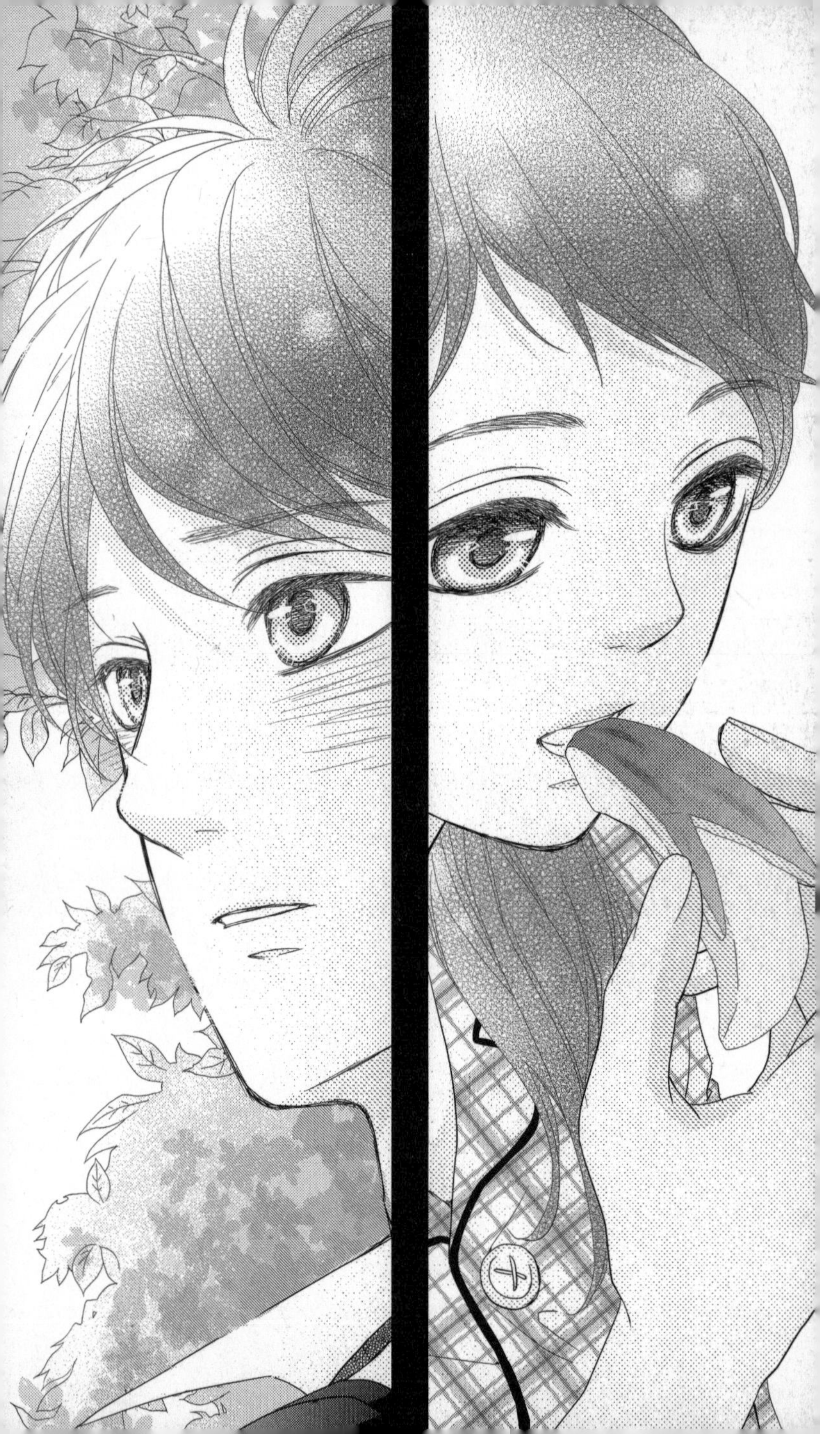

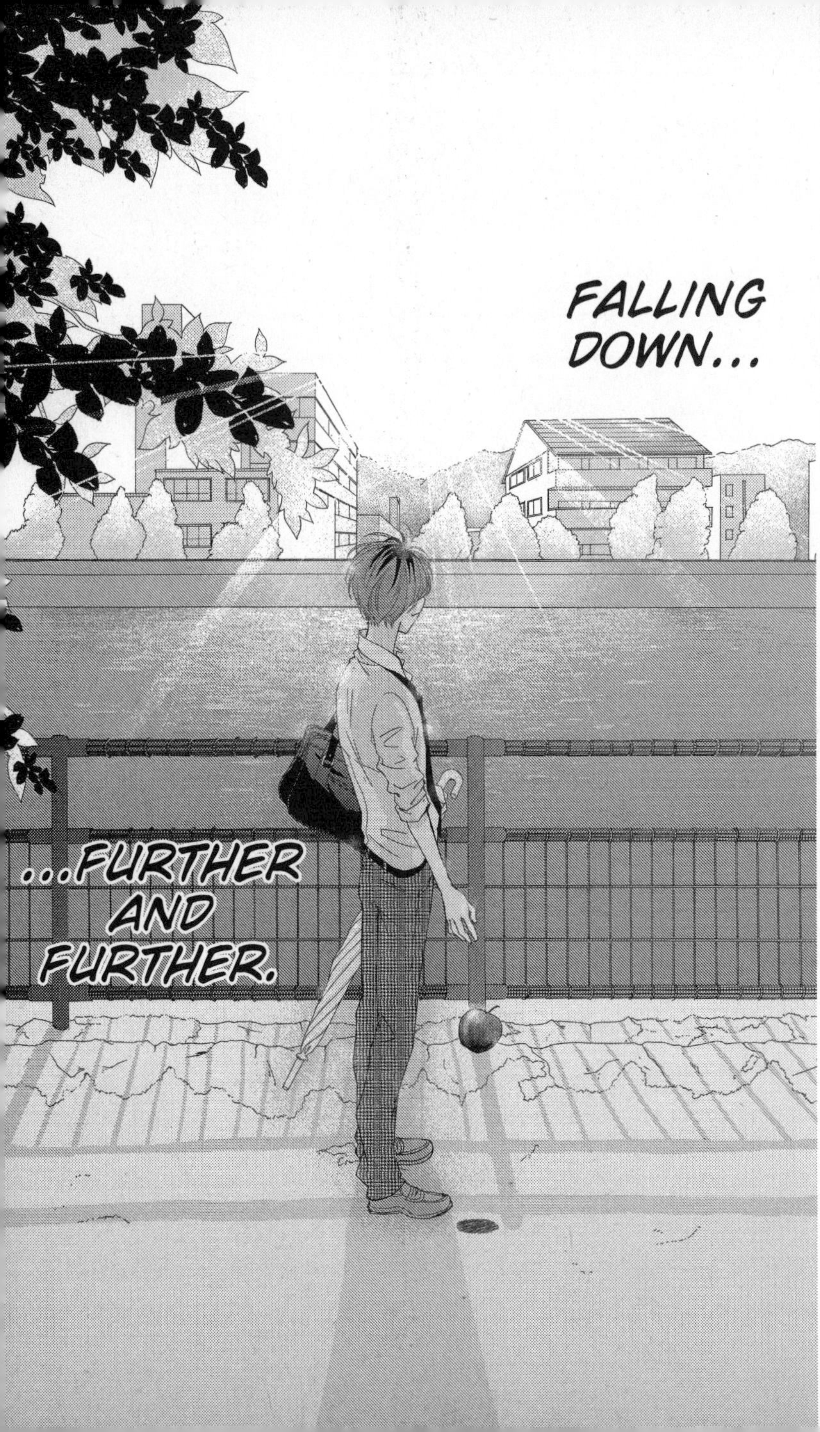
FALLING DOWN...
...FURTHER AND FURTHER.

A FINE DAY FOR BUNGLING Hatsu*Haru Tidbits

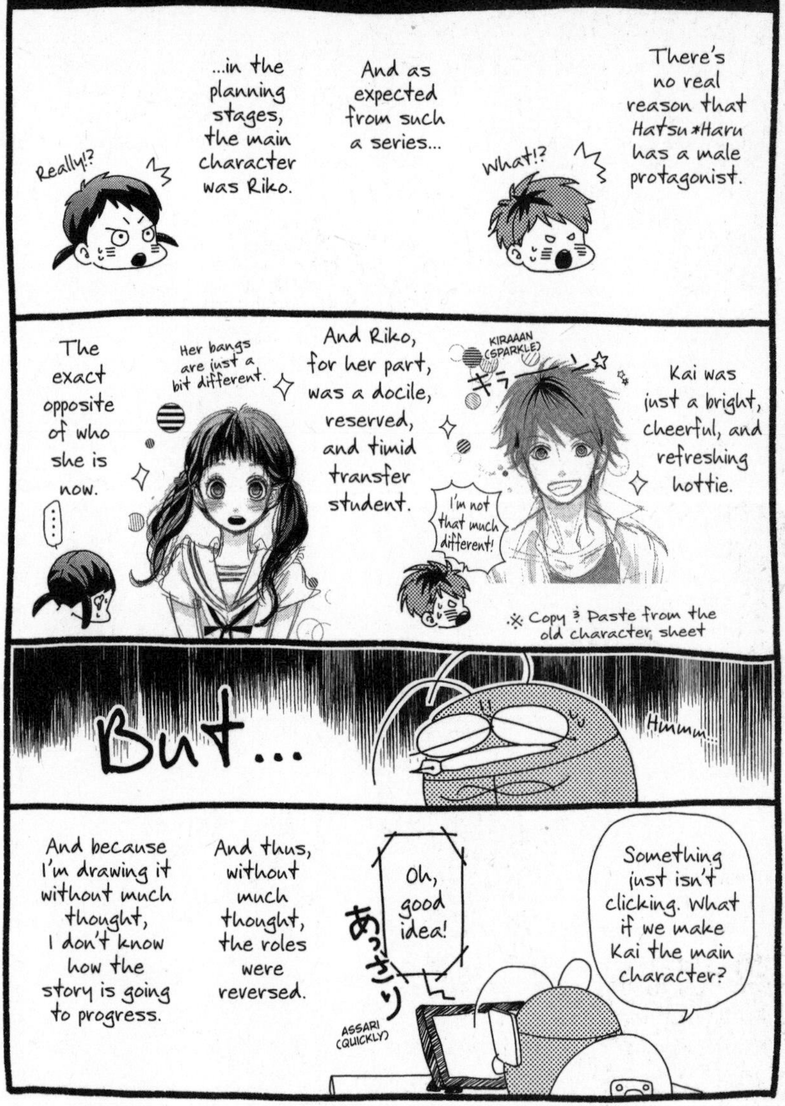

There's no real reason that Hatsu*Haru has a male protagonist.
What!?
And as expected from such a series...
...in the planning stages, the main character was Riko.
Really!?
Kai was just a bright, cheerful, and refreshing hottie.
KIRAAAN (SPARKLE)
キラ
I'm not that much different!
※ Copy & Paste from the old character sheet
And Riko, for her part, was a docile, reserved, and timid transfer student.
Her bangs are just a bit different.
The exact opposite of who she is now.
...
Hmmm...
But...
Something just isn't clicking. What if we make Kai the main character?
Oh, good idea!
あっさり
ASSARI (QUICKLY)
And thus, without much thought, the roles were reversed.
And because I'm drawing it without much thought, I don't know how the story is going to progress.

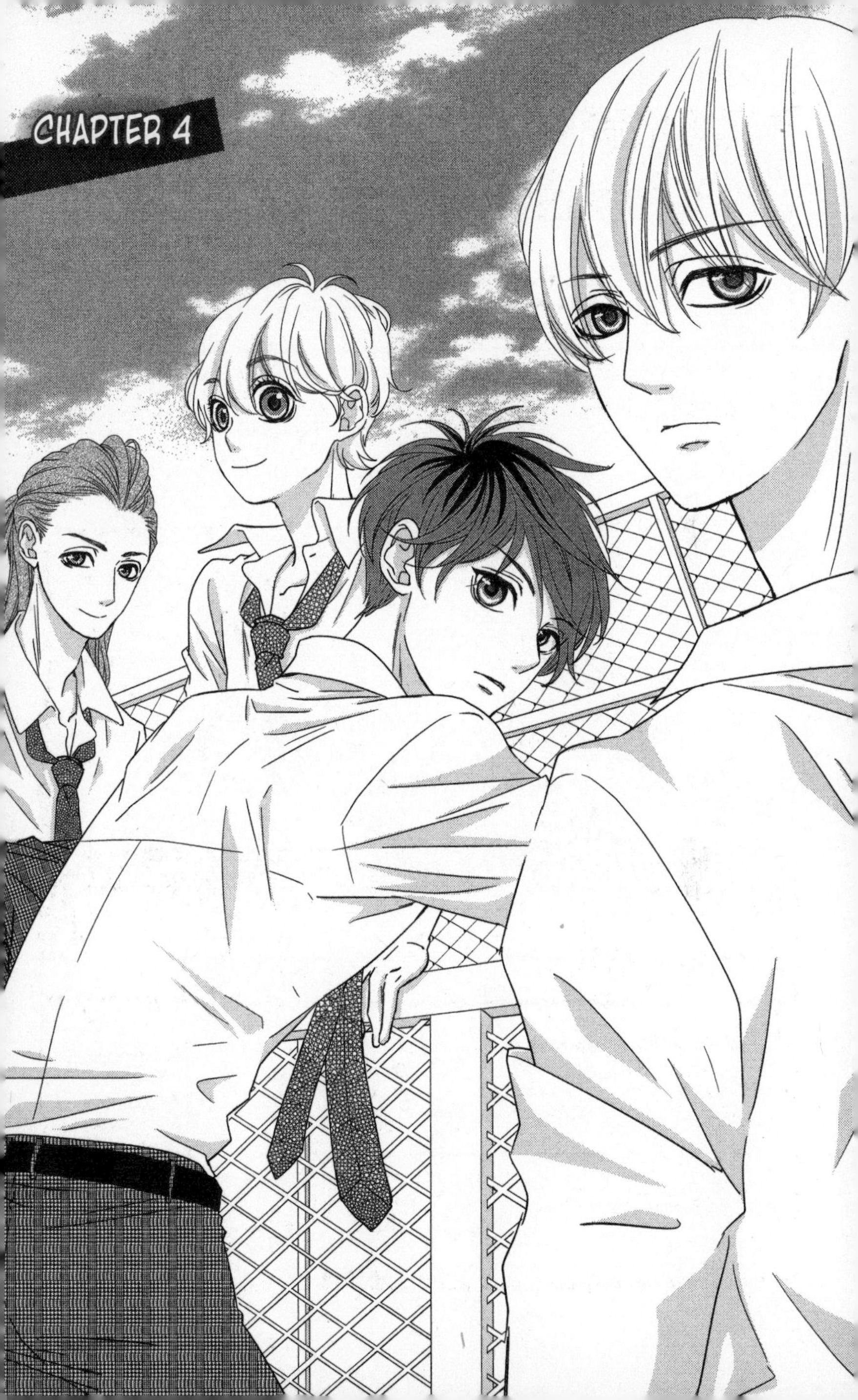
CHAPTER 4

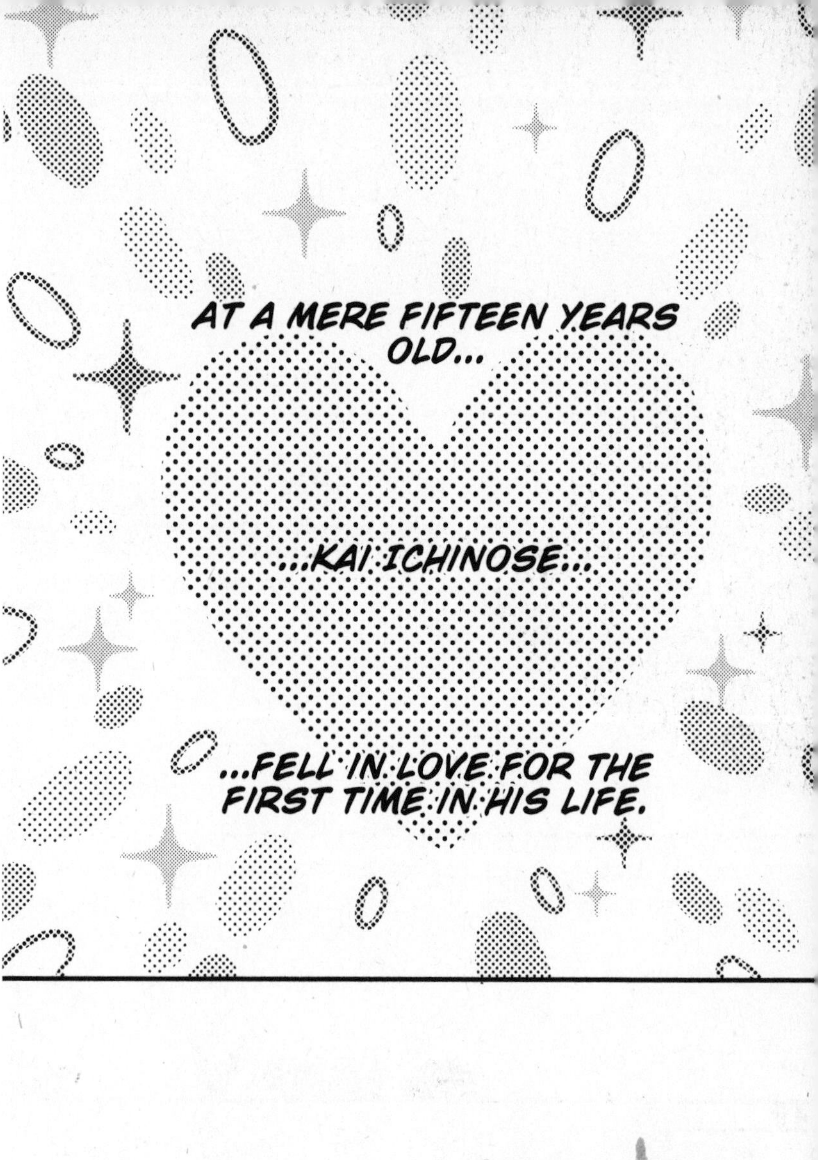
AT A MERE FIFTEEN YEARS OLD...
...KAI ICHINOSE...
...FELL IN LOVE FOR THE FIRST TIME IN HIS LIFE.

hatsu haru

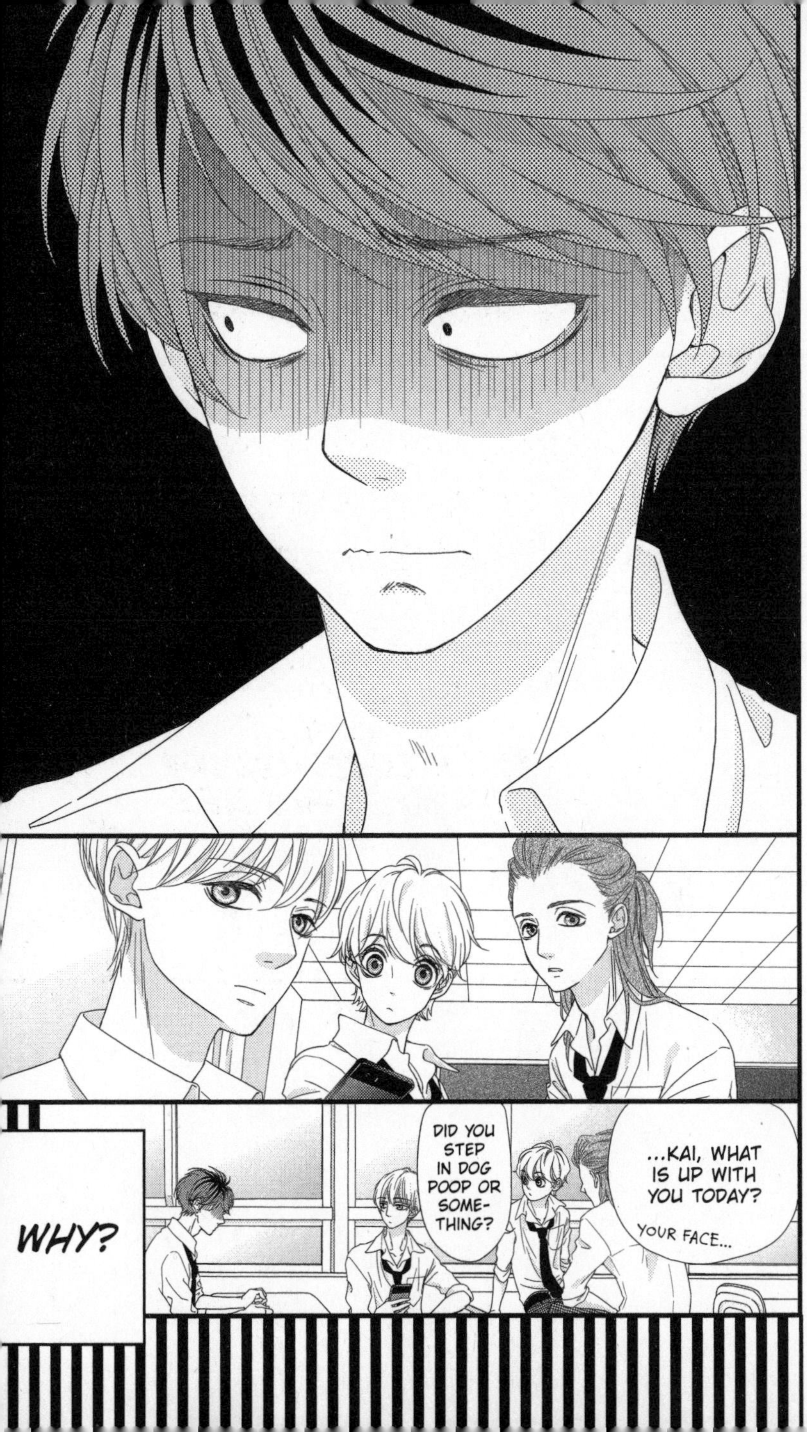
...KAI, WHAT IS UP WITH YOU TODAY?
YOUR FACE...
DID YOU STEP IN DOG POOP OR SOME-THING?
WHY?

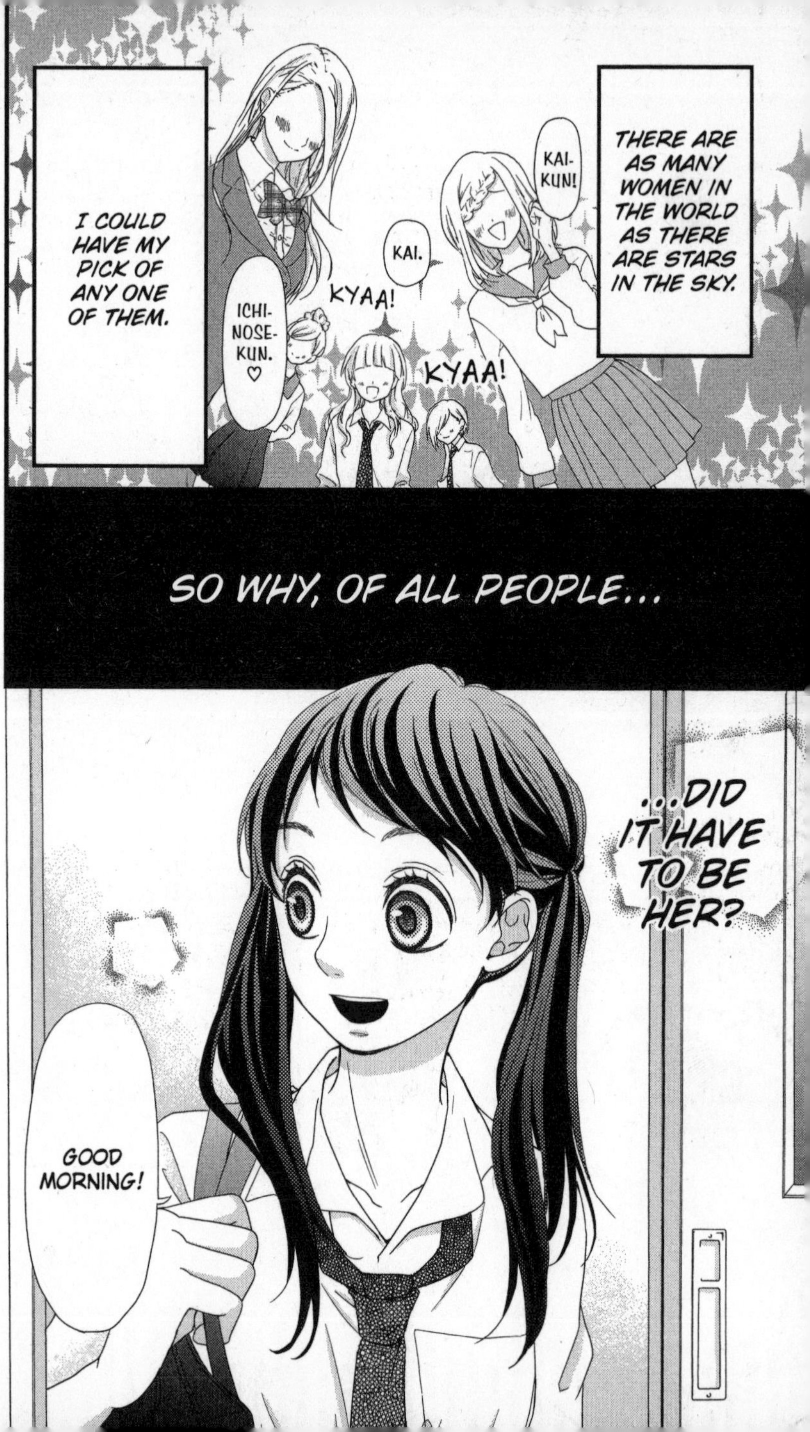
THERE ARE AS MANY WOMEN IN THE WORLD AS THERE ARE STARS IN THE SKY.
KAI-KUN!
KAI.
KYAA!
KYAA!
ICHI-NOSE-KUN. ♡
I COULD HAVE MY PICK OF ANY ONE OF THEM.
SO WHY, OF ALL PEOPLE...
...DID IT HAVE TO BE HER?
GOOD MORNING!

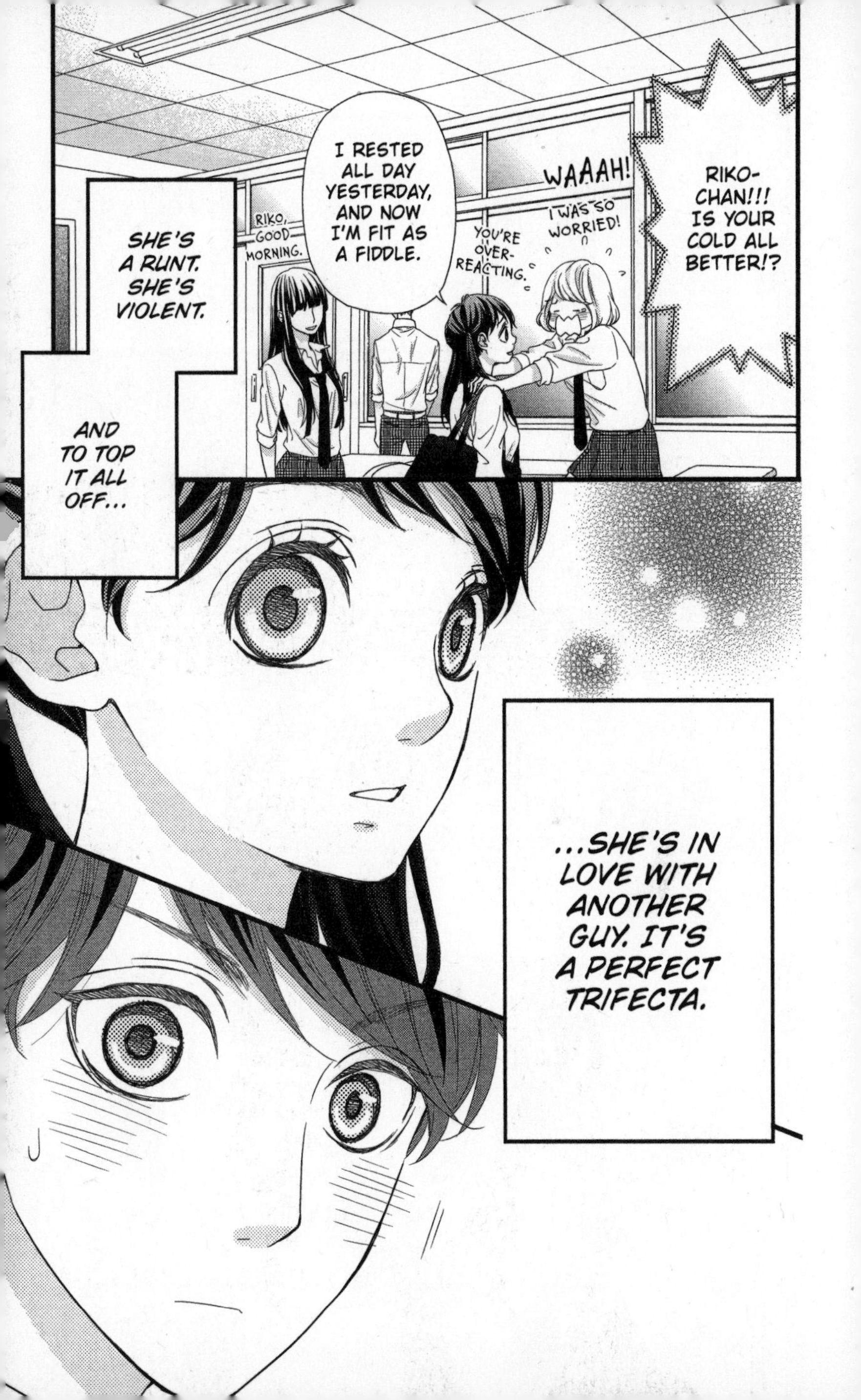
RIKO-CHAN!!! IS YOUR COLD ALL BETTER!?
WAAAH!
I WAS SO WORRIED!
YOU'RE OVER-REACTING.
I RESTED ALL DAY YESTERDAY, AND NOW I'M FIT AS A FIDDLE.
RIKO, GOOD MORNING.
SHE'S A RUNT. SHE'S VIOLENT.
AND TO TOP IT ALL OFF...
...SHE'S IN LOVE WITH ANOTHER GUY. IT'S A PERFECT TRIFECTA.

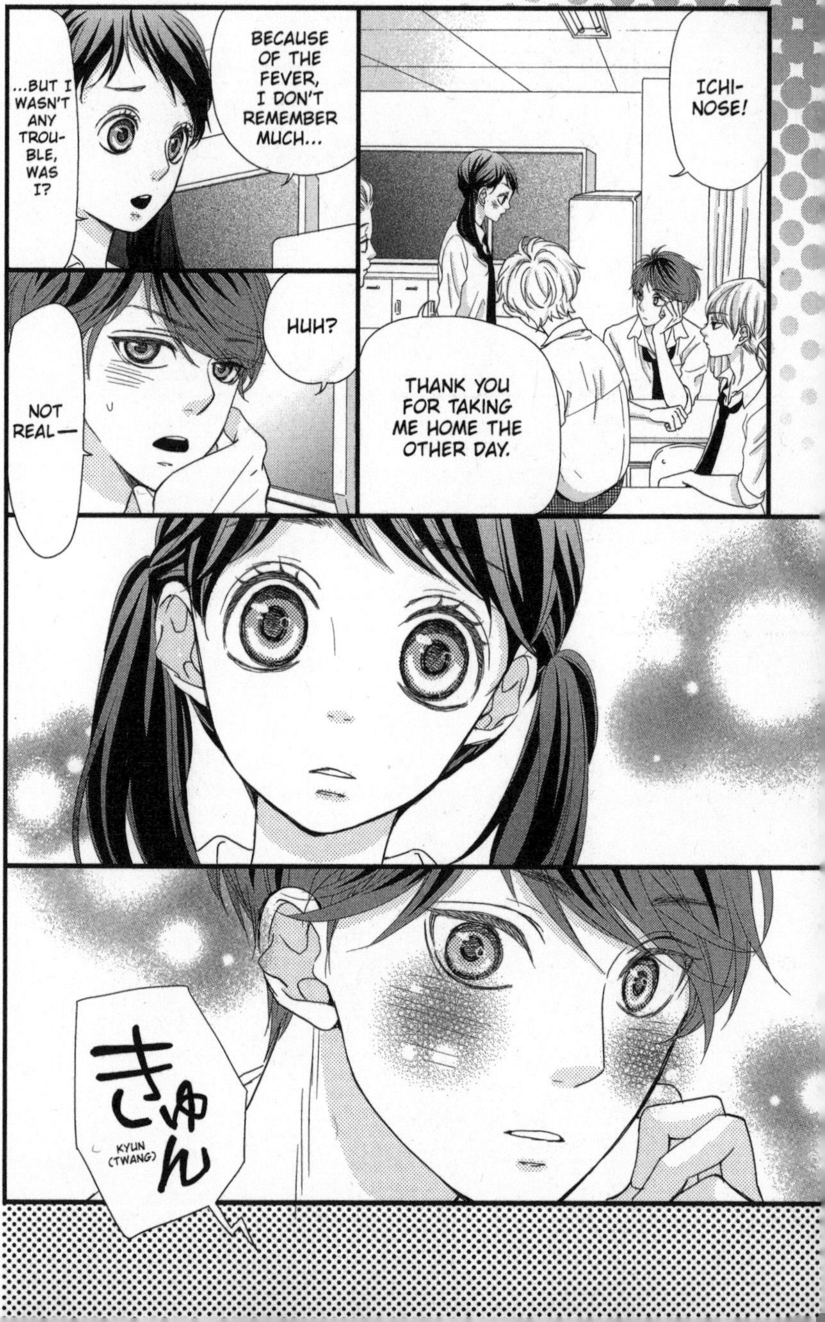
ICHI-NOSE!
THANK YOU FOR TAKING ME HOME THE OTHER DAY.
BECAUSE OF THE FEVER, I DON'T REMEMBER MUCH...
...BUT I WASN'T ANY TROUBLE, WAS I?
HUH?
NOT REAL—
きゅん
KYUN (TWANG)

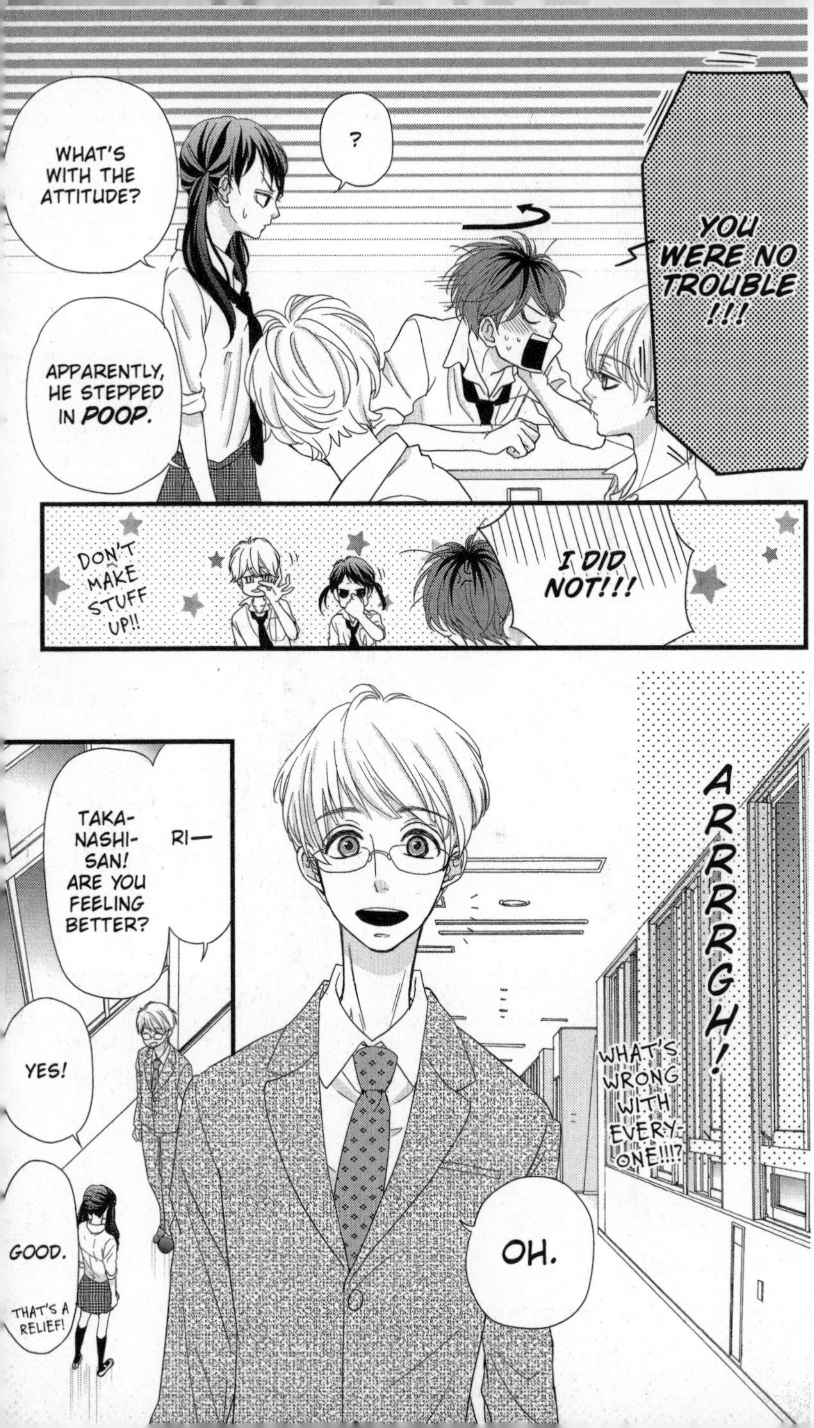
YOU WERE NO TROUBLE!!!
?
WHAT'S WITH THE ATTITUDE?
APPARENTLY, HE STEPPED IN POOP.
I DID NOT!!!
DON'T MAKE STUFF UP!!
ARRRRGH!
WHAT'S WRONG WITH EVERYONE!!!?
OH.
RI—
TAKA-NASHI-SAN! ARE YOU FEELING BETTER?
YES!
GOOD.
THAT'S A RELIEF!

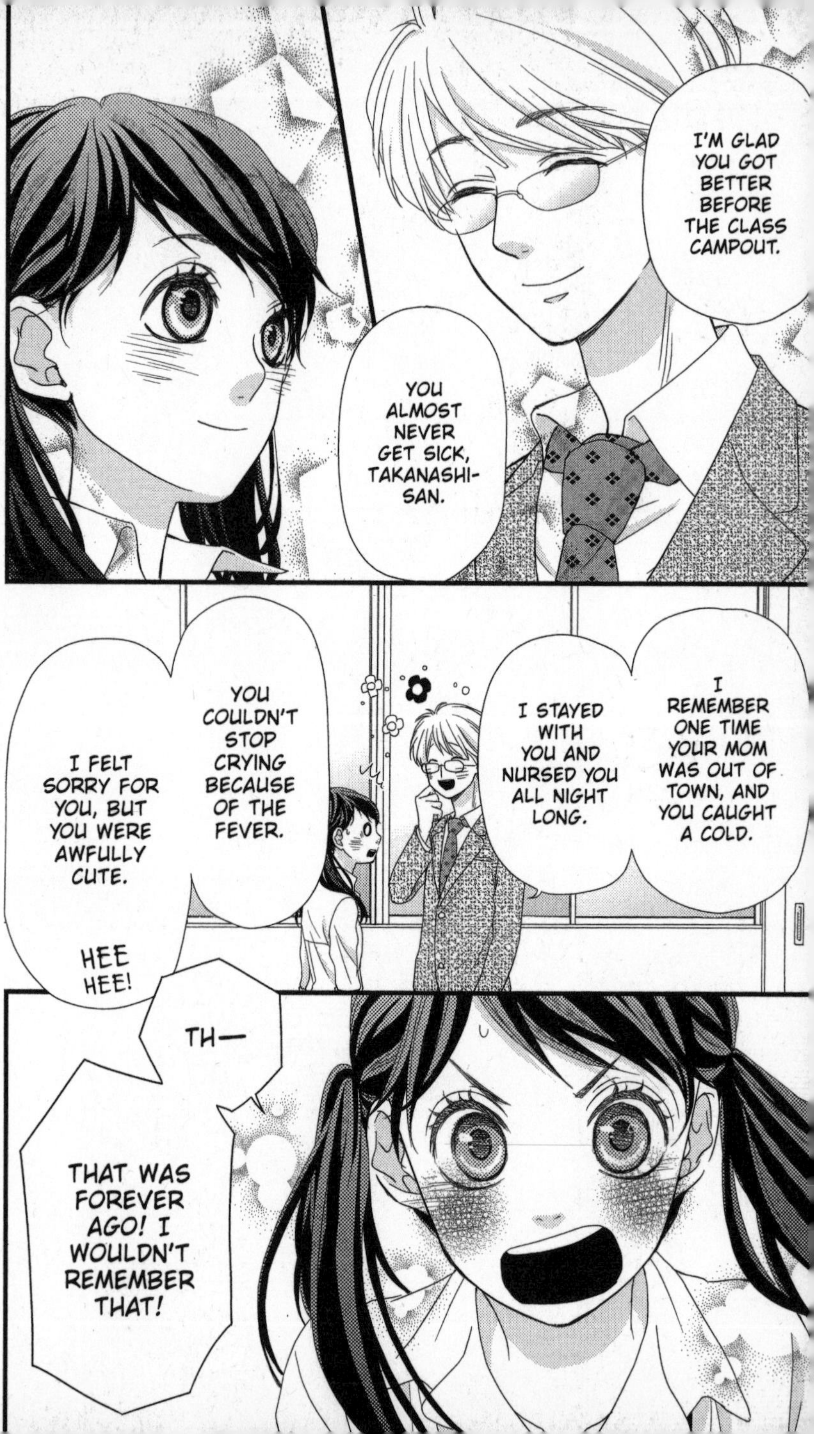
I'M GLAD YOU GOT BETTER BEFORE THE CLASS CAMPOUT.
YOU ALMOST NEVER GET SICK, TAKANASHI-SAN.
I REMEMBER ONE TIME YOUR MOM WAS OUT OF TOWN, AND YOU CAUGHT A COLD.
I STAYED WITH YOU AND NURSED YOU ALL NIGHT LONG.
YOU COULDN'T STOP CRYING BECAUSE OF THE FEVER.
I FELT SORRY FOR YOU, BUT YOU WERE AWFULLY CUTE.
HEE HEE!
TH—
THAT WAS FOREVER AGO! I WOULDN'T REMEMBER THAT!

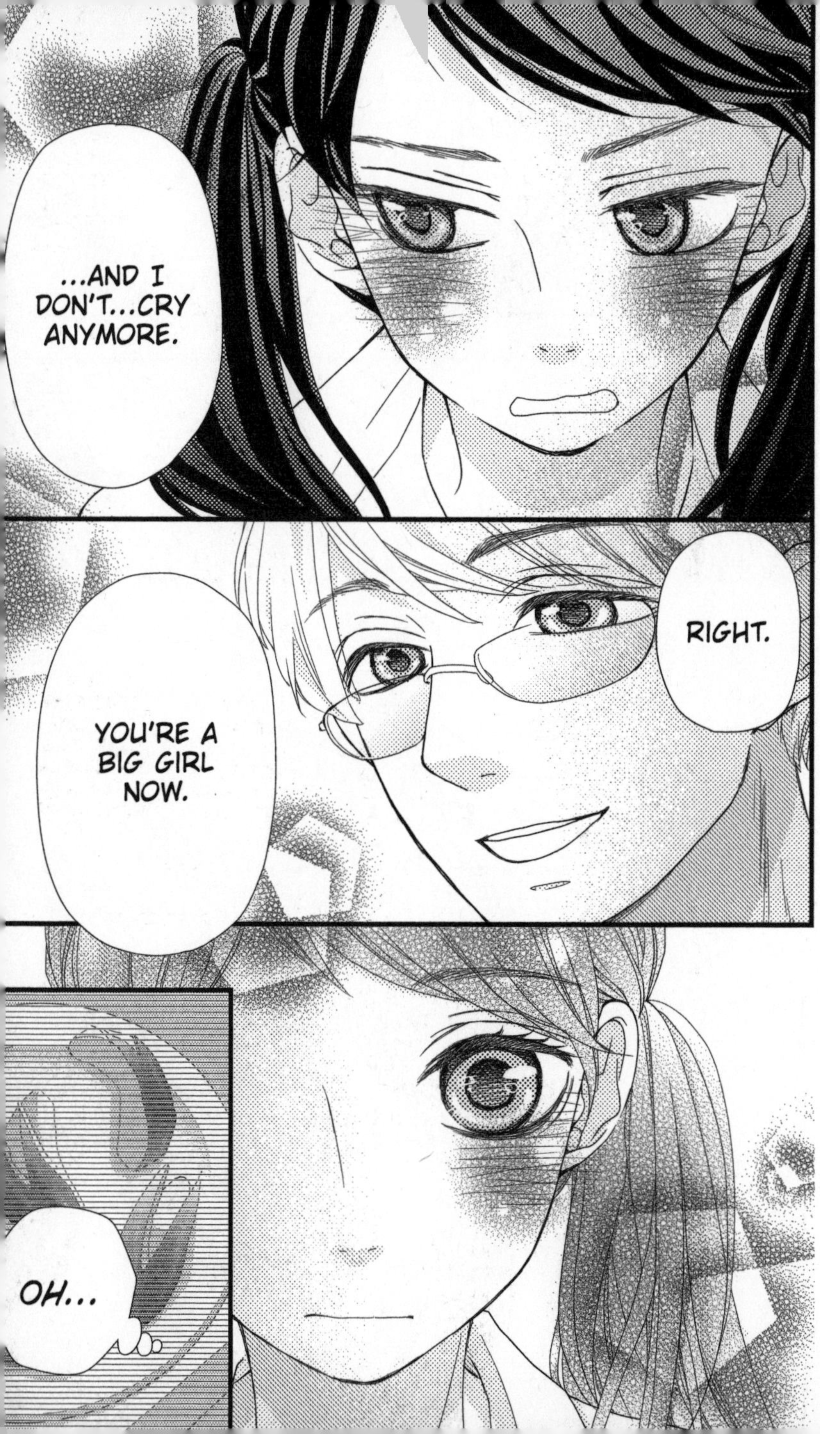
...AND I DON'T...CRY ANYMORE.
RIGHT.
YOU'RE A BIG GIRL NOW.
OH...

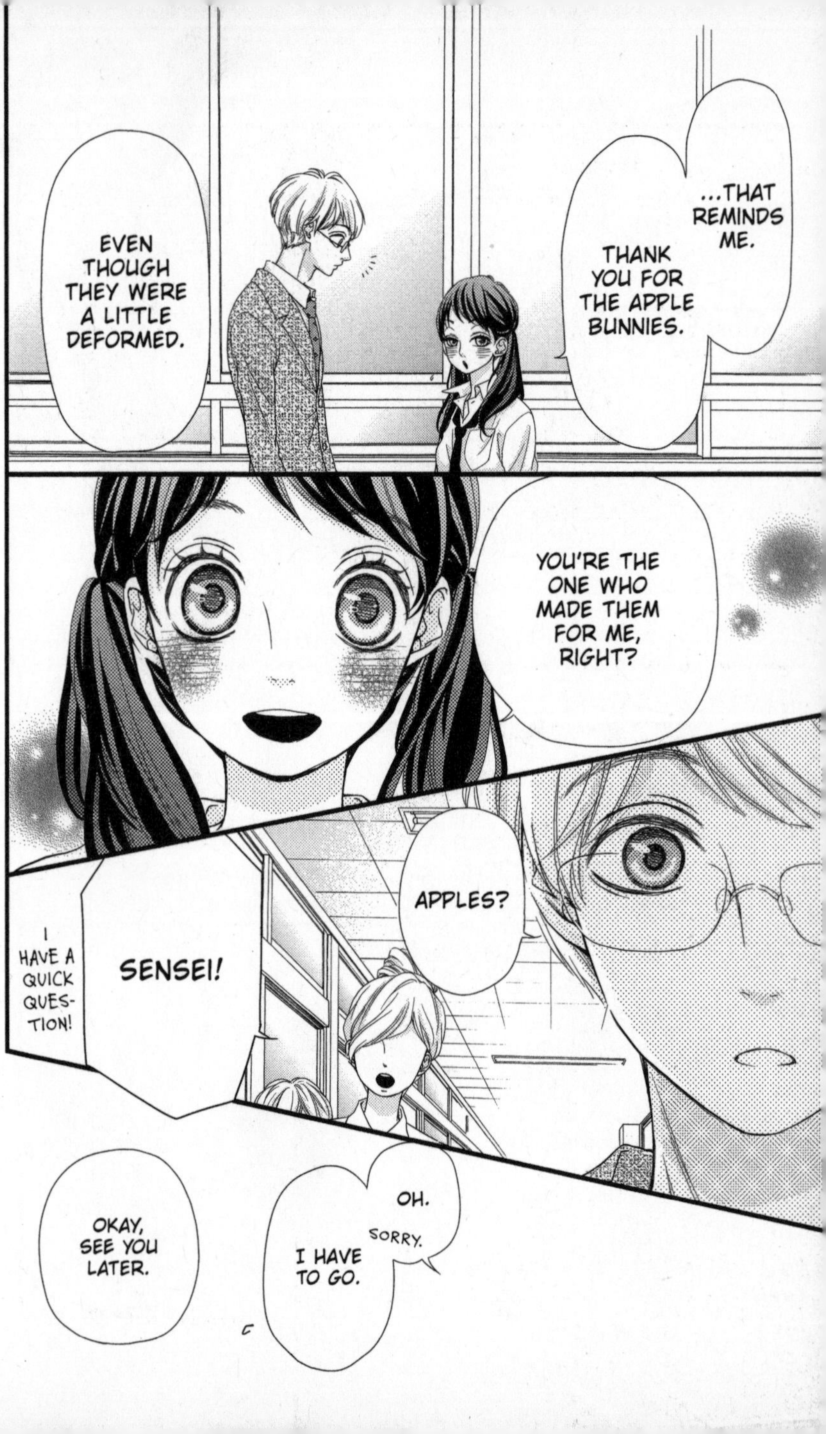

...THAT REMINDS ME.
THANK YOU FOR THE APPLE BUNNIES.
EVEN THOUGH THEY WERE A LITTLE DEFORMED.
YOU'RE THE ONE WHO MADE THEM FOR ME, RIGHT?
APPLES?
SENSEI!
I HAVE A QUICK QUES-TION!
OH.
SORRY.
I HAVE TO GO.
OKAY, SEE YOU LATER.

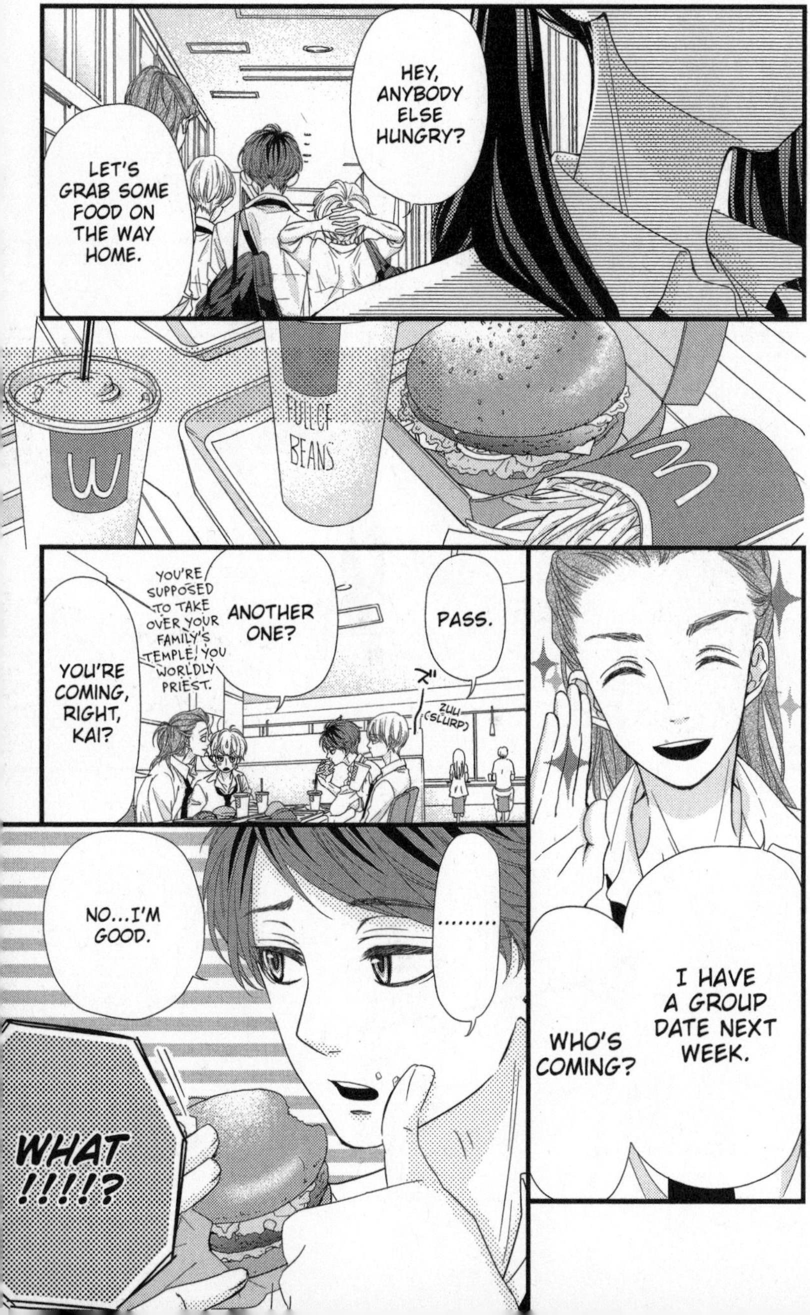
HEY, ANYBODY ELSE HUNGRY?
LET'S GRAB SOME FOOD ON THE WAY HOME.
FULL OF BEANS
I HAVE A GROUP DATE NEXT WEEK.
WHO'S COMING?
PASS.
ズ"
ZUU (SLURP)
ANOTHER ONE?
YOU'RE SUPPOSED TO TAKE OVER YOUR FAMILY'S TEMPLE, YOU WORLDLY PRIEST.
YOU'RE COMING, RIGHT, KAI?
....
NO...I'M GOOD.
WHAT!!!!?

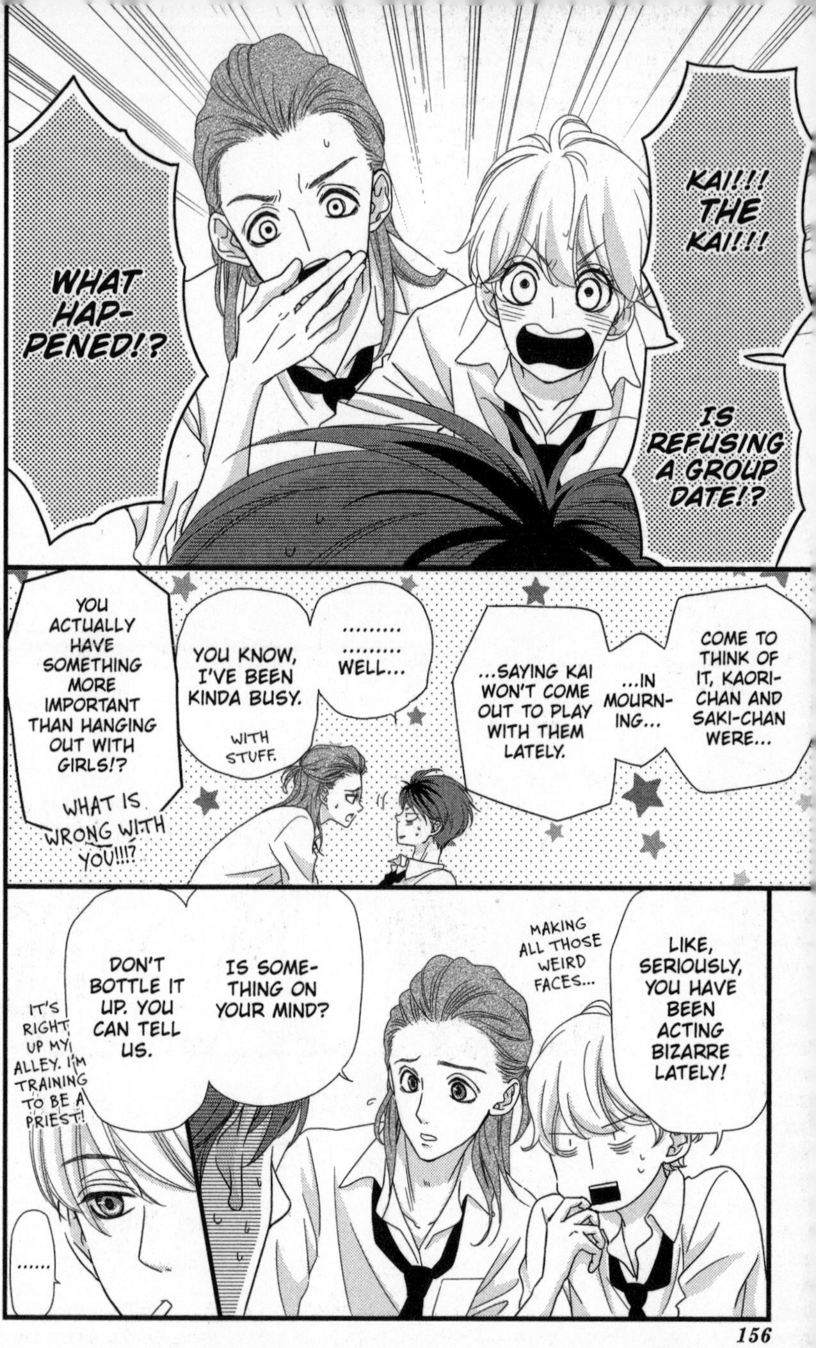
KAI!!! THE KAI!!!
IS REFUSING A GROUP DATE!?
WHAT HAP-PENED!?
COME TO THINK OF IT, KAORI-CHAN AND SAKI-CHAN WERE...
...IN MOURN-ING...
...SAYING KAI WON'T COME OUT TO PLAY WITH THEM LATELY.
.... WELL...
YOU KNOW, I'VE BEEN KINDA BUSY.
WITH STUFF.
YOU ACTUALLY HAVE SOMETHING MORE IMPORTANT THAN HANGING OUT WITH GIRLS!?
WHAT IS WRONG WITH YOU!!!?
LIKE, SERIOUSLY, YOU HAVE BEEN ACTING BIZARRE LATELY!
MAKING ALL THOSE WEIRD FACES...
IS SOME-THING ON YOUR MIND?
DON'T BOTTLE IT UP. YOU CAN TELL US.
IT'S RIGHT UP MY ALLEY. I'M TRAINING TO BE A PRIEST!
......

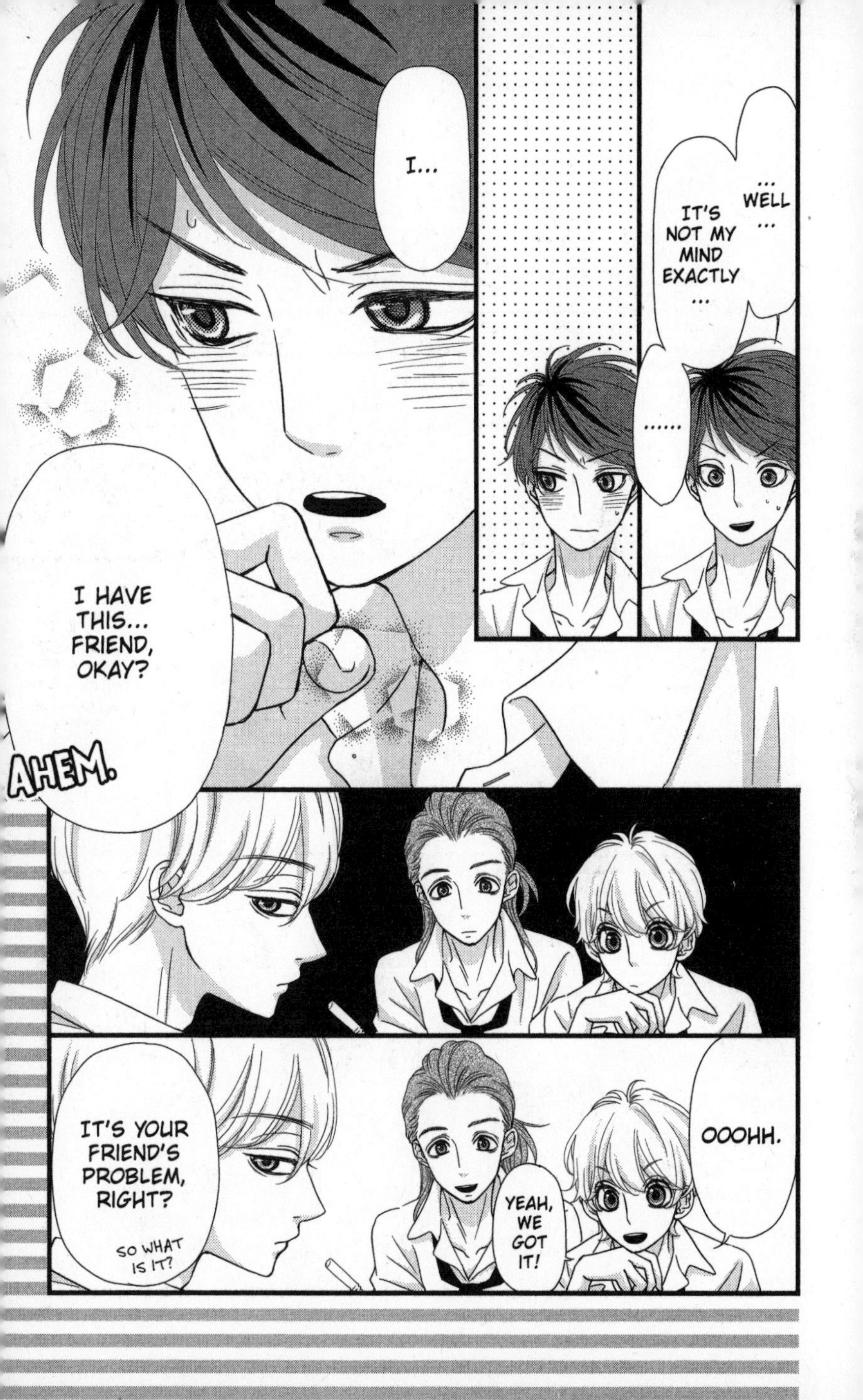
... WELL ...
IT'S NOT MY MIND EXACTLY ...
......
I...
I HAVE THIS... FRIEND, OKAY?
AHEM.
OOOHH.
YEAH, WE GOT IT!
IT'S YOUR FRIEND'S PROBLEM, RIGHT?
SO WHAT IS IT?

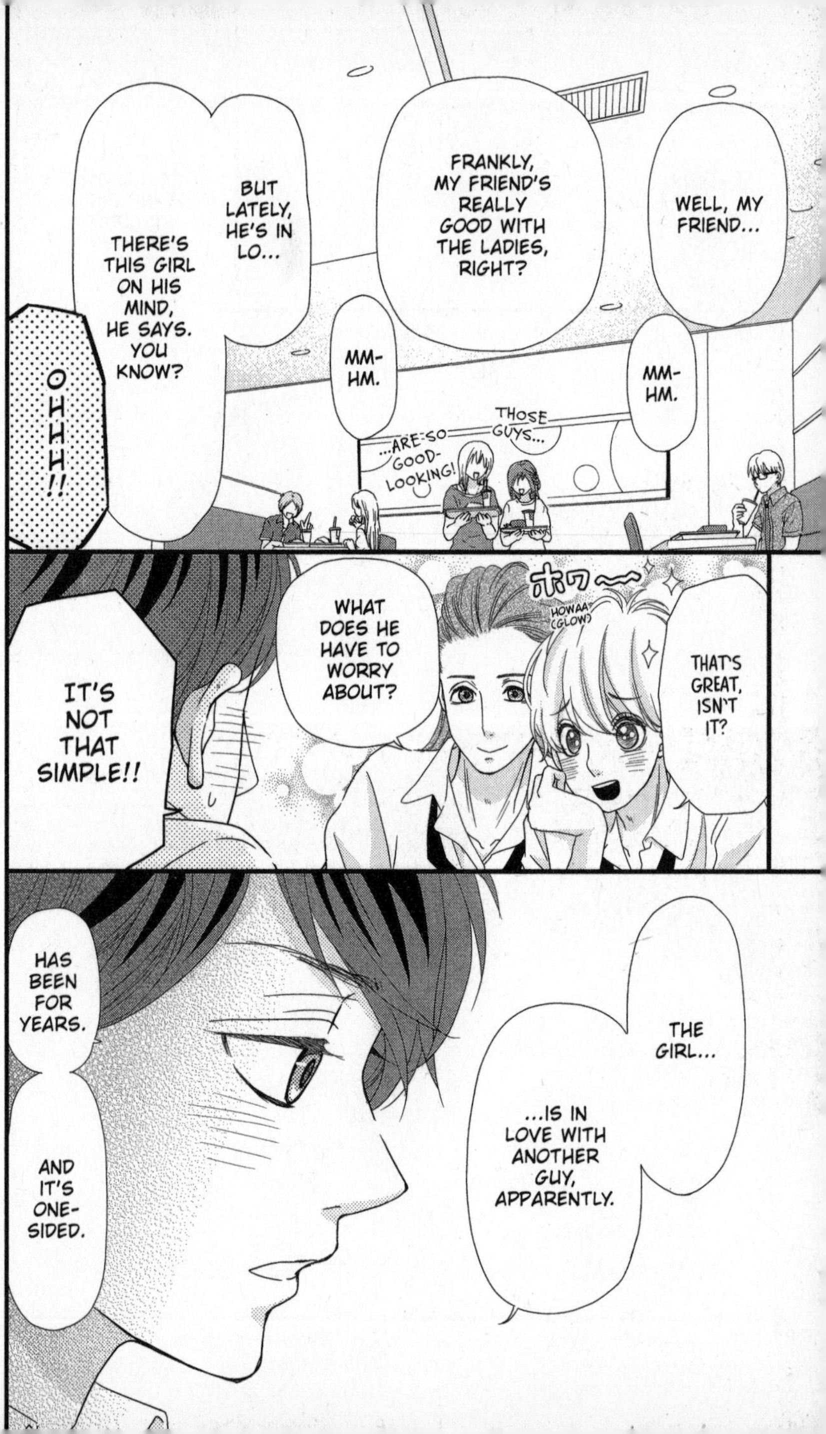
WELL, MY FRIEND...
MM-HM.
FRANKLY, MY FRIEND'S REALLY GOOD WITH THE LADIES, RIGHT?
MM-HM.
BUT LATELY, HE'S IN LO...
THERE'S THIS GIRL ON HIS MIND, HE SAYS. YOU KNOW?
THOSE GUYS...
...ARE SO GOOD-LOOKING!
OHHH!!
ホワ~~
HOWAA~ (GLOW)
THAT'S GREAT, ISN'T IT?
WHAT DOES HE HAVE TO WORRY ABOUT?
IT'S NOT THAT SIMPLE!!
THE GIRL...
...IS IN LOVE WITH ANOTHER GUY, APPARENTLY.
HAS BEEN FOR YEARS.
AND IT'S ONE-SIDED.

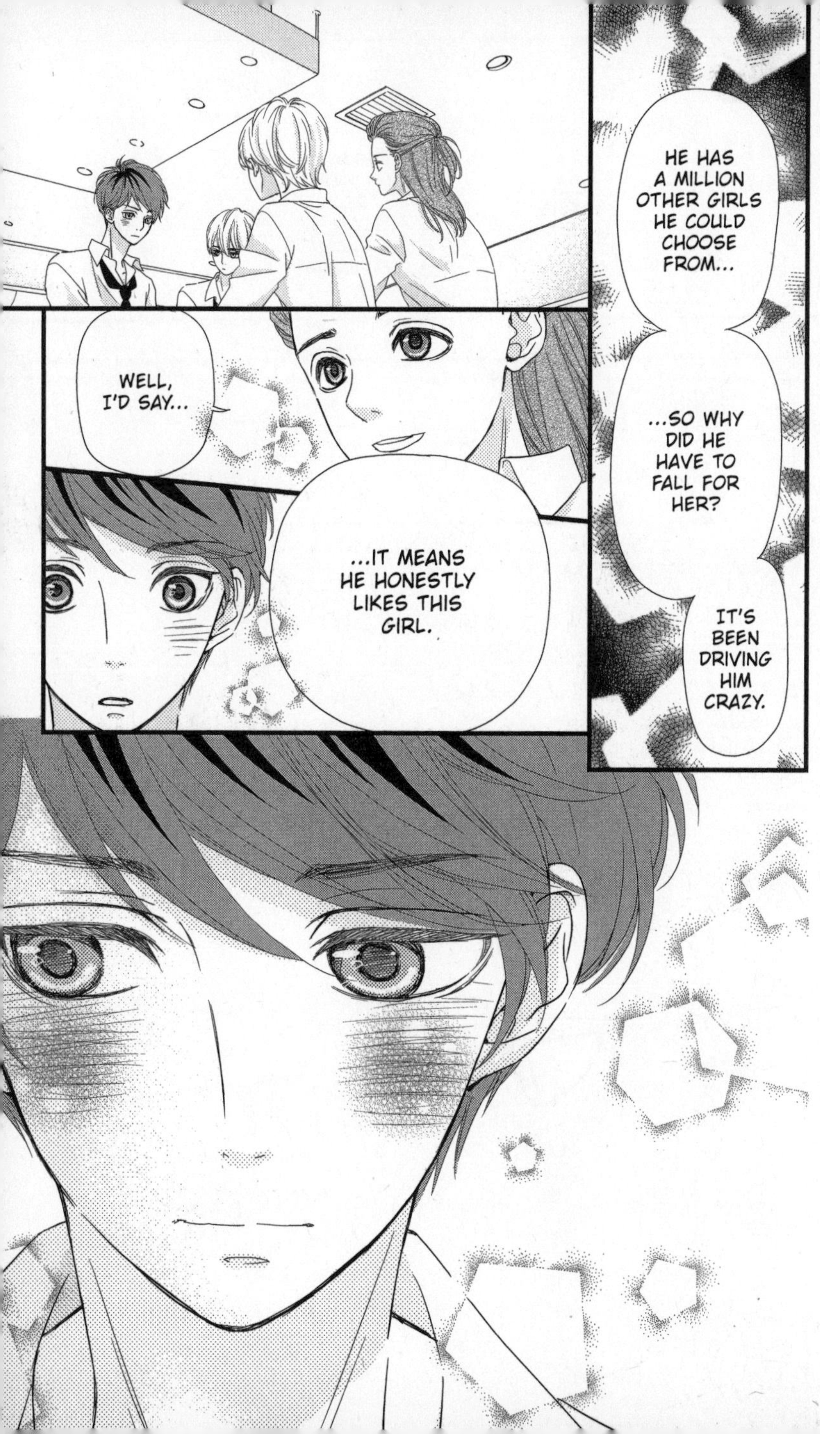
HE HAS A MILLION OTHER GIRLS HE COULD CHOOSE FROM...
...SO WHY DID HE HAVE TO FALL FOR HER?
IT'S BEEN DRIVING HIM CRAZY.
WELL, I'D SAY...
...IT MEANS HE HONESTLY LIKES THIS GIRL.

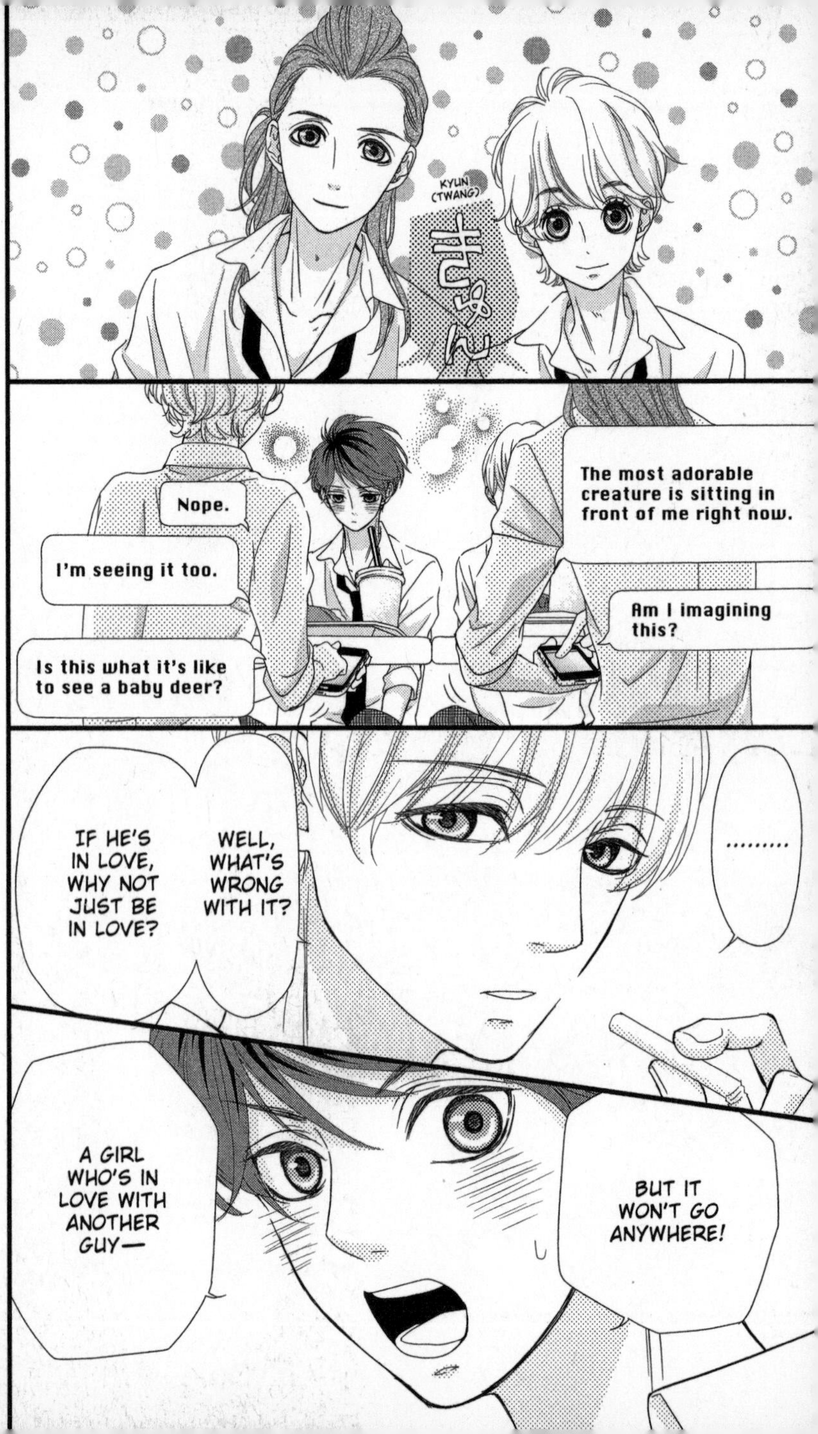
KYUN (TWANG)
きゅん
The most adorable creature is sitting in front of me right now.
Am I imagining this?
Nope.
I'm seeing it too.
Is this what it's like to see a baby deer?
....
WELL, WHAT'S WRONG WITH IT?
IF HE'S IN LOVE, WHY NOT JUST BE IN LOVE?
BUT IT WON'T GO ANYWHERE!
A GIRL WHO'S IN LOVE WITH ANOTHER GUY—

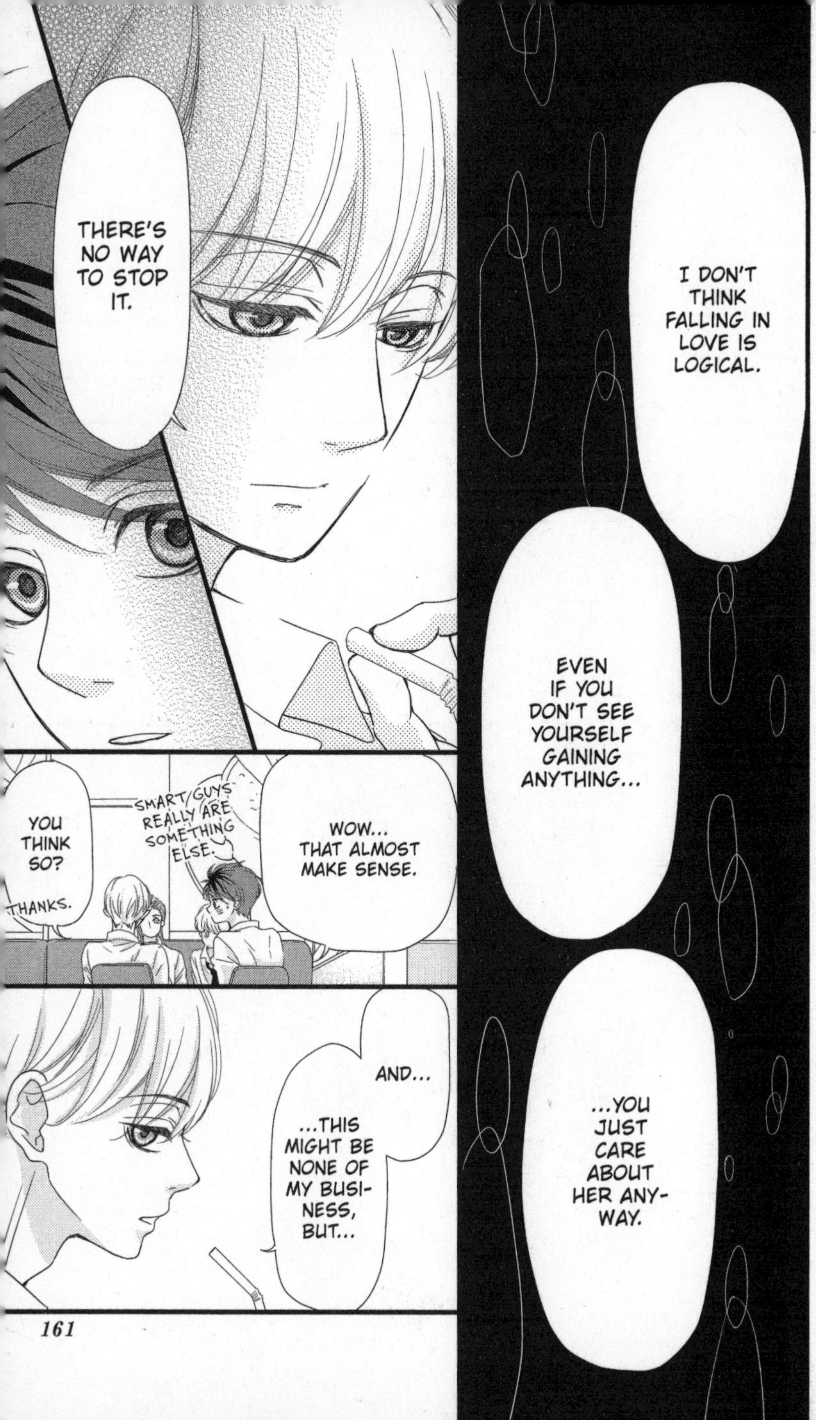
I DON'T THINK FALLING IN LOVE IS LOGICAL.
EVEN IF YOU DON'T SEE YOURSELF GAINING ANYTHING...
...YOU JUST CARE ABOUT HER ANY-WAY.
THERE'S NO WAY TO STOP IT.
WOW... THAT ALMOST MAKE SENSE.
SMART GUYS REALLY ARE SOMETHING ELSE.
YOU THINK SO?
THANKS.
AND...
...THIS MIGHT BE NONE OF MY BUSI-NESS, BUT...

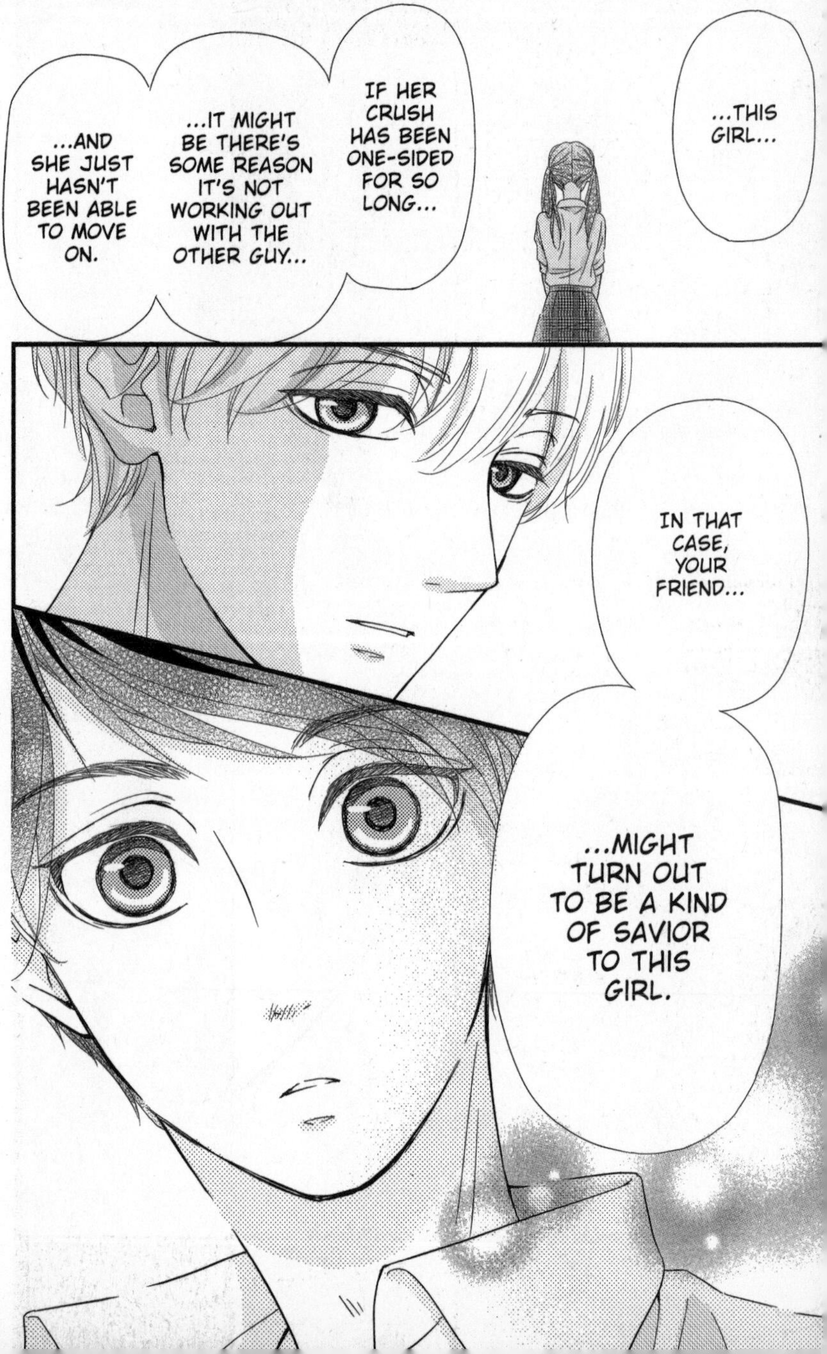
...THIS GIRL...
IF HER CRUSH HAS BEEN ONE-SIDED FOR SO LONG...
...IT MIGHT BE THERE'S SOME REASON IT'S NOT WORKING OUT WITH THE OTHER GUY...
...AND SHE JUST HASN'T BEEN ABLE TO MOVE ON.
IN THAT CASE, YOUR FRIEND...
...MIGHT TURN OUT TO BE A KIND OF SAVIOR TO THIS GIRL.

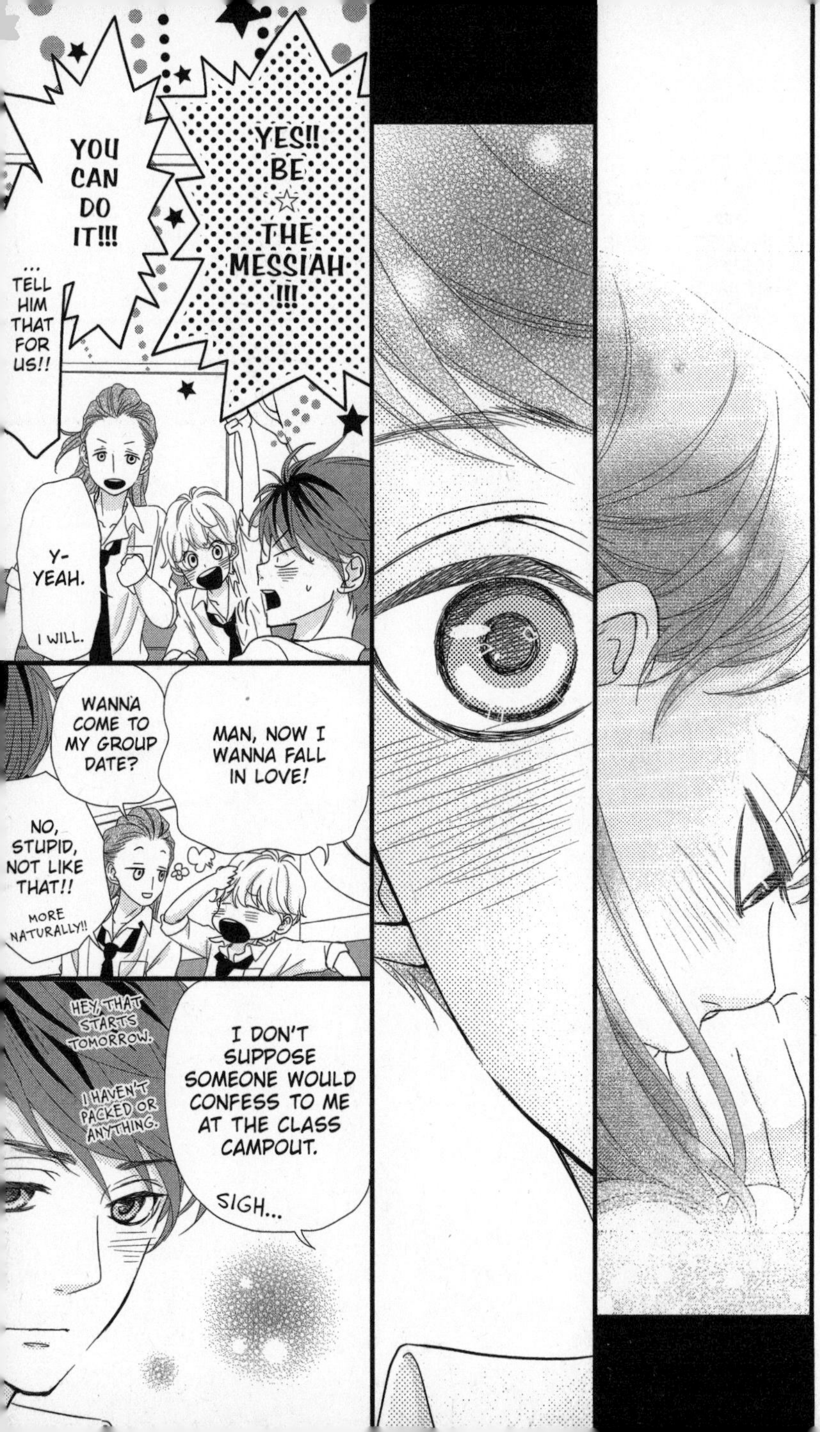
YES!! BE☆THE MESSIAH!!!
YOU CAN DO IT!!!
...TELL HIM THAT FOR US!!
Y-YEAH.
I WILL.
MAN, NOW I WANNA FALL IN LOVE!
WANNA COME TO MY GROUP DATE?
NO, STUPID, NOT LIKE THAT!!
MORE NATURALLY!!
I DON'T SUPPOSE SOMEONE WOULD CONFESS TO ME AT THE CLASS CAMPOUT.
SIGH...
HEY, THAT STARTS TOMORROW.
I HAVEN'T PACKED OR ANYTHING.

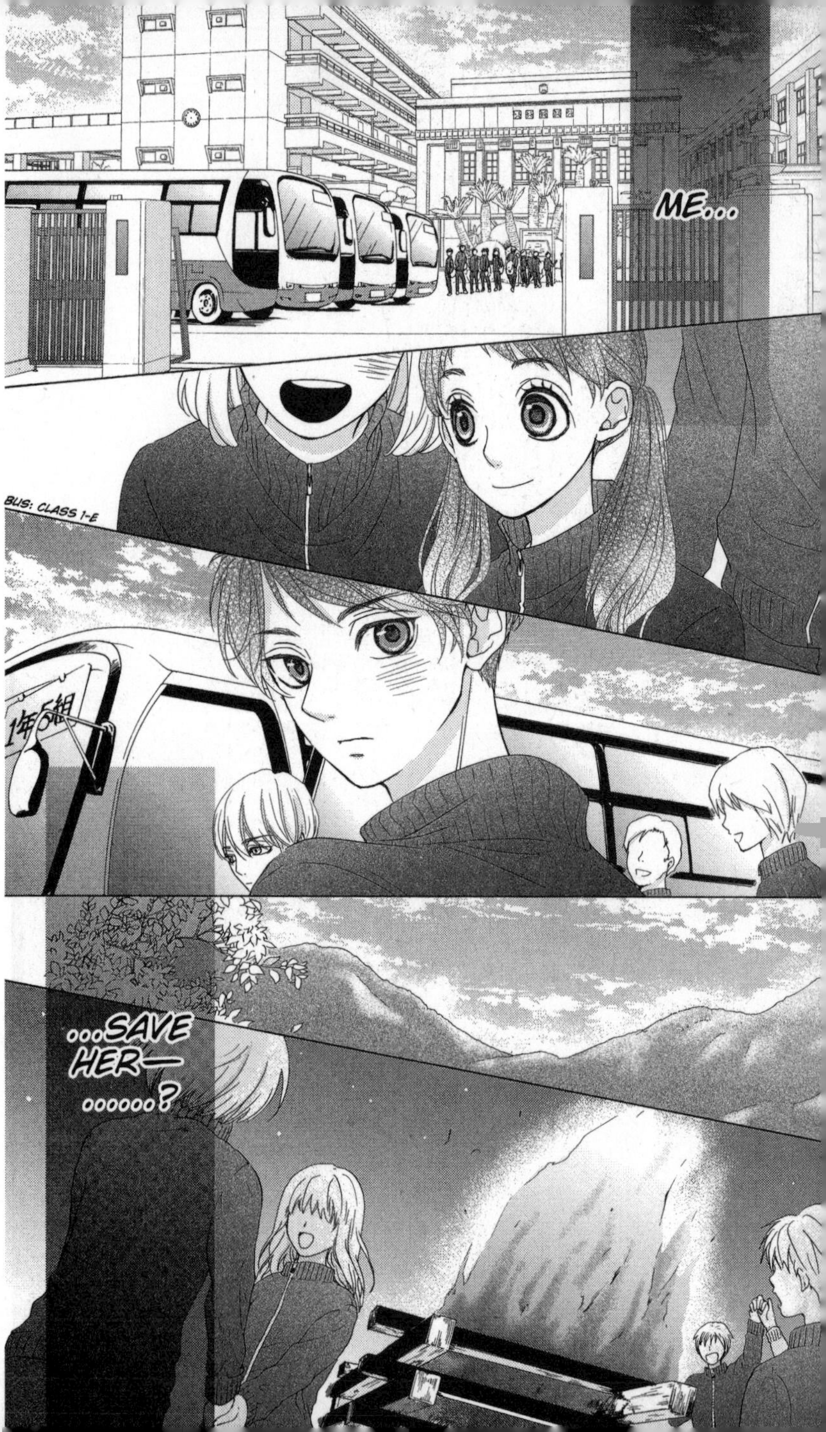
ME...
BUS: CLASS 1-E
...SAVE HER—
......?

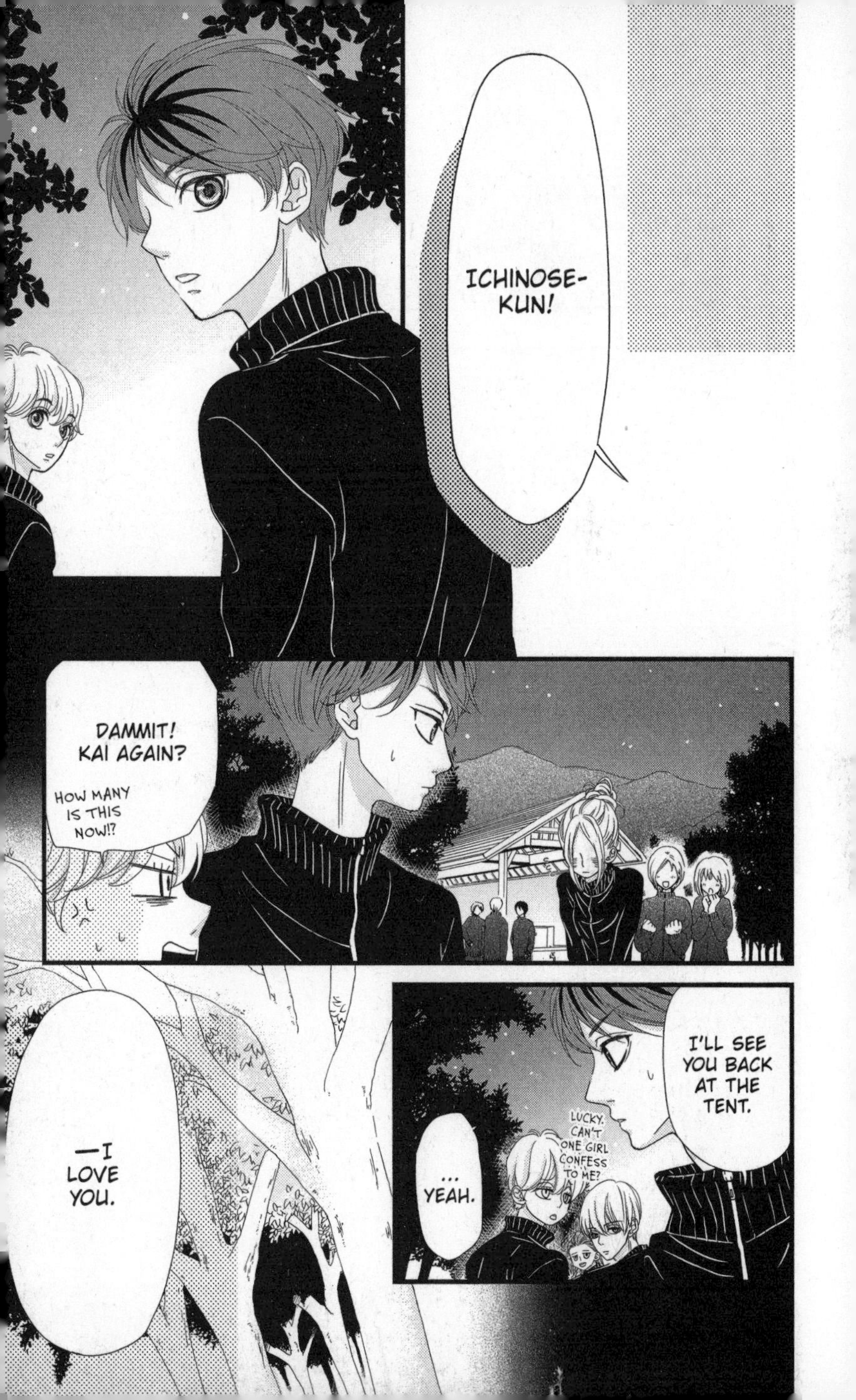
ICHINOSE-KUN!
DAMMIT! KAI AGAIN?
HOW MANY IS THIS NOW!?
I'LL SEE YOU BACK AT THE TENT.
LUCKY. CAN'T ONE GIRL CONFESS TO ME?
...YEAH.
—I LOVE YOU.

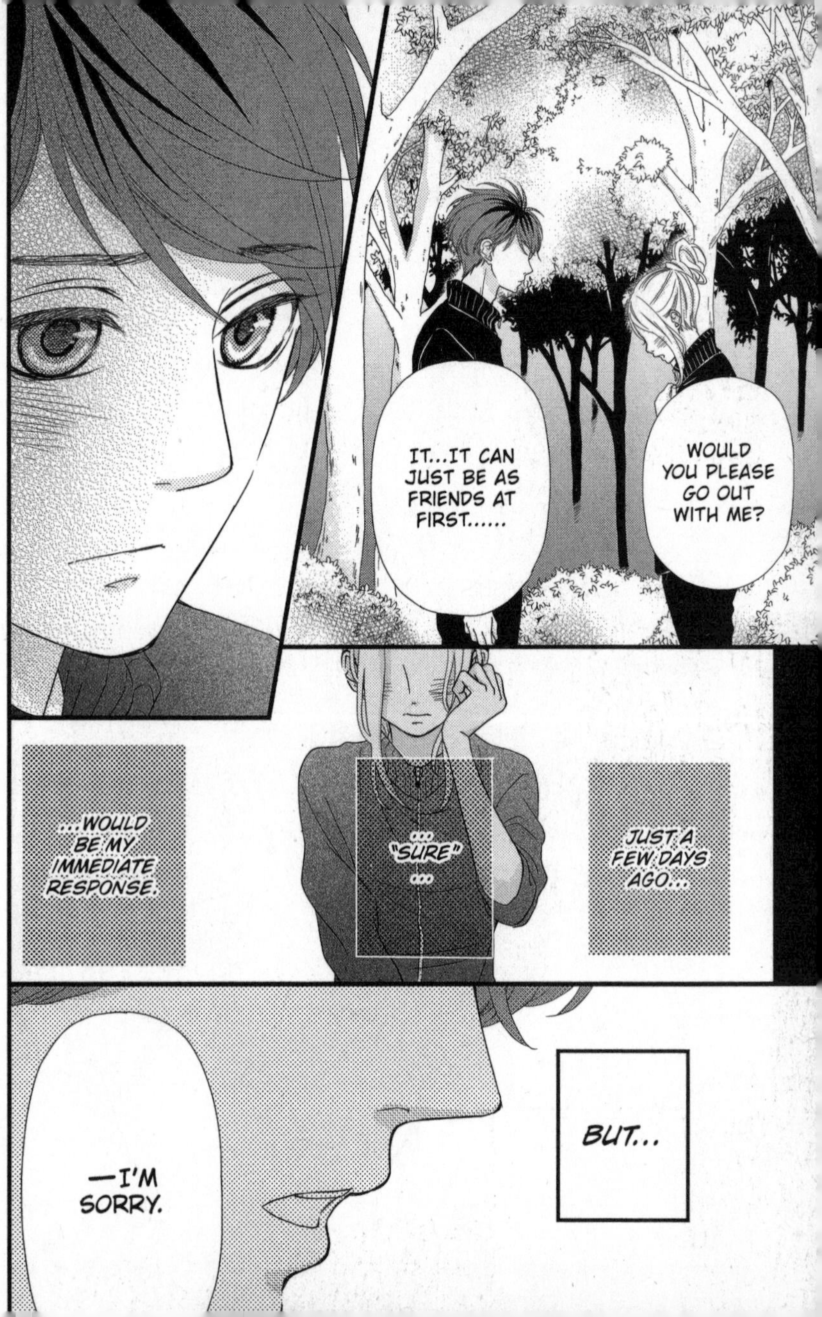
WOULD YOU PLEASE GO OUT WITH ME?
IT...IT CAN JUST BE AS FRIENDS AT FIRST......
JUST A FEW DAYS AGO...
"SURE"
...WOULD BE MY IMMEDIATE RESPONSE.
BUT...
—I'M SORRY.

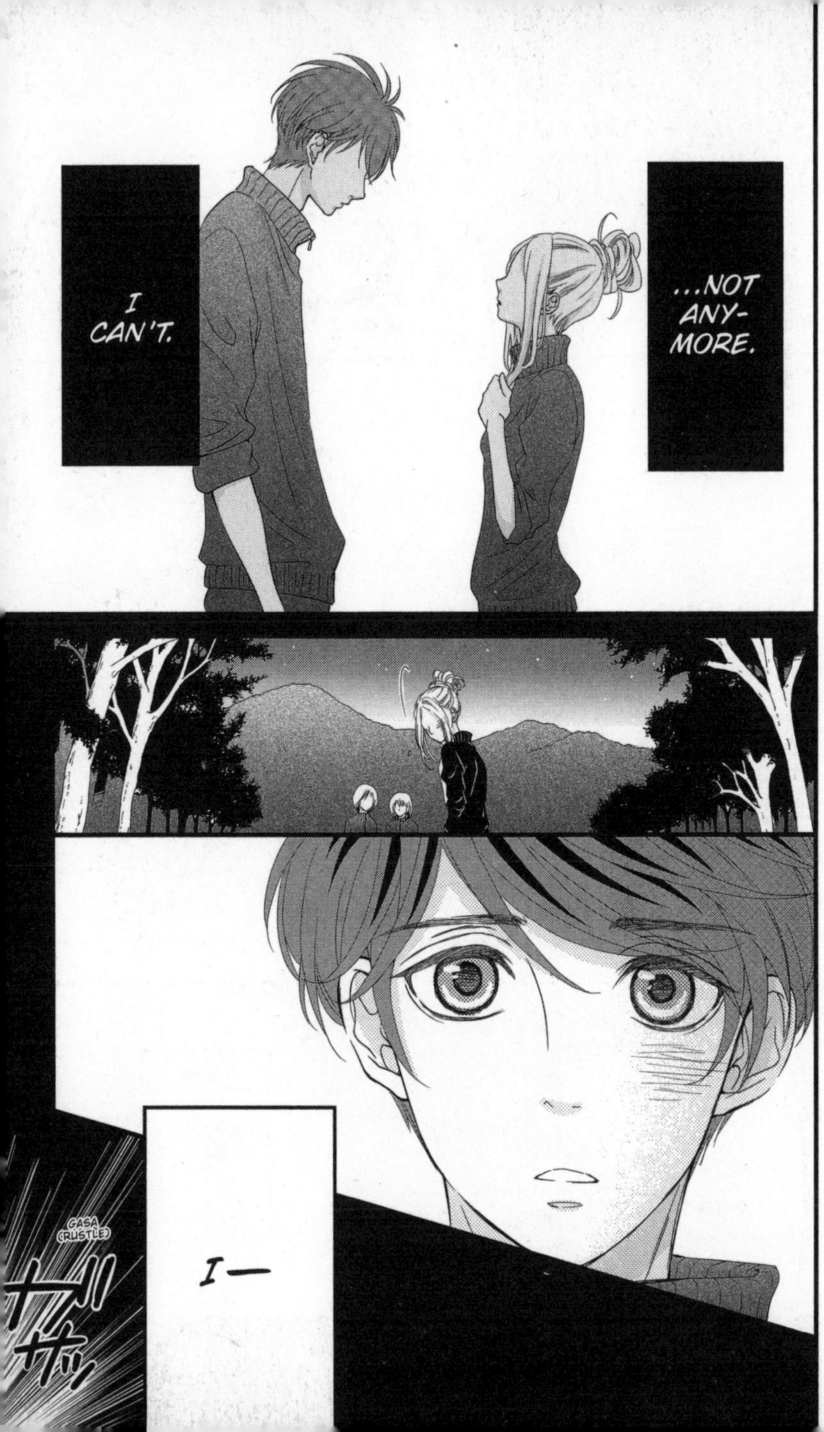
...NOT ANY-MORE.
I CAN'T.
GASA (RUSTLE)
I—

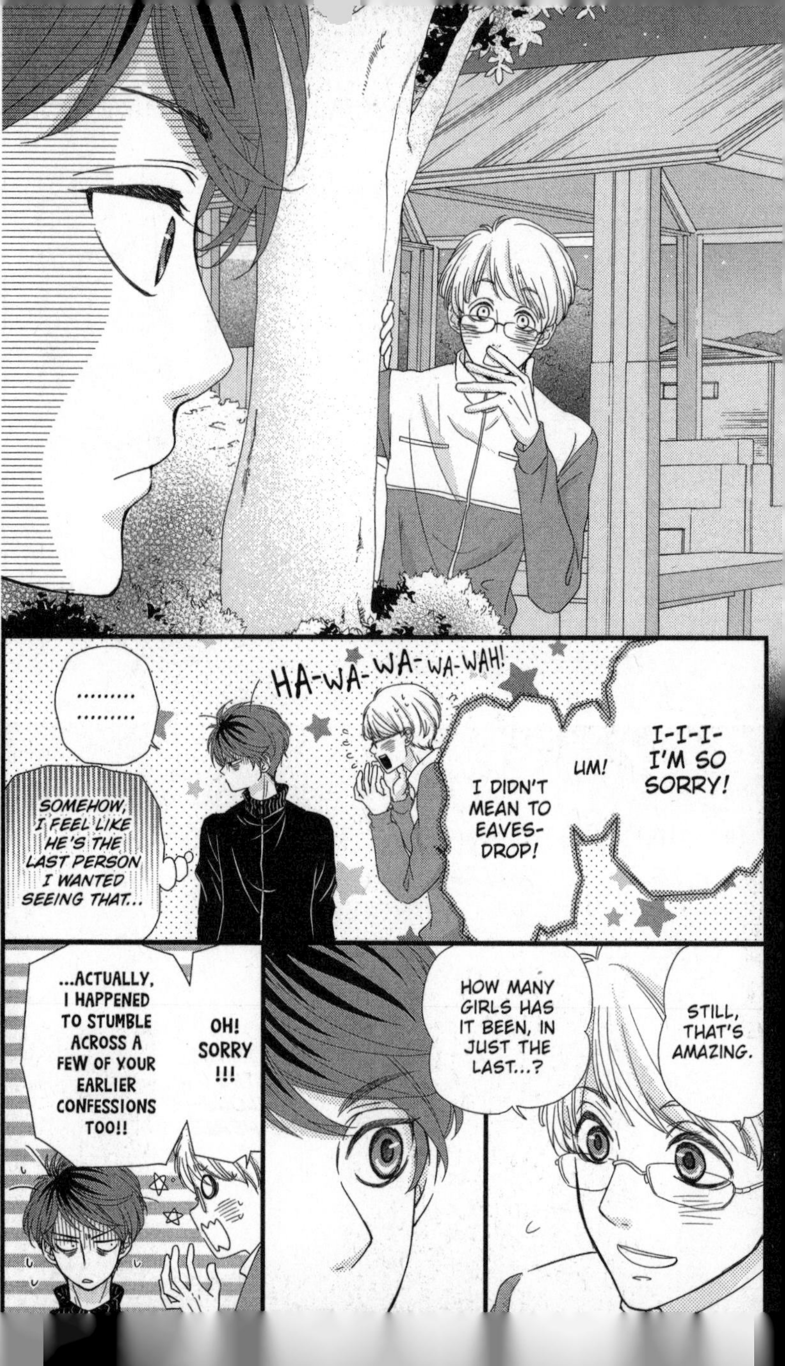
I-I-I- I'M SO SORRY!
UM!
I DIDN'T MEAN TO EAVES-DROP!
HA-WA-WA-WA-WAH!
....
....
SOMEHOW, I FEEL LIKE HE'S THE LAST PERSON I WANTED SEEING THAT...
STILL, THAT'S AMAZING.
HOW MANY GIRLS HAS IT BEEN, IN JUST THE LAST...?
OH! SORRY!!!
...ACTUALLY, I HAPPENED TO STUMBLE ACROSS A FEW OF YOUR EARLIER CONFESSIONS TOO!!

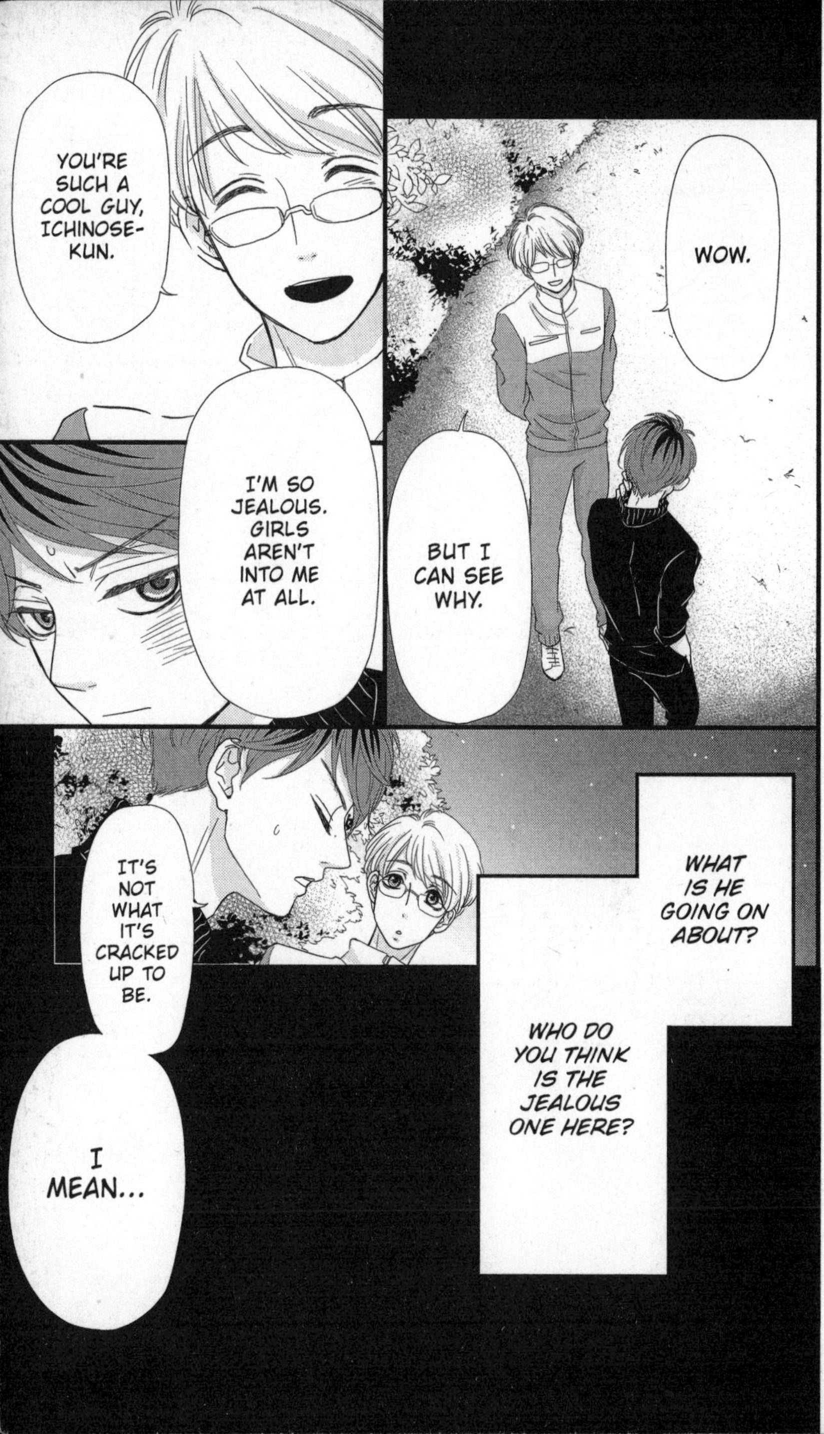
WOW.
YOU'RE SUCH A COOL GUY, ICHINOSE-KUN.
I'M SO JEALOUS. GIRLS AREN'T INTO ME AT ALL.
BUT I CAN SEE WHY.
WHAT IS HE GOING ON ABOUT?
WHO DO YOU THINK IS THE JEALOUS ONE HERE?
IT'S NOT WHAT IT'S CRACKED UP TO BE.
I MEAN...

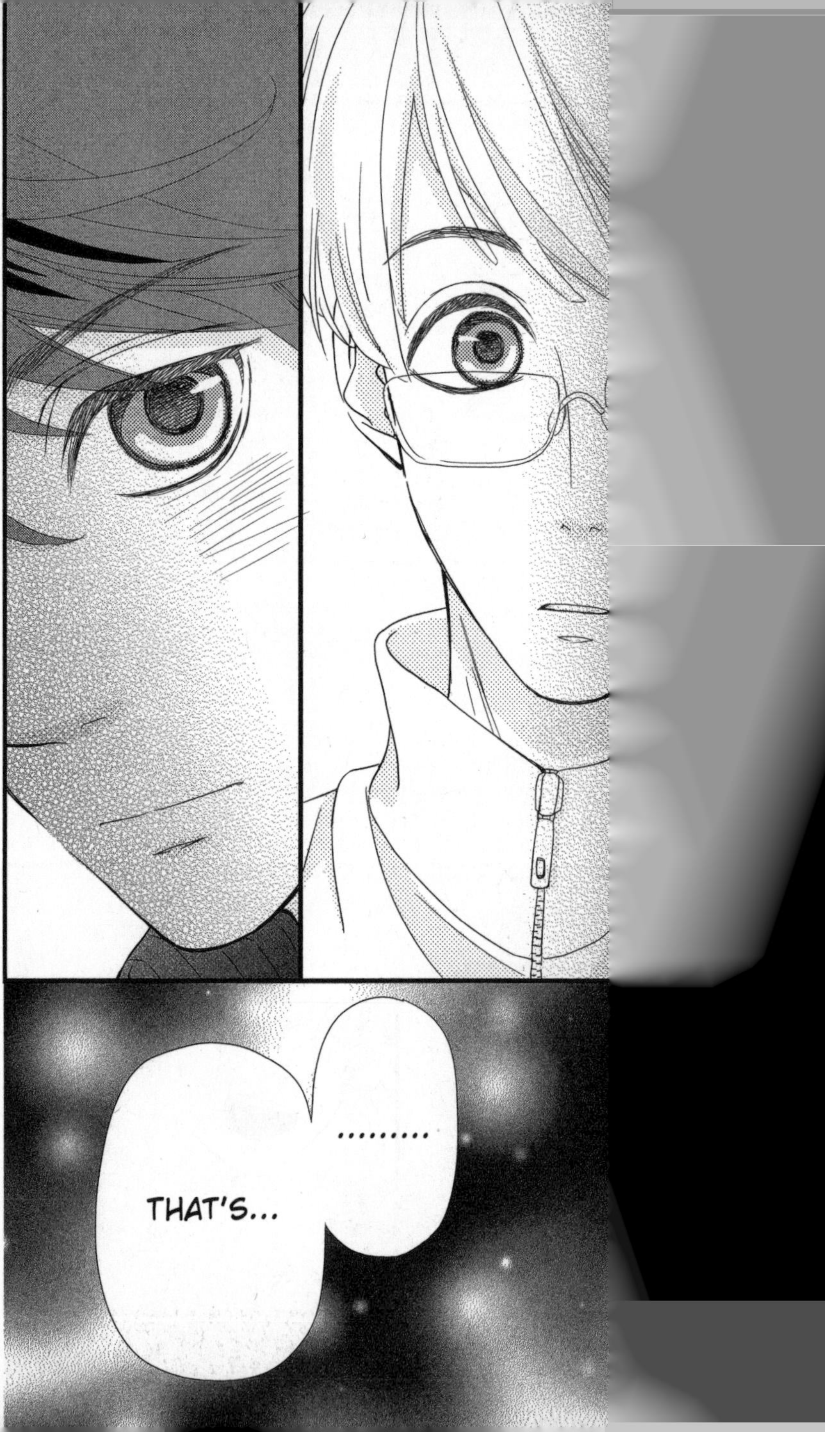
....
THAT'S...

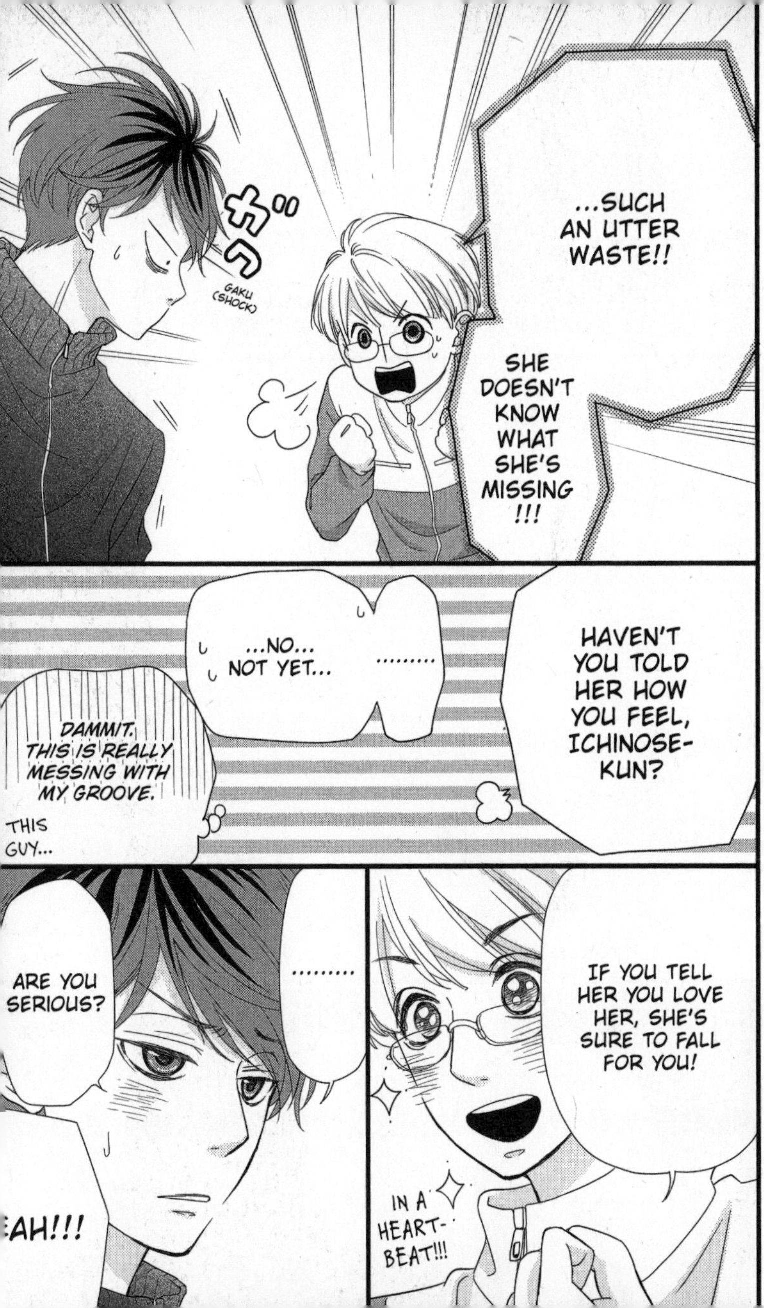
...SUCH AN UTTER WASTE!!
SHE DOESN'T KNOW WHAT SHE'S MISSING!!!
GAKU (SHOCK)
HAVEN'T YOU TOLD HER HOW YOU FEEL, ICHINOSE-KUN?
....
...NO... NOT YET...
DAMMIT. THIS IS REALLY MESSING WITH MY GROOVE.
THIS GUY...
IF YOU TELL HER YOU LOVE HER, SHE'S SURE TO FALL FOR YOU!
IN A HEART-BEAT!!!
....
ARE YOU SERIOUS?
EAH!!!

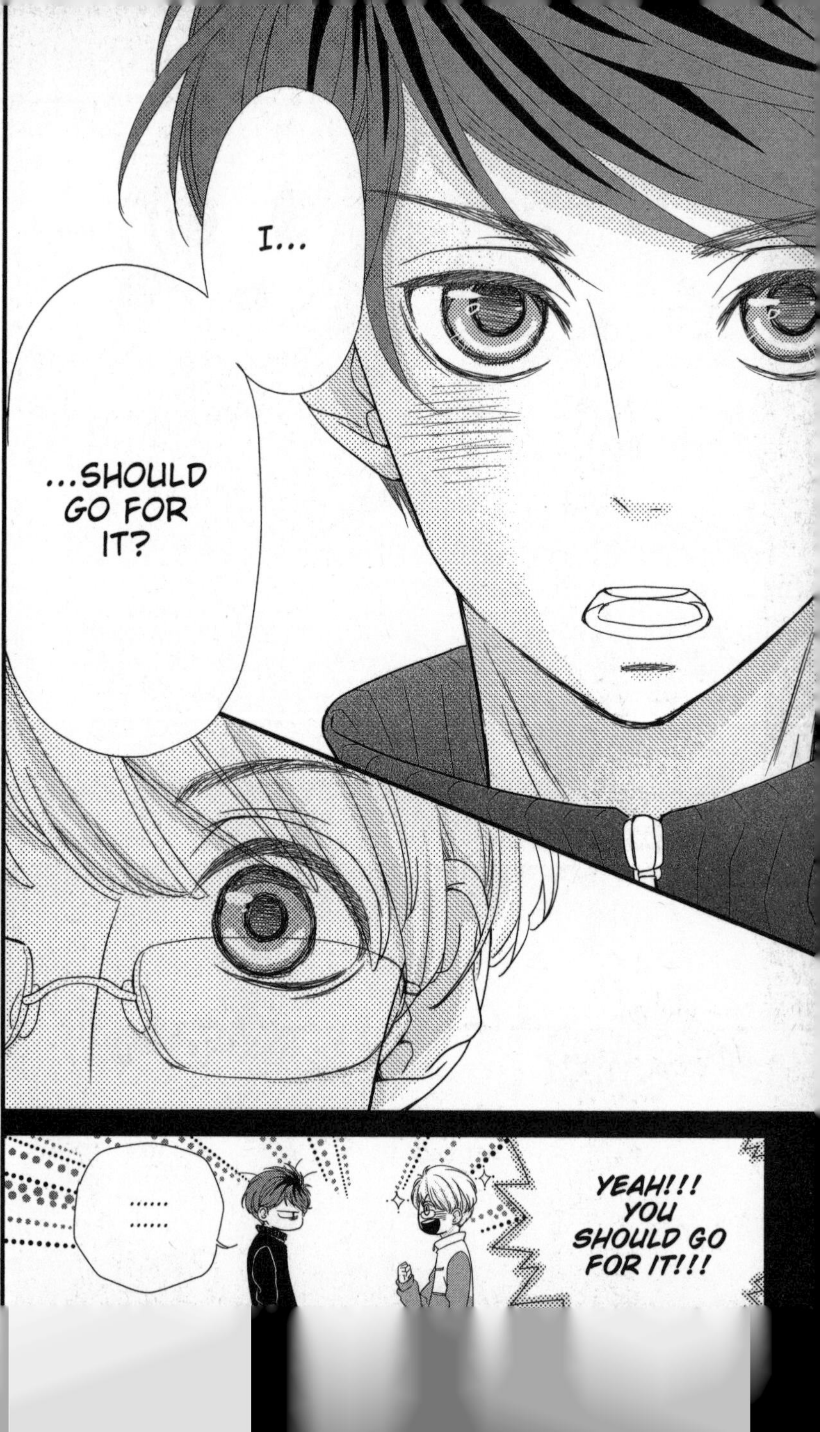
I...
...SHOULD GO FOR IT?
YEAH!!! YOU SHOULD GO FOR IT!!!
......
......

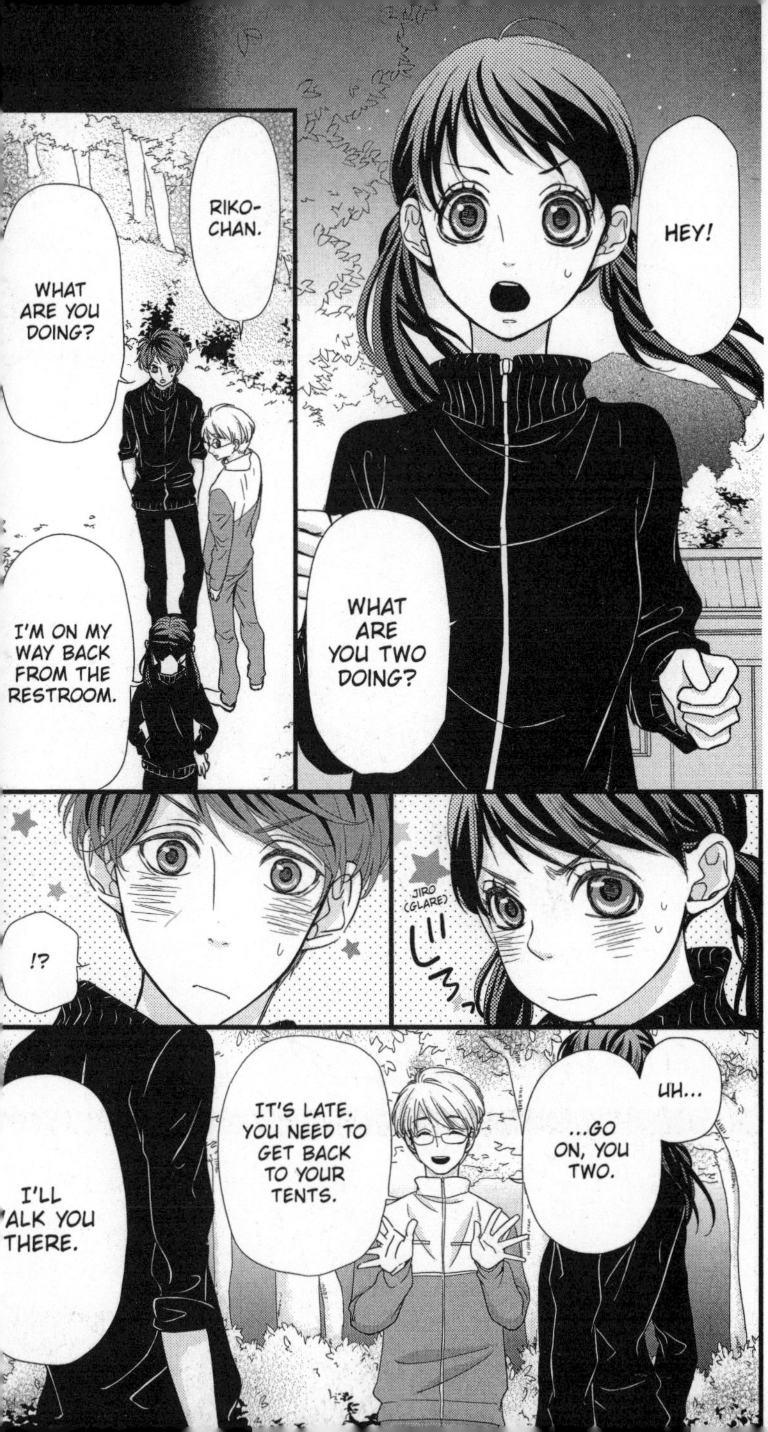
HEY!
WHAT ARE YOU TWO DOING?
RIKO-CHAN.
WHAT ARE YOU DOING?
I'M ON MY WAY BACK FROM THE RESTROOM.
JIRO (GLARE)
!?
UH...
...GO ON, YOU TWO.
IT'S LATE. YOU NEED TO GET BACK TO YOUR TENTS.
I'LL ALK YOU THERE.

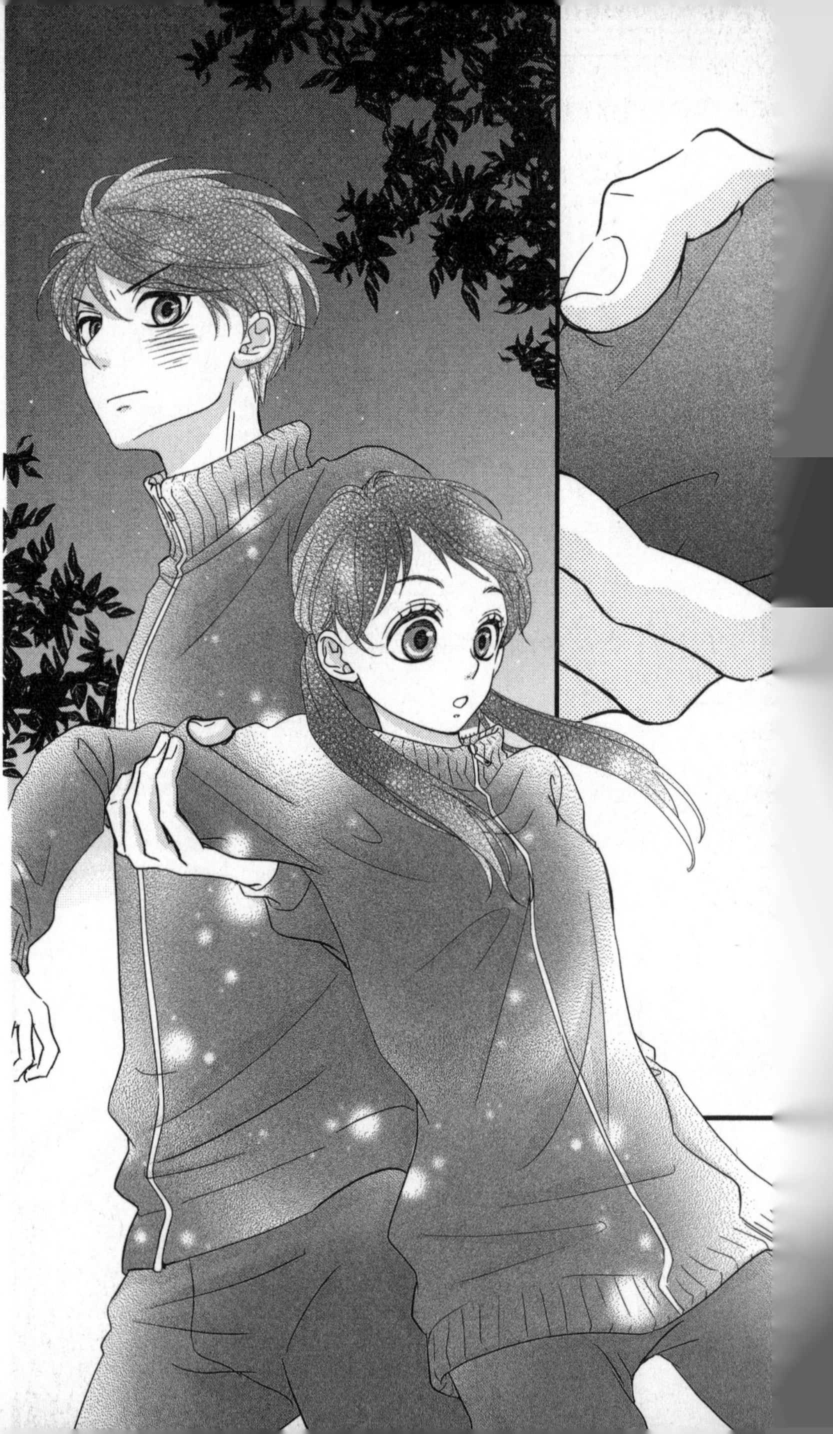

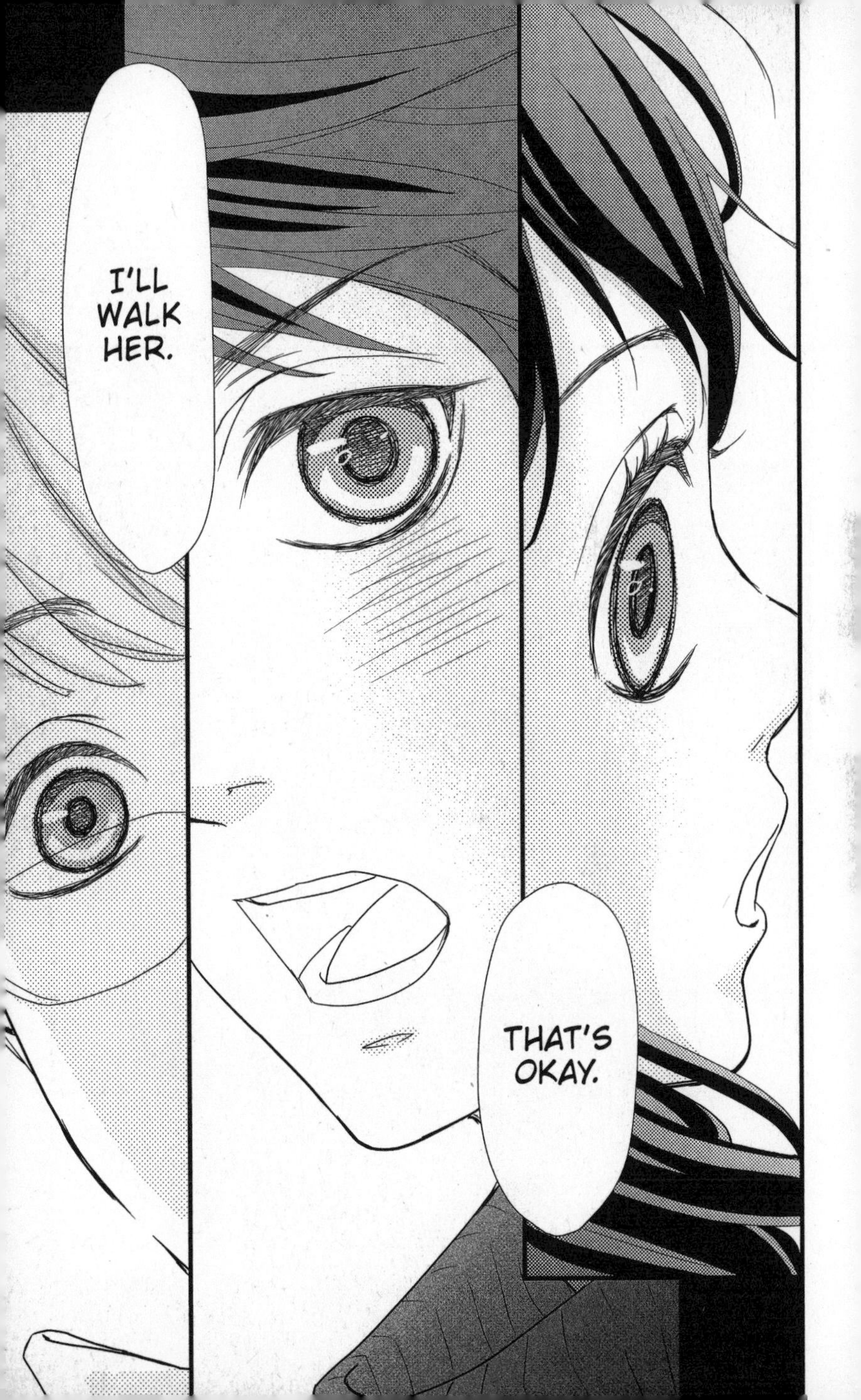
THAT'S OKAY.
I'LL WALK HER.

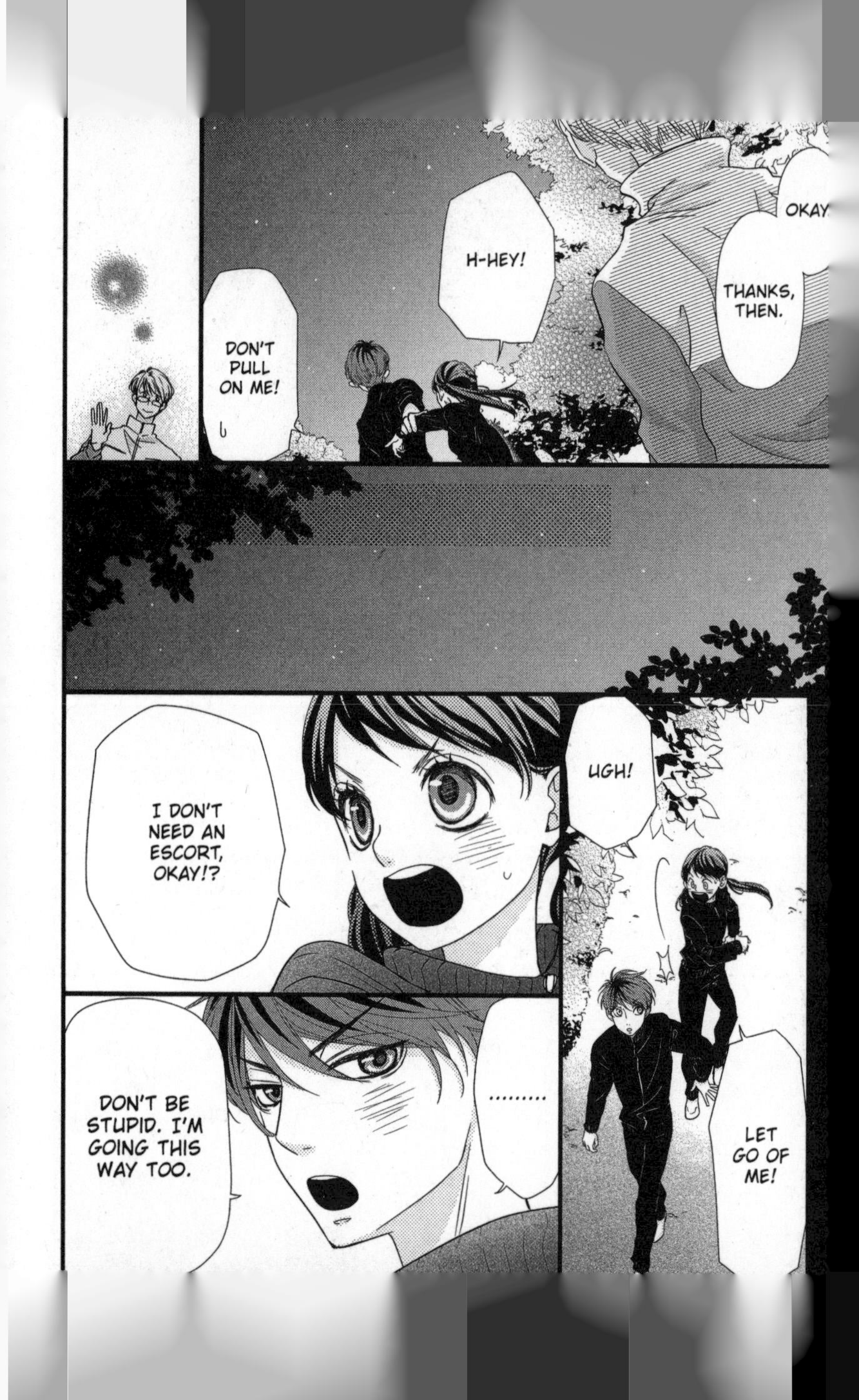

OKAY
THANKS, THEN.
H-HEY!
DON'T PULL ON ME!
UGH!
LET GO OF ME!
I DON'T NEED AN ESCORT, OKAY!?
....
DON'T BE STUPID. I'M GOING THIS WAY TOO.

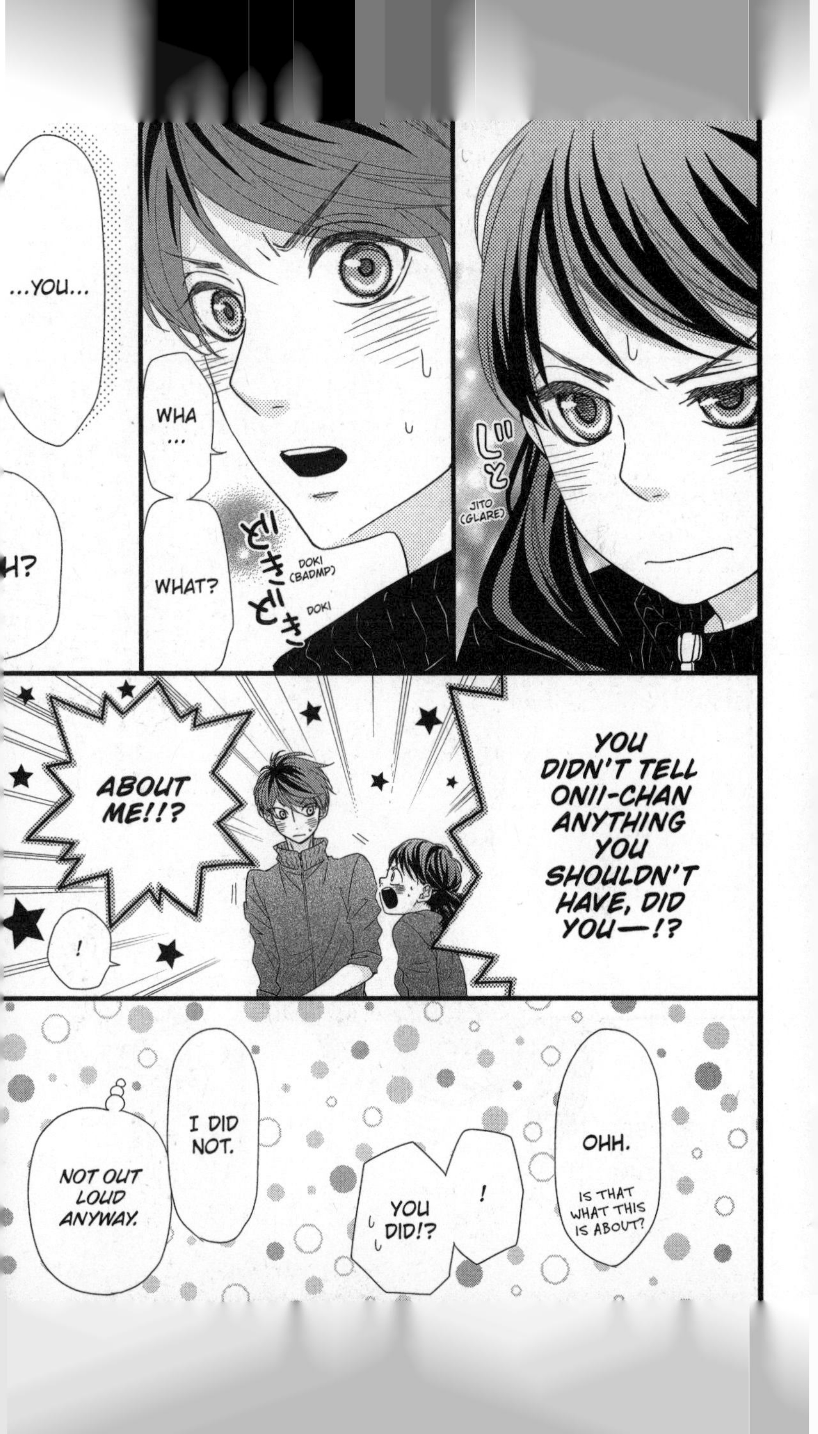

じと
JITO (GLARE)
WHA ...
WHAT?
どきどき
DOKI (BADMP)
DOKI
...YOU...
H?
YOU DIDN'T TELL ONII-CHAN ANYTHING YOU SHOULDN'T HAVE, DID YOU—!?
ABOUT ME!!?
!
OHH.
IS THAT WHAT THIS IS ABOUT?
!
YOU DID!?
I DID NOT.
NOT OUT LOUD ANYWAY.

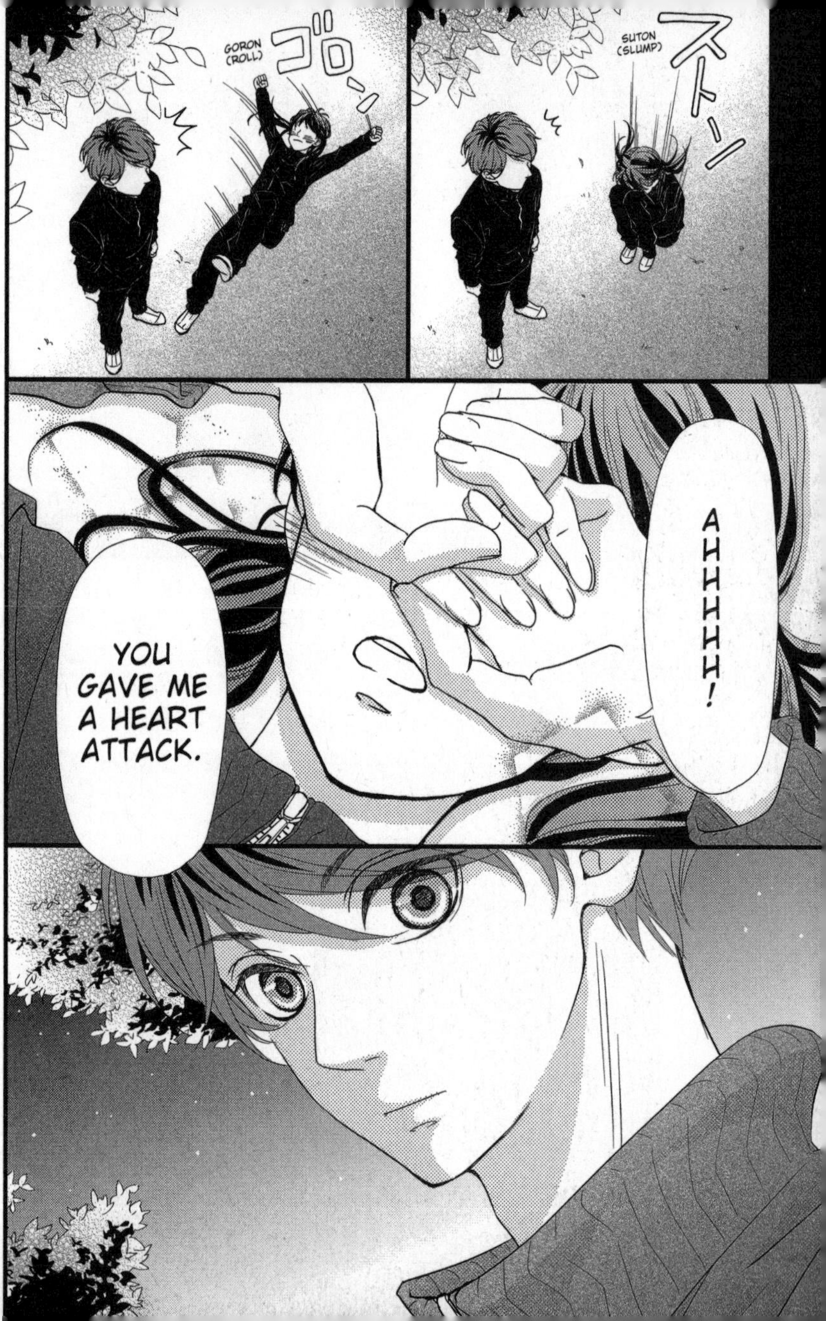
ストーン
SUTON (SLUMP)
ゴローン
GORON (ROLL)
AHHHHHH!
YOU GAVE ME A HEART ATTACK.

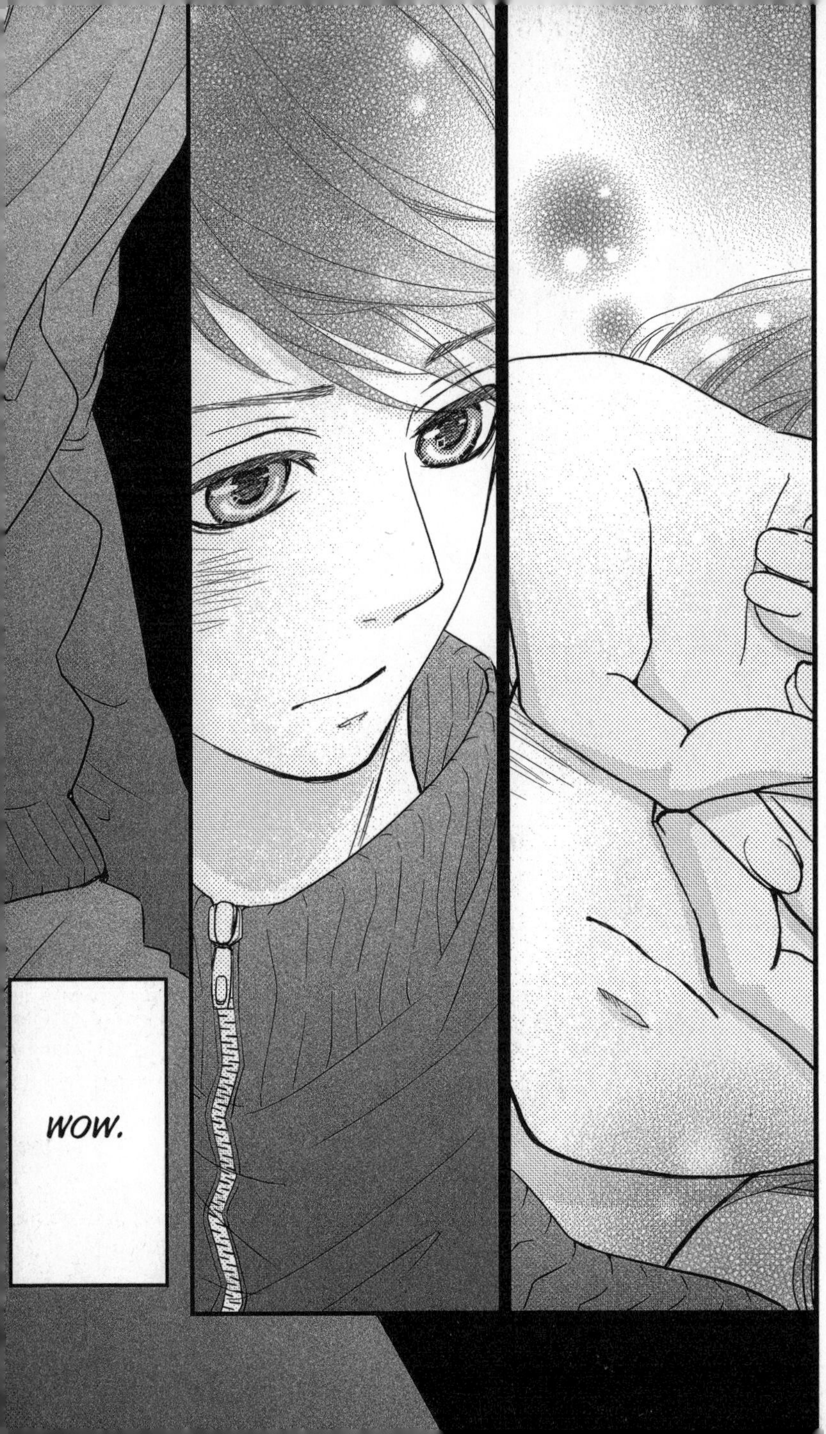
WOW.

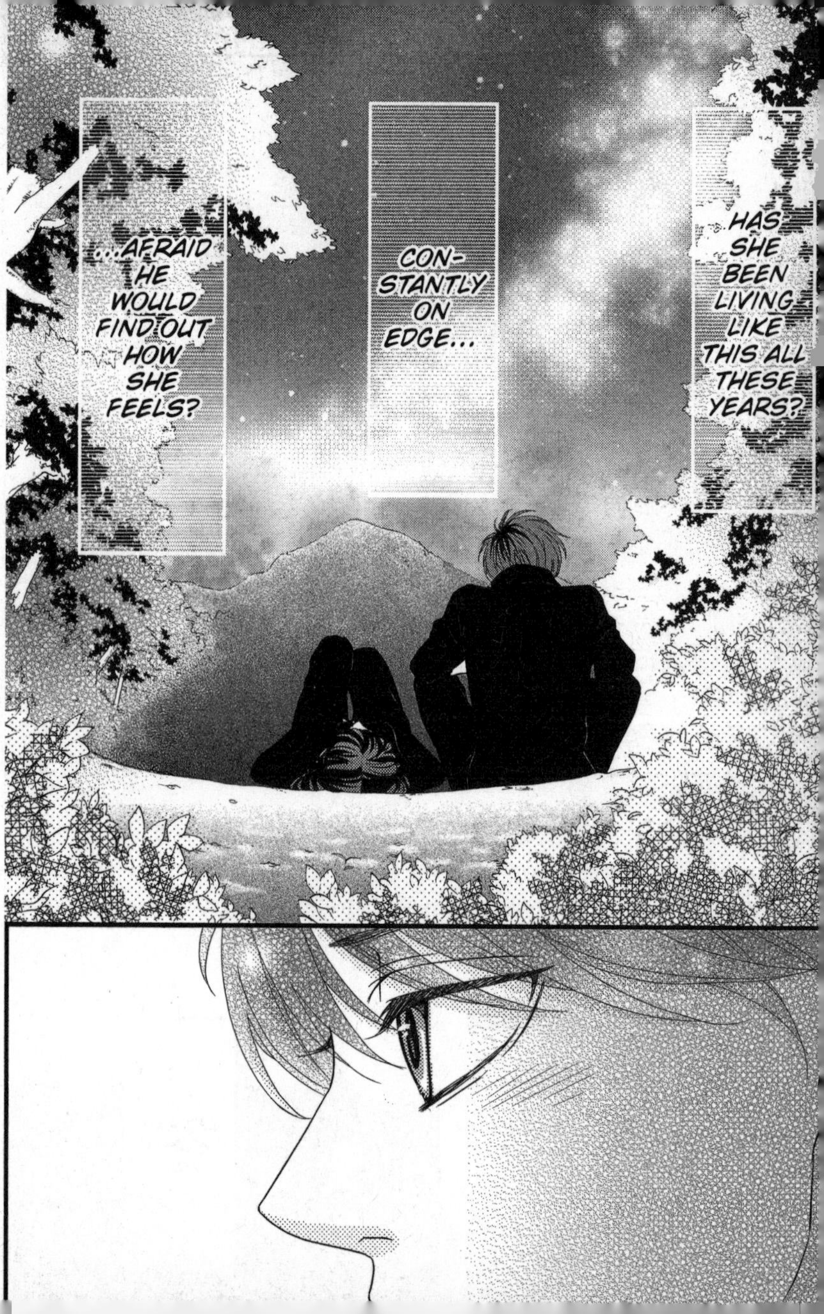
HAS SHE BEEN LIVING LIKE THIS ALL THESE YEARS?
CON-STANTLY ON EDGE...
...AFRAID HE WOULD FIND OUT HOW SHE FEELS?

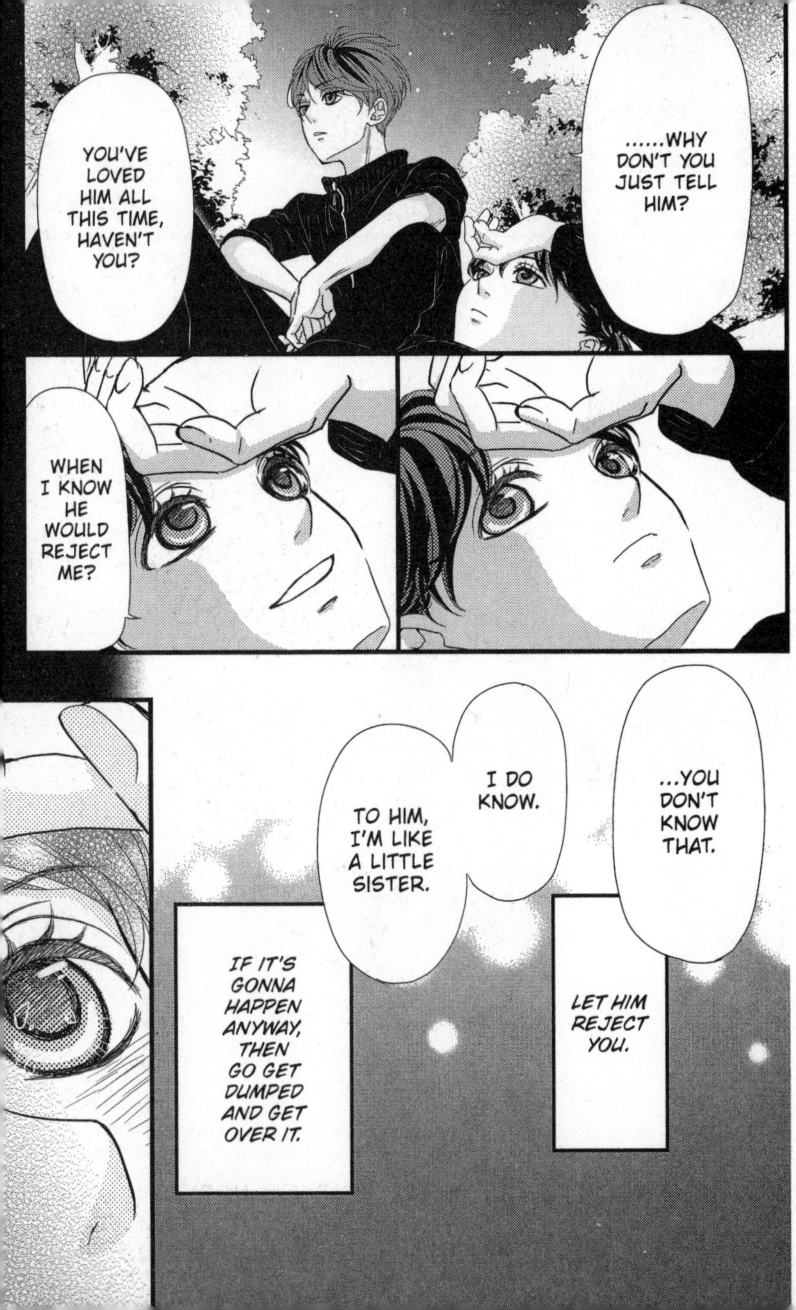
......WHY DON'T YOU JUST TELL HIM?
YOU'VE LOVED HIM ALL THIS TIME, HAVEN'T YOU?
WHEN I KNOW HE WOULD REJECT ME?
...YOU DON'T KNOW THAT.
I DO KNOW.
TO HIM, I'M LIKE A LITTLE SISTER.
LET HIM REJECT YOU.
IF IT'S GONNA HAPPEN ANYWAY, THEN GO GET DUMPED AND GET OVER IT.

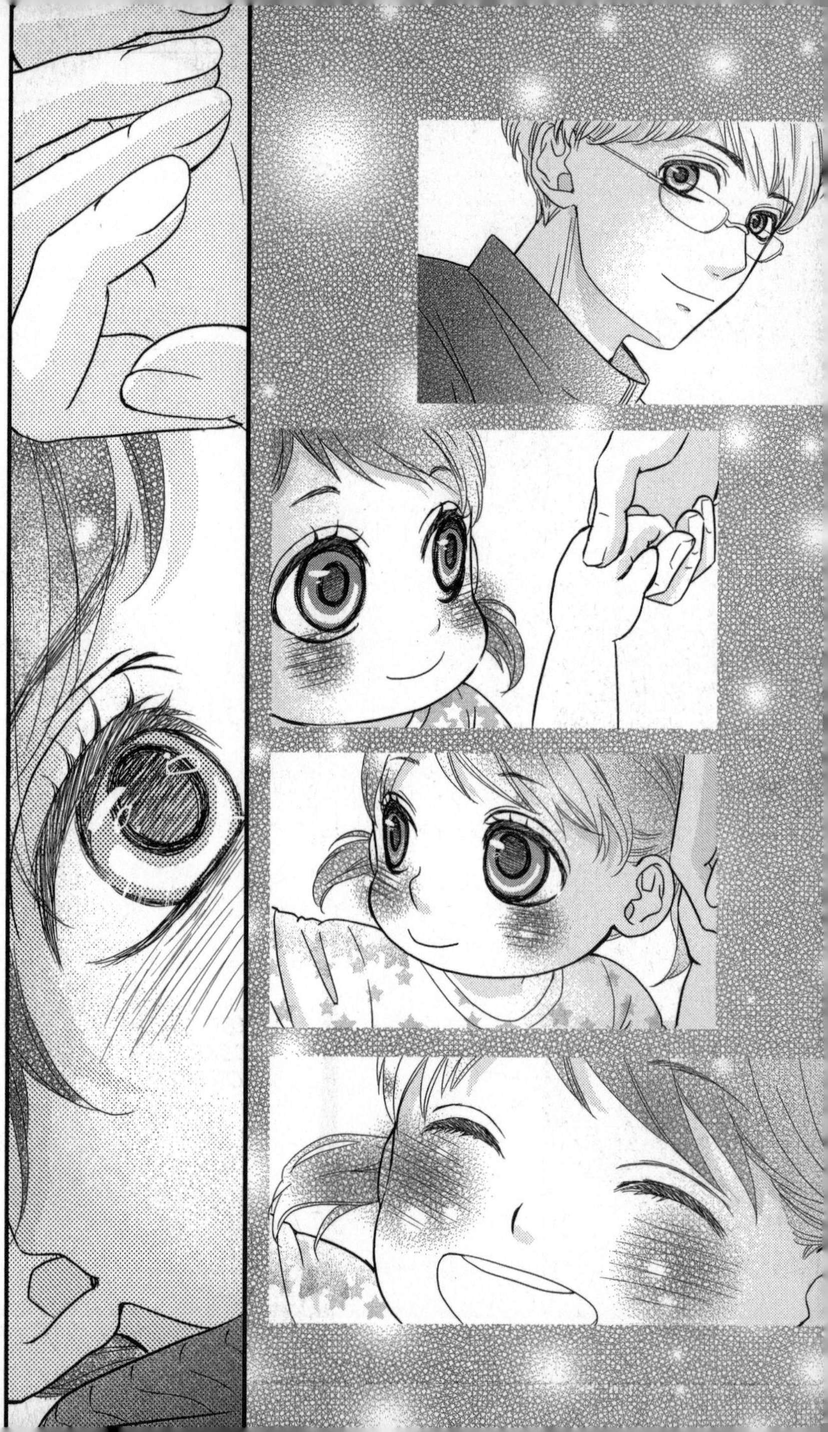

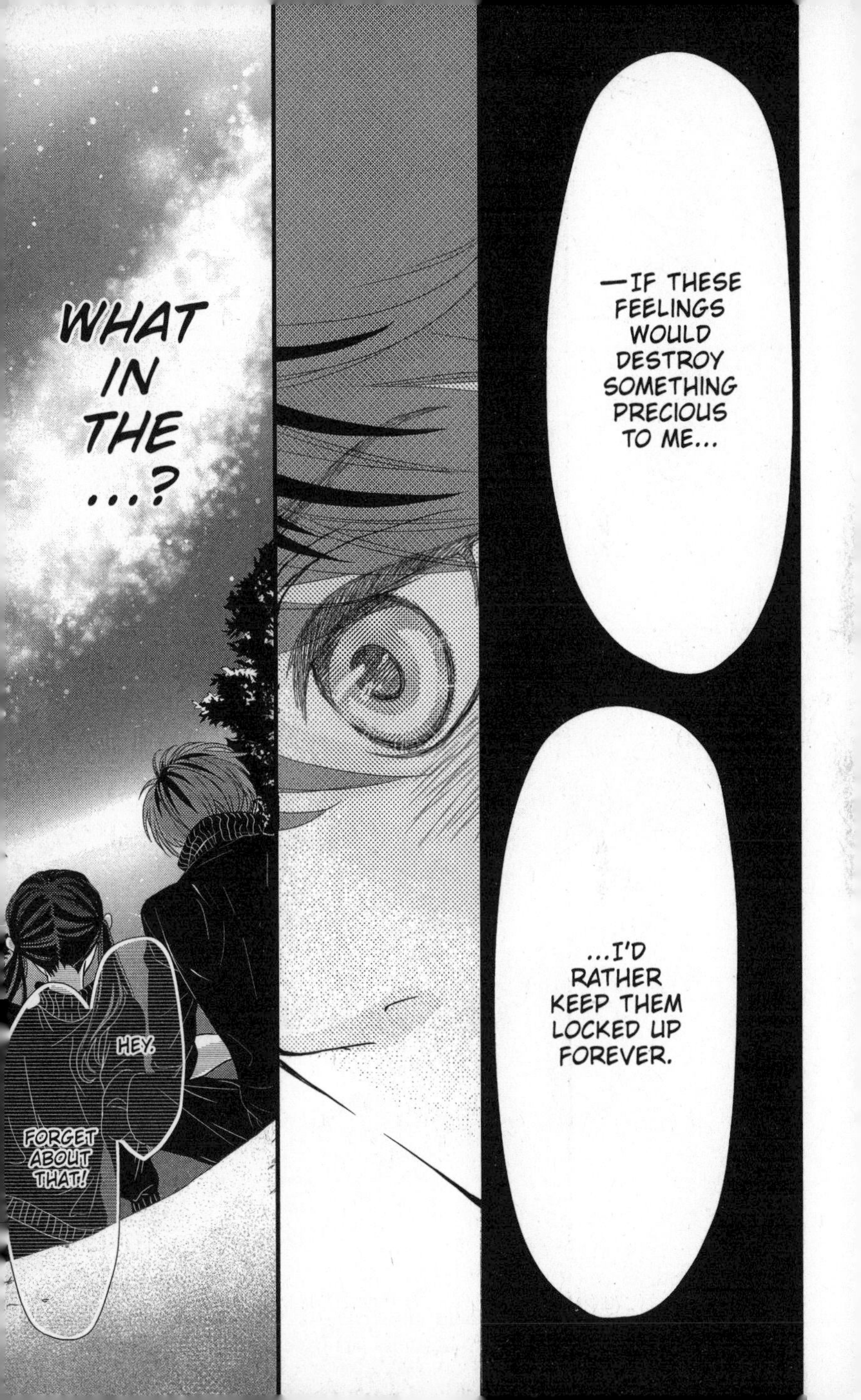
—IF THESE FEELINGS WOULD DESTROY SOMETHING PRECIOUS TO ME...
...I'D RATHER KEEP THEM LOCKED UP FOREVER.
WHAT IN THE ...?
HEY.
FORGET ABOUT THAT!

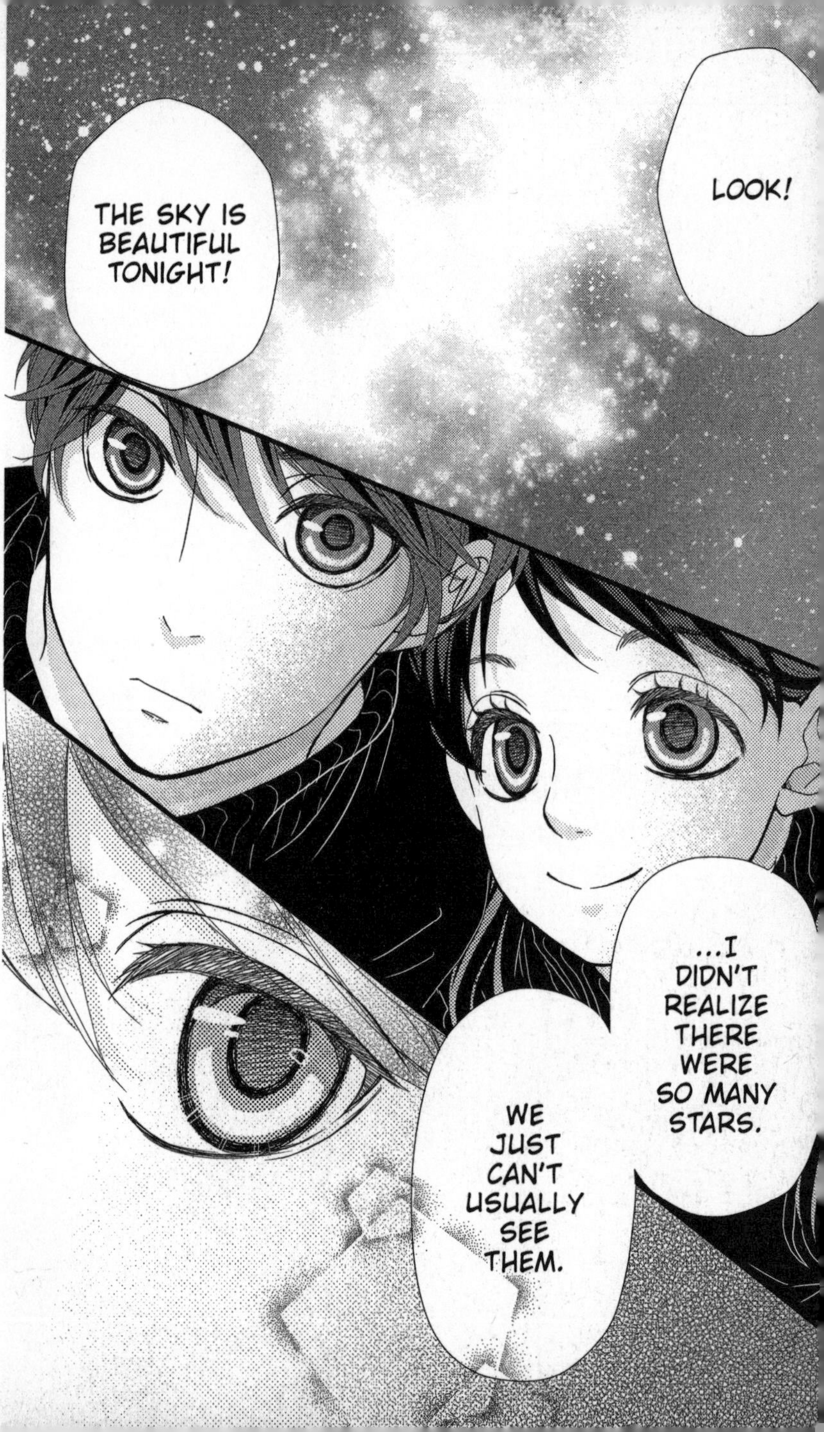
LOOK!
THE SKY IS BEAUTIFUL TONIGHT!
...I DIDN'T REALIZE THERE WERE SO MANY STARS.
WE JUST CAN'T USUALLY SEE THEM.

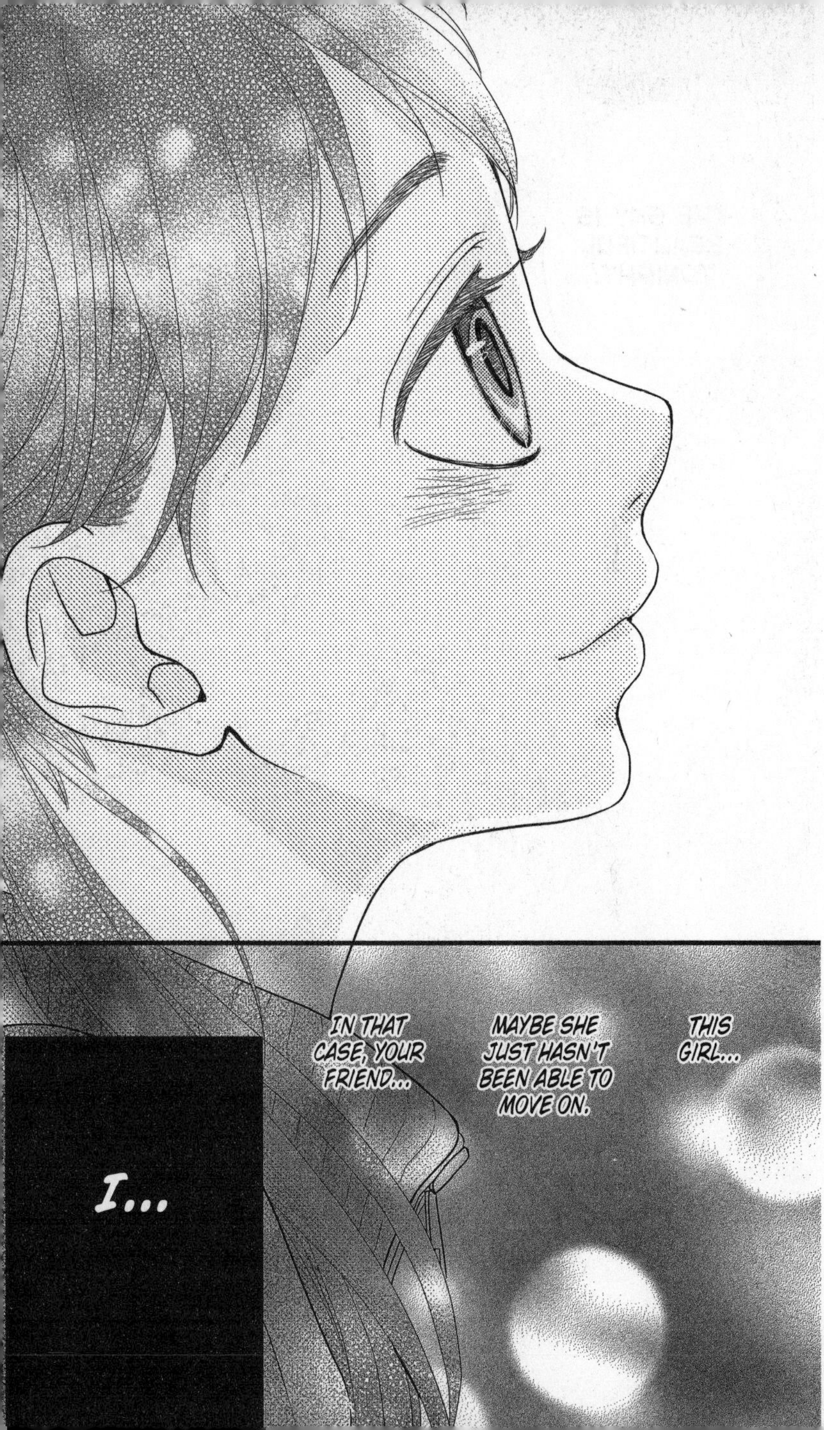
THIS GIRL...
MAYBE SHE JUST HASN'T BEEN ABLE TO MOVE ON.
IN THAT CASE, YOUR FRIEND...
I...

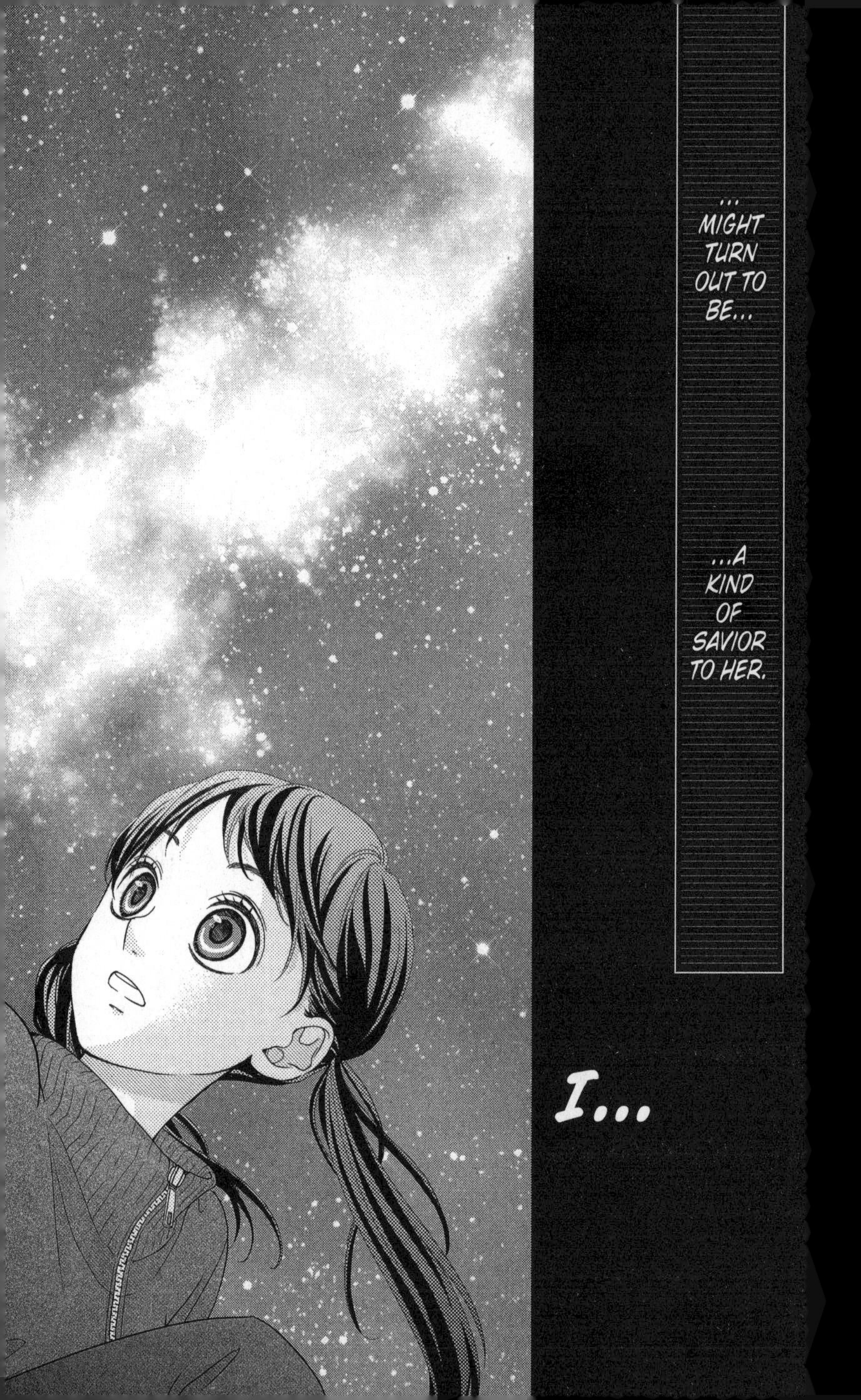
...MIGHT TURN OUT TO BE...
...A KIND OF SAVIOR TO HER.
I...

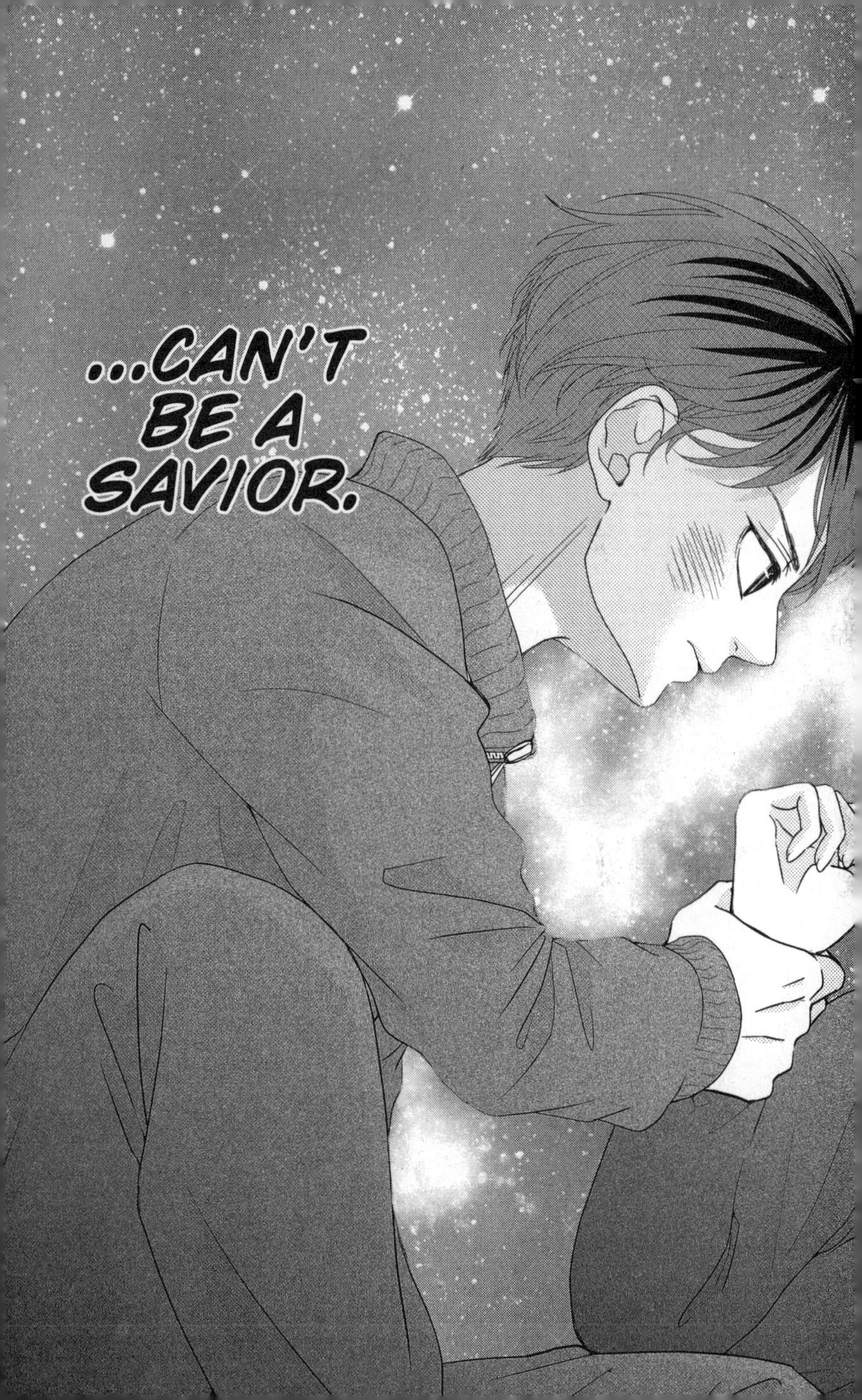
...CAN'T BE A SAVIOR.

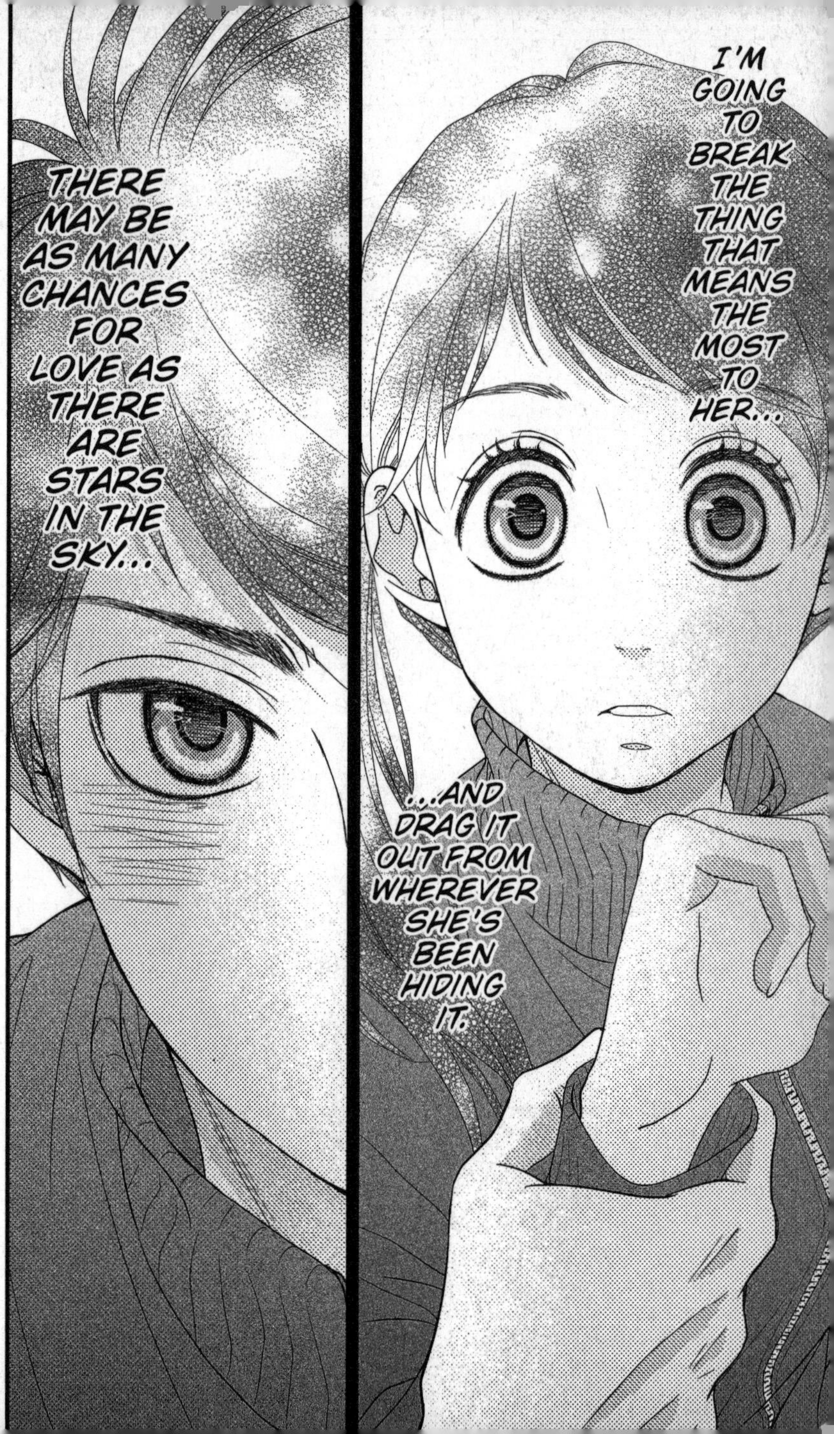
I'M GOING TO BREAK THE THING THAT MEANS THE MOST TO HER...
...AND DRAG IT OUT FROM WHEREVER SHE'S BEEN HIDING IT.
THERE MAY BE AS MANY CHANCES FOR LOVE AS THERE ARE STARS IN THE SKY...

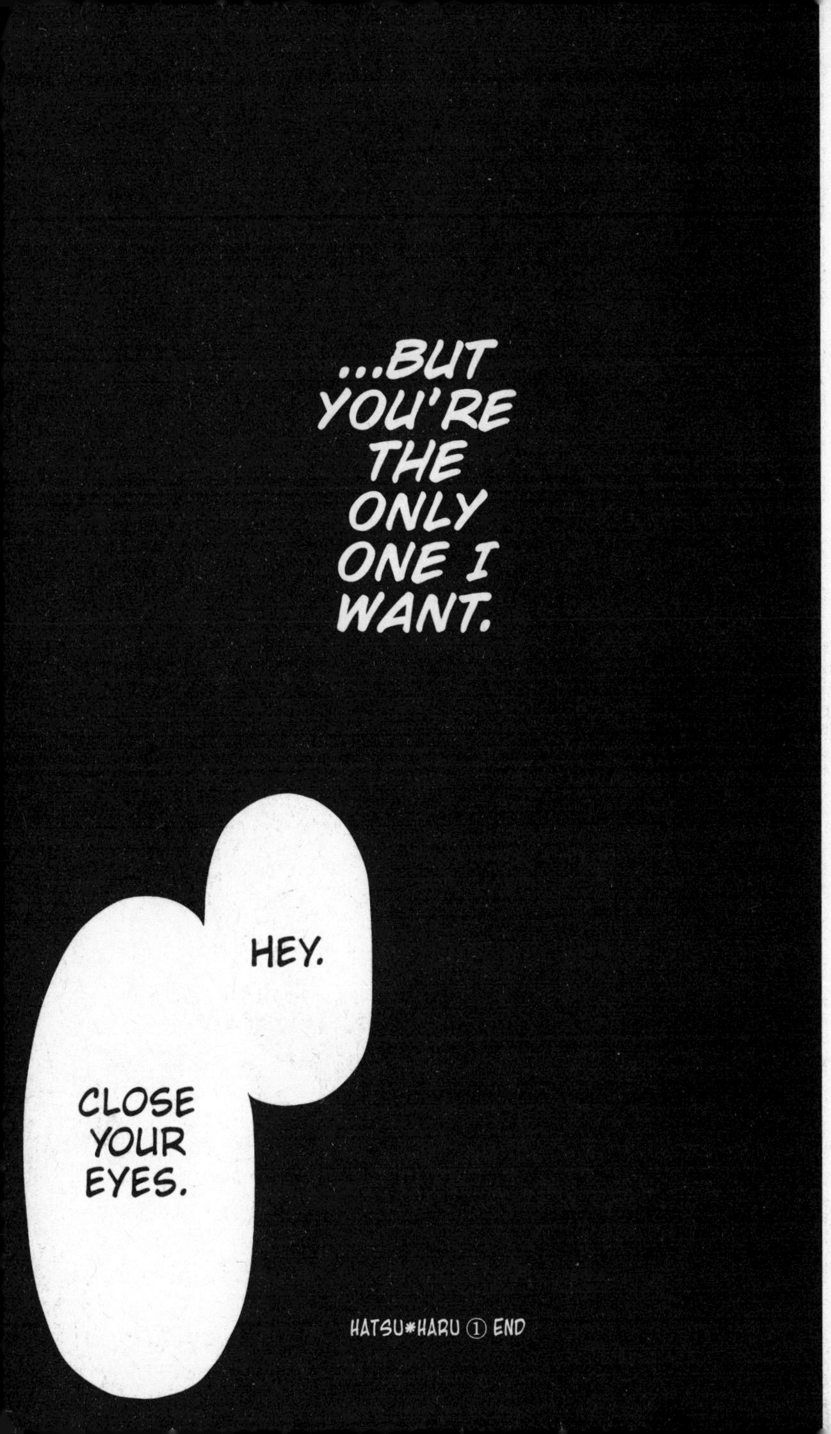
...BUT YOU'RE THE ONLY ONE I WANT.
HEY.
CLOSE YOUR EYES.
HATSU*HARU ① END

AFTERWORD

Hello. Thank you for reading. I asked myself if this series and its male lead would be interesting to my maidenly readers, but personally, male leads are ridiculously easy to draw, and I've never felt like something fit so perfectly before. Especially the scenes where Riko is beating the snot out of Kai—it was abnormally fun drawing the first layouts that I couldn't suppress my doubts about my drawing *shoujo* manga. And by some twist of fate, at the same time I started a series called *My Girlfriend Doesn't Know Love* in *Deluxe Comics* (a special edition of *Betsucomi*), and that has a male lead too. It's not that I'm going through a male lead phase; that's just how things happened. *Doesn't Know* began with the concept of having a male lead, but *HATSU * HARU* really did just randomly change to a male lead. So I'm not really sure if it's okay, but as a result, I am having a lot of fun drawing it, and I hope you all get some enjoyment out of this series too.

Of course, nothing would make me happier than to hear that not only girls but boys too are enjoying it.

So I hope you pick up Volume 2.

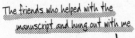

The friends who helped with the manuscript and hung out with me

Roku-san
Adacchan
Asamin
Kanchi
Mae-chan
Eda-chan

2014.05.05 藤沢志月
Shizuki Fujisawa

Blog → "Shizu Diary"
shizukifujisawa.amebaownd.com

Twitter ID → shizukifujisawa

Fan letter address:

I can't wait to hear from you!

Yen Press
1290 Avenue of the Americas
New York, NY 10104

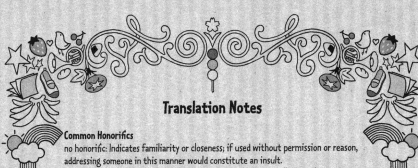

Translation Notes

Common Honorifics

no honorific: Indicates familiarity or closeness; if used without permission or reason, addressing someone in this manner would constitute an insult.

-san: The Japanese equivalent of Mr./Mrs./Miss. If a situation calls for politeness, this is the fail-safe honorific.

-sama: Conveys great respect; may also indicate the social status of the speaker is lower than that of the addressee.

-kun: Used most often when referring to boys, this honorific indicates affection or familiarity. Occasionally used by older men among their peers, but it may also be used by anyone referring to a person of lower standing.

-chan: An affectionate honorific indicating familiarity used mostly in reference to girls; also used in reference to cute persons or animals of either gender.

-sensei: A respectful term for teachers, artists, or high-level professionals.

PAGE 8

The Japanese term used here is *konpa*, short for *goudou konpa* or "combined company." This particular style of **group date** is a little get-together with equal numbers boys and girls who may or may not have all known each other previously. The idea is for people to pair up and, in the perfect situation, become official couples or, in Kai's case, friends with benefits.

PAGE 9

A Japanese urban legend has it that if a man or woman reaches the age of thirty (or, in more recent versions, forty-five) without having sexual relations, that person will gain the ability to use magic and become a **wizard**.

PAGE 37

When Kai calls Riko **"a softie pretending to be strong,"** what he originally says is *tsundere*. Readers may be familiar with the *tsundere* trope, which describes characters who are often sarcastic and mean but will occasionally reveal hints that they actually do care about another character. In this case, Kai assumes that Riko is acting bad-tempered to hide her feelings for him.

PAGE 111

Pocari Sweat, or **Pocari**, this sports drink sounds somewhat unappetizing, but it is not meant to imply that sweat is an ingredient. Rather, the drink supposedly supplies the body with the nutrients and electrolytes lost when sweating.

hatsu haru II

Shizuki Fujisawa

Translation/Adaptation: **Alethea and Athena Nibley**

Lettering: **Lys Blakeslee**

This book is a work of fiction. Names, characters, places, and incidents are the product of the author's imagination or are used fictitiously. Any resemblance to actual events, locales, or persons, living or dead, is coincidental.

Original Japanese edition published by SHOGAKUKAN.
English translation rights in the United States of America, Canada, the United Kingdom, Ireland, Australia and New Zealand arranged with SHOGAKUKAN
through Tuttle-Mori Agency, Inc.

Yen Press
1290 Avenue of the America
New York, NY 10104

Visit us at yenpress.com ❀ facebook.com/yenpress ❀ twitter.com/yenpress
yenpress.tumblr.com ❀ instagram.com/yenpress

First Yen Press Edition: June 2018

Yen Press is an imprint of Yen Press, LLC.
The Yen Press name and logo are trademarks of Yen Press, LLC.

The publisher is not responsible for websites (or their content) that are not owned by the publisher.

Library of Congress Control Number:
2018935618

ISBN: 978-1-9753-2743-9

10 9 8 7 6 5 4 3 2 1

WOR

Printed in the United States of America

NOMO